MW00354980

The Education Trap

THE

Education Trap

Schools and the Remaking of Inequality in Boston

Cristina Viviana Groeger

Harvard University Press

Cambridge, Massachusetts   London, England   2021

Copyright © 2021 by the President and Fellows of Harvard College
All rights reserved
Printed in the United States of America

Publication of this book has been supported through the generous provisions
of the Maurice and Lula Bradley Smith Memorial Fund.

First printing

Library of Congress Cataloging-in-Publication Data

Names: Groeger, Cristina Viviana, 1986– author.
Title: The education trap : schools and the remaking of inequality in Boston /
    Cristina Viviana Groeger.
Description: Cambridge, Massachusetts : Harvard University Press, 2021. |
    Includes bibliographical references and index.
Identifiers: LCCN 2020042443 | ISBN 9780674249110 (cloth)
Subjects: LCSH: Economic development—Effect of education on—Massachusetts—
    Boston—History. | Labor supply—Effect of education on—Massachusetts—
    Boston—History. | Equality—Massachusetts—Boston—History. | Income
    distribution—Massachusetts—Boston—History. | Occupational training—
    Massachusetts—Boston—History.
Classification: LCC HD75.7 .G76 2021 | DDC 306.3/60974461—dc23
LC record available at https://lccn.loc.gov/2020042443

To my parents, Margarita and Chris, who first taught me that learning happens everywhere, not just in school

Contents

The Education Trap

Introduction

Education and Social Inequality

"The great equalizer." In the mid-nineteenth century, that's how Horace Mann, the leading promoter of public schools, described education in the United States.[1] Today, on the face of it, not much seems to have changed to contradict this view. Education is still seen as an essential tool to reduce the gap between the rich and the poor and to create a more egalitarian society. In his 2010 State of the Union address, President Barack Obama announced to applause that "in the 21st century, the best anti-poverty program around is a world class education."[2] Not only politicians, but popular public intellectuals have promoted faith in the capacity of education to diminish socioeconomic inequalities. Economist Thomas Piketty, whose work on inequality has attracted widespread scholarly and public attention, noted in his landmark *Capital in the Twenty-First Century* that "the best way to increase wages and reduce wage inequalities in the long run is to invest in education and skills."[3]

The evidence, however, points to a fundamental paradox. The United States has long had among the highest rates of school enrollment and graduation in the world.[4] In 2017, the United States ranked second-highest globally for the average years of schooling for individuals over the age of 25.[5] Simultaneously, however, the United States has among the highest levels of economic inequality and lowest levels of social mobility across the Global North.[6] Even though Americans are attending school at comparatively high rates, the US economy is increasingly polarized between a wealthy few and the rest. In short, high levels of education coexist with high levels of inequality. If Horace Mann were right, this could not be true.

At a time when half of Americans live paycheck to paycheck while the wealth of some CEOs increases by millions of dollars an hour, the gross inequalities of our contemporary moment have spurred interest in the sources of these disparities, and in remedies for them.[7] Many contemporary explanations of American social inequality have focused on developments since the 1970s, at the moment when inequality began its recent rise.[8] But nearly a century earlier, at a time when educational enrollment was surging and schools made up the largest public expenditure, social inequality reached heights similar to our own. This book turns our attention to this early twentieth-century moment. As a case study in which to explore the paradox of expanding access to education and persistent inequality, it focuses on the city of Boston, famously home to many institutions of learning and a wealthy patrician elite. Based on the historical evidence, I argue that education became a central means of social mobility at the same moment that it became a new infrastructure for legitimizing social inequality. While providing economic opportunities to some workers, the expansion of schooling actually undercut the power of others. By obscuring the broader question of worker power in the economy, a focus on education as the primary means to remedy economic inequality became a pernicious policy trap.

This book explains the seemingly paradoxical role of education by analyzing the intertwined growth of the US educational system (primary, secondary, and higher) and the modern corporate economy in the city of Boston between 1880 and the Great Depression. In this period of rapid economic transformation, formal education reshaped the occupational structure and became a medium through which inequalities were remade and legitimated. Fundamental to this process was the transformation of pathways into employment from workplace training to school-based training. In the late nineteenth century, training for work was decentralized and loosely regulated. Few stayed in school beyond the primary grades and even professionals such as lawyers did not typically attend specialized schools. Most accessed jobs through informal family and ethnic ties and learned occupational skills on the job. Between 1880 and 1930, conflict and coalitions between a variety of interest groups—employers, unions, government officials, professional associations, educators, parents, and students—reshaped the training pathways leading into occupations. This was a contradictory process of both opportunity and exclusion rather than a simple story of educational expansion bringing greater equality.

The Education Trap lays out two parallel transformations that together restructured labor markets and training in this period. Schools intended to train workers for low-wage and industrial jobs never successfully structured access into this work. Despite the dogged efforts of progressive reformers to use vocational training to "elevate" the status of low-wage occupations, those who performed these jobs—overwhelmingly recent immigrants and African Americans—by and large chose not to enroll, whether for lack of time and interest or the failure of these programs to meet their needs. In manufacturing and the trades, conflict between employers and craft unions over control of craft skills and apprenticeship undermined new attempts at industrial education. The failure of industrial education for the trades and manufacturing encouraged employers to seek labor sources that were less costly and less subject to craft-union control.

Among these new labor sources were white-collar employees. In contrast to the failure of school-based vocational training for low-wage and industrial work, schools that offered training for new business employment attracted thousands of students. Office and sales jobs were the fastest-growing occupations in the early twentieth-century economy, and schools that provided pathways into this work garnered tremendous support from students, employers, and public officials across the political spectrum. Competition between public schools and proprietary schools (private establishments run by a proprietor to make a profit) fueled unprecedented school expansion and the rapid rise of clerical and managerial staff in corporate bureaucracies. For many students—especially women, working-class students, and second-generation immigrants—these schools provided social mobility, fueling faith in education as a central tenet of the American dream. However, this expansion provoked a reaction among Boston's elite, who pursued "professional" strategies based on exclusive credentials obtained at degree-granting colleges and universities to control access to the most lucrative positions. Through the successful marriage of elite universities and the most well-paid professional and business careers, formal education became a means of intensifying existing concentrations of wealth and power.

By the early twentieth century, formal education allowed previously underrepresented groups to grasp higher rungs on the occupational ladder, eroding elements of the nineteenth-century kinship-based labor market. However, the transformation of these decades reveals the significant limits of education as a means of reducing inequality. Existing gender, ethnic, and racial hierarchies in the labor market were reproduced alongside and through an expanding school system. Moreover, employers used school-based training to consolidate power over workers. The failure of industrial education and the success of white-collar education were in fact two sides of the same coin. Employers undercut the basis of craft-union power by pursuing mass production, shifting their workforce away from craftworkers and toward nonunionized machine operatives and educated white-collar staff. At the top of the economic hierarchy, elites used exclusive educational credentials to secure the power of a professional, managerial class. In response to the influx of women and second-generation immigrants into the white-collar workforce, this work differentiated into high school–educated female clerical and retail workers supervised by a small number of college-educated male managers. Institutionally, public schools displaced some for-profit competitors but also laid the foundation for the expansion of private higher education, the advantages of which accumulated at the top.

Prior to the New Deal, municipalities were the most developed level of American governance.[9] For that reason, this book analyzes the full cross section of economic, political, and educational institutions in the city of Boston. In this urban center, we can observe the emergence of a consensus around education as the primary policy solution to a wide range of social ills.[10] The Massachusetts state capital was a financial and industrial center with a diversified economy and heterogeneous immigrant population. Home to some of the oldest public schools in the nation, Boston was unique in its well-developed public school infrastructure, and its high taxes provided the city with one of the top per-capita public incomes in the country.[11] It was also home to an unusually high number of private institutions, and this rich and competitive institutional ecology allowed Boston to play a pioneering role in national movements for common schools, curricular reform, and professional standards. Through Boston's history, we can observe the rise of a national process in which schools, and the credentials they provided, remade American inequality.

To put together this encompassing analysis of one city, this book uses both quantitative and qualitative data. It is among the first book-length studies to use new 100 percent samples of IPUMS historical census microdata—individual-level data taken directly from the US federal manuscript censuses—from 1880 to 1940. This dataset offers complete coverage of fine-grained demographic, occupational, and educational attributes for all individuals living in Boston through this period, and it reveals, for example, the profound rise in white-collar work and school enrollment among second-generation immigrants, coupled with persistent gender, ethnic, and racial exclusion by leading professions. This data is contextualized with qualitative sources from seventeen local and regional archives, including the institutional records of schools, colleges, and universities in the Boston area; trade journals from each major occupational sector; local newspapers offering detailed political coverage; personal correspondence about everyday life and aspirations; student yearbooks and testimonials; and employee personnel files. These qualitative sources allow the historian to interpret the meaning of quantitative trends in the words of students and workers as well as their educators and employers.

Boston's local politics reveal the ways in which racial, ethnic, class, and gender hierarchies were inscribed into a new, school-dependent political economy. The "cradle of liberty" boasted a tradition of abolition and racial tolerance, but city politics in this period reveal stark fault lines. Ethnic conflict between Boston's traditional Yankee "Brahmin" elite and increasingly powerful Irish Catholics was the most prominent fissure, but conflict and alliances between Boston's southern and eastern

European immigrant population and its African American community also shaped the emerging economy. Compared to other American cities, Boston had a small Black population, less than 3 percent during this period, but as in other cities, African Americans were consistently marginalized in the labor market. Boston's elite women attended college at a rate higher than in most American cities, but gender segregation in schools was more entrenched. While Boston's particular demographics were unique, the political dynamics of interethnic conflict, Black marginalization, and gender segregation exemplify patterns across the urban North.[12]

The historical account I offer in this book challenges some of the most common narratives about education that dominate public discourse and policy making. Perhaps the most common is the framework of "human capital," derived from the field of economics.[13] In this framework, individual earnings reflect one's level of skill and knowledge, typically acquired through schooling or work experience. In order to participate in and reap the benefits of the modern "knowledge economy," individuals must gain more human capital through education and training.[14] At a macro level, according to this framework, human capital also facilitates economic growth, which can foster shared prosperity. Much of human-capital scholarship is focused on individual productivity and economic growth rather than social inequality per se. However, according to some scholars in this tradition, as well as popular interpretations of these ideas, the policy implications are straightforward: more education is needed to reduce social inequality.[15]

This framework gets a piece of the story right—the piece that best complements our national faith in education. In the early twentieth century, the expansion of schools was driven to a significant extent by grassroots demand for education, and this training facilitated social advancement for many. Students sought access to job-related skills and the culture and knowledge that had long been the exclusive realm of the elite. At an individual level, many did benefit economically from their investment in education. At a larger scale, the labor of millions of educated workers made a booming industrial economy possible. Yet the human-capital framework obscures the ways in which returns to education in the marketplace reflect not only skills but also power.[16] The "unskilled" labor of women cooking complex dishes or performing needle-work at home required skill, albeit often learned informally, undervalued in the labor market, and compensated with meager wages, if any at all.[17] In addition, "skills" required or preferred for many jobs—flawless and perfectly accented English, tact, sociability, neatness, appropriate dress, trustworthiness, and character—are extremely specific historical con-structions in which technical knowledge, learned behaviors, gender per-formance, and proxies for class or ethnic background cannot be easily disentangled. Skills must therefore be contextualized to reveal the ways in which they reflect and naturalize power differentials and ideological assumptions about gender, race, and class.[18]

Furthermore, the growth of schools did not simply feed human cap-ital into an autonomous economy, but actively reshaped the nature of work, the economy, and indeed, society as a whole.[19] Far from a simple imparting of skills, the expansion of schools was a contested, political process in which some won and others lost. Across different countries, political scientists have shown how conflict between major interest groups forged distinct "skill formation regimes."[20] Within liberal market economies like the United States, characterized by limited employment protections, this political struggle was particularly pronounced between craft unions and employers. This struggle impeded the development of vocational training for industrial work, and was an important reason that firms increasingly shifted their labor force away from craftworkers and took advantage of an abundance of school-educated women to fill new clerical positions. On the one hand, this shift allowed for the rapid entry of women into clerical work and helps us historically account for the relative openness of the American economy to women wage earners.[21] On the other hand, the shift to a school-educated workforce helped un-dercut the power of craftworkers by replacing them with lower-wage op-eratives, women white-collar workers (or "pink-collar" staff), and a small number of highly paid engineers and managers. If we pay atten-tion only to rising levels of education, we miss how conflict within the contested arena of training helped shift the overall distribution of work-place power to employers.

Elites successfully used professional credentials to maintain their positions of power. This certainly reflected some degree of skill and expertise, or human capital, but not exclusively. Rather, sociologists have shown how the top of the educational hierarchy was a key arena for strategies of stratification that effectively perpetuated class distinctions.[22] Rather than seeing education as an indicator of productive skills, Marxist scholars have stressed its role in socializing a compliant, capitalist workforce.[23] Other "credentialist" theories emphasize the role of degrees and diplomas as an "abstract cultural currency," disconnected from the actual content of schooling, which can be used to control entry into lucrative jobs and legitimize the status and authority of these positions. Status-seeking through education can drive up degree requirements for the same work, leading to "credential inflation."[24] Historically, credentialism can best be observed in the cooperation between elite professionals and elite universities, with the latter channeling their graduates—selected for a range of qualities collectively deemed "merit"—into the top of the corporate ladder.[25]

In theorizing what exactly education provides to individuals in the labor market, credentialist theories are the primary challenger to the dominant human capital framework. However, the credentialist minimization of the content of schooling hampers a more precise analysis of the nature of job-related skills imparted in schools.[26] In addition, Marxist and credentialist theories tend to underplay the important bottom-up demand from students for valuable skills to enter white-collar employment, especially at the primary and secondary levels, and the ways in which changes at these lower levels of education drove profound transformations of the economy as a whole.[27] Here is where a historical approach, attentive to the ways in which different types of schools related to distinct sectors of the labor market, can offer a narrative that combines bottom-up and top-down pressures in the mutual development of education and the economy.

Despite its centrality in public life and scholarly debate, education, surprisingly, has not been a chief focus of political or economic histories of the modern United States.[28] The role of schools, however, has been fundamental to American historical development in several key ways. Politically, education was a key driver of American state-building from the local level up. Nineteenth-century public school enrollment rates in the northern United States surpassed those of France and Great Britain, and schools made up the largest share of municipal expenditures during the early twentieth century. The United States relied on schools as the basis of its decentralized welfare state, as opposed to robust social insurance or job protections characteristic of leading European welfare states, and school systems became vehicles for the provision of many social services.[29]

Economically, schools played a central role in the making of American capitalism, structuring access to employment and serving as the training grounds for the new staff of the American corporate economy. By providing exclusive credentials, educational institutions gave economic elites a tool for controlling entry into the most well-paid positions. *The Education Trap* shows how the Progressive Era—popularly named for efforts to rein in the excesses of capitalism—in fact deepened and legitimized long-standing forms of inequality.[30] Indeed, it was during this period, rather than in the late nineteenth-century Gilded Age, that income inequality reached its height.[31] This book also bridges common divisions within labor history to examine the working lives of domestic workers, pink-collar staff, and highly paid professionals alike, contextualizing work within families and communities and highlighting the relation between groups of workers that shaped the development of each.[32]

Culturally, schools also helped consolidate an ideology of individual advancement. This ideology is often characterized as a belief in equality of opportunity in contrast to equality of outcome.[33] While rooted in a long American tradition of favoring reward for individual talent over hereditary privilege, this ideology was not static, nor should we imagine it operating autonomously.[34] Rather, it was grounded in, fortified, and validated by experiences of schooling in the early twentieth century.[35] As schools were imagined as a social panacea, they became a new foundation for individualized policy solutions to structural inequalities. "Educationalizing" social problems reduced pressure for more direct measures of reducing poverty and inequality.[36] A growing body of scholarship has highlighted the ways in which American policymakers have persistently turned to solutions that place the blame, and the burden of reform, on individuals rather than society.[37] The triumph of schooling in this era can help us understand why.

The ideology of education as a path toward social advancement was premised on the belief that one's economic success reflected one's skill level, or educational "merit." Recent critics of meritocracy have pointed to the role of elite professionals in exacerbating social inequality, but many still cling to a faith in meritocracy in theory and point to educational solutions to address the problem.[38] This book challenges us to reinterpret "merit" as a culturally constructed set of knowledges, behaviors, and values that reflect historically specific personal preferences and prejudices, often used by elites to maintain their power. Moreover, this book shows how the reconstruction of economic opportunity on the basis of education created a new institutional and ideological infrastructure for upholding socioeconomic inequality. As schools remade pathways into work across the employment structure, educational achievement (or lack thereof) became a new way of explaining and justifying the wealth of some and the poverty of others.[39]

While education has many different meanings, this book focuses specifically on the role of education in shaping paths to work. The "vocationalization" of education, or the use of schools for economic reward, has long been criticized by educational reformers, from the early twentieth century through to the twenty-first.[40] Many nonvocational roles of education—such as education for democratic citizenship, intellectual and artistic creativity, and emancipation—are under threat, and are absolutely worth fighting for.[41] But it is important to acknowledge that schools' vocational role was enormously meaningful to those able to use schools, including "nonvocational" academic and liberal arts programs, to access better employment. Indeed, we can only explain the dramatic expansion of schools in this period if we acknowledge the role of parents and students who, by voting with their feet, pushed the educational system to expand its offerings and provide instruction that they believed would benefit them in the workplace.

To understand changes in training for work, we also need a wide lens that contextualizes schools as just one institutional form within an ecology of many sites of learning. By examining the full landscape of job-training institutions (including schools, universities, workplaces, the family) and the contested processes through which they forged links to distinct economic sectors, this book challenges long-standing silos in the field of educational history: between public and private, secondary and higher, formal and informal, "vocational" and "liberal" education.[42] Public high schools and private universities a century ago were substantially shaped by competition with a flourishing ecology of proprietary and parochial schools, and the emerging public-private educational "system" was a distinctive feature of the American welfare state.[43] While vocational education has often been interpreted and studied predominantly with reference to men's industrial training, this book broadens the focus to encompass women's occupational trajectories, as well as service-sector, white-collar, and professional jobs.[44] In doing so, this book challenges the dichotomy between vocational and liberal (or academic) education by showing how forms of liberal education served as key paths to specific future employment opportunities.[45] Liberal arts education, imagined in opposition to vocational concerns, was held up as an ideal across the political spectrum toward a variety of ends. In practice, however, this idealization became an important tool used by leading educational institutions to secure their status and prestige, as well as a means of legitimating the economic benefits attained by those with a supposedly nonvocational degree.

This book begins in the late nineteenth century, at a time when American pathways into employment looked haphazard. As detailed in Chapter 1, for nearly all wage earners in Boston, paths to work were based on family and social networks, and learning took place in the workplace rather than in school. Despite its lack of formal channels, the occupational structure was defined by many overt gender, ethnic, and racial inequalities.

The rest of the book moves through each economic sector to illustrate the two interrelated patterns of transformation that restructured the labor market in the next decades: the failure of education intended to train students for low-wage and industrial work, and the success (and hence proliferation) of schools that trained students for white-collar and professional jobs. These two dynamics together reveal how education offered advantages for some, while simultaneously undercutting the power of organized workers and strengthening the power of elites. Faith in education as a way of mitigating a growing class divide was solidified just as the educational system provided a new institutional basis for reproducing class advantage. As a means of addressing social inequality, education became a dangerous trap.

Chapter 2 examines the failure of reformers' efforts to improve the precarious employment of recent immigrants and African Americans in the lowest-paying service and manual-labor jobs. Based on the common diagnosis that low-wage work was due to a lack of skills, many progressive reformers pushed for the expansion of vocational training schools, such as "schools of housekeeping," in order to elevate the status of household work. These efforts were largely unsuccessful. More popular services for low-wage workers included nurseries, kindergartens, English-language instruction, and citizenship classes, yet these services proved equally ineffective in reducing patterns of exploitation at the bottom of the occupational hierarchy.

For jobs in manufacturing and the trades, the subject of Chapter 3, conflicts between unions and employers over control of the training process hindered new industrial schools in both the private and the public sectors. Employers pursued managerial strategies to undercut the power of craft unions, and in place of the small shop with several craftworkers, sprawling assembly-line factories with immigrant operatives would come to define industrial America. Instead of receiving an education in specific industrial schools or industrial tracks within schools, which suffered from declining reputations and low enrollments, these factory workers learned basic literacy and numeracy in public elementary schools.

This reorganization of the workplace was made possible by an army of school-educated white-collar workers that firms deployed to staff their corporate bureaucracies. Rather than the "organization man," it was women who were the chief protagonists in this transformation.[46] Chapter 4 traces the changing landscape of training for clerical and sales work. With broad public support and without organized opposition, proprietary "commercial" schools and public high schools multiplied. The success of many women and second-generation immigrants entering positions as clerks, secretaries, and retail workers challenged some labor market inequalities and solidified the link between education and social mobility. Their entry, however, also sparked a reaction among a predominantly male, white, native-born elite. Upper-class Bostonians used professional strategies, relying on advanced educational credentials, to control access to the most remunerative jobs. An expanding white-collar sector became a differentiated hierarchy, with a vast pool of feminized pink-collar clerical and sales workers at the bottom and a new managerial class at the top. Thus, this new landscape of schools, while offering some opportunities, did not empower workers as a whole; rather, schools provided an opportunity for employers to centralize power.

Professional strategies of control are traced in the professions of law and education (Chapter 5) and the "new profession" of business (Chapter 6). By forging pathways from elite schools into corporate law, educational administration, and financial and business management, professionals and universities became coarchitects of the top rungs of the managerial ladder that undergirded twentieth-century corporate capitalism. In so doing, they defined the meaning of "merit" on the basis of academic knowledge as well as cultural norms, personal characteristics, and family background. They also shaped steep internal ladders within each profession, differentiating the corporate lawyer from the courtroom advocate, the administrator from the teacher, and the executive from the low-level manager. Rungs on the professional ladder not only corresponded to a hierarchy of schools, but also to hierarchies of gender, ethnicity, and race.

This book ends when these trends were consolidated in the 1930s. During the Great Depression, when youth employment collapsed, school enrollment continued to grow.[47] By this point, employers across sectors had come to prefer school-educated employees, and formal education structured the majority of pathways into jobs. The triumph of school-based training had significantly reshaped the employment structure and the balance of worker power.[48] While the expansion of formal education opened up many new pathways into work and limited the overall supply of labor by keeping youth out of the labor market, this transition also undercut earlier forms of worker control by facilitating the transition to a nonunionized workforce and a credentialed elite. The 1930s and 1940s marked the beginning of a new chapter in the American political economy, when workers launched more inclusive organizing strategies for building power through industrial unions and the role of the federal welfare state greatly expanded.

Additional studies of other places and eras will be necessary to fully piece together the historical relationship between education and inequality in the United States. But the case of Boston challenges deeply rooted assumptions among both scholars and the general public about how education works. In early twentieth-century Boston, education expanded as socioeconomic inequality increased. The contested history of this development suggests that our national faith in education may be obscuring how schooling can in fact deepen economic inequality and conceal the ways in which educational merit has become a new foundation on which this inequality is justified.

By shifting the contemporary conversation about social inequality from the 1970s to the early twentieth century, the historical narrative presented in this book should also prompt a change in our understanding of the "great compression" between 1940 and 1970, when inequality was substantially reduced.[49] The expansion of public higher education in that period has been heralded as a key contributor to the decline in inequality during those years. This golden age is also the basis upon which economists have rested claims that the best policy solution to address inequality in the present is more education. According to these scholars, we can think about the relationship between education and technology as a race, in which, if education falls behind technology, inequality increases.[50] From the late nineteenth century to the late 1970s, educational attainment rose faster than "skill-biased" technological change (or technological change that favors highly skilled workers), causing a reduction in social inequality. After the 1970s, however, educational attainment slowed as technological change continued apace, disproportionately benefiting those with the most human capital, and thereby increasing social inequality.

The evidence presented in this book suggests that many other political and economic factors were necessary preconditions and supplements to education during the midcentury decline of inequality. These include the expansion of social and economic protections by New Deal and Great

Society welfare programs, progressive taxation, minimum wage laws, and the broad economic power of industrial labor unions led by the Congress of Industrial Organizations (CIO), which increased the power of workers and ensured that the jobs they entered had living wages and good working conditions.[51] Education has always operated within a broader political and economic context that shapes its impact on social inequality. In addition, rather than imagine "education" monolithically, this book shows the very different roles played by distinct institutional types, some of which were much more effective as tools for concentrating wealth than redistributing it.

Beginning in the 1970s, social welfare protections, labor rights, and workers' collective power began to be stripped away. Wages stagnated and middle-class jobs were "hollowed out."[52] Educational enrollment, meanwhile, continued to grow. Between 1963 and 2006, enrollment in public and private four-year colleges and universities nearly doubled, and community college enrollment increased by over 700 percent.[53] To human-capital economists, this educational expansion has not been enough to mitigate the benefits accruing to those with the highest human capital. But the equation of skill and economic reward cannot explain the surging income and wealth of the top 1 percent, nor why the economic payoff of advanced education is so much higher in the United States than in other countries.[54] As observed in the early twentieth century, educational expansion can trigger reactions from distinct organized political interests, in particular those at the top of the economic ladder who seek to preserve their power. Credentialist theories of occupational control seem better equipped to explain why the primary beneficiaries of rising inequality today are concentrated in highly credentialed professions in key positions in the corporate economy.[55] Without a corresponding increase of power for working people, the benefits of additional educational attainment can be captured at the top. The historical perspective offered in this book suggests that focusing only on expanding educational opportunities traps us into a narrow policy framework that can exacerbate the very problem it seeks to address.

In our new Gilded Age, we can look back to the first Gilded Age over a century ago for insight. The role of education in amplifying unequal opportunity was not a unique product of the neoliberal turn of the 1970s or the corporatization of higher education, but a deeply rooted out-growth of the historical relation between education and the economy in the United States. In an era of skyrocketing inequality, we need a new historical understanding of the consequences—sometimes for the better but more often for the worse—of the American faith in education as *the* panacea for social inequality.

ONE

Nineteenth-Century Networks

The pursuit of economic advancement through education is such an entrenched feature of today's public discourse and lived experience that it is difficult to imagine a time when this was not the case. But we only need to go back 150 years to find the operation of a very different world—one in which education played a marginal role as a pathway into employment. In late nineteenth-century Boston, most people did not need diplomas, degrees, or licenses to obtain and practice their jobs. Indeed, in 1880, only 8 percent of boys and girls aged 14 to 17 in Boston attended a public high school.[1] Nationally, secondary school enrollment for this age group was no more than a few percentage points.[2] Few working adults had a formal education beyond eighth grade. What they had instead was informal training, shaped by a range of social and cultural institutions, including extended families and ethnic networks.

We can envision the population of Boston as being divided into three "worlds of work." The first was that of low-wage workers, made up of recent immigrants and members of Boston's African American community employed as day laborers, teamsters, factory operatives, cooks, waiters, and household staff. A second world of work was made up of craftworkers, clerks, and small proprietors. These workers were predominantly native-born, with a minority of Irish, Canadian, German, and English immigrants.[3] A third world of work was inhabited by Boston's upper classes, including merchants, bankers, brokers, large-scale manufacturers, and

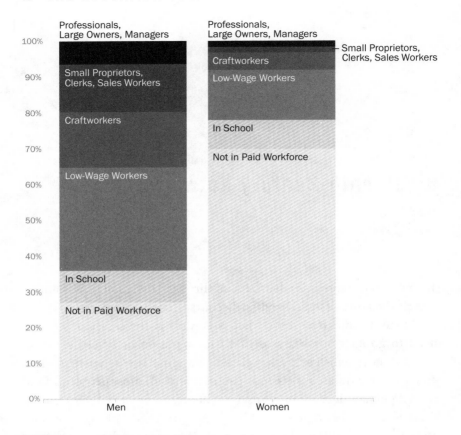

FIGURE 1.1: Workforce participation of Boston population, 1880.

DATA SOURCE: IPUMS 1880. © Cristina Groeger.

NOTE: For details about this classification scheme, see note 5.

professionals. The social norms and culture of Boston's business and professional class were shaped by Boston's most elite group of Protestant families, known as the Boston Brahmins, some of whom traced their ancestry back to the time of the Mayflower.[4] These "worlds" were not the same size—low-wage workers made up nearly half of the workforce while only a sliver belonged to the elite. As Figure 1.1 shows, a significant proportion of men and women did not report a wage-earning occupation to the census at all, yet many of them worked: taking care of children and family members, preparing meals and cleaning the home, or participating in the informal or illicit economy.[5]

Across these diverse worlds of work, what is striking is the extent to which paths into them did not lead through formal education. Michael Walsh, an Irish immigrant whose family came to Boston at the turn of the century, explained his father's entry into a manual labor job that would have been typical: "[My father] got a job the second day he was in the country. They were putting in a sewer on Wood Avenue and it was all pick and shovel then. . . . He went out and got a pick and shovel job."[6] Walsh's father might have had some farming experience in Ireland before migrating, and a relative may have told him where to go to get a pick-and-shovel job once he arrived. Carmela Cerqua, an Italian immigrant in Boston's North End, described a learning path characteristic of a working-class woman in late nineteenth-century Boston: "We had to stay home and work. We did housework—cooking, cleaning, ironing, washing by hand. . . . I learned through other people. You see, you ask, and you learn. . . . We did a lot of crochet. We used to make neckties; we used to make sweaters. I made bedspreads, tablecloths, and linen handkerchiefs."[7] Cerqua would have carefully watched her mother or aunt at home cooking dishes or crocheting before attempting it herself. For entering the world of craftworkers, young apprentices learned on the job. As Lewis Lyne, a mechanical engineer, recalled in 1881: "I used to closely watch the process of hanging shafting whenever I got the chance, which was very seldom. [I] would have given any of my earthly possessions at one time, in exchange for a knowledge of the various details . . . laid out in a very mysterious way by the 'boss.'"[8] Lyne might have had a relative help him get started in a workshop, where he would have learned to be patient and attentive while an older experienced master craftsman performed "mysterious" tasks. From a young age, girls and boys learned specific behaviors and skills within their families, workplaces, and communities, socialized into the networks that would shape their future trajectories.

These trajectories were informal and loosely regulated. With few exceptions, Bostonians did not need specific credentials to enter occupations. Craftworkers had far less control of training than their artisanal counterparts in continental Europe, and professionals such as lawyers and doctors did not need to attend professional schools. But these trajectories were, in other ways, inflexible. The labor market was structured unequally based on gender, class, race, and ethnicity. Many doors into employment in the trades or white-collar work were closed to all but white, native-born Bostonians. Reliance on racial and ethnic networks for finding jobs opened some opportunities but also demarcated their boundaries. Fine distinctions between those performing similar work— bookkeepers and clerks, clothing cutters and clothing finishers, chambermaids and general houseworkers—preserved hierarchies of power.[9]

This chapter surveys Boston's three worlds of work in the year 1880. At this time, the city of Boston, depicted in Figure 1.2, was a commercial and cultural center of nearly 400,000 people. Almost 90 percent of them had arrived in the previous sixty years, and the labor of immigrants transformed the city into New England's hub for textile trade and manufacturing, shoe and leather production, shipyards, and fishing. After the Civil War, Boston lost financial preeminence to New York and industrial preeminence to Western railroads, oil, and steel, but the city rebuilt a diversified economy based on custom- and ready-made clothing, the building trades, foundries and machine works, and commerce in a wide range of goods.[10]

The inhabitants of Boston's three worlds of work—from deck hands, to dressmakers, to wholesale merchants—were not completely cordoned off from each other. Indeed, the most common occupation for women involved working in the well-furnished homes of wealthy employers. There were possibilities for movement and mobility, especially for Boston's immigrants after one or two generations. But restrictions remained rigid for others, especially Black Bostonians. Schools, as we will see, were just one among many institutions that shaped these worlds.

THE WORLD OF LOW-WAGE WORK

The world of low-wage work, which encompassed about half of all wage earners in Boston, centered around the immigrant neighborhoods near Boston's port: the North End, Charlestown, East Boston, and South Boston. It also included Boston's African American community in the West End and north slope of Beacon Hill, where domestic workers had

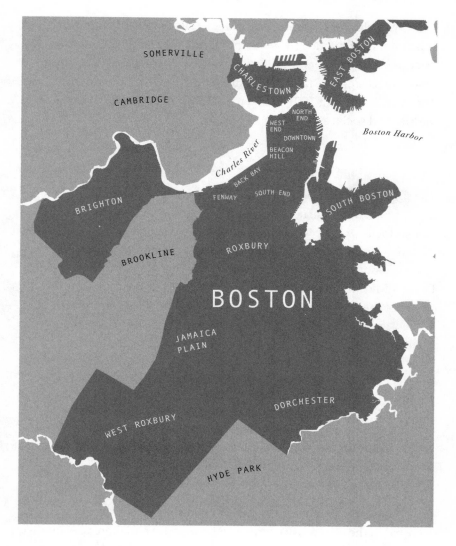

FIGURE 1.2: Boston in 1880.

DATA SOURCES: Steven Manson, Jonathan Schroeder, David Van Riper, and Steven Ruggles, IPUMS National Historical Geographic Information System: Version 14.0 [database] (Minneapolis: IPUMS, 2019), http://doi.org/10.18128/D050.V14.0; Robert W. Fogel, Dora L. Costa, Carlos Villarreal, Brian Bettenhausen, Eric Hanss, Christopher Roudiez, Noelle Yetter, and Andrea Zemp, Historical Urban Ecological Data Set (Chicago: Center for Population Economics, University of Chicago Booth School of Business, and the National Bureau of Economic Research, 2014). © Cristina Groeger.

long lived close to Boston's wealthiest households.[11] While work was fundamentally divided by gender, both the sons and daughters of low-wage manual laborers and personal service workers tended to leave school by the age of 14 to work and contribute to the family income. The most important institutions were ethnic networks that provided financial and social support.

Men's Low-Wage Labor

The single most common occupation for men in Boston, making up one-fifth of male wage earners, was that of a laborer.[12] Laborers worked on ships, docks, wharves, and in warehouses; helped construct houses, buildings, streets, and railways; and served as helpers in workshops. They earned about $300 to $400 per year ($9,500 to $12,600 in 2020 dollars).[13] Dennis Manning, an Irish immigrant to Boston born in 1883, recalls, "Most of the greenhorns went to work on the boats, or on the railroads. Some went in groups into the wool houses. Some did sugar hauling."[14] Eighty percent of Boston laborers were Irish, although they only made up 40 percent of the male workforce. Despite their sizeable presence in the city, in 1880 no person of Irish descent had yet been elected mayor.[15] In the years to come, the Irish would be joined by Italians, Poles, and Lithuanians in the poorly paid, difficult, dangerous, and unregulated work of manual labor.

One-fifth of men and one-seventh of women wage earners in Boston labored in the lower ends of factory work or operated vehicles (as teamsters, hack drivers, and sailors).[16] Thomas McNulty, who was born in Canada to Irish parents, went to work in a shoe factory at the age of 12. As listed in the 1880 census, he lived with his father, a laborer, his mother, who kept house, his sister, a tailor, and his 14-year-old brother, who worked as a clerk in a store.[17] He was likely one of the many generic "shoemakers," machine hands, and table men who made laborer's wages or slightly more. His sister, if she worked in a garment factory, likely earned even less than her brother. Many industries had already shifted from customized craftwork to low-wage factory work by 1880, including the boot, shoe, and leather industries.[18] The conditions of factory labor, especially the employment of women and children, had mobilized labor unions and upper-class reformers in Massachusetts in the 1870s to push for the passage of what were among the first state laws in the country implementing factory inspections and a ten-hour day for women and children, although these laws were routinely violated.[19]

Hucksters, peddlers, and street vendors also belonged to the world of low-wage work, making up about 1 percent of men wage earners. These sellers, predominantly Irish but accompanied by eastern and southern European immigrants, sold produce and wares on carts in the commercial districts of Boston and door-to-door in the suburbs.[20] A range of service occupations—porters, coachmen, waiters, janitors, barbers, and bartenders—occupied the bottom 6 percent of the men's occupational hierarchy. While Black Bostonians were 2 percent of the male workforce, they were largely confined to the bottom rung, representing 16 percent of male service workers. A typical family was the Wilsons. Samuel Wilson was a 47-year-old cook who was listed as "mulatto" in the 1880 census. He had moved from Virginia with his wife and family a few years prior and lived in a tenement on Shawmut Avenue in the South End. Neither he, nor his wife, nor his 23-year-old son who worked as an upholsterer could read or write. His 18-year-old son worked as a bellboy and his 15- and 13-year-old daughters worked as "baby tenders," likely looking after their six younger siblings, ages 1 to 10.[21]

Women's Unpaid and Low-Wage Labor

Working-class families were as dependent on the unpaid labor of wives, mothers, and children as they were on the labor of fathers and husbands. Caring for young, elderly, or sick family members was almost entirely women's work. Household cleaning, cooking, washing, sewing, and mending clothes took hours of often strenuous labor. Women also performed this work for wages. A husband or father's unemployment due to illness, injury, disability, or economic downturn often pushed women into the wage economy to earn additional income.[22]

Such was the case of the family of "P-D," a laborer who in 1870 reported to the Bureau of Statistics of Labor that he "had not been able to obtain work since Christmas, with the exception of a few days; wages $1.67 per day." Due to these circumstances, his wife went "out washing" to support them and their two children. Many women tried to find piece-work for the clothing industry that could be done at home. For example, "P-C," an unemployed laborer, and his wife and daughter earned income by "making flannel shirts at $1.25 per dozen; the two [could] make a dozen a day with help of [a] sewing machine." Children's labor was especially important for low-wage families, particularly if a parent was absent. Many girls left school to work at home caring for parents and siblings or helping with cooking, cleaning, and laundering. In the case of one Irish laborer's family, it was noted that "the mother is dead, and the eldest, a girl of fifteen years, takes entire charge of housework, and performs her many duties with great care."[23]

While homes were the center of unpaid work for the majority of women, the most common paid occupation for women—about 40 percent of all women wage earners, and nearly 50 percent of Black women wage earners—required living in someone else's home as a domestic servant. Most domestic workers were between the ages of 18 and 25 and were disproportionately Irish, Canadian, and African American. Nearly 70 percent used their earnings to help support their families. In a specialized position such as a chambermaid, laundress, seamstress, cook, or nursery governess, a woman might earn between $6 and $9 per week, or $300 to $500 per year. The majority of domestic workers, however, were hired for "general housework" and paid less than $2 per week. With board included, they earned the equivalent of $5 per week. The average domestic worker performed 10.5 hours per day, beginning at 6:00 a.m. or 7:00 a.m. with a 10:00 p.m. curfew, and would have had to receive permission before going out or receiving visitors.[24] While domestic workers complained about their lack of freedom, limited employment options and entrenched ethnic and racial networks channeled many women into this type of work.

Some women turned to prostitution for wages. While the number of women is difficult to measure, based on estimates from New York in the late nineteenth century, between 5 and 10 percent of young women engaged in prostitution at some point in their lives. Of a sample of Boston prostitutes surveyed in 1884, a majority had previously worked in personal service, typically as domestic workers. Most of these women were in their late teens or early twenties, born in Ireland or with Irish parents, and had experienced the death of a parent that instigated their turn to sexual labor for income.[25] Massachusetts laws against adultery, fornication, keeping a "bawdy house," and "night walking" were on the books by the early eighteenth century. Although being a prostitute itself was not a crime before 1917, women were routinely apprehended for vagrancy, loitering, or disorderly conduct. Until early twentieth-century anti-vice campaigns, brothels and parlor houses in Boston's North End were mostly tolerated by the police. However, an uptick in police raids drove prostitution into more private quarters in rooming or lodging houses in the West and South Ends by 1880. Women could earn a lot of money performing sexual labor: some earned in one night what a factory or domestic worker earned in several weeks. For most women, prostitution was not a permanent or full-time job but was temporary work during periods of unemployment, or it was performed in addition to another job to supplement their income. Many found paid sexual labor in the same way other wage earners did—through personal connections provided by neighbors, relatives, and friends.[26]

Ethnic and Kinship Networks

Some immigrants found work quite literally as they walked off the boat. Dan Doherty, who ran a coal yard in Dorchester, "used to go over to East Boston and hire the greenhorns off the boat for very little pay."[27] Friends and relatives often helped to finance the costs of long-distance migration and provided advice about where to travel and what do to upon arrival. These contacts often provided new immigrants with temporary housing and further instruction on acquiring work. John Devlin, a North End resident whose father emigrated from Ireland in the late nineteenth century, recalled the central role of the "Glen Guard House," a combination boarding house, employment agency, and central social site for Irish immigrants in the North End:

> When the greenhorns came over from Ireland, they were met at the boat in Charlestown or in East Boston. They'd be allowed to stay at the Glen Guard House for a week. . . . They'd talk about conditions at home; they would exchange information, so after

a while they had a vast network of information of all the immigrants coming from that particular section of the country. . . .
During that week they had an employment committee which
was going out to seek gainful employment for them.[28]

African Americans who migrated to Boston from the southern United
States also relied on a community of previous migrants to establish themselves. In most cases of southern Black families in Boston taking in
boarders in 1880, both boarder and householder were from the same home
state. Like recent immigrants, Black Bostonians created their own social
spaces to facilitate the transition of newcomers. Neighborhood taverns
and barbershops in the West End and South End became lively social centers where information about lodging and employment was exchanged.[29]

Once these initial networks were established, chain migration patterns reinforced them. Not only did local ties aid recent arrivals, but
employers also benefited from and encouraged these social connections,
fortifying ethnic and racial niches within the labor market. From the
perspective of employers, hiring the relatives and friends of current employees facilitated rapid orientation to a new job and instilled a sense of
personal obligation to remain. As Carmela Cerqua described the process of getting her job in a Cambridge candy factory, "To get the jobs,
you had friends and they talk about you to the boss."[30] However, the
ability of employees to assist others in finding work varied by job sector
and ethnic or racial group. African Americans, who were relegated to
the most menial jobs and often scattered across private homes could less
easily assist each other in finding employment.[31]

Recent immigrants joined a pool of precarious workers. Once a
building or infrastructure project was over, laborers' employment search
would begin anew. Many factory workers sought employment directly
at factory gates and were subject to the whims of employers, foremen,
and production schedules. Eric Wartmaugh described his experience
seeking employment at Walworth, a valve-manufacturing company in
South Boston, in the 1890s:

They used to call that the madhouse. They had iron gates. The
whistle blew at 7 o'clock and you're crossing the street and those

gates closed, so you went into the hall and you stood there and the man telephoned upstairs. I called him my Uncle George. . . . If the boss liked you he'd say, "Well, send him up." If he didn't he'd say, "Tell him to come back at noontime." So you could lose a half day's pay. I've seen men go in Monday and they didn't have many orders from the main office so they say, "Well, come in Wednesday." You could lose two or three days a week.[32]

Outdoor work on streets, sewers, trolley lines, and railways was even less secure than factory work, and seasonal patterns left many laborers unemployed for months each year.

Those without ready access to personal contacts or networks turned to employment agencies to secure work. The majority of these "employment bureaus" or "intelligence offices" were for-profit enterprises that relied on fees from both employers and employees, and the aid they could provide depended upon the social contacts of their owners. The state of Massachusetts required intelligence offices to be licensed starting in 1848, but these offices still operated in a fairly unregulated market.[33] By 1894, Boston was home to 119 licensed private intelligence offices and fourteen licensed philanthropic employment agencies.[34] Deception of unsuspecting applicants was common. Mrs. M. from Nova Scotia, who had moved to Boston in 1877 seeking employment after her husband died, wrote to the *Boston Globe:*

On my arrival [in Boston], seeing an advertisement that five Nova Scotia girls were wanted, I started for the place, and on entering met a lady who informed me that she had plenty of nice situations. I made an application for one and paid my fee. [Later that day, I] was very rudely told that there was none. . . . I asked for my fee and was refused. I tried four others during the week and paid fees in all three of them, and the result was the same in all.[35]

Since the eighteenth century, Boston newspapers had featured advertisements for both goods and personal services, and as circulation expanded, employers or employment agencies took out "Male Help" and

"Female Help" want ads.[36] Even though newspaper ads played a minor role in facilitating employment, they shed light on the qualities that were important to employers for low-wage workers. Many ads simply speci-fied what kinds of workers were needed and when: "Corset stitchers, at once," and "Laborers, this morning." For manual labor, physical abili-ties were specified: "Smart, able-bodied men for good jobs on farms," "Stout men for laboring."[37] Many ads specified an age range: "A girl, about 14 years old to take care of children and assist in house work," "A middle-aged woman to take charge of a small family."[38] Religion, eth-nicity, and race were common qualifiers: "A Protestant girl, either Amer-ican or Nova Scotian," "German preferred," "A colored boy to run a passenger elevator."[39] Personal behavioral traits were also cited in lists of prerequisites for employment: "Must be an industrious and sober man," "A colored inside man: must be of good habits, pleasant and willing," "A smart, honest girl for housework."[40] These qualities had little to do with formal schooling and much more to do with employers' calculus of the gender, ethnic, racial, and personal traits they believed to be best suited for low-wage labor.

The Role of Schools for Low-Wage Workers

Some low-wage workers and their children took advantage of Boston's expanding school system. In the late 1830s, Horace Mann, the secretary of the Massachusetts board of education, spearheaded the common school movement that became a model for public, free, graded schools around the country. Common school advocates urged support for the expansion and centralization of public services, and they drew on a re-publican, Protestant tradition of education as character-building and moral formation, intersecting with both racial and ethnic politics of the mid-nineteenth century.[41] The nation's first legal challenge to segregated schools in 1849 originated in Boston, when Benjamin F. Roberts sought to enroll his daughter Sarah in a white school closer to their home in-stead of Boston's underfunded Black school. The Massachusetts courts ruled against Roberts in an opinion that would later be cited in *Plessy v. Ferguson* upholding the doctrine of "separate but equal." Only a few years later, however, Massachusetts became the first state to prohibit seg-regated schools on the basis of race or religion in 1855. Rising anti-Irish nativism was likely responsible for this shift. Irish Catholics sought to gain public funding for their own parochial schools, and racial segregation was an obvious precedent for their efforts. Thus, the desire to assimilate immigrants into Protestant culture undoubtedly served to motivate Boston leaders to tolerate racial integration and hinder the growth of Catholic schools.[42]

After the Civil War, decentralized local governance, white manhood suffrage, and popular support fostered high levels of school enrollment in northern states.[43] While the antislavery Republican Party had been the leading champion of expanding public services before and after the Civil War, public schools were also driven by working-class support for practical instruction within the Democratic Party, the party associated with Catholic immigrants in many northern cities.[44] Most of Boston's school budget, which was the city's single largest expense in the late nineteenth century, went to public primary (the first three grades) and grammar schools.[45] In these schools, which also effectively functioned as free day care for parents, young people were taught basic literacy, numeracy, proper manners, and discipline. At a time when school grading by age was in its infancy, many older students were still enrolled in grammar school, such that, although only a small fraction of 14–17-year-olds in Boston were enrolled in public high school in 1880, about one-third of the 14–17-year-old children of low-wage workers reported that they had attended school within the last year. This likely reflects some degree of exaggeration to the census reporter, but also the reality that grammar school, rather than high school, was the upper limit of education for the vast majority of Boston's population.[46]

Most of Boston's Irish Catholic families sent their children to public schools instead of parochial schools. Public schools were free and were seen by many lay Catholics as a means of accessing the status of more affluent Bostonians. By 1880, Irish Bostonians had some influence over public schools through their political representation on the school committee and in ward-level political offices. Boston's archbishop from 1866 to 1907, John Joseph Williams, also promoted conciliation with Protestants and saw the benefits of one system of public schools as opposed to a separate system of parish schools.[47] Only about 10 percent of Boston students were enrolled in parochial or private schools in 1880, at a time when 75 percent of Irish school-age children (age 5 to 15) attended school, about the same average attendance rate of school-age Bostonians overall.[48]

Among low-wage workers, formal schooling did not play a very significant role in facilitating work patterns. Many adult immigrants and African Americans were illiterate, and remained so. After the age of 13, there was a steep drop-off in school enrollment. Among children of laborers in 1880, at least 40 percent of 14-year-olds and 80 percent of 16-year-olds went to work instead of school—most commonly as factory workers, domestic workers, messengers, or sales clerks.[49] Massachusetts passed the first compulsory school law in the country in 1852, requiring all children 8 to 14 to attend school for a minimum of twelve weeks a year, and Boston appointed its first truant officers that year. However, attendance laws were routinely violated.[50] Notably, African American children, for each age cohort up to the age of 19, attended school at higher rates than the white sons and daughters of low-wage workers, reflecting both the strong aspiration of African Americans to achieve literacy as well as the employment discrimination that lowered their opportunity cost of remaining in school.[51]

According to an 1879 survey of working-class men, 90 percent of those who responded expressed confidence that their children were receiving the appropriate amount of schooling. At the same time, some laboring families expressed a desire to send their children to school longer. One wool sorter lamented the trade-offs his family had to make: "My wages have been reduced forty per cent in the last three years; and, if my children were old enough, I should be obliged to set them at work, thereby causing them to lose the education they ought to have, and that I would give them had I the means." Even though many working-class families required the assistance of their children to survive, some believed schooling to be something their children "ought to have."[52]

THE WORLD OF CRAFTWORKERS AND SHOPKEEPERS

Craftworkers, clerical workers, and small proprietors altogether made up over one-third of Boston's wage earners in 1880. They predominantly hailed from New England and Canada; a small number were from

Ireland, England, Scotland, or Germany. These families lived in central industrial districts of the South End and South Boston, or in Boston's recently annexed suburbs of Roxbury, Dorchester, or Brighton, likely making use of Boston's system of streetcars.[53] For a small "skilled aristocracy" of male craftworkers, pathways into employment were structured through a craft-union regulated apprenticeship. Others entered this work through kinship and social networks rooted in a variety of organizations: churches, social clubs, benevolent organizations, and fraternal societies. Sons and daughters of craftworkers and shopkeepers typically attended public school but left after age 15 or 16. Public high schools, known at the time as "people's colleges," were celebrated as institutions that opened higher learning to all, but in practice only a small percentage of working-class youth ever enrolled, and an even smaller minority attended parochial or private secondary schools.[54]

The Trades

About one-quarter each of working men and working women in Boston were craftworkers. Most worked as carpenters, builders, masons, bricklayers (in the building trades), machinists, mechanics, and engineers (in the metal trades), and tailors, dressmakers, milliners, and seamstresses (in the needle trades). While the majority of craftworkers were native-born, immigrants from England, Germany, Scandinavia, Canada, and Ireland also populated these trades.

Carpentry was the most common trade for men in Boston in 1880, with Canadians significantly overrepresented. "No. 10" was an "American" carpenter who earned $716 annually, slightly above average for this trade. He lived with his wife and four children in a six-room tenement with "a small flower-garden attached." His 15-year-old son also worked, earning an extra $300 for the family. His 16-year-old daughter sometimes "[helped] the mother at home," but also regularly attended school. As signs of respectable status, the family had a carpeted parlor and a piano.[55] As the city grew, carpenters were in demand to build houses, and construction proceeded rapidly in an unregulated housing market. Many amateur carpenters would build one or two homes; others worked for contractors or builders.[56] Contractors and builders lived even more comfortably. William Rand, a 61-year-old carpenter-builder from New Hampshire, lived in a single-family home in Roxbury with his wife, three children, one boarder, and two domestic servants.[57]

Machinists, who comprised the second-most common trade for men in Boston, were at the center of the technological change transforming major industries in the late nineteenth century.[58] Some machinists made a business out of designing specialized metalwork and machinery. W. R. Hanks, raised in Wellesley, ran his own shop in downtown Boston. In addition to manufacturing locomotive tire heaters and brass oil burners, he also designed and sold a new welt cutter for boot manufacturers that was put on the market in the fall of 1886.[59] The average machinist, by contrast, worked for an employer and might have made $13 to $15 per week, or $700 to $800 per year.[60] Walworth, the pipe fitting and valve company, occupied thirteen acres and over 500,000 feet of floor space in South Boston and employed over 800 men in 1880, many of whom were machinists and mechanics.[61]

Needle-trade workers made up almost one-third of all craftworkers in Boston, and nearly 90 percent of these needle-trade workers were women. Tailors and tailoresses made men's suits: designing patterns, cutting fabrics, sewing garments together, finishing them with details such as buttons or hooks, and pressing them with a heavy iron. Although men dominated the top positions as clothing cutters and pressers making between $700 and $800 per year, women working as sewing machine operators and finishers outnumbered their male counterparts two to one. The lowest-paid women finishers often made just $150 to $250 (an amount equal to or less than that earned by domestic workers) per year. The majority of Boston's tailors were Irish, with a high representation of German Jewish tailors as well. Many recent immigrants brought experience in the clothing industry with them when they immigrated to the United States.[62]

Dressmakers and milliners (hatmakers) made up what historian Wendy Gamber has called the "female aristocracy of labor." Dressmakers ran stores in downtown Boston or went "out by the day" to visit clients, primarily women in the wealthier districts and suburbs of Boston. The typical dressmaker made between $400 and $500 per year, but the lowest-paid seamstresses might have made $200 annually. Dressmakers and milliners were primarily white women from New England and Canada and, as family responsibilities would have precluded many women from pursuing this work as a full-time occupation, tended to be single or widowed.[63]

Craft Union Apprenticeships

In Boston, as in most other American cities, family networks served as conduits through which young workers entered the trades. The countless small establishments with "Brothers" or "& Sons" appended to their names is just one indicator of these family connections. The 1880 census also reveals that of young carpenters still living at home, 58 percent had fathers who were also carpenters; of young male tailors, 57 percent had fathers who were tailors. One-third of all apprentices were in the same trade as their fathers.[64]

The majority of craftworkers in the late nineteenth century trained through apprenticeships, whether of the formal or informal variety. Those migrating from England, Germany, and Canada conducted their apprenticeships abroad, but most craftworkers were native-born and had learned their trade in the United States.[65] While traditional artisanal guilds never developed in the United States, since the seventeenth century, apprenticeships, like indentured servitude, had been structured according to formal legal contracts between the family of an apprentice and a master craftworker (almost always a master craftsman). Traditionally, apprentices would work their way up to the status of journeyman and then proceed to open their own shops as masters. Through the nineteenth century the number of master craftsmen shrank, and larger shops hired more permanent wage earners.[66]

Among wage-earning craftworkers in the mid-nineteenth century, journeymen were the first to organize craft unions. In the nineteenth century, workers' right to organize a union was precarious, and courts often upheld the business ideology that union organizing was akin to criminal activity. Before the 1930s, employers were not legally obligated to recognize a union or to engage in collective bargaining.[67] However, workers pursued multiple strategies for building their power. Boston was home to the first eight-hour league in 1865, dedicated to promoting an eight-hour workday, and journeymen unions formed the Boston Central Labor Union (BCLU) in 1878. The Knights of Labor, which counted between 5,000 and 12,000 Bostonians among its members in 1886, made Boston its "banner city" that year.[68] The Knights' vision of an encompassing union across gender, race, and skill level quickly gave way to the craft union model of the building trades and the American Federation of Labor (AFL), based on limited membership among those who possessed specific craft skills. The craft union approach of the AFL, which dominated the BCLU, was premised on the exclusion of newer eastern and southern European immigrants, as well as African Americans. Racial discrimination was often written into craft union local bylaws, especially as white workers came to view African Americans as strikebreakers.[69]

Regulating apprenticeship was a crucial way that craft unions maintained their power. Craft unions specified pay and working hours to prevent young apprentices from being used to undermine the pay scales or replace the jobs of journeymen. They set upper limits to the number of apprentices per journeymen in workshops to ensure that new workers would not overcrowd the market. They also specified the number of years of apprenticeship training—typically three to seven years—to ensure that only high-quality workers entered the trade.[70]

Building-trade unions were among the strongest craft unions. Among the reasons for their strength was the decentralized nature of construction. Construction projects were local, one-off endeavors and work was seasonal and highly weather dependent. Tradesmen moved rapidly from one project to the next, and unions came to play an indispensable role in coordinating this work as a labor bureau. Numerous types of craftworkers—carpenters, bricklayers, plasterers, plumbers—worked side by side on a project and could threaten to strike if non-union workers showed up to the worksite.[71] When contractors entered politics, their cooperative relationship with building-trade unions became the basis of political machines, and hence a major source of emerging strength for Irish Democrats in Boston.[72] Building-trade workers also secured licensing laws beginning in 1885, specifying prerequisites to engage in construction projects, plumbing, and electrical installation, as another form of regulating entry.[73]

By contrast, union presence in other trades was weak. Across the United States, high geographic mobility, an underdeveloped tradition of craft guilds, and a limited regulatory state hindered the power of craft unions to formalize apprenticeship. Craft unions battled employment associations eager to break their power, and gender and racial divisions also fractured worker solidarity. In practice, "apprenticeship" was often used colloquially to refer to the employment of young workers or helpers, whether or not the shop was abiding by union standards. Apprentices, as such, were frequently exploited as a source of inexpensive labor.[74] But whether through a formal or informal apprenticeship, young craftworkers primarily learned their work on the job.

Learning technical craft skills was an essential aspect of training for craftwork. Help wanted ads for craftworkers reveal that experience, skill, and speed were necessary qualities. For example, an employer sought to hire "a first-class custom tailor to take charge of a back shop" who "must be . . . capable of turning out first-class work," and "a [female] compositor" who "can set a good proof."[75]

The process of training, however, was about more than learning the technical skills of the trade. Initiation into the "shop culture" of young apprentices, and the hazing rituals that went along with it, were essential to craft identity and the socialization of youth.[76] In the building and metal trades in particular, craftsmen embraced a masculine culture based on a shared white identity that excluded eastern and southern European immigrants, African Americans, and women. Master craftsmen and employers also used apprenticeship to groom future foremen and supervisors who possessed the right technical, behavioral, and personal characteristics. Employers viewed the training process as a way to instill loyalty to the firm and root out union "agitators." The preferred traits for "promotable material" also reflected racial and ethnic stereotypes. As foreign workers increasingly entered the trades, employers expressed concern with the declining number of native-born apprentices.[77]

If craftsmen switched jobs, they might rely on references from a previous employer to substantiate their technical mastery and moral character. Henry Pickford, a Boston locksmith, accumulated a collection of reference letters that he could share with prospective employers. The owners of a hardware dealership, Bogman and Vinal, wrote in 1881, "We the undersigned have had business relations with Mr. Henry Pickford for the past 15 years and consider him a thorough mechanic and perfectly honest and trustworthy, for any position in which he may be placed."[78] Honesty and trustworthiness may have been as important to prospective employers as Pickford's mechanical ability. Craftworkers were evaluated based on a wide range of qualities beyond their technical expertise.

Schools as a Working-Class Demand

Trade union leaders had long supported the expansion of public schools. In the late nineteenth century, labor support for education stemmed from multiple reasons: the belief that free universal education was essential to democracy, skepticism of privately controlled schools aligned with the interests of capital, a desire to assimilate immigrants and foster solidarity across ethnic groups, and, in their support for compulsory education laws, keeping youth out of the labor market to prevent them from undercutting adult wages. George McNeill, a leader of the eight-hour movement in the 1860s and later director of the Massachusetts Bureau of Statistics of Labor, espoused a common belief that education was a key means of both alleviating poverty and instilling the values that would prevent the abuses of wealth. Observing factory conditions in the 1870s, he expressed horror at the violations of child labor laws that denied children access to education. As he put it, "Who can doubt that if every child in America was properly trained and educated . . . that the degradation of abject poverty would be removed with its cause, and that the worst degradation, the degradation which great and misused wealth brings to its possessor . . . would no more exist?"[79]

The AFL similarly gave a prominent place to education, resolving in 1888 "that the education of the people is the fundamental principle upon which the success of every proposed piece of social reform depends."[80] On the basis of their belief in egalitarianism, union leaders supported free public higher education. In 1888, the Boston Central Labor Union "most heartily and unqualifiedly" endorsed a proposition to introduce a university-level course into the public school system "so that our children may have the same educational advantage now only attainable by rich men's sons and daughters."[81]

If these positive educational demands represented aspirations, they were limited in practice for the majority of craftworkers. Although Boston craftworkers took advantage of primary schools where their children could learn basic literacy and numeracy, few of their children attended high school. Some craftworkers criticized public schools for their failure to teach respect for labor. As one machinist wrote in 1881, "Too many of our boys are silently taught . . . to shun labor, and think trade a disgrace."[82] A related critique of public schools pointed to their problematic focus on training for business. An editorial in *The Carpenter* argued that the "mercantile and banking house education of our schools" trained youth to dislike the trades and believe that "the most respectable occupation is that in which a man becomes rich the quickest."[83] Public school officials acknowledged the limitations of their curriculum. Although some trade instruction had been introduced into the public schools, including mechanical drawing for boys in the 1830s and sewing for girls in the 1850s, the school board observed in 1870 that "our present school education is too exclusively the preparation either for professional life or for a mercantile or shop-keeping life," and recommended expanding trade instruction.[84] The critique of public schools as training schools for business would become central to efforts to expand industrial education in future decades.

Shopkeepers and White-Collar Workers

Small proprietors, clerical, and sales workers occupied a similar economic position to Boston's craftworkers in this period. While owning a small shop was a central avenue for immigrant entrepreneurs, most proprietors in 1880 had well-established roots in Massachusetts and New England. The most common proprietors were traders and dealers in groceries and produce who often belonged to one of Boston's trade associations, such as the Boston Grocer's Association, the Boston Fruit and Produce Exchange, or the Boston Fish Bureau.[85] The families of these small proprietors lived in double- or single-family homes, in the South End or on the outskirts of Boston; they were often aligned with the Republican Party. About 3 percent of working women, predominantly natives of New England and Canada, were recorded in the census as proprietors, running retail stores and boarding or lodging houses.[86]

Clerks, sales workers, bookkeepers, and accountants made up 15 percent of wage-earning men and 6 percent of wage-earning women in Boston. In the early nineteenth century, a clerkship was in effect a merchant's apprenticeship. Clerks assisted with the handling of accounts in small offices with a handful of other employees. As corporate and state bureaucracies expanded in the late nineteenth century, clerks began to work in larger settings, performing more specialized tasks, and most would remain in the middle ranks of office work despite aspirations of economic independence.[87] Women also entered these positions. In Boston, prompted by periods of recession in the 1870s, employers increasingly drew from a growing pool of predominantly native-born, Protestant, educated women who were willing to work for half of the salaries of their male counterparts. As one employer wrote in 1883: "Young women are more contented with their lot . . . more cheerful, less restless, more to be depended [upon], more flexible than young men."[88] In 1880, the feminization of clerical and sales work was just in its early stages. At the lowest levels, messengers, errand and "cash" girls and boys relayed information and assisted with sales transactions. These jobs could pay as little as $2 a week (or $100 per year) and were most likely to be occupied by second-generation Irish and women employees. Further up the white-collar hierarchy, cashiers would conduct sales, and copyists would transcribe letters and bills. Canvassers, salesmen, and saleswomen were employed in stores or sent to travel (in this capacity, they were known as commercial travelers or "drummers") to sell their companies' goods. At the highest level, commission clerks, bookkeepers, and accountants were almost entirely white men with parents from Massachusetts and New England. While Boston's male bookkeepers and accountants might have earned $800 to $1,000 annually in 1884, the average female bookkeeper only earned $300 to $350.[89]

The diary of a traveling salesman provides a window into the daily routines and cultural norms of this late nineteenth-century white-collar world. Augustus Ayling was born in Boston in 1841; his parents were both from Massachusetts, and his father had been an actor. Between 1865 and 1910 Ayling worked for R. P. Hall & Co., a hair-product company based in Nashua, New Hampshire, plying wares around New England. In his diary from 1867 to 1869, Ayling detailed his day-to-day travels, which ranged from fifty to one hundred miles per week. Every few days, he moved to a new inn, tavern, boarding house, or hotel. He regularly found himself at the mercy of rain, sleet, and snow, as well as unreliable transportation due to a sick horse or a broken "sleigh" that would prevent him from traveling for days on end.[90]

While the life of a traveling salesman was a lonely one, Ayling spent his evenings playing billiards, dominoes, or crib; playing guitar; smoking; dancing; chatting with fellow boarders in the bar room; and occasionally attending a circus show, baseball game, or lecture. Several times he attended a minstrel show such as "Comical Brown's"; on one occasion, he noted that his hotel "got some darkeys in with violins and violin-cellos and they played very well."[91] On the weekends he would write letters to his family and friends, or read novels, detective stories, popular history, and periodicals such as *Harper's Weekly*. While on the road, he crossed paths with business acquaintances: a "Fox Sewing Machine Agent," or a "Rennes Magic Oil" agent. He also belonged to the Ancient York Lodge of the Masons, a fraternal organization representative of his respectable status, and he regularly encountered fellow Masons along his business routes.

The judgments expressed in Ayling's diary reveal a portrait of a man who sought to maintain an elevated sense of propriety and who looked down upon people and forms of entertainment that he considered cheap and vulgar. One night he "got acquainted with a Mr. Pinny of NY in the liquor trade and played a game of billiards with him—he didn't amount to much—can talk of nothing but women."[92] A magician's show was "Humbug," and a village debate on the subject "Is the world advancing in morality?" was "a big display of eloquence & bad grammar."[93] Ayling's comments also reflect the role of ethnic and racial exclusion in policing the boundaries of the respectable businessman. When staying in Hotel O'Brien, he wrote, "Deuced poor accommodations—*Irish*."[94] On the other hand, Mr. Tracy, an assistant teacher from West Stockbridge he met on a different occasion, was "a very fine fellow," and he was similarly impressed with Mr. Lawrence, "a man of education and has traveled extensively . . . had a very pleasant and instructive talk."[95] Ayling exemplified what would have been typical leisure activities, social networks, and attitudes among white, native-born male clerks and salesmen in the late nineteenth century.

Entering White-Collar Work

Like craftworkers, many children of small proprietors followed their parents into the business world. Clerks were typically the sons, nephews, and brothers of proprietors working in the family business or a related business. Want ads, such as one seeking "a young man of ability to grow up in a counting room," reveal that apprenticing informally in an office, store, or counting room was common practice.[96]

Technical job skills such as penmanship, writing, reading, and mathematics were essential for these occupations. One ad stipulated the need for "a young man about 18 years of age as entry clerk in wholesale fancy dry goods house; must be rapid penman, quick and correct at figures. Address in own handwriting."[97] Also sought after was "a lady bookkeeper; must write a good business hand."[98] In addition to technical skills, these ads indicate the behavioral traits required for both entry-level and advanced positions. For salesmen who worked in stores, tact, sociability, and proper manners were crucial. One ad for a salesperson read, "An American gentleman of several years business experience; must be very polite and know how to carry himself with lady customers."[99]

Even more so than in the trades, letters of recommendation were often required to attest to candidates' honesty and reliability: "A boy, age not less than 15, of American parentage, who can offer perfect evidence of trustworthiness in the way of recommendation."[100] As historian Brian Luskey argues, "Young men in nineteenth-century America depended for their advancement on revealing their good character to patrons who would use their own connections to propel these youthful associates into well-paid jobs."[101] For those entrusted with important business transactions—either in office work, sales, or work involving long-distance travel—reliability was an important trait for which employers wanted to have evidence. "American parentage" was often preferred and was likely, in the eyes of predominantly Yankee employers, a proxy for dependability.

While established families were able to pass down norms of politeness and sociability to their children, other skills were learned in schools. Beginning in the eighteenth century, Boston's public grammar schools offered English, reading, writing, spelling, and arithmetic; bookkeeping was added in the 1820s. The English High School, founded in 1821 as an alternative to the college-preparatory Latin High School and located in the South End in the 1880s, was in effect a school for business, offering bookkeeping, algebra, trigonometry, and foreign languages, intended to fit boys "for all the departments of commercial life."[102] By the late 1880s, the majority of men who only pursued one to two years of public high school without graduating went on to become clerks.[103] Women in the same period might have attended a few years at the Girls' High School, also in the South End, or one of the six co-ed neighborhood public high schools.[104] A typical businessman in 1880, however, would have considered practical experience far more important than formal education for succeeding in the business world.[105]

Schools existed among a wide range of cultural institutions organized along religious and ethnic lines. By 1880, 150 Protestant churches (predominantly Congregationalist and Episcopal), thirty Catholic churches, and seven synagogues made up key social nodes for Boston's native-born and immigrant communities.[106] Churches sponsored charities to help those within their own religious communities and provide social activities for their more affluent members. One example was the Charitable Irish Society, whose annual St. Patrick's Day dinner in one of Boston's fashionable hotels was a central occasion for privileged Irish Bostonians. Fraternal organizations such as the Ancient Order of the Hibernians offered their Irish Catholic members benefits such as life insurance, as well as social events and annual parades.[107] Boston's Catholic and Jewish communities were largely excluded from Boston's elite clubhouses, but they organized a few of their own. The Elysium Club, founded in 1871 in the South End, was a social club for Jewish businessmen and professionals.[108] The Catholic Union was founded in 1873 at the suggestion of Archbishop Williams to foster a Catholic intellectual elite that could participate on equal footing with Protestant Boston in the leadership of the city.[109] The Catholic Union—whose clubhouse featured a library, billiard room, and a bowling alley—sponsored weekly discussions, public lectures, concerts, and "assemblies" for entire families.[110] These religious and ethnic organizations established norms of propriety for their members and forged the social networks that shaped entry into jobs.

THE WORLD OF BOSTON'S ELITE

Boston's upper class of businessmen and professionals made up about 10 percent of Boston workers. They lived in the posh Beacon Hill or Back Bay neighborhoods or in suburban Brookline, Chestnut Hill, or Wellesley.[111] Boston's private clubs served as places to eat meals, socialize, and host events. Wives, sisters, and daughters managed the household and their domestic workers, entertained guests, raised children, and helped run charity and benevolent societies. Sons and daughters of businessmen attended school until the age of 16 or 17 and might enroll in Boston's public high schools or a private academy, learning appropriate behaviors and developing contacts with other upper-class families. Boston Brahmins, who dominated the top financial and professional positions, developed a distinct culture within exclusive private social clubs such as the Somerset and Algonquin, trade associations, churches, charitable societies, academies, colleges, and universities, which facilitated entry into the economic elite.

Merchants and Manufacturers

Boston was a global center of commerce in cotton, wool, shoes and leather, fish, produce, lumber, and other manufactured goods, and its merchants, traders, and dealers busily directed the movement of goods in and out of Boston's port. Commission merchants and brokers facilitated these transactions. Presidents, executives, and business managers might earn several thousand dollars annually.[112] Successful businessmen typically got their start through family contacts. For example, in 1880, B. S. Snow took over a wholesale fish dealer located on Boston's T Wharf from his father, Franklin Snow, who had established the business in 1853. They handled varieties of dry, salt, pickled, and boneless fish, and maintained a three-story brick building for storage and a store on Long Wharf. They sold to wholesale as well as retail dealers across the United States, especially large grocers in Boston, and employed twenty people.[113] The social network of businessmen cut laterally across sectors of the business community, and unlike craftsmen trained in a specific trade, businessmen traveled easily across industries.[114] A shared opposition to organized labor helped unify the ranks of management.[115]

Manufacturers produced a wide range of goods in shops and factories located in Boston and its environs. In some cases, master craftsmen worked their way up to become proprietors themselves. The founder of Walworth Company, James Jones Walworth, was an apprentice engineer before starting what became a successful heating and later pipe-fitting and valve company.[116] Most presidents and managers of companies, however, were those with a background in business.

Entering Management

Most proprietors of large businesses learned on the job through informal apprenticeships, working alongside a merchant or manufacturer, rather than in schools. The rates of school enrollment for their children were second only to professionals, but even secondary schooling was not essential. From a sample of thirty-five prominent business leaders in Boston in 1880, about half had received only a grammar school education. Thirty percent continued on to some form of secondary education. Only 10 percent attended a degree-granting college. One student, Frederick Prince, the son of a mayor of Boston, left college before graduating to pursue business opportunities and became a successful banker and broker.[117] At a time when many students who attended college did not earn a degree, a year or two would have served as a period of cultural finishing and social networking, regardless of the credential obtained.[118]

Proprietors were skeptical of the classical education dominant in high schools and colleges. As one businessman complained, "What shall we say then of the colleges—and their number is legion—which, after four years of so-called training for life, turn out of their doors a helpless creature whose whole stock in trade consists in his ability to scan you a Greek verse, or to give you on demand a Latin quotation 'to point a moral or adorn a tale'?"[119] The president of the National Retail Shoe-Dealers' Association, I. B. Arnold, stressed practical experience first, observing "the man with a common school education [and] much knowledge of the world. . . . outstrips the man of high literary and scientific attainments." Experience, rather than formal schooling, was the most important factor in business employment. At the same time, businessmen recognized the cultural power of colleges and universities. "I would not be understood to disparage literary education; far from it," Arnold clarified. He admitted, "I desire all my children to take a course in college." However, he still insisted that "a knowledge of men and things is fully as important as all they gain from text books."[120] Collegiate education was a sign of cultural prominence and prestige, which even a skeptical businessman might want for his child.

The Learned Professions

The traditional professions of law, medicine, ministry, and teaching were the most structured by formal education in 1880. It was common for Boston professionals to have obtained some postsecondary education. However, most professionals had not attended a dedicated professional school, and with the exception of the ministry and public high school teaching, a college degree was not required.[121] Like entry into other occupations, training took place on the job in the form of an informal apprenticeship.

Lawyers and teachers illustrate opposite poles in the experience of "professionals" in late nineteenth-century Boston. Law was the most exclusive profession: nearly 90 percent of Boston lawyers were white, native-born, Protestant men and could make $3,000 per year or more.[122] The legal profession was controlled by a small number of attorneys and judges who comprised the Suffolk County Bar Association. In law, educational requirements actually went down from the early to mid-nineteenth century. In 1808, in order to practice before the Suffolk County lower court, one was required to have a college degree or have completed seven years of "literary pursuits" (equivalent to high school

and college), in addition to three years of study in an attorney's law offices. One was also required to pay $150 a year, which was raised to
$500 in 1810. The majority of Boston lawyers in this period received an
undergraduate education at Harvard College. In 1836, Democrats in the
Massachusetts legislature pushed through a new law that eliminated the
formal education requirement for practicing law. Aspiring lawyers were
required to either spend three years studying with a practicing lawyer
or simply pass an exam administered by the courts. While this populist
deregulation marked a shift away from formal educational requirements,
there were many other mechanisms to keep law practice restricted, especially in a Northeastern city like Boston. The bar exam was an oral
exam administered by a judge, who was often a member of the local bar
association. To enter into an apprenticeship with a practicing attorney,
one needed a contact to facilitate an introduction and offer a recommendation. In addition, after acceptance into the bar, practicing lawyers
participated in rituals of socialization while on the judicial circuit that
reinforced their exclusive status.[123]

"Law" was practiced by many individuals without any formal legal
training. Laypeople without any standing before the court, including
many women, regularly provided legal assistance to resolve small disputes. However, these practitioners were excluded from the bar. There
were a handful of African American lawyers in the nineteenth century,
including Robert Morris, who, alongside Charles Sumner, argued the
1849 case to desegregate Boston's schools. However, African Americans were not allowed into the Boston Bar Association (formally organized in 1876) until the twentieth century. Similar to craft unions, professional associations would play a key role in regulating entry to an
occupation.[124]

The earliest law schools were primarily meant to supplement, not substitute for, a legal apprenticeship. When Harvard Law School was
founded in 1817, it offered an eighteen-month course leading to a bachelor's of law degree (LLB)—with no required final examination—that
was taught by law instructors who were also practicing attorneys. After
receiving their LLBs, students would then conduct a period of office
study. In the nineteenth century, law schools thus primarily functioned
as sites for networking among practicing members of the bar.[125]

Teaching was the most commonly listed profession for men and women in late nineteenth-century Boston. Compared to other professions, teaching had one of the most formalized school-based training processes as well as the lowest status. The common school movement of the mid-nineteenth century sought to professionalize and standardize teacher training. Massachusetts opened its first normal school, or teacher training school, in Bridgewater in 1840, and Boston opened a city normal school in 1852. A mandatory examination to teach in the Boston public schools was introduced by 1858, and by 1884, to apply for an examination to become a primary or grammar school teacher, one needed to have one year of teaching experience or to have graduated from the Boston Normal School.[126] To teach in public high schools, a college degree was required.[127]

Unlike the legal profession, the teaching profession was already majority female by the mid-nineteenth century, and in 1880, 85 percent of all Boston teachers were women.[128] Horace Mann was a chief promoter of the idea that women were the "natural" teachers of young children and, thus, that professional opportunities should be open to them.[129] Gender shaped a steep internal ladder. At the top, public high schools were until 1852 solely for male students and taught by male college graduates. To become a primary or grammar school teacher, women typically trained in private academies or seminaries, since strong resistance to women's education in Boston kept public high schools and private colleges closed to them.[130] When the Boston Normal School opened to women students, compared to the impressive buildings of some of Boston's male high schools, it shared cramped quarters with the newly founded Girls' High School and subsequently a public grammar school in the South End.[131] Gender structured occupational titles: male teachers were "masters," and female teachers, the numeric majority, were "assistants." The position of principal, stemming from the designation "principal teacher," was reserved for men. Men could earn between $1,440 and $3,780 annually, while women earned between $504 and $1,800. Salaries for women teachers in nineteenth-century Massachusetts were an average of 40 percent of those paid to their male counterparts, constituting one of the largest gender wage gaps in the country.[132]

The first teachers' association, the Boston Grammar School Masters Association, was organized by men in 1845 to protect their status in response to the feminization of the teaching force.[133] Women also formed organizations, such as the Lady Teachers' Association, founded in 1874, "to furnish relief in case of sickness or disability, social intercourse and fellowship." Distinguishing itself from labor unions as well as "radical" women suffragists, the Lady Teachers' Association organized petitions against salary cuts based on appeals to the norms of feminine gentility and public service, rather than on the basis of workers' rights or gender equality.[134] While early women teachers' organizations faced hostility from both men teachers and the school committee, women teachers' advocacy helped Boston public schools gain increases in municipal funding that kept wages and benefits for teachers in Boston among the highest in Massachusetts.[135]

Women teachers in late nineteenth-century Boston, occupying one of the only professional positions available to women, were a relatively well-off cohort. Of students entering the Boston Normal School in 1880, 21 percent came from families with a domestic servant (only 3 percent of all Boston households employed domestic workers) and 6 percent of students had fathers who were laborers or operatives (compared to 50 percent of Boston's male workforce). Eighty-five percent were born in Boston, and 18 percent had an Irish parent (compared to 42 percent of Bostonians).[136] Women schoolteachers were almost all single, as marriage would "operate as a resignation of her position," and a particularly high rate of teachers lived with widowed mothers.[137] For many, the death of a parent was the reason they pursued employment. For example, Zoa Balch was a 25-year-old teacher born in Massachusetts who lived with her widowed mother, aunt, and sisters. Her family ran a boarding house for twenty-one boarders in Beacon Hill, a genteel neighborhood that developed a reputation for housing many affluent, single women. Five domestic workers helped run the boarding house.[138] For Boston women, teaching was a respectable occupation with high status relative to their limited alternatives.

Boston Brahmins

Boston Brahmins exerted oversized influence over the city's economy, politics, and culture. Since the eighteenth century, a small number of "Proper Bostonian" families had made their wealth in commerce, especially trade with China and in New England textiles, and turned Boston into a major center of finance and banking by the early nineteenth century.[139] These "First Families" partnered with one another in business endeavors and became further related through marriage. They held an "intense belief in themselves, their race, and their traditions," according to Henry Cabot Lodge, Brahmin historian and senator, to which they attributed the "successes of the New Englanders."[140] They attended the same churches: already by 1850 about two-thirds of the wealthiest Bostonians were Unitarian, dubbed the "Boston religion."[141] Many attended Harvard College, to the extent that one resident in 1844 could write, "By living in Cambridge a few years you get the run of the families and then recognize each new set of youths by their resemblance to their older brothers!"[142]

When Oliver Wendell Holmes dubbed these leading families the "Brahmin Caste of New England" in the *Atlantic Monthly* in 1860, these proper Bostonians had already passed the peak of their power.[143] In the years after the Civil War, although Boston financiers continued to play a key role providing capital to western railroads and manufacturing, New York overshadowed Boston as a center of finance.[144] Boston patricians were wary of the nouveau riche industrialists who pursued the "low instinct" of "money-getting" without "thought or refinement," as well as the growing immigrant population in their own city.[145] The "task of assimilating [immigrants]," Lodge wrote, was essential to prevent the "worst evils" of the "ignorant and vicious vote."[146] In local politics, while most of Boston's elite were associated with the Republican Party, in 1880 a new Yankee-Irish alliance emerged within the leadership of the Democratic Party. This alliance drew disaffected Republican "mugwumps" opposed to political corruption, as well as Unitarians and other liberal Protestants committed to "stewardship" of the Boston Irish. Although temporary, cooperation between "Harvard College and the slums" shaped a generation of Boston's Brahmin political leaders between 1880 and 1900.[147]

Participation in school affairs was a popular stepping-stone for leading Bostonians to enter politics, including women, who had served on the school committee since 1874 and voted for its members since 1879. Pauline Agassiz Shaw was one such leading Bostonian. The daughter of Harvard professor Louis Agassiz and the wife of wealthy Boston investor Quincy Adams Shaw, she played a leading role in the establishment of kindergartens and new forms of industrial education in the 1880s and 1890s.[148]

Shaw and members of Boston's elite sponsored a variety of charities and philanthropies, including local hospitals, libraries, museums, and schools. While many Brahmins ascribed to a laissez-faire philosophy and were hostile to forms of collectivism such as labor unions, they also saw themselves as guardians of the city's moral and cultural life. Brahmins prided themselves on their patronage of the arts, music, and academics, institutionalizing a "high culture" ideal.[149] Philanthropic activities became key modes through which patricians displayed their commitment to public service, maintained their social networks, and passed cultural advantages and social connections on to their children.[150] Social clubs were another arena for cultural formation. The Saturday Morning Club, founded in 1871 to promote "culture and social intercourse" for young women, featured lectures and plays, and sponsored parties.[151] Men's social clubs such as the Temple Club or Somerset Club on Beacon Hill were joined in the 1880s by new clubs such as the "opulent" Algonquin Club with its palatial clubhouse in the Back Bay. Within the walls of these clubhouses—over lunches, afternoon teas, and dinner parties—proper Bostonians groomed younger generations in the intellectual life and the cultural norms of the elite.[152]

Schools and Elite Formation

Boston's colleges and universities chiefly served Boston's upper-class men in 1880. In this era, colleges admitted virtually all who applied, but cost and social norms kept these institutions exclusive.[153] With the exception of a few who received scholarships, students at private institutions paid from $60 to $250 per year, the high end of which was equivalent to the annual salary of a domestic worker or a laborer.[154] These rates did not include the cost of room, board and living expenses, nor the opportunity cost of attending school instead of working. While a significant proportion of students used these schools to access professional careers, they also served as sites to develop relationships among Boston's upper class. In the 1870s and 1880s, student extracurricular activities—literary and debating clubs, athletic teams, fraternities, social clubs, religious organizations, and musical and dramatic clubs—proliferated on college campuses, creating a student subculture that rivaled academics in importance. Collegians took part in hazing rituals and a sports culture that characterized the "muscular Christianity" of the era.[155] The commencement ceremonies of colleges and universities were extensively covered in local newspapers and were the occasions of many festivities for Boston Brahmins.[156] For more affluent Catholics, Catholic colleges operated in a similar fashion, serving as important symbols of cultural and intellectual achievement.[157]

The oldest public school in the United States, Boston Latin School, was founded in 1635 in the North End to give the sons of proper Bostonians a classical education (including the classical language of Latin) and prepare them for Harvard. As the North End became a working-class immigrant center, the school moved incrementally farther south, relocating to the South End by 1880.[158] Many sons also attended private preparatory schools such as Roxbury Latin, founded in 1645 as a free school for local boys, or Noble's Classical School, founded in 1866 on Beacon Hill, both of which catered to boys preparing for Harvard.[159] Other private schools, such as Chauncy Hall, founded in 1828 on Boylston Street in downtown Boston, offered a traditional classical course (for $200 annually in 1880) or a discounted "English" course with business-related subjects.[160] By this date, as a growing number of families sent their children to public high schools, Boston Brahmins increasingly sent their sons outside of the city to private boarding schools in rural New England, such as Phillips Exeter, St. Paul's, or Groton, many of which had been founded by wealthy Bostonians.[161]

Fewer daughters of elite households attended college, but many received a secondary education in the Girls' Latin School, opened in 1878 in a building shared with the Girls' High School in the South End, or one of many small private denominational academies. Mrs. Hayes' Home and Day School, for example, was a Congregationalist academy that enrolled forty women who paid up to $200 in annual tuition. Several Catholic academies for girls also existed, such as the Academy of Notre

Dame in the Back Bay or the Academy of the Sacred Heart in the South End. Compared to men's college preparatory schools, the curriculum of girls' schools typically placed a heavier emphasis on elocution, visual arts, and music.[162] Some of these schools effectively provided private tutoring. For example, Henry Williams, a former public school principal, began his own private school for young ladies in 1856 and taught many daughters of Boston's elite, including Julia Howe, the daughter of abolitionists Julia Ward Howe and Samuel Gridley Howe. The register book for his school from 1856 to 1881 indicates that only one or two young women each year had previously attended public schools; the majority came from other private tutors or home instruction by a "governess."[163]

Only a small fraction of Bostonians attended college in 1880: about 5 percent of 18–24-year-old men in Boston, and less than 1 percent of women of that age group.[164] New England colleges were founded to train ministers and foster an educated male laity in specific denominations, but by the late nineteenth century, facing uneven enrollment, most had turned away from sectarianism and broadened their curriculum to boost interest among the sons of wealthy industrialists and professionals.[165] The oldest colleges in New England were gender segregated, and even after colleges in western states became co-ed, gender segregation was touted by supporters such as Harvard president Charles Eliot as a sign of institutional prestige.[166]

Harvard College, established in 1636 to provide a classical education to future Puritan ministers, had by the early nineteenth century become the chief institution where Boston Brahmins sent both their sons and their charitable contributions. By 1860, about half of students attending Harvard College came from families with estates over $100,000 (about $3.5 million in 2020 dollars).[167] A reorientation to modern sciences and practical subjects was prompted in 1869, when alumni of Harvard College, including many business leaders, gained control of the university's board of overseers. This new board helped to secure the appointment of Eliot, then professor of chemistry at the Massachusetts Institute of Technology, as president. Inspired by the research universities and technical schools of Europe, Eliot sought to modernize university education along scientific lines.[168] While Eliot, a Boston Brahmin himself, did not ascribe to the hereditary race science of some of his associates, he hoped that the "educated classes"—deploying expert knowledge to serve the public good—could maintain enlightened leadership of the city and the nation.[169] Harvard offered a classical collegiate education to nearly 1,000 men in 1880, as well as a smaller scientific program through its attached Lawrence Scientific School. While Harvard only had two listed graduate students in 1880, it also served several hundred students enrolled in its law school, medical school, dental school, school of veterinary medicine, and divinity school. Harvard charged $150 per year for all students except medical school students, who paid $200.[170] A few members of Boston's small but significant Black elite attended Harvard, including William Monroe Trotter, activist and founder of a leading Black newspaper, the *Boston Guardian,* and W. E. B. Du Bois, the first African American to receive a PhD from Harvard, in 1895.[171] Campus social life enforced strict racial and class boundaries, and only patrician students maintained residences along the Mt. Auburn Street "gold coast" or were invited into fashionable "final" clubs.[172]

While Harvard was the largest and most prominent university in the Boston area, it existed within a rich landscape of private institutions in 1880. The Massachusetts Institute of Technology (MIT), founded in 1865 as a part land grant, part privately funded school of industrial science in the Back Bay, enrolled 140 undergraduate and a handful of graduate students by 1880 and was as expensive as Harvard.[173] Boston University, which originated as a Methodist seminary before it was chartered as a co-ed research institution in 1869, was slightly less expensive and enrolled about fifty men and thirty women in its collegiate program, and over 200 professional students in its school of law and its theological seminary. Boston College (BC) opened in 1863 in the South End as a seven-year preparatory and collegiate program for Catholic men, paralleling the sequence from Boston Latin to Harvard for Protestants. Consistent with the Irish Catholic demographic to which it catered, BC was the cheapest option, at $60 per year. By 1880, it enrolled over sixty men in its high school preparatory department and nearly 200 in its collegiate program.[174] Women might attend one of the new women's colleges, such as Wellesley College (opened in 1875) on the outskirts of Boston, which enrolled nearly 400 students at $60 per year. The Harvard

Annex (later Radcliffe) opened in 1879 to twenty-five students who paid the same tuition as their male counterparts, but due to the opposition of the Harvard board of overseers, it did not offer women bachelor of arts degrees until 1894.[175]

While many upper-class Bostonians were educated in secondary and collegiate institutions, these schools existed among a broad range of cultural institutions through which affluent families maintained their status. For women in particular, this status was linked to activities and events outside formal education. The diary of one such woman, Marian Lawrence Peabody, provides a window into the world of Boston Brahmins. Marian's father, William Lawrence, was the bishop of the Episcopal Diocese of Massachusetts, and her grandfather, Amos Adams Lawrence, was an abolitionist and textile industrialist. She was educated in a number of small private schools and by private tutors. Peabody remarked of her education that "I boarded the little horse car . . . to Charles, where I got off and walked to Miss Folsom's School. There I received instruction from Professor Kittredge of Harvard, Professor Dewey of MIT, Frau Grote, a wonderful German teacher, and others."[176]

Extended formal education was not the norm for elite women. Peabody noted that "I knew one or two who [went to college], but none of my group of friends did." Rather, activities that trained young women in the norms of high society were more valuable. Peabody and her sister moved from Cambridge to her aunt and uncle's home in the Back Bay because, as she put it, "Aunt Sue, I think, felt we needed a little polishing up, and more social contacts, which the big city could give." Social activities such as evening dance classes were opportunities to meet eligible bachelors. "Every girl of fifteen or sixteen went to [Papanti's] Friday evening if she could . . . and danced with freshmen from Harvard." Most importantly, "coming out" into high society marked an introduction into the world of the wealthy. At the age of 18, Peabody wrote that "in our year, there happened to be so many debutantes . . . that there was a dance, or sometimes two, practically every night from December 5th to February 7th."[177] For Boston's elite, social events in which leading families intermingled were as important as schools for securing one's place in the upper class.

CONCLUSION

In the late nineteenth century, educational credentials did not facilitate the paths of most Bostonians into their jobs. While letters of reference could serve as introductions to employers, job applications had yet to be invented. Most types of work were acquired informally, through word of mouth and personal contacts. One would learn the skills required for a job while at work alongside a mentor or practitioner.

As chaotic as this labor market may appear in retrospect, it was also governed by strict hierarchies. Men and women, African Americans and white immigrants, did not compete for the same positions. One's ability to enter a job depended on access to specific kinship or ethnic networks, and most employees were unable to access work outside these boundaries.

By 1880, schools already defined a key phase in the lives of most children, up through the age of 13 or 14. Existing high schools and colleges also played an important role in preparing Bostonians for a few professional occupations, such as teaching, and for initiation into the social world of the elite. However, schools were not essential as sites of job-training for the vast majority of the population. Schools functioned within a much wider range of organizations in which personal contacts were made and social networks were forged.

Changes, however, were clearly visible on the horizon. By this date, the effects of industrialization were undercutting traditional ways of learning in many occupations. Boston's political and economic leaders were becoming aware of both economic and demographic changes that were throwing social norms out of balance, such as heightened labor conflict and the rising power of immigrants in the political life of the city. The corporate economy was opening up entirely new types of work, whose status was not yet fixed in the economic order. Diverse constituencies sought to shape this changing landscape. By and large the most popular medium through which Bostonians sought to address the dislocations of a rapidly expanding economy was through schools. Schooling would not replace the role of informal family and ethnic networks in securing work, but the schools that were successful would add a new institutional layer to this process. In the next decades, schools both expanded students' circles of social contacts and taught skills and behaviors to constituencies who would not otherwise have had access. Schools also served as institutions through which traditional networks, and the inequalities they reproduced, continued to operate, now legitimized on the basis of educational merit.

TWO

Uplifting the "Unskilled"

Pietrina Maravigna emigrated from Italy to Boston's North End in 1913. Her father was one of the thousands of early twentieth-century workers who did the difficult, dangerous manual labor of building modern Boston. Maravigna explained her father's experience performing this type of work:

> [Dad] was used to hard work [but] not used to the bitter cold, to working underground, pushing wheelbarrows up scaffolds, or digging ditches. Here they toiled ten to twelve hours a day. . . . It was all back-breaking work—and they had to work fast, because if they slowed down, other men would replace them. Dad told us about when they were building Filene's, digging the two stories that are underground, some mornings they would find two or three men who had slipped while they were working and had died.[1]

From 1857 onward, laborers played a vital role in the massive effort to convert a swamp on the Boston side of the Charles River into what would become the Back Bay, filled with high-end town houses for Boston's upper class.[2] They dug the subway tunnels and built the elevated rail lines of an extensive public transit system that enabled over 600,000 commuters to enter downtown daily by 1926.[3] By 1930 the population of the city was double what it had been in 1880, and Boston was the second-largest and second most densely populated metropolitan area in the country after New York.[4] At this date, "laborer" remained the most common occupation of men wage earners in Boston. Despite the difficulties that Maravigna's father and others like him encountered on the job, many workers would have gladly taken their places. Laborer's wives, sisters, and daughters performed unpaid labor in their homes or served as cooks, laundresses, and domestic workers in the homes of the wealthy.

Many low-wage Bostonians were able to move out of this world of work. Ellen Ahearn, born to Irish parents in the North End in 1860, worked as a cook in 1880. Her parents relied on the labor of all their children and extended family to support a household of eight. Ellen continued working as a cook until she married John Mahoney, an Irish-born teamster, in 1887. By 1910, John had become a street paver for the city of Boston, and while their son Daniel worked as a stock boy, their daughter Mary attended high school and their son John Jr. attended school until the age of 20. In 1920, Ellen's family moved into a triple decker, or three-story multifamily home, in Dorchester, a clear sign of upward mobility. Mary entered the white-collar workforce as a stenographer in a grocery store, while Daniel worked as an elevator operator at a telephone company. John became a schoolteacher in a Boston grammar school.[5]

Between 1880 and 1940, many Boston families followed similar trajectories. Historian Stephan Thernstrom found that about half of the children of those that he classified as "low manual" workers in Boston in this period became craftworkers or white-collar workers.[6] Moving out of poverty is a dominant theme in Boston biographies of this period, and it was a reality for many second-generation Irish Catholic, Jewish, and Italian immigrants, as well as a few African Americans.[7] New technologies eliminated many routine forms of manual labor, and household appliances and public infrastructure projects such as water systems and electrification reduced the heaviest labor of women in the home.[8]

Despite instances of intergenerational mobility and large-scale social transformations, those who performed manual labor, worked as factory or vehicle operatives, and provided personal services still made up a strikingly large percentage of Boston's workforce by 1940, as depicted in Figures 2.1 and 2.2.[9] While the share of men working as laborers

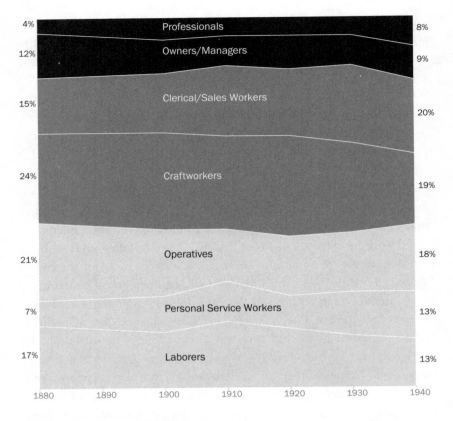

FIGURE 2.1: Men wage earners by sector in Boston, 1880–1940.

DATA SOURCE: IPUMS 1880–1940, 1890 estimated. © Cristina Groeger.

NOTE: These categories follow those used in Figure 1.1. Hucksters and peddlers, 1 percent or less of men wage earners in this period, are included in the "personal service" category.

declined, those in personal service expanded. Women service workers fell dramatically but still made up one-fifth of the women's workforce in 1940. In addition, many of the same informal and often exploitative channels of recruitment and dismissal persisted into the mid-twentieth century and, indeed, into the twenty-first.[10]

These informal pathways persisted despite a multitude of reform efforts aimed at the low-wage labor market. A broad coalition of reformers sought to respond to growing immigrant poverty in urban America through private philanthropies and public services. Many architects of industrial and public policy believed that low-wage workers' lack of

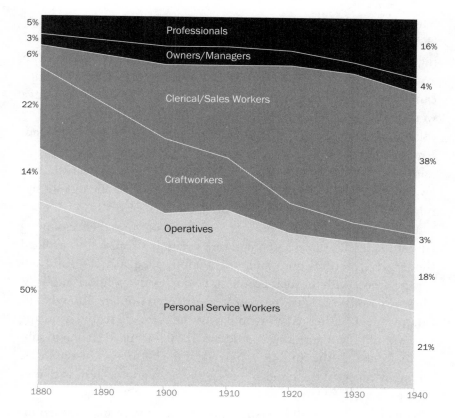

FIGURE 2.2: Women wage earners by sector in Boston, 1880–1940.

DATA SOURCE: IPUMS 1880–1940, 1890 estimated. © Cristina Groeger.

NOTE: These categories follow those used in Figure 1.1. In addition, since only 1 percent of women wage earners were recorded as "laborers," they are included in the "personal service" category.

training was the primary problem. "Unskilled" jobs came with meager wages, they reasoned, because workers lacked skill. Hopes ran high that vocational training, based on a model of professionalization, could be used to lift up these low-wage workers and "dignify" their occupational status.

Vocational training for low-paying jobs, however, never attracted significant enrollment. Impoverished workers were not interested in training geared toward specific skills used in low-wage work. Voting with their feet, some recent immigrants sought out other educational offerings such as English-language and citizenship instruction, or services like nursery schools and kindergartens that alleviated the burden of childcare. The children of service workers and manual laborers increasingly attended public day schools, which provided many of them with an array of labor market advantages. Black youth in particular were significantly more likely to attend school than the white children of low-wage workers throughout this period, although the economic advantages they could reap from their additional education were far more restricted. Among adults who performed low-wage work, however, only a small minority ever took advantage of formal education. Furthermore, with little leverage to "elevate" the status of low-paying jobs, education did not significantly change the pathways into or nature of this work.

Educational solutions to poverty found supportive audiences among educators, intellectuals, and employers precisely because they avoided the larger structural questions of economic inequality and did not threaten those with the most economic resources and political authority. These solutions placed the burden of reform onto workers through self-improvement, rather than on employers or the state through raising wages or improving working conditions. The failure of education to substantially change the conditions of work at the bottom of the economic hierarchy reflected the limits of education as an approach to working-class poverty.

Low-wage workers did pursue other strategies to reshape the conditions of their labor. Some of the earliest efforts to organize industrial labor unions across skill, gender, and racial lines emerged among service workers and laborers. Yet successes were often short-lived and undercut by these same divisions. Some direct interventions in the labor market by the state, including minimum wage laws and public employment, expanded in the early twentieth century and had a small but significant impact. By 1940, the political economy had transformed dramatically, but informal and often exploitative channels in the low-wage labor market remained.

This chapter first surveys the landscape of low-wage work and progressive efforts to reform it: first in the sector of women's domestic work, then for men's manual labor. These efforts often began with employment assistance before shifting to educational approaches. I also describe among the first efforts to organize unions led by these service workers and laborers. I then turn to public school services intended for working-class immigrant adults and youth workers, and contrast the failure of occupationally specific training with the success of basic literacy, numeracy, and citizenship instruction. Examining the case of African Americans, I explore the limits of education in addressing the structural disadvantage of those at the bottom of the occupational ladder. Finally, I describe the scope of alternative public policy interventions in the labor market undertaken in Boston before the Great Depression.

WORKING-CLASS POVERTY

Those who performed the lowest-paying jobs in Boston were overwhelmingly recent immigrants. Between 1880 and 1920, over 23 million immigrants came to the United States. Boston's foreign-born population nearly doubled, making up 30 percent of the city's population during those decades.[11] As shown in Figure 2.3, first- and second-generation immigrants made up the majority of Boston's population between 1880 and 1930. Immigration fell during World War I and was heavily restricted in the 1920s, leading to a dramatic decline of Boston's foreign-born population by 1940.

The low-wage labor market remained highly segregated in these years, based on the premigration backgrounds of workers as well as chain migration patterns and employer prejudices. While many Russian Jewish emigrants fleeing religious violence came from shopkeeping and handicraft backgrounds, the majority of Italian immigrants were peasants or farm laborers.[12] By 1920, Italians replaced Irish as the most overrepresented ethnic group among Boston's laboring population. The former Irish enclave of the North End became an almost entirely Italian neighborhood, with smaller numbers of Polish and Lithuanian immigrants.[13] Greeks and Middle Eastern immigrants commonly worked as peddlers or in service occupations in the North End, South End, and West End. As Nabeeha Hajjar, a Syrian immigrant to the South End, recalled, "The Syrian people . . . they'd take stuff in a suitcase, little articles, and they'd take a streetcar and go out of Boston to the suburbs and sell from door to door."[14]

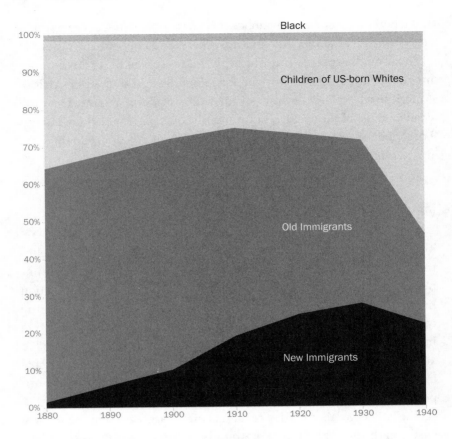

FIGURE 2.3: Boston population by race and ethnicity, 1880–1940.

DATA SOURCE: IPUMS 1880–1940, 1890 estimated. © Cristina Groeger.

NOTE: "Old" immigrants include those of Canadian and northern and western European backgrounds. "New" immigrants are those of southern and eastern European backgrounds. Other groups, including Asian, Middle Eastern, or Latin American and Caribbean immigrants, each made up less than 1 percent of the population and are included in the "new immigrants" category. Immigrant background is calculated based on whether or not that individual was born or had a parent born in a foreign country, according to census listings for mother's and father's places of birth. As such, this metric only captures first- and second-generation immigrants. "Black" includes both African Americans (1 to 3 percent of Bostonians during this time period) and Black immigrants (about 0.1 percent of the population).

Chinese immigrants came to Boston in increasing numbers in the late nineteenth century, settling in a part of the South End known as South Cove. They remained less than 1 percent of the workforce through 1940, concentrating in the service sector operating laundries and restaurants.[15] Black men and women, who made up less than 3 percent of Boston's workforce through 1940, continued to be overrepresented in personal service work. At the turn of the century, many African Americans moved to the South End close to the hotels of the Back Bay and Copley Square and train lines such as the New York, New Haven, and Hartford Railroad, where they worked as porters and stewards.[16] Irish women remained the majority of household workers through 1930, but as new opportunities in clerical and sales work opened for white women, Black women were increasingly overrepresented as maids and cooks in private households, as depicted in Figure 2.4.

Boston's immigrant poor were the objects of a wave of philanthropic and public reform efforts in the last decades of the nineteenth century. In 1880, public and private charities provided some assistance to poor families but made up an uneven social safety net. The Boston Overseers of the Poor, dating back to the seventeenth century, operated a lodge for unemployed men who were required to perform manual labor, and a temporary home for poor women and children in return for their household labor. These institutions were premised on a long-standing notion that indiscriminate charity would undermine the work ethic of the poor. The Board of Overseers also oversaw the distribution of public and privately donated funds to provide "partial" (but not full) relief in the form of "food, fuel, medicine" (but "rarely money") to families who applied, and would visit the homes of recipients to ensure these beneficiaries were not squandering their assistance.[17] Church-affiliated philanthropies also provided some assistance. The Associated Charities was founded in 1879 to centralize Boston's Protestant charity efforts and draw a more careful distinction between the "deserving" and "undeserving" poor. Catholic churches and religious orders sponsored a wide range of relief services, aid societies, asylums, temporary homes, and orphanages, as did Boston's synagogues, which organized the Federation of Jewish Charities in 1895.[18]

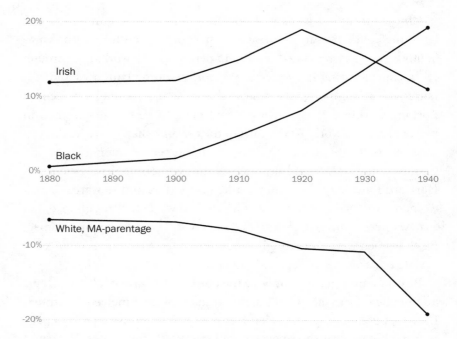

FIGURE 2.4: Overrepresentation by race and ethnicity of women domestic workers, Boston, 1880–1940.

DATA SOURCE: IPUMS 1880–1940, 1890 estimated. © Cristina Groeger.

NOTE: "Overrepresentation" is calculated by subtracting the percentage of the Boston workforce made up by workers of a specific racial or ethnic group from that group's percentage in an occupation. For example, if Irish women made up 30 percent of the women's workforce but 50 percent of women domestic workers, they would be overrepresented by 20 percent. This metric only captures first- and second-generation immigrants, likely underestimating the representation of specific ethnic groups.

By the 1890s, philanthropic social services, often in the form of settlement houses, flourished in neighborhoods where recent immigrants lived. Based in an emerging professional milieu, the leaders of these settlements were primarily Protestant, college-educated, upper-class men and women. They shared a hostility to partisan politics and championed civil service reform. Between 1880 and 1900, a segment of Boston's reformist elite aligned themselves with the Democratic Party; however, the depression of 1893 and the growing power of Irish Democratic ward bosses eroded the stability of this alliance, and after 1900 most of Boston's affluent reformers were associated with Boston's Republican Party.[19]

Mary Morton Kehew was one such reformer. Born into a long line of Boston Unitarians and married to an oil merchant, she became president of the Women's Educational and Industrial Union in 1892, a philanthropic organization dedicated to social services for immigrant women. Women like Kehew embodied the "new woman" of this era: the independent, college-educated woman who entered the public arena through reform movements, including women's suffrage, and claimed public and political power on the basis of her maternalist virtues.[20]

Robert Archey Woods was another typical reformer. An Amherst College graduate who trained as a theologian, Woods helped organize the first settlement house in Boston, the Andover (subsequently South End) House, in 1891. Progressive reformers such as Kehew and Woods believed that the right social institutions and interventions, guided by scientific knowledge, could remake industrial society on a Christian model of fellowship. While supporting labor legislation and the trade union movement, these reformers identified the chief cause of industrial conflict as a lack of understanding between employer and employee that could be resolved through dialogue and empathy. They believed in the responsibility of Boston Brahmins to alleviate poverty and stem labor conflict in order to prevent societal upheaval on a larger, potentially revolutionary scale.[21]

Above all, these reformers placed their faith in education, and vocational education in particular. Education for the immigrant poor, they believed, could foster understanding across class and ethnic lines, acculturate recent immigrants into respectable American norms, as well as teach specific occupational skills. Vocational or "industrial" education was an especially promising solution to the problem of youth entering "dead end" or "blind alley" jobs (i.e., menial jobs with no opportunities for advancement or promotion) at the bottom ends of expanding industries. For Woods, "this period of juvenile employment" represented "wasted years." Practical instruction would prompt youth to stay in school longer by offering them useful skills, and subsequently, their enhanced skills would "result in a stimulous [sic] to investment in productive enterprises," thereby benefiting society as a whole.[22]

Protestant reformers drew on a long tradition of using education to teach the poor industrious habits, premised on an understanding of poverty as the result of individual moral failings.[23] In the Progressive Era, reformers began to approach poverty as the result of wider social conditions beyond individual control, but aspects of this earlier philosophy of individual responsibility persisted. This assumption was particularly apparent in the belief that if workers acquired more skills and knowledge, their entire occupation could be "dignified" and its status elevated.[24] A focus on industrial training was shared with Boston's Catholic and Jewish philanthropies. Catholic asylums such as St. Vincent Female Orphan Asylum in Boston's South End made sewing and housekeeping central to their curriculum, and the Hebrew Industrial School for Girls, founded in 1890 in the North End by Boston's German Jewish community, aimed to aid as well as to assimilate newer Russian Jewish immigrants through industrial training.[25]

The tendency of progressive reformers to focus on occupational skills was also informed by their professional orientation. The increased training requirements for professions such as law and medicine, as well as new academic disciplines, were justified through appeals to scientific expertise and improved service to society.[26] Success in these professions led reformers to imagine recasting the entire occupational structure in the image of the rising professions. Their numerous "professionalizing projects" were premised on a faith that the labor market would reward the acquisition of knowledge and skills.[27]

The assumption that additional skill would elevate the status of an occupation, however, ignored the power imbalances that kept certain jobs at the bottom of the occupational hierarchy and allowed others to rise to the top. Professions such as law and medicine were able to be "elevated" because of their structural positions in the economy and the economic relevance of their specific knowledge base, which made it possible for practitioners to use advanced educational credentials to restrict access.[28] In addition, the assumption that wages would reflect "skill level" in the labor market naturalized the political process that shaped what types of work were deemed "unskilled" or "skilled." These labels did not describe inherent qualities of the work but were themselves politically constructed categories. The skilled / unskilled dichotomy was first popularized in the United States by nineteenth-century craft unions to claim a monopoly on a specific set of skills that were not to be per-

formed by an "unskilled" worker.[29] "Unskilled" work, however, necessitated numerous skills. Upper-class norms of service were the acquired
skills of domestic workers, and dexterity, strength, and balance were all
necessary for manual laborers to survive under dangerous conditions.
Skills passed down generationally within the home or that were invis-
ible to outside observers were some of the least recognized and least
remunerated forms of labor.[30] Despite the array of historical factors
determining the market value of work, reformers treated this low
value as rooted in a lack of training. The strategy of uplift is exemplified by efforts to reform the most common occupation for women: domestic service.

ELEVATING DOMESTIC SERVICE, 1877–1909

According to a survey in 1898, women disliked domestic service due to
its long hours, social stigma, isolation, lack of independence, and the dis-
tastefulness of the work. Even though domestic worker pay, factoring
in room and board, tended to be higher than factory or entry-level sales
work, it was still insufficient to entice women, and the prospect of even
higher wages did not change respondents' minds.[31] In a subsequent study
of Boston domestic workers in 1901, 85 percent admitted to disliking
their jobs. "One says she hates housework, and has no time to see her
friends or relatives. . . . [Another] feels that housework is slavery. . . . One
says she prefers other work but she is saving money in order to learn stenography. One is discouraged because her work is not appreciated."[32]
As white native-born and second-generation Irish women left this sector,
women who were the most marginalized or excluded from other jobs,
especially Black women, remained.[33] In turn, the association of domestic
work with foreign-born or Black workers became an additional reason
that "self-respecting" white native-born women were determined to
avoid it.[34]

The "servant problem," referring to the trend of women avoiding this
type of work and the dissatisfaction of matrons with their household
workers, was widely featured in popular journals of the time. One of the
most important philanthropies dedicated to solving this problem was

the Women's Educational and Industrial Union (WEIU), located in the heart of downtown adjacent to the Boston Common, founded in 1877 "for the purpose of increasing fellowship among women, in order to secure the best practical methods for securing their education, industrial and social advancement."[35] The WEIU first addressed what it considered to be the abuses committed by employment bureaus. The decentralized nature of work in private homes, as well as the class and racial differences between employers and employees, made it difficult to find domestic work without the aid of an employment bureau. An 1897 study by Vassar College professor of history Lucy Maynard Salmon found that employment bureaus were replacing word of mouth and "girl wanted" signs in large cities.[36] Philanthropists were particularly concerned that these agencies would send women to a "house of ill-fame" to engage in prostitution.[37] In 1882, the WEIU intervened in this realm by opening an employment bureau of its own, which aimed "not only at finding employment for [women], but at giving them kindly advice as well." It expanded with the addition of a dedicated domestic service department in 1885.[38]

Philanthropic organizations such as the WEIU, which were dominated by upper-class leadership, had a complicated relationship with these reform efforts.[39] On the one hand, the WEIU was among the first organizations to approach the servant problem as a labor problem. As diagnosed by the WEIU, service work was conducted on a "do-as-I-please" principle, with some employers acting "as if for $2.00 or $3.00 a week they had a right to seven days' unremitting labor." The WEIU's legal protection department helped many women resolve cases of wage theft; their primary clients were domestic workers. At the same time, WEIU leaders also placed equal blame on domestic workers for creating the conditions that gave rise to discord. Their annual report of 1889 noted that "some domestics behave as if they, in turn, should dictate what should be done and when." To ameliorate conflict, they urged employers to keep a record book for wages, so that agreements could be confirmed and verified. The best way to solve the servant problem, they believed, was to encourage "a better state of feeling between the mistress and maid."[40] Their domestic service bureau aimed to do just that, by pairing domestic workers and matrons under the guidance of the WEIU.

The WEIU bureau was soon overwhelmed with applications from employers, which far outnumbered applications from service workers themselves. Workers who applied were described by the bureau as women "who have not been accustomed to general labor, or trained to service of any particular kind." Their lack of training was most likely a reflection of the fact that these women were engaged in their employment of last resort. The philanthropists of the WEIU, however, thought it reflected a presumption among these women that they could get hired without acquiring any skills. According to the annual report of 1895, "The competent general housework girl is practically a thing of the past. . . . The demand for household servants is greater than the supply, thus giving little incentive to maids to become really skilled in their work."[41]

Over the years, the WEIU pursued several strategies aimed at remedying this perceived skills deficit. In 1891, it reorganized its employment bureau with a different focus. The new Domestic Service Bureau did not aid everyone, but only those who were ostensibly "fitted for" domestic service. To make sure that it sent out "only reliable and satisfactory women," the bureau asked employers to report back on their experiences with each domestic worker.[42] Over the next several years, it conducted what it described as a "weeding-out process" of removing the names of "unfit workers" from its books, which, it believed, would "strengthen the character for reliability at which the Union aims."[43] In 1897, this bureau was refashioned as a membership-based Domestic Reform League. Employers could still join for free, but domestic workers had to pay $2 per year plus 10 percent of their first month's wages. Notably, this was two to four times the cost of other private employment agencies in the city. Adding an employee fee, not surprisingly, limited the applicant pool to "girls of a higher class" who were said to "appreciate the worth of the League and wish to join."[44] By excluding those deemed "unskilled," the WEIU narrowed its original project of improving working conditions of domestic service work and instead served a more advantaged group of women.

The WEIU also began a School of Housekeeping in 1897. The idea was pioneered by Mary Kehew, who argued that new modes of training would "dignify housework in the eyes of both employer and employee by lifting it to the level of other trades."[45] The school offered an eight-month course for young women between the ages of 16 and 30 in kitchen, laundry, chamber, and parlor work, as well as special instruction in "house sanitation, personal hygiene, or economy of foods." Prospective students were required to garner two endorsements as to their "character and general intelligence." Once accepted, they were required to live at and work for the WEIU in exchange for tuition, room, and board. A steep fee was charged for early departure from the program. In addition to the class for domestic workers, the school also offered a course for employers on sanitation, interior design, food chemistry, and best practices for managing domestic servants.[46]

The WEIU quickly learned the limits of its educational model for "uplifting" low-wage work. Only a few domestic workers enrolled in this school. One did so in order to get a better position, another aspired "to be a housekeeper and oversee others," and a third hoped to become "a specialist in parlor work for the sake of greater independence."[47] However, overall interest in these classes was low. Women domestic workers likely did not have time for classes, and if they did, they would have chosen forms of training relevant to preferable employment in the needle trades, shops, or offices. After only five students enrolled in 1900, the WEIU gave up entirely on classes intended for domestic workers.[48]

During the same time period, enrollment in classes on household management designed for employers increased. These classes attracted an increasing number of "young women just out of college." As a result of this interest, the WEIU opened a professional course to train women college graduates in "leadership in the various branches of Home Economics." In 1902, this school was incorporated into the department of home economics at the new Simmons College, a private college for women endowed by a clothing manufacturer offering bachelor of science degrees. The college was located in the Fenway, a district of parks west of the Back Bay that became home to many of Boston's renowned cultural and educational institutions. Women college students were far from the domestic workers that the WEIU had originally aimed to reach. In 1910, after closing its office to domestic workers, the WEIU opened a new "appointment bureau" that catered to college-educated women.[49]

The unsuccessful trial of the WEIU's School of Housekeeping was repeated by other philanthropic organizations in Boston, such as the North Bennet Street Industrial School (NBSIS), founded by Pauline Shaw. After its inauguration as a settlement home in 1880, the NBSIS offered a range of services to immigrants in the North End, including an employment office for domestic workers. But like their peers at the WEIU, the reformers of NBSIS were discouraged by the clientele that their office attracted. Shaw wrote in 1887 that "[we] became more and more convinced that most of the poverty and suffering by which [this] building was surrounded were caused by inability, together with a want of ambition, to do anything really well." Thus, the leaders of the NBSIS decided to shift their focus to occupational training. As they explained, "The giving of industrial training to those willing and young enough to learn . . . [was] the really hopeful work waiting to be done."[50] Their industrial training courses in carpentry, clay modeling, shoemaking, printing, cooking, sewing, and dressmaking attracted dressmakers, teachers, tailors, and students from suburban neighborhoods, but not those working as domestic servants. An almost identical trajectory was repeated by the Boston YWCA.[51] The Hebrew Industrial School, while including housekeeping and cooking instruction, primarily provided sewing and dressmaking skills to Russian Jewish immigrants who became garment workers, not domestic servants.[52]

An informal color line segregated most of Boston's philanthropies, but a focus on education also characterized the approach of Boston's Black cultural institutions, exemplifying a strategy of racial uplift among Boston's Black elite. Josephine St. Pierre Ruffin, founder and editor of the first Black women's newspaper, *The Women's Era,* also helped found the Women's Era Club in 1893 for the "betterment, intellectually and morally, of colored women." Among its many cultural activities and political discussions, the Club hosted classes in civics, literature, and domestic science. The Robert Gould Shaw House in the South End, established in 1908 and led by both white and Black residents, was one of the few settlement houses that did not primarily cater to European immigrants but instead to the city's Black community. The Shaw House temporarily implemented an employment bureau before launching classes in housekeeping.[53]

On a national scale, the emerging field of home economics reflected a shifting focus of reformers away from reforming domestic work and providing employment assistance to providing women's education. In the first presidential address of the National Household Economics Association (NHEA) in 1893, Laura Wilkinson, a Unitarian and Massachusetts native, described the transition from employment bureaus to schools of housework to help "the girl at service." It was her conviction, Wilkinson stated, "that two-thirds of the trouble in having housework done is because the majority will not make a study of the dainty ways of doing the work."[54] Wilkinson went on to urge the national organization to promote training schools around the United States.

In the next years, state branches of the NHEA grew rapidly across the country.[55] Instead of schools of housework, however, an emerging group of women scientists, interested in carving out new professional fields for women in industrial chemistry, nutrition, and sanitation, shifted the focus to women's higher education. Chemist Ellen Henrietta Swallow Richards, for example, was denied a doctoral degree for her advanced studies at the Massachusetts Institute of Technology (MIT) but was hired to establish and run MIT's new Women's Laboratory. Richards believed that women, as professionals, would play a key role in socially engineering a healthier society. She cultivated relationships with members of the NHEA, and in 1909 the NHEA was absorbed into the American Home Economics Association (AHEA), with Richards as its first president.[56]

As the field of home economics developed, the original project of reforming the domestic worker labor market was discarded. The new scientific fields of domestic science and home economics did spawn new collegiate programs and employed women professionals as home economics teachers in public elementary and high schools. However, it did little to reach the world of domestic workers. As a public school elective, home economics classes predominantly trained students to perform the domestic duties expected of them as daughters and future wives, rather than paid private household labor. Ultimately, even these courses only reached a small number of women: a 1923 study of eastern city high schools found that only one in twelve female students enrolled in the home economics course.[57]

On the face of it, the shift from assisting household workers to educating homemakers and women professionals seems to have been a clear abandonment of the original project of reformers such as Kehew and Wilkinson. However, in her 1897 study of domestic service, Lucy Maynard Salmon explained the logic of professionalization that guided this shift. Salmon readily admitted that "no father or mother born under the Declaration of Independence will ever send a child to be trained as a servant." The conclusion that she drew from this fact, however, was not that other labor reforms were necessary to improve conditions for domestic workers. Rather, it was that domestic service needed a body of scientific knowledge to legitimate advanced training and elevate its occupational status. Only with this body of expert knowledge could domestic service hope to become a "profession." It appeared not to concern Salmon that it would have been nearly impossible for a domestic worker herself to access these new professional positions. More affluent women who could afford extended college education were those who entered this new scientific field.[58]

SERVICE WORKER ORGANIZING, 1890–1916

Household workers devised alternative strategies to advocate for themselves and were among the first to organize inclusive industrial unions. In 1908, Boston's Independent Order of Culinary and Domestic Workers of America sought to organize "all the help employed by boarding houses, caterers, cafes, clubs, families, hotels, lunch rooms, restaurants, and institutions." The inclusion of "families" indicated that this union encompassed private household workers. The general organizer, Paolo Contestabile, was an Italian chef who came to the United States in 1898 and became the business agent of a local cooks union in 1904. By 1910, the Culinary and Domestic Worker Union (CDWU) included women housekeepers, white and Black waiters and bellboys, culinary workers, pantry workers, and even office helpers. One of its primary grievances was the "exorbitant commissions" charged by private employment bureaus.[59]

The CDWU faced numerous obstacles. Some were inherent to the landscape of organized labor at the time. The dominant American Federation of Labor (AFL) favored locals who organized on specific craft lines, rather than across multiple occupations with both "skilled" and "unskilled" workers. In addition, while in some cases the national organization encouraged the creation of local unions representing women and African American workers, members were often hostile.[60] The CDWU attempted to affiliate with the AFL several times, but it was repeatedly rejected. By 1911, the union had dissolved. A separate AFL-affiliated Domestics Protective Union No. 12996 was formed in 1911 in Boston with women in leadership positions, likely with the assistance of wealthier women allies in the WEIU, but it disappeared from the historical record after 1912. In the meantime, Contestabile returned to the Cooks Union No. 328. Italian cooks like Contestabile may have seen the benefit of organizing along craft and ethnic lines and distancing themselves from predominantly Irish and African American domestic workers. In 1910, on the grounds of health and safety, Contestabile supported a law that would have required every cook in Massachusetts to obtain a license.[61] By erecting barriers to entry, the cooks revealed that the policing of boundaries to their occupation, rather than broader worker solidarity, was their preferred organizing strategy.

Organizing efforts among Black service workers in Boston faced similar challenges. After the founding of a white AFL-affiliated Waiters Union, Local 80, African American members split off in 1893 to form the only Black union in Boston, the Colored Waiters Union Local 183. These two locals were governed by a joint board within the national Hotel and Restaurant Employees Union and had an agreement not to compete with each other.[62] The African American president of Local 183, Forrest B. Anderson, had migrated to Boston from Missouri in 1904. While he worked as a waiter and rose into union leadership, he also attended evening law school and would subsequently go on to become a lawyer and politician.[63] Anderson regularly wrote for the national union journal, *The Mixer and Server,* about the difficulties of maintaining membership and the need for additional support from the union.[64] While his local succeeded in joining Boston's Central Labor Union in 1907, just a year later the local was suspended when Local 80 filed a complaint that the

Black local had been providing a Boston caterer with waiters for fifty cents less than agreed union rates.[65] The Black local was reorganized as Local 226 in 1909, but it lasted only a few years. In 1916, when a white local from Lynn, Massachusetts, complained of Black waiters from Boston taking jobs from its members, the Black local was deemed a "menace" by the General Executive Board and its charter was again revoked.[66]

The susceptibility of Black unions to attacks by white unionists was exacerbated by a growing number of white immigrants who entered jobs in the service sector. In particular, Canadian and Irish women employees increasingly displaced Black male workers. In Boston, Black men and white women comprised about one-third each of all waitstaff in 1880, but by 1940, Black men were less than 10 percent of waitstaff and white women over half. The first women's waitress union was formed in Boston in 1912, and it became Local 112 of the national Hotel and Restaurant Employees union in 1916, the same year that Boston's Black local was suspended.[67] The displacement of Black men by white women in some of the few occupations traditionally available to African Americans, including waiting tables, catering, and barbering, further marginalized Black Bostonians.[68] The racial, ethnic, and gender divisions among those performing low-wage service work repeatedly undercut efforts to organize collectively.

REFORMING MANUAL LABOR, 1885–1911

In the decades after 1880, labor agents and recruiters facilitated the mass migration of immigrant laborers from Europe into the United States, and transatlantic migration became an extensive business.[69] An 1885 federal contract labor law banned direct employment contracts for immigrants, but indefinite promises of employment fell outside the law's reach. The *padrone,* an Italian word meaning "boss" or "manager," was a labor agent, typically an immigrant and fluent in English, who facilitated these labor flows. Labor agents cooperated with steamship officials to spread circulars and letters abroad advertising employment opportunities. Steamship agents might employ "agitators" or "runners" to travel from village to village, local money lenders to finance the transport of immigrants, and "traveling labor agents" to lead a group from Europe to the United States and navigate interactions with immigration officials.[70]

Padrones were the primary target of reformers, who held them responsible for much of the exploitation of immigrant laborers. The 1911 multivolume US Immigration Commission Report, or Dillingham Report, singled out padrones as those responsible for the "evils" of this unregulated transnational labor market. As used by reformers, "padrone" was more a racialized term of denigration than a specific occupational title, and it became a stand-in for a range of abuses across this transnational industry. Labor agents held significant power over recent immigrants, especially those who didn't speak English. Labor agents commonly picked up workers and transported them to factories outside of the central city, leaving laborers isolated from other workers with little oversight. Such arrangements sometimes meant that workers had to stay in lodgings rented from their employer, who might charge exorbitant rates. Reformers were also concerned about the exploitation of young boys brought to the United States by padrones. The threat of deportation could be used to keep these youth compliant and discourage them from seeking assistance.[71]

Some of these padrone networks opened up possibilities for low-wage workers to organize along ethnic lines. "Italian residents are determined [to form] Italian-speaking locals of every international union of lines in which the Italians are engaged," reported the *Boston Globe* in 1904.[72] That year, Dominic D'Allessandro, a Boston Italian padrone turned union organizer, channeled discontent with the padrone system among laborers themselves into a movement for worker power, helping to organize the Union Generale dei Lavoratori, or General Workers Union, which affiliated with the AFL as the Laborers and Excavators Union. Taking advantage of his extensive labor network, D'Allessandro became the primary leader of Italian unionization across the East Coast, organizing ten Italian unions in previously padrone-dominated workplaces by 1909. These unionized Italian laborers predominantly worked on city streets, sewers, subways, and tunnels. Each local union replaced the role of the padrone with a union-run employment bureau that helped the union enforce a closed, or union-only, shop.[73]

By 1911, the Laborers and Excavators Union had become part of the International Hod Carriers and Building Laborers Union, an AFL-affiliated union founded in 1903 that organized laborers and hod carriers in the building trades. ("Hods" were boxes of brick and mortar that were carried to bricklayers.)[74] D'Allessandro, who had been a hod carrier himself, was president of the international union until his death in 1926.[75] Like the Italian cooks union, this shift reflected a narrowing of the previous general workers union to one defined along craft lines. The building-trade unions were some of the most successful of all craft unions, but laborers in the building trades were a small proportion of the laboring population at large.

Another solution proposed by labor reformers to the problem of the unregulated market for immigrant labor was the creation of public employment bureaus, first pioneered to address temporary unemployment. Labor unions such as the short-lived Culinary and Domestic Workers' union joined a broad coalition that advocated for the public sector to take over a service still mostly in the hands of private fee-charging agencies.[76] The Massachusetts Bureau of Statistics of Labor first investigated and reported on free employment agencies in 1894, and advocated for their establishment repeatedly over the next twelve years.[77] In 1906, the state legislature authorized the creation of a free employment office in Boston, which opened that December. Between 1907 and 1922, the Boston office made about 15,000 job placements annually. The largest occupational categories for men were laborers, general workers, farm hands, and errand boys; for women they were houseworkers, kitchen workers, and waitresses. In 1907, over 70 percent of male positions offered and two-thirds of female positions offered were in low-wage positions.[78]

The public employment bureaus that sprung up nationwide in the early 1900s provided an important service, especially for men and women workers without access to alternative employment networks. They also ran up against several limitations. In particular, public employment bureaus did not have access to the ethnic networks of many private agencies and padrones, which limited their work contacts.[79] Leaders of these bureaus also continued to diagnose the problem of low-paying labor as a reflection of workers' lack of skill and training. In his 1907 annual report on the public employment office, the chief of the Bureau of Statistics of

Labor, Charles F. Gettemy, wrote that "one of the most difficult problems with which the free public employment offices have to deal . . . is the large number of persons who register for employment but are lacking in suitable equipment for any particular trade or occupation where some degree of skill or experience is required." To address this problem, Gettemy pointed to formal education: "Every child should have an opportunity to learn to do one thing well and should be trained in such a way as to become an effective industrial and social unit." Since, Gettemy continued, "this training cannot safely be trusted to private agencies it follows that the field of public education must be broadened. Nowhere are these facts more apparent than in the daily experience of the free employment office."[80] Like Mary Kehew and Pauline Shaw, Gettemy saw applicants' lack of skill as the central problem facing the employment bureau, for which the solution was to broaden educational opportunities. This could not be the responsibility of the private sector; it required the involvement of Boston's public schools.

PUBLIC SCHOOLS FOR LOW-WAGE WORKERS

In the minds of reformers such as Gettemy, the public school system offered the best institutional infrastructure through which to provide essential social services. In this period, local educational bureaucracies were the most well-developed public agencies available for social welfare provision in the United States.[81] From the mid-nineteenth century onward, Boston's public school system served students from all class and ethnic backgrounds. In the 1920s, school officials such as superintendent Frank Thompson championed the public schools as "a cross section of the sum total of progressive social effort."[82] Importantly, educational services were also palatable to large business owners, who believed schooling would foster the right kinds of skills for their employees, political stability, and economic growth. As anti-immigrant sentiment and fear of labor radicalism peaked around World War I, many public officials also supported Americanization and citizenship programs through the school system.[83]

By the turn of the century, as public school programs were added at a rapid pace, Boston's educational services reflected a negotiated meeting point between educators' ideals and low-wage workers' needs.[84] Due to the high opportunity cost of attending classes instead of working, most impoverished wage earners did not take advantage of education themselves. However, among those who did make use of educational services, we see a clear preference for some types of classes over others. Classes in specific occupational skills for low-paying jobs, although promoted by reformers as the most appropriate for the working poor and their children, did not draw significant enrollment. By contrast, many adult immigrants enrolled in English language and citizenship classes and sent their children to nursery and primary schools. The evidence suggests that low-wage workers used public services not to train for their jobs, but to address their immediate social needs and to aid their children.

Public Services for Immigrant Families and Adults, 1883–1924

Among the earliest and most popular services for immigrant families were nurseries and kindergartens that offered free day care. Private and philanthropic services were on the scene first before public schools took over this role. In 1883, the North Bennet Street Industrial School Nursery, run by Pauline Shaw, served the children of twenty-three Italian families, fourteen Irish families, and a diverse mix of Canadian, Portuguese, German, Russian Jewish, and Swedish families who lived in the immediate North End neighborhood. The fathers of these children were predominantly fruit peddlers, organ grinders, fishermen, and laborers, and many mothers earned extra income by washing and ironing.[85]

This popular nursery quickly exceeded the capacity of the NBSIS, which reduced admissions by two-thirds by introducing a selective process. In 1908, children suffering from a parent's illness or absence were accepted, but children whose parents were "lazy," unemployed, in debt, in prison, or children who were the offspring of an illegitimate marriage, were refused.[86] As philanthropic organizations became more selective, they sought to shift the burden of assisting immigrant families onto the public school system. In the late 1880s, Shaw succeeded in

Does not acknowledge that this was a common strategy to acquire an empansion of city services

lobbying the Boston School Committee to launch public kindergartens.[87] By 1900, over 4,000 children were enrolled in fifty-four public kindergartens across the city, and the Hancock school kindergarten, located in the North End, was by far the most highly enrolled. These public institutions became the dominant providers of preschool education in Boston.[88]

Other public services, including English language and citizenship classes, more directly aided adult immigrant workers. Immigrants took advantage of courses that aided them in the naturalization process, and English-language classes allowed them to participate more fully in the life of the city, to improve their ability to seek work, and to communicate with their children and coworkers. Evening elementary schools had been founded in the early nineteenth century to cater to working youth, but by 1910 they had become almost entirely schools for adults from eastern and southern Europe. Out of 12,000 students enrolled in evening elementary schools in 1915, 86 percent were born outside the United States.[89] Many immigrant workers, including night-shift workers and mothers, were not able to attend evening courses, so the school committee launched a day school for immigrants downtown in 1916, with an accompanying kindergarten for young children.[90] New branches of the day school were quickly established in school buildings in Roxbury, the West End, and the North End.[91] According to Superintendent Thompson, "Mothers have been most enthusiastic."[92] By 1915, classes in citizenship had been organized in all evening schools, including instruction in US government, history, basic English comprehension, and technical requirements for naturalization. School administrators recognized the demand for citizenship and English-language classes among immigrant adults and repeatedly requested better textbooks, more appropriate teaching materials, additional teacher training or interpreters (in languages including Italian, Yiddish, Greek, Armenian, Syrian, and Lithuanian), and extensions of the evening school term.[93]

Public educational services for immigrants were promoted by Boston's political and economic leaders for various reasons. Reformers such as Robert Woods feared the displacement of Protestant authority and cultural mores by what they believed to be inferior immigrant customs, culture, and religious practices, and they hoped that education would

"Americanize" recent immigrants. Woods, along with many of Boston's leading philanthropists, belonged to the Immigration Restriction League, founded by Harvard graduates in 1898, whose advocacy contributed to restrictive national immigration policies in the 1910s and 1920s.[94]

Others, such as Frank Thompson, expressed a more tolerant, even celebratory view of cultural pluralism. The descendant of a long line of New Englanders, Thompson had been a math teacher before becoming the headmaster of Boston's High School of Commerce in 1906 and worked his way up to the position of superintendent. His superintendency (1918–1921) overlapped with the height of the Red Scare in the wake of the 1917 Russian Revolution, World War I mobilization, and the arrest and conviction of two Italian anarchists in Massachusetts, Nicola Sacco and Bartolomeo Vanzetti, on unsubstantiated charges, which became the center of international outrage.[95] As superintendent, Thompson rejected "100-percent-Americanism" and stressed the role of public schools in promoting the best democratic values of the United States. In his 1920 book *Schooling of the Immigrant,* Thompson argued that native-born Americans must "assume fundamental racial equality" and rid themselves of the "delusion" that they constituted a "superior race." He claimed that recognition of the "virtues of other nationalities" was what "we offer to the immigrant when asking him to join the fellowship of our democracy."[96]

Employers tended to support Americanization programs as a means of countering labor radicalism. The Boston Chamber of Commerce formed a Committee on Americanization of Immigrants in 1916, and an internal document listed as one of its Americanization Plan talking points, "Boston is one of the cities where the anti-American and pro-Bolshevist agencies are most firmly entrenched. Their propaganda is making undoubted headway, and it must be crushed by the united opposition of loyal and powerful American institutions of the type of the Chamber of Commerce."[97] School officials coordinated with employers to bring classes directly to immigrants at the workplace. In 1911, the school committee began to organize and promote "classes for non-English speaking people in factories or other places of business" such that "attendance cannot be avoided."[98] School administrators sat on the

Committee on Americanization of Immigrants of the Boston Chamber of Commerce from its inception, and one of the primary activities of this committee was to promote these classes to member firms.[99] The Boston-headquartered paper-product company Dennison Manufacturing was one firm that cooperated with the public schools to launch a citizenship class, "as a result of which ten employees are securing their final papers for naturalization."[100] By 1919, over 800 firms nationwide had initiated Americanization courses for employees, either privately or in conjunction with public schools.[101] In Boston, these courses for immigrant employees, housed under the Day School for Immigrants, peaked in 1924, with an enrollment of 769 men and 1,254 women in eighty-five classes throughout the city.[102]

The demographic profile of one 1916 class of graduates of the Eliot school, a North End evening elementary school, offers a window into how adult immigrants used public educational opportunities. The vast majority of these graduates were foreign-born Italian men, reflecting the composition of the neighborhood. Their ages spanned from 15 to 38, with the majority in their late twenties. Most graduates began the process of naturalization within several years of completing evening school. They tended to work in the trades (as tailors, cobblers, printers, or machinists), as sales clerks, or as small proprietors. Many used their education to shift into white-collar positions or to advance in their trades. For example, Albert Compagnoni was a machinist who enrolled in the Eliot evening school in his early twenties. In 1915 he was naturalized as a US citizen, and by 1920 he was working as a bookkeeper and supporting his widowed mother at home. From this cohort, it appears that those who could take advantage of these classes long enough to graduate tended to be those in trades and clerical positions, not the most impoverished laborers or service workers.[103]

While public school officials and employers had varied and sometimes grand aspirations for the impact of their Americanization courses, the immigrants who took advantage of them likely did so for practical reasons. These courses offered adult immigrants the opportunity to learn English and aid in becoming US citizens, which, while not explicitly focused on occupational training, would have provided strategic advantages in the labor market. At the same time, these courses had limited reach. Administrators like Frank Thompson repeatedly complained about the irregular and low attendance of adult immigrants.[104] Based on enrollment numbers and the information available about attendees, it appears that the vast majority of the most impoverished workers did not participate in the education services intended for them.

Public Schools for Youth Workers, 1879–1930

School administrators were even more concerned about the children of working-class immigrants than about their parents. Children between the ages of 13 to 16, they feared, would leave school to enter jobs with little promotion prospects and be subject to an "entirely new set of temptations." As the school committee reported in 1902, it was the responsibility of the schools to ensure that children were given opportunities to "become good and helpful citizens."[105] Daytime primary and grammar school enrollment of immigrant children increased steadily after 1880, and teachers and school officials implemented new strategies to accommodate them. Beginning in 1886, those who did not know the English language were placed in "ungraded classes" in the Eliot and Hancock school districts in the North End. Ungraded classes were first organized in 1879 for students too old for their grade, but they quickly became repositories for non-English speakers, those deemed "dull and backward," and students who worked part-time.[106] In 1883 the ungraded population was 834 students; by 1900 it had increased to 2,364 students. When students deemed "mentally deficient" or "feeble-minded" were separated out into the first special education classes in 1899, ungraded classes became almost completely English-language classes for immigrants.[107] They were dubbed "steamer classes," perhaps because immigrants came to the United States by steamship and because, once they arrived, they needed further educational "transportation" to enter into the regular grades.[108]

In 1902, the Boston School Committee launched evening "education centers" across the city. Modeled on social settlements, these centers offered "more extended use of the school plant for the especial benefit of those children who are obliged to leave school at the age of fourteen or thereabouts." To distinguish these centers from the "purely educational" classes of the regular day and evening schools, students in these courses were to spend their time "acquiring knowledge and skill likely to be of service in their daily occupations."[109] In other words, these centers offered vocational courses to help young workers advance in their jobs. Like their philanthropically sponsored equivalents, however, the courses offered in the crowded immigrant district of the North End—in sewing, dressmaking, embroidery, millinery, and cooking—proved unattractive to immigrant youth. While some students did enroll, they were not 14-year-olds but rather women with the average age of 20. These women were likely already employed as dressmakers, tailors, or seamstresses, or pursuing these courses in their free time.[110]

Other services proved much more popular for the children of low-income families. During the summer months, a "vacation school" in the North End featured a playground, sports games, excursions, public baths, and kindergarten classes. As reported by the superintendent, "the large yard of the Hancock school was equipped with swings, tilting horses, and various games, and kept open all day, for boys and girls not over ten years of age." In 1902, this summer day camp had an average daily attendance of 250 in the morning and 350 in the afternoon—higher than the school's course offerings for the entire week combined. "Many mothers came every day with their . . . little ones to watch the games and sports, and to hundreds of children in the North End it was an ideal resort." Additionally, "every pleasant day classes of 15 to 20 pupils went to the woods, parks or seashore," including the Arnold Arboretum and Revere Beach. Services that offered childcare and entertainment, not occupational training, were the most popular for immigrant families.[111]

Another public school initiative was the creation of "continuation schools," inspired by the German practice, which offered part-time vocational instruction for youth who worked during the day.[112] In 1912, a continuation school opened for immigrant girls who worked in large candy factories to provide part-time instruction in household arts.[113] In 1913, Boston's school officials made continuation classes compulsory for 14–16-year-olds, following a state law that mandated these youth either be in school full-time, or obtain an employment certificate and take classes for four hours per week in a continuation school.[114] Vocational instruction—especially manual training for boys and household arts such as sewing and cooking for women—was considered a promising way to entice students with a record of truancy to remain in school longer.[115]

Franklin Dyer, superintendent from 1912 to 1918, had established mandatory continuation schools in Cincinnati before he was recruited to help usher in Boston's new policy.[116] Boston's first compulsory continuation school, with classes housed either within employers' firms or at a rented building in downtown Boston, opened in September 1914 and enrolled a total of 4,000 students in the first year.[117] Students received both vocational and academic instruction, and vocational classes were divided into trade extension classes for "pupils in skilled employment," prevocational classes for those "whose employment does not afford preparation for such vocation," and general continuation classes for those without "specific vocational aim."[118] These continuation classes also devoted time to citizenship instruction and imparting lessons in "the nobility of work."[119] In the 1920s, similar compulsory continuation schools became a popular phenomenon in cities nationwide.[120]

Working-class immigrant youth had uneven experiences attending evening and continuation schools designed for them, and the evidence suggests that these courses offered basic instruction rather than occupationally specific training. For example, after arriving in Boston from Kiev, Russia, in 1911, Minnie Corder worked at a large clothing company sewing buttonholes on men's coats. Because she was under the age of 16, she was required to attend school in the evening and "bring an attendance certificate to the bookkeeper every week." For Minnie, even after a tiring day of work, attending school was a gratifying experience: "The schoolroom was the nicest place I had ever seen. It was warm and well lit. The teacher was a law student during the day and taught young immigrants at night, treating us as if we were his lost relatives. I was in school at last."[121] Carmela Cerqua had a different experience. After finding her candy factory job in 1905 at the age of 12, she recalled, "I didn't have any education. I went to the Cushman School [in the North End] at night, but we didn't have to learn too many subjects, just your name, your address. We had a teacher, her name was Miss Hatch. She was a young girl. She'd say 'Who knows how to sing Italian songs?' So we didn't learn too much. That's why I don't know how to read and write too good."[122] Minnie Corder and Carmela Cerqua's experiences anecdotally suggest the varied and nonoccupational nature of their mandatory evening classes.

A survey of over 1,000 continuation school students in 1915 offers additional evidence about the youth experience and curriculum of these schools. This survey found that, like Minnie, a strong majority (85 percent) of students enjoyed the school, but only 30 percent reported that the school helped them in their current employment. The survey also suggests that the primary role of this school was support in basic primary school subjects: 90 percent of students surveyed said that the continuation school had helped them in English, and 85 percent in arithmetic. Rather than training for a specific occupation, these continuation schools provided students with basic academic skills.[123]

To the extent that continuation schools coordinated with employers, they primarily provided job placement services. Because unemployed youth were also required to attend, continuation schools served as an employment bureau during recessions. According to the superintendent of continuation schools, the school system established a "flourishing" cooperative relationship with employers during the postwar recession in 1922. He noted with apparent satisfaction that "literally, hundreds of employers now know that it is possible to telephone to the school when boys or girls are needed and that in the out-of-work class may usually be found the particular type necessary to fill the particular vacancy."[124]

While compulsory continuation schools offered some advantages to employers and youth workers, they were a short-lived phenomenon from 1914 to 1930, due to the decline in child labor and the Depression-era youth labor market collapse. Adult immigrants provided a ready and more steady supply of labor than young teenagers, and many low-paying jobs performed by children were mechanized. Upper-class opposition to child labor and new conceptions of the sanctity and emotional value of childhood also exerted cultural pressure on working-class families to send their children to school over work. As the opportunity cost of attending public school declined, more children enrolled.[125]

The Triumph of Public Day Schools

Rather than occupationally specific training, the most popular forms of education for the children of service workers and laborers was basic elementary instruction. After 1906, "primary" and "grammar" schools were merged into an eight year "elementary" school sequence, and growing youth enrollment in daytime elementary schools dramatically reconfigured the social class composition of Boston's public school system.[126] Figure 2.5 breaks down reported school attendance among the 14–16-year-old children of professionals, clerical and sales workers, craftworkers, and laborers in Boston. In 1880, only 40 percent of the 14–16-year-old children of laborers reported being in school, compared to 65 percent of the children of professionals. By 1940, however, the reported attendance rates of 14–16-year-olds across all classes had reached 90 percent or above.

What benefits did elementary school offer students, especially those of lower-class backgrounds? A human capital explanation of the advantages of education would typically focus on the technical and academic skills offered. In 1922, the school committee sent a questionnaire to employers asking what 14–16-year-old youth workers in continuation schools should be taught, inviting "any other suggestions which would enable us the better to serve the employers of Boston." Their replies suggest that indeed, academic skills were important, but basic literacy and numeracy were prioritized over specific job-related skills. Employers' suggestions tended to stress academic basics: "Brace up the weak spots in the three R's by practice and review"; "Ground the pupils in the fundamentals of general education."[127]

The most common suggestions of employers, however, did not refer to academic skills, but to cultural norms and behavioral qualities. In response to the question, "what qualities necessary in their work do your fourteen-to-sixteen year olds lack?," employers replied (as summarized by a school principal): "Neatness, a sense of responsibility, initiative, willingness, reliability, ambition, real interest in the work, ability to follow instruction, punctuality, and general intelligence."[128] Other than the last, these traits refer to the personal conduct and cultural

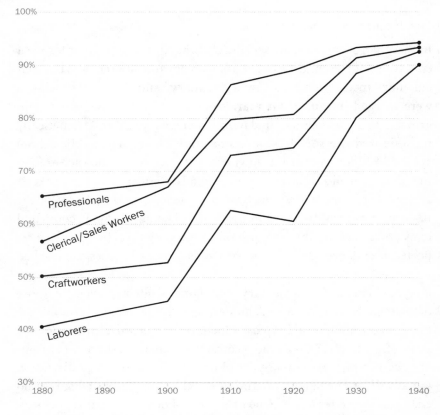

FIGURE 2.5: Rising school attendance by class: school attendance of 14–16-year-olds by father's occupation, Boston, 1880–1940.

DATA SOURCE: IPUMS 1880–1940, 1890 estimated. © Cristina Groeger.

norms taught in public schools, rather than the academic content of the curriculum.

The combination of academic and cultural education was reflected in the curriculum of early twentieth-century public elementary and high schools. In addition to the academic subjects of English, history, foreign languages, mathematics, and science, as well as popular commercial courses such as bookkeeping, accounting, and shorthand, and a few electives in industrial or domestic arts, public schools had long served as institutions to acculturate youth into the norms of the upper class.[129] Public school leaders believed schools would compensate for the negative influence of homes, especially those of immigrant families, where youth purportedly acquired incorrect speech, untidiness, and social improprieties. For women in particular, schools were imagined to guard against urban dangers and the influence of "vicious and exciting amusements."[130] The introduction of school nurses in 1905, medical examinations for eyesight and hearing in 1906, expanded facilities for recreation and physical education in 1907, and school lunches in 1910 turned Boston's school system into a health-care provider, which, like many other urban school systems at the time, aimed to instruct students in healthy habits of hygiene, physical fitness, and good nutrition.[131] Extracurricular activities, including athletics, became a central feature of public school education in these years. Advocates championed their cultivation of teamwork and civic values, and student participants helped shape a new youth culture that carried over into the workplace. These forms of knowledge and acculturation, as well as the wider circle of social connections that schools facilitated, opened up more job opportunities for young people than were available to their parents.[132] The benefits of schooling, in addition to changing ideas of childhood and the declining employment of youth workers, all fostered high participation in the public school system.

THE LIMITS OF EDUCATION FOR LOW-WAGE WORKERS

Between 1880 and 1940, while public elementary and high schools opened up employment opportunities for many sons and daughters of low-wage workers, their parents were largely stuck in their occupations. Many mature adult immigrants simply did not have time for schooling. As youth entered rapidly growing clerical and sales positions, service sector and laborer positions were increasing performed by an older demographic. The median age of domestic workers rose from 24 to 40 between 1880 and 1940. Among laborers, the median age rose from 35 to 39.[133]

Help wanted ads placed in newspapers reveal the sorts of traits employers believed to be relevant for low-paying positions, and as late as 1920, education was not one of them. Employers sought variously to hire the following: an "experienced Protestant chambermaid assistant to working housekeeper, not over 40 years old"; a "colored nursemaid with experience"; a "garage night-man: must be sober and industrious"; and an "errand boy: must be neat and clean."[134] Some desirable qualities, such as industriousness and cleanliness, would have been acquired in the elementary schools that young people attended. Experience, however, was more important than formal education, and references to race and religion reflected long-established labor market patterns.

Even with enhanced opportunities for public education, discrimination in the labor market pushed certain groups into low-wage work. The limits of schooling were nowhere more apparent than in the case of African Americans. In 1920, the illiteracy rate of Black Bostonians over the age of 21 was 2.6 percent, far lower than the rate for foreign-born white adults, which was 10.5 percent.[135] If we examine reported rates of attendance between 1880 and 1930, Black children ages 14 to 18 were more likely than white children of the same age to attend school, and this higher rate of attendance is especially apparent among the children of low-wage workers, as Figure 2.6 shows. The attendance rate of Black girls is also striking. In 1880, among the children of laborers and service workers, nearly half of 14–18-year-old Black girls attended school, compared to one-third of Black boys of this age group. Throughout this period, Black girls were more likely to attend school than their male counterparts, while white Irish-born girls of this age were less likely to attend school than Irish-born boys until 1930.[136]

These high rates of attendance reflected several factors. Black Bostonians, especially Black youth, faced difficulties finding employment, and the high rates of attendance among Black girls likely reflected the even more limited range of jobs available to women. The Black community also cultivated strong aspirations to receive an education denied to them in the antebellum and Jim Crow South.[137] Boston's Black community leaders upheld a long tradition of racial uplift through education, exemplified by Julius C. Chappelle, one of the only Black state legislators in late nineteenth-century Massachusetts. Born in South Carolina, Chappelle moved to Boston in 1870 and worked as a barber while earning a high school diploma at night. After being elected to the state legislature, he championed education as a crucial means of effecting Black social and economic advancement. Accordingly, he pushed for free text-

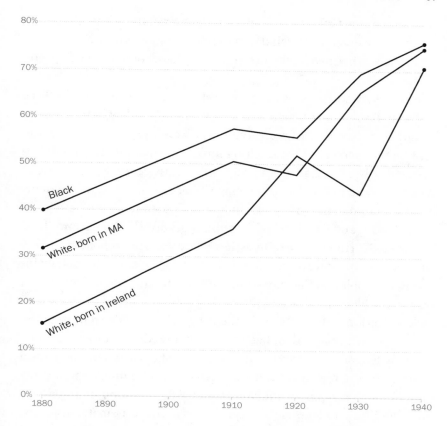

FIGURE 2.6: Rising school attendance by race: school attendance of 14–18-year-old children of laborers and service workers by race and birthplace, Boston, 1880–1940.

DATA SOURCE: IPUMS 1880–1940, 1890 estimated. © Cristina Groeger.

books, free evening high schools, and an employment bureau for Black women.[138]

After 1890, the political climate became more hostile for Boston's Black community. In the last decades of the nineteenth century, Black Bostonians made up over half of Republican voters in one city ward representing the West End, and through their local concentration could exert some political power. However, redistricting in 1895 broke up this ward and diminished their strength.[139] Although fewer African Americans migrated to Boston than to other northern cities during World War I, as in other urban centers, racial tolerance deteriorated during these years. According to W. E. B. Du Bois, at the turn of the twentieth century "not a single hotel in Boston dared to refuse colored guests," but by the 1930s there remained "few Boston hotels where colored people [were] received."[140]

Boston's schools were by no means welcoming environments for Black children. Black students faced an almost complete lack of representation among their teachers. African Americans were 2 percent of students in 1928, but 0.1 percent of the teaching force.[141] Boston public schools had been racially mixed since the mid-nineteenth century, and African Americans did not make up the majority of any one Boston neighborhood, which meant that Black students attended local public schools with the sons and daughters of white immigrants.[142] School committees across the North were loath to assign Black teachers to predominantly white schools. Ironically, therefore, northern US cities with racially integrated schools had the lowest rates of Black teachers, while those with segregated Black schools had the highest rates.[143] There were some notable exceptions: Maria Baldwin, the daughter of a Haitian immigrant, became a teacher and then headmaster of a predominantly white elementary school in Cambridge in 1915, earning her entry into the genteel circle of Boston reformers and suffragists.[144] But, tellingly, she was the only Black woman in an equivalent leadership position in all of New England. Black students faced prejudice from their classmates, teachers, and in their textbooks. In 1903, one student told a Boston newspaper that her textbook described African Americans as "slaves and niggers."[145]

Despite all of these impediments, the children of Black Bostonians had among the highest rates of school attendance. In the labor market, however, racial discrimination kept them in the lowest-paying laborer and service jobs. Many employers believed African Americans to be inferior workers and also feared unrest among white employees if they hired them.[146] Edwin Walker, elected one of Massachusetts's first Black assemblymen during Reconstruction, noted in 1893 that "no matter how well our boys and girls are educated . . . the business portion of the community will not employ colored children for anything but menial work."[147] George Adams, a resident of the South End, identified the same pattern thirty years later: "I remember my sisters doing summer work in the laundries on West Newton Street. There were Jews, Italians and

Irish in the laundries also, but only because they lacked formal education or any other opportunity at the time. A Black who had talent, some capability, was still forced to accept employment in those areas."[148] The experience of African Americans should shatter historical illusions that education alone could open doors to better employment or improve one's working conditions.

STATE INTERVENTIONS IN THE LABOR MARKET

If the experience of Black Bostonians underlines the limits of education for reforming low-wage employment, it should also be noted that other efforts were attempted in this era that showed greater promise. While the vast majority of public services for Boston's most vulnerable communities came through the school system, the city and state also implemented policies that more directly reshaped the labor market. To limit the most blatant abuses by employers, progressive reformers like Mary Kehew were instrumental in passing the first state minimum-wage law in the country in 1912. However, like much "protective" labor legislation prior to it, this law only applied to women and children, and although backed by organized labor, the 1912 law did not attach any legal penalties for violation, just sanction in local newspapers. Minimum wage laws were ruled unconstitutional in 1923 and would only be implemented on a national level in the 1930s. Boston also established a program for Mothers' Aid in 1914, which became a state program including dependent children in 1923, and both city and state funding for public relief increased in the 1920s, administered through the renamed Overseers of the Public Welfare. On the eve of the Great Depression, the amount of monthly public relief awarded in Boston to each recipient was among the highest in the nation.[149] The city of Boston expanded direct welfare relief during the 1930s, increasing the number of families aided by 500 percent. Compared to other cities, political disputes impeded the implementation of New Deal programs, but Bostonians did take advantage of new federal works projects and funding.[150]

Direct public employment also significantly shaped the low-wage labor market. In the decades after 1880, Boston itself became one of the single largest employers of low-wage workers. In 1900, the city employed about 2 percent of all laborers; in 1920, 10 percent, and in the first year of the Great Depression in 1930, 20 percent.[151] Throughout the nineteenth century, public employment was commonly used as a means of "spoils" to reward loyal party members and provide assistance to those in need. Political patronage was subject to increased public scrutiny in the late nineteenth century, and in 1884, Massachusetts established its own civil service commission, which implemented new hiring practices for the "labor service" of the city of Boston. This service employed day laborers to work on streets, sewers, lamps, public grounds, parks, and cemeteries. In addition to name, age, residence, and citizenship status, applicants for laborer positions were required to report their dependents, previous occupations including military service, and evidence of "their habits as to industry and sobriety." When a request was made for laborers, the officer would make "an impartial selection by lot or otherwise, giving preference [to veterans] and to those having families depending upon them for support."[152] A preference for supporting families in need was thus built into the guidelines of public employment. At the same time, these criteria were used to exclude those who did not meet proper "habits of industry and sobriety," as well as those who lacked references. Noncitizens, conspicuously, were excluded entirely from public employment.[153]

Civil service reform did not eliminate channels of patronage. Robert Woods noted in 1898 that labor appointments were still "distributed through the wards and allotted to the local politicians."[154] Ward bosses who dominated Boston politics at the turn of the century reinforced their support through these patronage channels.[155] Woods estimated that in 1902 about one-third of Irish families in the West End included a bread-winner employed by the city. The most common city jobs at the time were laborers, patrolmen for the police department, hosemen and lad-dermen for the fire department, teachers, clerks, inspectors, and jani-tors.[156] One such city employee was John Mahoney, the Irish street paver and husband of Ellen Ahearn who helped support his family's move from the North End to Dorchester by 1920.[157] Non-Irish workers were significantly underrepresented on the city payrolls. In 1919, when Italians and

Irish each made up around one-third of all Boston laborers, Italians made up less than 10 percent of Boston's public sector laborers.[158] Yet for those able to obtain it, public employment offered among the best manual labor jobs in the city. Boston city laborers constituted an "aristocracy of the unskilled," earning on average 27 percent more per hour and working 10 percent fewer hours per week than those in the private sector in 1896.[159] Many public laborers—street cleaners, sewer workers, or water department workers—organized unions around the turn of the century, giving them additional security.[160]

Protective legislation, public relief, and public employment helped many, but this was far from a secure safety net. For the majority of private sector low-wage workers, the effects of regulatory legislation or public services were minimal. An important shift in the nature of domestic work had taken place by 1940: most household workers now worked by day instead of living in their employer's home. About 70 percent of domestic workers were live-in employees in 1900; in 1940, that number had dropped below 35 percent. This shift reflected the growing reality that older women with families of their own, especially Black women, took these positions. However, these women day workers were as subject as male day laborers to fluctuations in demand.[161] While eastern and southern Europeans, as well as African Americans, had replaced the Irish as the most overrepresented demographic groups in the lowest-paid jobs, many aspects of the jobs they performed and the ways in which they accessed them would have been similar to their nineteenth-century counterparts.

CONCLUSION

In the late nineteenth century, leading philanthropists, public officials, and reformers looked to education to address the problem of poverty. Within Boston's most impoverished districts, reformers sought to address immigrants' immediate needs by offering a wide range of services. In their analysis, one of the chief reasons that workers were stuck in low-paying jobs was because they lacked skills. They believed that education would uplift workers out of poverty by elevating the status of their work. Boston reformers, like progressives in cities across the northern United States, used school systems to provide a range of social services. Their ideological preference for educational services dovetailed with more practical considerations. Public education was a service that catered to and drew substantial political support from a broad political constituency and offered the most developed vehicle for public sector expansion in this period. Educational services were also embraced by employers themselves.

Without strong opposition, school systems became the leading edge of American state-building in the early twentieth century, but their effects on low-wage labor did not bear out the assumptions of many progressive reformers. The provision of occupational training was by and large ignored by low-wage workers themselves. Rather, educational services came to reflect a negotiation of interests between more affluent reformers and working-class attendees. Some adult immigrants took advantage of classes to learn English and train for citizenship tests, and many sent their children to nurseries, kindergartens, and elementary schools to learn basic academic skills and norms of respectability.

Ultimately, private and public educational services did not significantly impact the status, pay, or conditions of low-wage work. Informal modes of obtaining jobs through ethnic networks persisted, and in many regards the primary features of this work changed very little. While household amenities may have altered the nature of work in the home, domestic workers continued to labor in isolation with little to no oversight. Employers picked up groups of day laborers to travel out to work sites as they had in 1880. By the Great Depression, personal service and manual labor jobs remained among the largest sectors of employment for men and women. For workers across the employment structure, the Depression revealed just how little their "skill" protected them from the vagaries of the market. Service workers and laborers, already the most vulnerable, were hit the hardest.

It was not adult low-wage workers but rather their children who were the primary beneficiaries of expanding public elementary and secondary schools. Schooling would primarily aid the Americanized children of European immigrants in finding employment, as the Black children of wage earners, despite assiduously pursuing education, remained relegated to the lowest-paying jobs. Between 1880 and 1940, reformers looked approvingly at increasing school enrollment rates. In these years, the expanding educational system was also at the heart of one of the chief conflicts of the early twentieth century: the battle between employers and organized labor. This conflict would shape both the emerging educational landscape as well as the industrial workplace, with consequences for the entire economy.

THREE

Craft Power in the Industrial Workplace

"Millions of boys and girls [are] waiting and starving for the mere chance of learning standard trades," wrote a concerned observer for the labor reform journal *Progressive Age* in 1881. The problem of modern industry, according to this author, was that it had "abolished apprenticeship."[1] That same year, Lewis Lyne had recalled the mystery and excitement of learning new craft skills as an apprentice by watching a master craftsman. Over the next decades, even fewer opportunities for learning craft skills in this way would remain. Although Boston continued to have a relatively high number of small machine shops and family-owned workshops, the city also exemplified changes taking place across industrial America.[2] Between 1880 and 1920, the value of manufactures produced in Boston more than doubled.[3] Factories, tanneries, breweries, and foundries expanded in Boston's industrial districts of the South End, South Boston, and Roxbury. Large plants were constructed in Hyde Park, Charlestown, and Dorchester, as well as neighboring Cambridge and Watertown. Increasingly, small shops of master craftsmen and their apprentices gave way to larger factories with greater division of labor and streamlined production.[4]

Training was at the heart of industrial conflict in this era. Across all trades and manufacturing in the United States, while many specific craft skills were rendered obsolete, the total number of highly trained craftworkers rose.[5] Manufacturers across the United States complained about a "skills shortage," arguing that there were not enough well-trained craftworkers to meet their needs. Business leaders such as Anthony Ittner, president of the National Brick Manufacturers Association, blamed "the arbitrary and tyrannical methods of organized labor" for imposing unfair restrictions on the number of apprenticeships.[6] In reality, many employers, who wanted to avoid having to defer to union training standards, did not take on the full number of apprentices allowed by unions.[7] Formal apprenticeships were costly for large firms, especially given the possibility that apprentices might "steal a trade" by moving from one shop to another.[8] In addition, firms wished to avoid devoting resources to those under the ideological influence of craft unions. Employers thus sought alternatives to unions for training their workforce and, simultaneously, maintaining control of the workplace.

Among the alternatives was "industrial education," which employers imagined operating free from union oversight.[9] In their pursuit of industrial education, employers found many willing allies. Philanthropists were eager to provide social and cultural uplift for immigrant children, and many public officials hoped to revitalize craftsmanship as a youth vocation and boost American industrial prominence. Progressive reformers such as John Dewey championed industrial education to foster the tools of democratic collaboration and scientific inquiry; other reformers, including Massachusetts commissioner of education David Snedden, hoped to train more efficient producers.[10] Employers even counted as allies many craftworkers themselves, who supported teaching youth respect for craft traditions in school. The concerned writer for *Progressive Age* believed education was the best solution to counter a dangerous trend toward the "pauperism of the masses," urging "the introduction of compulsory industrial education . . . affording our school children a chance to learn the rudiments of trades."[11]

Given the enthusiasm of many constituencies and the important role of craftworkers in the city's diversified industries, Boston was in many ways the ideal location for the implementation of industrial education. Yet, by 1930, industrial education had largely failed to provide reliable pathways into industrial jobs. The primary reason for its failure was that organized interests—employers and unions—clashed as they vied for control of the training process. Because craft union power depended on controlling access to specific craft skills, the struggle over training was a struggle for workplace power. In Boston, as well as Chicago, New York, St. Louis, San Francisco, and other cities, strong craft unions fiercely opposed employer-sponsored private trade schools, and they had some success in shuttering these schools or reorienting them away from teaching specific trade skills.[12] Public instruction offered an alternative, but attempts to develop public programs simply moved the terrain of contest into the school system, leaving all parties unsatisfied. Without the joint investment of employers and craft unions, industrial schools faced prohibitive costs as well as difficulties in securing qualified instructors. Across the country, the reputation of industrial education (either as separate schools or tracks within schools) declined, becoming repositories for academically underperforming students instead of pathways into well-paying jobs.

The failure of industrial education ultimately helped shift workplace power toward management. Without reliable and inexpensive forms of industrial training, business models based on small-scale custom production, which required a high proportion of craftworkers, grew less attractive to US employers, especially during the surge of economic production during World War I. The decentralized nature of some trades, such as the building trades, allowed craft unions to hold on to their power and traditional union apprenticeships. But in most trades, employers pursued managerial strategies to centralize technical knowledge and restructure the labor process.[13] They were able to do this by hiring a different set of workers, who had received formal education in schools. Across the industrial north, employers increasingly hired machine operatives with some public school education, high school–educated white-collar staff, and a small number of university-educated engineers or supervisors, rather than those trained via union-regulated apprenticeships.[14]

Nationally, business models of mass production relied on many factors beyond training, including the appropriation of abundant natural resources, creation of internal domestic markets, transportation technologies, and the inexpensive labor of recent immigrants, women, and African Americans.[15] But the failure of industrial education, especially in cities such as Boston without the natural resources of western states and with many of the preconditions for competitive small-batch production, was a significant contributing factor. By the onset of the Great Depression, the training landscape for workers in industry had been transformed. Although Boston's craftworker wages were among the highest in the country in 1929, craftworkers as a percentage of the Boston male workforce fell from a height of 27 percent in 1920 to 19 percent by 1940.[16] Outside of the building trades, union-regulated apprenticeship was nearly eliminated.

The weakening of craft union power in the 1910s and 1920s had several implications. The power of the skilled, white, native-born male aristocracy of labor diminished as women, immigrant, and Black workers found opportunities working in industrial jobs in large factories. The erosion of craft union power also opened up space for alternative modes of building worker power, such as industrial unions. At the same time, the decline of craft union–regulated jobs increased the ability of employers to tighten managerial control over a nonunionized workplace. Working-class immigrants with little job security mostly filled the lowest factory positions, while a small number of engineers and managers occupied the top. Despite the growing salience of formal education, certain communities, particularly African Americans, continued to be pushed into the lowest-paying jobs regardless of their educational achievement.

In this chapter, I explore first the conflict over training in trades with strong unions, exemplified by the metal and building trades. Then I turn to battles over industrial education in the private and public sector. I examine the ways in which the failure of industrial training contributed to new large-scale business models that shifted the industrial workforce away from craftworkers. I then turn to the needle trades as a counterexample of a trade that had very weak craft union power and, thus, had successful trade schools for a time due to lack of political opposition. The lack of craft union power, however, ultimately limited needle-trade workers' ability to prevent the rapid "deskilling" of this industry, and by 1930, even in this sector, industrial education declined as a pathway into well-paying jobs. The lack of entrenched craft unions, however, allowed the garment industry to pioneer some of the earliest industrial unions in manufacturing, based on solidarity across skill levels, gender, and ethnicity rather than control of the training process. Their organizing efforts, which peaked around World War I, foreshadowed the strategies of worker control that would be powerfully exercised by the Congress of Industrial Organizations (CIO) after the Great Depression. By this date, the reputation of industrial education had declined, and employers preferred academic education for managers and rank-and-file operatives alike rather than the graduates of industrial programs.

CRAFT UNION CONTROL AND MANAGEMENT STRATEGIES

The 1893 depression spawned a wave of populist uprisings nationally, and between 1897 and 1904, union membership in the United States grew from 440,000 to over 2 million.[17] Unionization surged in Boston at the turn of the century: 65 percent of Boston union locals in 1909 were founded after 1900.[18] By 1910, over 20 percent of Boston workers were union members.[19] Even with a small percentage of unionized workers in a trade, a union could exert significant power. The Boston Central Labor Union (BCLU), the voice of organized labor in Boston, forged close ties to the Democratic Party. Democratic mayor Josiah Quincy IV, elected in 1895, launched a program of "municipal socialism" that included hiring union labor for public works projects and launching a union-run municipal printing plant.[20] Irish and Canadian workers continued to dominate the building trades, while English and Scandinavians were significantly overrepresented as machinists. When Russian Jewish and Italian workers organized craft unions, they tended to do so via segregated locals. Women and African Americans did so in the rare cases that they were not excluded entirely.

The regulation of apprenticeship allowed unions to control entry into their craft, maintain the "quality" of their members, and prevent apprentices from being used as cheap labor. Employers, for their part, sought to use apprenticeships to groom loyal future foremen and managers. A manager at Brown & Sharpe, a Rhode Island–based machine tool company, wrote in 1906 that there was "a demand and an absolute necessity for . . . thoroughly trained men—men from whom we can select our foremen and heads of departments" and that there was "no better way to maintain the vitality and keep up the standard of a shop than by training young men in the shop itself." [21] Managers, however, saw craft union membership as antithetical to the qualities of good leaders. Foundry company president George Thornton argued that the foremen of today "should be wholly free from any sort of trades-union affiliation, either directly, as by actual union membership, past or present, or indirectly, as by social ties, or class prejudice." Only a foreman untainted by union ties could "represent his employer fully."[22] The fight over training was thus a fight over the ideological and cultural formation of both new workers and future foremen.

In the metal trades, employers' anti-union orientation helps to explain the origins of the mechanical engineer as a different occupation than that of the machinist. The two terms were interchangeable in late nineteenth century; both referred to mechanics who worked in metal shops or foundries and became proprietors of their own businesses. The American Society of Mechanical Engineers (ASME) was formed in 1880 by owners of metal shops. The ASME was an exclusive engineering group, and its professional identity was linked to its members' position as businessmen and their opposition to trade unionism. Their technical journals made it clear that joining a union disqualified one from being considered a potential engineer, and they denigrated "grumblers" and "tramps" who agitated for strikes as a bad influence.[23] This political orientation was also reflected in the demographic composition of engineers. In 1880 Boston, 77 percent of engineers were native-born men with native-born parents, compared to 47 percent of machinists.[24]

Engineers were among the first to pioneer new practices that aimed to improve labor relations while maintaining managerial control. As labor turnover became a debilitating problem for employers in the 1880s and 1890s, "industrial betterment" and "welfare work" became buzzwords in managerial circles. These programs of betterment encompassed initiatives such as mutual aid associations, profit-sharing schemes, the provision of company nurses and medical care, housing, picnics, lunchrooms, vacation plans, suggestion boxes, lectures, and English-language learning for immigrants.[25] By 1900, scientific management had emerged out of the field of mechanical engineering, led by Frederick Taylor, president of ASME in 1906. Its practices included cost accounting to manage expenses, increased division of labor, and incentive pay schemes and piecework to individualize remuneration for work. These forms of rationalization helped centralize power among a small cohort of foremen, engineers, and managers. Firms hired engineers to help with technical troubleshooting, sales and distribution, as well as mediating employee grievances with the goal of preventing labor disturbances.[26]

Rationalizing the process of hiring, training, and firing also became the purview of the new field of personnel management. In 1911, Meyer Bloomfield, leader of the Civic Service House, a settlement house in Boston's North End, organized a meeting of sixty Boston employers to discuss best practices for efficient employee hiring and training, especially for young workers. Out of this meeting emerged the Employment Managers Association, a local iteration of the National Employment Management Association, which later became the American Management Association (AMA).[27] The field of employment management became more widely known as personnel management, and by 1920, one-quarter of large firms across the country were tasking specialized managers with personnel decisions.[28]

The management practices of new personnel departments allowed firms to be more precise in selecting employees. Firms identified those who might become troublesome agitators, as well as those who had potential as foremen or managers. Personnel departments often kept records of applicants on file, including information such as employment history, performance evaluations, union affiliation, and personal characteristics such as physical appearance and race. The director of one national employer association described the importance of race as a criterion for selection as follows: "It would obviously be unwise to expect Russian Jews as a class to be proficient in high-grade mechanical work, whereas most Scandinavians possess natural ability for such work."[29] Personal information could also be used to reward specific employees through merit-pay schemes, a favored tactic to undercut craft union pay scales based on seniority. W. Herendeen, New York manufacturer and commissioner of the National Founders Association, urged his colleagues in 1906, "Be quick to recognize merit and the labor agitator will find it difficult to get your workmen to exchange their independence for a union card."[30] Some personnel departments adopted school-based grading systems, such as Dennison Manufacturing, which graded employees on a scale of A-plus ("very capable") to D ("mediocre"), as well as E ("too new to determine").[31]

In the first two decades of the twentieth century, the largest, best-endowed firms opened their own training departments or corporation schools, which were publicized by trade journals as a cutting-edge management practice.[32] The National Association of Corporation Schools, an association founded in 1913 that would eventually merge into the AMA as well, included among its members large utility, railroad, and steel companies such as General Electric and Carnegie Steel.[33] To avoid the perceived problem of union-controlled apprenticeship, these schools served as an alternative training process to select employees for leadership positions.[34] Employers justified expenditure on employee education on the basis that it would "develop loyalty."[35] One master builder stressed the importance of employer-controlled training schools as an anti-union tactic: "Educate them . . . [;] let students feel that [employers] are their best friend; let them grow up under better influences than constant association with union men . . . [;] do your duty to them and toward the future of the trade."[36] With full control over the curriculum and instructors, these schools allowed firms to counter growing union influence.

CRAFT UNIONS AND EMPLOYER ASSOCIATIONS

While smaller companies often lacked the resources to finance their own personnel departments and training schools, many belonged to industry-wide employer associations that performed similar functions. The National Metal Trades Association (NMTA) was founded in 1899 in New York to oppose a growing movement of organized machinists.[37] In 1901, the NMTA broke a union agreement with the International Association of Machinists (IAM), and a rash of strikes broke out across the country, including in Boston. On June 11 of that year, 270 Boston machinists, millwrights, pattern makers, blacksmiths, and apprentices at the American Tool and Machine Company walked out.[38] In the wake of such episodes, the NMTA enhanced its efforts to counter the collective action of workers.

In 1903, the NMTA began to publish a monthly bulletin "devoted *exclusively* to the discussion of the many evils and enormously uneconomic rules which organized labor is constantly endeavoring to enforce." The bulletin consisted of reports on union activity and advice on breaking strikes and limiting union power.[39] In 1904, it announced the renaming of the monthly bulletin to *The Open Shop,* a reference to a nonunion workplace.[40] In 1908, the bulletin published an extensive list of "Open Shop and Non-union Foundries," including seven Boston companies, touting their open-shop status.[41]

These associations organized employment bureaus with explicit anti-union agendas. The NMTA's labor bureau served as "a clearing house for the members . . . from which to procure their labor supply."[42] By 1904, NMTA had labor bureaus in thirteen cities. Member employers of these labor bureaus reported employee information including name, address, age, nationality, employment history, and performance traits such as "efficiency" ("first class hustler, average, poor"), "disposition" ("pleasant, lazy, bad"), and "habits" ("good, irregular in attendance, talkative, intemperate").[43] On a daily basis, employers were also asked to report the workmen leaving their employment, including reasons why they were leaving, as well as any open positions in their establishment. Workers seeking positions could apply to the local NMTA labor bureau free of charge, and the secretary would coordinate placement on a daily basis. Employers were also required to report the hiring of anyone on the list, which served as a safeguard against apprentices stealing a trade.[44] The labor bureaus also developed reward systems for loyal employees. In October 1904, they began issuing "certificates of recommendation" to "such men as have proven themselves faithful and given efficient service to a member during a labor difficulty." These certificates took the form of a "handsome booklet, bound in deep red, flexible, morocco leather, the cover of which is lettered in gold."[45] Those with certificates were given top priority in placement.

Because of their usefulness in selecting workers with the proper skills and ideological orientations, employment bureaus immediately became one of the most powerful and prized institutions of the NMTA.[46] By 1913, the Boston bureau alone had records of 23,454 workmen in the city.[47] Employers kept close tabs on union membership and used records to help them break strikes by funneling workers into positions when needed.[48]

The NMTA labor bureaus celebrated their positive influence on community life through "educating" against socialism and political radicalism. One promoter of these bureaus wrote, "Education of the right sort cannot come through socialistic and revolutionary trash, but through sane and matter-of-fact literature." Political radicalism was often presented by employers as a foreign influence brought into the United States by immigrant "criminals and agitators," which appealed to the racist prejudices of native-born white employers and workers alike. These labor bureaus presented themselves as "[safeguards] against an undesirable class of citizens," and, like personnel departments, they helped to maintain a compliant workforce.[49]

Employer associations in the building trades had far less success in establishing labor bureaus. Unlike the centralized firms of the metal trades, construction work depended on one-off jobs with dozens of small contractors, making employer coordination much more difficult. In the aftermath of a breached agreement with the Mason's Union in 1903, the Master Builders Association (MBA) in Boston experimented with establishing its own labor bureau. It asked workmen to fill out registration cards with their name, place of apprenticeship, length of service, name of last employer, and a declaration that they would not let any affiliation they might have cause harm to any member of the MBA. Unions refused to allow their members to sign the cards of the MBA, rendering the project futile.[50] Instead, building-trade unions were able to control access to jobs and functioned as labor bureaus themselves.

Employer associations such as the MBA and NMTA complained bitterly about union control of apprenticeships. Anthony Ittner, speaking to the National Association of Manufacturers in 1905, claimed, "Formerly the apprenticeship system offered to the American boy the opportunity to learn a trade, but . . . the bitter and cruel opposition of [unions] have nearly destroyed this former safeguard of opportunity. . . . [It is] a crime against the youth of the whole nation." He sought to demonstrate the "utmost necessity" of the establishment of trade schools that would take the place of apprenticeships.[51] These schools, Ittner hoped, would be free from the influence of craft unions. The argument that craft unions represented a threat to individual liberty was widespread among Boston's elite, including Harvard president Charles Eliot, who claimed that labor unions were dangerous "social and industrial evils" worse than capitalistic monopolies.[52] By the turn of the century, a growing chorus of advocates pushed for new initiatives in industrial education.

THE MANUAL TRAINING MOVEMENT, 1876–1896

In the late nineteenth century, the few existing technical and industrial schools in Boston were closely aligned with anti-union employer interests. Instead of grooming their own rank-and-file workers to take on managerial positions, employers began to draw on graduates of technical institutes. Beginning in 1895, Westinghouse recruited "executives and technical experts from among those who . . . enter the organization directly from engineering schools."[53] Among the nation's leading technical institutes was the Massachusetts Institute of Technology (MIT), whose graduates, since the school's founding, overwhelmingly entered supervisory positions in industry and aligned themselves against organized labor.[54]

In addition to training for foremen and engineers, employers were attracted to educational schemes intended for their rank-and-file craftworkers. Some of Boston's first industrial schools were "manual training" schools. Manual training drew on a long tradition of charity and reform schools and paralleled the Reconstruction-era movement for African American industrial education in the South, funded by Northeastern philanthropists.[55] In northern urban centers in the 1880s, manual training was championed by upper-class reformers concerned with the declining status of craftsmanship and the replacement of native-born white men by immigrant workers. These reformers were also influenced by progressive educational theories that stressed active, hands-on learning.[56]

Promoters of manual training expressed the same professionalizing logic that Kehew had used to justify schools as a way to "elevate" low-wage work. In 1888, philosopher and popular lecturer Thomas Davidson wrote an impassioned plea for raising the status of "mechanical arts" to that of the liberal arts by teaching it in schools. As he declared, "It may be laid down as a general rule, that whatever is taught in school will soon become respectable and gentlemanly, while that which is picked up in the home or the workshop will always be regarded as menial."[57] As we have seen, manual training was a central component of urban settlements in Boston's poorest immigrant neighborhoods, including the North Bennet Street Industrial School (NBSIS), which partnered with the public schools in 1883 to offer trade instruction to local grammar school students, and the Unitarian-affiliated North End Union Trade School, founded in 1894.[58]

One of the manual training movement's leading champions, MIT president Jon Runkle, opened a private School of Mechanic Arts in 1876 that aimed to prepare both craftsmen and prospective MIT students. Boston's superintendent of schools, Edwin Seaver, formerly an assistant professor of mathematics at Harvard, also advocated for a full-fledged public "Mechanic Arts" high school, which, like Runkle's school, would not teach "any one trade, but the mastery of the fundamental principles."[59] In June 1888, MIT gave notice that it would be closing its School of Mechanic Arts, arguing that this type of school should be a public responsibility.[60] The precise timing of this closing was likely precipitated by the planned opening of the new Manual Training High School in Cambridge that fall, with funding from Frederick Hastings Rindge, son of a wealthy textile merchant and Harvard graduate.[61] In Boston, Edwin Seaver continued his canvassing for public and private funding until 1893, when the Boston Mechanic Arts High School, for male students only, opened its doors in a "commodious and substantive" new building in the Back Bay.[62]

Employers and employer associations lauded the manual training movement. One article in the NMTA bulletin optimistically predicted that manual training courses would soon replace union apprenticeships and weaken union power.[63] The author of a promotional feature on an Indianapolis trade school argued that trade schools could avoid the "poisonous" atmosphere of union rules and "teach a boy, not only the art of molding, but also good morals, and the art of the 'open shop.'"[64]

Boston's first manual training schools, however, did not succeed in training a new cohort of craftworkers free from union influence. Due to strong pressure from building-trade and printing unions, philanthropic schools such as the North End Union Trade School limited enrollment for courses in plumbing and printing to those already employed in their trades, rather than new recruits.[65] Other schools did not train craftworkers at all. Based on a list compiled in 1886 of graduates of MIT's School of Mechanic Arts and their subsequent occupations, these students were similar to those who matriculated at MIT. Out of twenty-five recorded graduates, six became either professors or instructors of mechanical arts and eleven became merchants (in oil, provisions, fancy goods) or manufacturers (of typewriters, sewing machines, wire nails, watches, or gold and silver refiners). Only one was listed as what was likely a mechanic's position in a "repair shop of Lower Pacific Mills."[66] With $150 in annual tuition, the School for Mechanic Arts catered to students from more affluent families who aimed to become technical instructors or enter industrial management, not future mechanics.[67]

Like students at MIT's School of Mechanic Arts, students at Boston's public Mechanical Arts High School also entered the supervisory ranks of industry. A list of the pursuits of the school's first graduating class of 1896 reveals that of the 55 male graduates, 22 continued on to higher education, including 14 who entered MIT. Four became draftsmen in architects' offices; six became salesmen. Within five years, many had become manufacturers themselves, or industrial chemists, city officials, or instructors. By this date, only 12 percent of the original 55 graduates worked as machinists, pattern makers, electricians, or employees of larger manufacturing companies.[68] Other than a slightly higher number of engineers, the occupational patterns of the graduates of the Mechanical Arts High School did not differ significantly from Boston's English High School.

Why did these schools fail to reach their target demographic? For youth entering the trades, actual experience in a workshop was far more significant than formal schooling. In addition, high schools, even mechanical arts high schools, were still exclusive institutions. The opportunity cost of attending school during the years one would otherwise begin gaining on-the-job training and work experience was high. The first manual training institutions, public and private, left employers' aspirations for reshaping the craftworker training process unfulfilled.

PRIVATE TRADE SCHOOLS, 1900–1919

In the first decade of the twentieth century, industrialists across the country supported a new wave of private trade schools to meet their training demands. In 1900, the Massachusetts Charitable Mechanics Association (MCMA) opened a school in Boston's Back Bay for the purpose of teaching young men a trade. The MCMA had been founded in 1795 by Paul Revere and other craftsmen to promote the mechanic arts and provide funding for members' widows and families. By the turn of the twentieth century the MCMA was part charity, part social club, and part an employers' association of leading craftsmen and manufacturers in the state.[69]

The MCMA's "pioneer evening vocational school" offered courses in plumbing, carpentry, masonry, drawing, reinforced concrete construction, sheet metal work, heating and ventilating, steam and gas fitting, and electricity, in the basement of its Mechanics Hall. Courses cost $12 per year and met three times per week from 7:00 to 9:00 p.m. The students it attracted were those who intended to become craftsmen. In 1904, according to the school's first report, 57 percent of those registered were "regularly employed as apprentices or helpers in the trade they [were] studying," and several others were "learning the trade that they [might] be of more value to their employers."[70]

The MCMA collaborated with a number of employers' associations. For a new tile-laying class offered in 1908, the Tile Dealer's Association provided supplies free of charge.[71] The MCMA even established formal agreements with employers for the training of apprentices. The Massachusetts Association of Sheet Metal Workers took "a great interest" in the school and incorporated into its four-year apprenticeship program a requirement that the apprentice attend the MCMA trade school for three years at the employer's expense.[72]

The new MCMA trade school, however, repeatedly ran into difficulties. In its first year, despite plans for a wider array of courses, it secured only enough students for plumbing, masonry, carpentry, and drawing. The challenge of enrollment was not only due to lack of student interest, but also to the power of unions in each respective trade. In 1903, the MCMA blamed the Mason's Trade Union for difficulties in procuring a suitable instructor.[73] In 1908, the Tile-Setter's Union mobilized to prevent the enrollment of any students in the MCMA tile-laying class, forcing the cancellation of the class.[74] Enrollment remained below 100 during the school's first years of existence, and even fewer students remained for the full three or four years required to receive a diploma. At its peak in 1913, the MCMA trade school had ten instructors and 205 students; in subsequent years, enrollment declined substantially.[75]

One Boston union leader, Frank Foster, was at the forefront of many debates over Boston's new trade schools. A printer by trade, Foster had been a leader of the Knights of Labor before helping to found the American Federation of Labor in 1886.[76] He edited Boston's trade union newspaper, *Labor Leader,* where he championed shorter working hours, higher wages, women's rights, and ethnic pluralism.[77] A strong believer in education, he was also critical of the private interests that controlled much of Boston's educational landscape. In 1895, he supported a BCLU resolution that rejected MIT's attempt to secure $25,000 annually from the state legislature, on the basis that such private institutions were "not free to the people" and diverted funds away from the "children of wage workers.[78] In 1904, he gave a public point-by-point rebuttal to Charles Eliot's address on capital and labor, in which Eliot had praised the scab as "a fair type of hero" and criticized unions for "destroy[ing] free competition" and "rotting the individual man's moral fibre."[79]

Foster played an active role in the debate over the next private trade school, Franklin Union, which opened its doors in 1908 in the South End. The funding for this school came from the Franklin Fund, a bequest to the city of Boston by Benjamin Franklin in 1789 for "forming and advancing other young men," as well as a matching grant from Andrew Carnegie to found a school on the model of New York's Cooper Union.[80] Because of the public status of the Franklin Fund, the board of trustees included Foster as a labor representative, and unions pushed strongly to shape its direction. While the plans for the school were still being determined, Foster helped to craft a BCLU resolution opposing trade schools, which was issued on December 18, 1904:

> Whereas it is impossible for any young man to acquire a trade
> in any trade school;

Whereas, there is no dearth of mechanics in any skilled trades; and

Whereas, the advocates of trade schools are either men who pay small wages, or work their help long hours, or are dilettante labor reformers; therefore, be it

Resolved, by the representatives of organized labor of the city of Boston, that we protest against the establishment of a trade school by the board of managers of the Franklin Fund.[81]

Despite BCLU's blanket condemnation of trade schools in this statement, its position was in fact more nuanced. A BCLU statement the following year explained, "We are . . . in favor of wider opportunities for the higher industrial and technical training, by means of which mechanics may perfect themselves in the theoretical and practical branches of their trades."[82] The BCLU supported trade education for those who were already employed as craftworkers, but did not support the teaching of specific craft skills to those not employed, because employers could then use these students to evade union regulations.

When Franklin Union opened in 1908, its courses and policies reflected a compromise with the BCLU. It offered evening courses in elementary mechanics, drawing and drafting, industrial arithmetic, steam and gas engines, heating and ventilation, structural materials, and chemistry. Courses were only open to men who were already employed in the trades. In addition, relative to those offered by the MCMA, these courses were more theoretical and math- and science-based than workshop-based. The first students at Franklin Union were engineers, firemen, machinists, steamfitters, and carpenters, with an average age of 29. The majority were born in Massachusetts, with a minority from Canada, Britain, Ireland, Scandinavia, and Russia. Organized labor was likely heartened that the students at Franklin Union were, on the whole, not young learners skirting union apprenticeship but rather mature craftworkers who sought more advanced scientific knowledge.[83]

Unions were less successful in shaping the instruction provided by the "avowedly antiunion" private trade school, Wentworth Institute.[84] Arioch Wentworth, the descendent of a wealthy New Hampshire family,

died in 1903, leaving $7 million in his will to found "a school for the pur-
pose of furnishing an education in the mechanical arts."[85] The new
school, which opened in 1911 in the Fenway, offered workshop-based
courses in specific craft skills: machine work, carpentry, electrical wiring,
foundry work, plumbing, machine tool and design, and electrical construction. Rather than evening courses for those already employed,
Wentworth's day classes targeted high school–age boys. Unlike the
MCMA, which offered three-to-four-year extensive training programs
similar in duration to a standard apprenticeship, Wentworth offered
one-year courses explicitly so that students could avoid "[having] to
spend two or three years as apprentices."[86]

Wentworth's leaders were not subtle in their anti-union stance. O. M.
Wentworth, one of the trustees, was known for his numerous antilabor
columns in the *Boston Globe*, in which he accused workers who advocated for shorter workdays and higher wages of laziness and unreason-
able demands.[87] Speakers at the graduation exercises of Wentworth, including former president William Taft, criticized unions, accusing
them of "destroying initiative" and creating "poor citizens." Politically,
Taft suggested, unions created a "field for anarchy and Socialism."[88]
During the Boston police strike of 1919, Wentworth allied with the Massachusetts state government, as well as administrators of Boston's other
private universities, to oppose the strike. Wentworth students were
joined by hundreds of Harvard, MIT, and Boston University students
to serve as strikebreakers, encouraged by their respective university administrations to fulfill their civic duty.[89]

Wentworth successfully attracted its target demographic of students.
Of the first class of graduates in 1912 who had taken the daytime foundry
practice class, the majority were under 19 years of age. Almost all had
been born in Massachusetts, and the majority of their parents were from
New England, Canada, or England. Their fathers were predominantly
craftsmen and small proprietors, and most students themselves worked
in factories, in the trades as mechanics and plumbers, or as clerks or
salesmen. After graduating, a minority became proprietors, foremen,
and managers in manufacturing firms, while the majority of students
became craftsmen themselves, as printers, plumbers, machinists, city
wire inspectors, and blueprint designers.[90] Wentworth thus offered the

type of instruction to the type of students that craft unions most strongly opposed, and in this case, unions were unable to effectively counter it.

Across the country, craft unions continued to oppose employer-funded trade schools, with some successes. Anthony Ittner blamed union opposition for shuttering his trade school in St. Louis: "We met with this same determined opposition [from unions] in St. Louis, and there is no doubt in my mind that it had much to do with our failure to establish a trade school at that time."[91] Given the repeated challenges facing private trade schools, employers reasoned, the public sector had a responsibility to address this need. Hence, the political struggle over efforts to expand industrial education in many cities, including Boston, shifted into the public sector.

PUBLIC INDUSTRIAL EDUCATION AND THE 1906 DOUGLAS COMMISSION

In the midst of debates over private trade schools such as MCMA and Franklin Union, Massachusetts governor William Douglas made public industrial education central to his political platform. Douglas, a Democrat, was a shoe manufacturer who was willing to work with organized labor. In his inaugural address in January 1905, he echoed the arguments of reformers who had diagnosed lack of training opportunities as the problem afflicting a changing economy. Douglas pointed out that due to the "practical abolition of apprenticeship systems" and the specialization of labor, it was nearly impossible for a young person to learn a trade. He claimed that the achievement of German and English industry could be attributed to their system of industrial and trade schools, and that Massachusetts would be well served by following their lead.[92] In his first months in office, Douglas received authorization from the state legislature to appoint a commission on industrial and technical education, known as the Douglas Commission, to investigate industrial and technical education in the state.[93]

Unionists mobilized to shape the new state initiatives. Some rejected the plan for more industrial schools outright. At a BCLU meeting in March 1905, "flat-footed declarations in opposition to trades schools

[were] made by many," including the secretary-treasurer of the state branch of the AFL, Dennis D. Driscoll.[94] In a subsequent debate in April, Peter W. Collins, business agent of the Boston Electrical Workers Union No. 103, claimed that trade school instruction "makes an indolent worker, a novice without thorough knowledge and practice . . . [and] their graduates are willing members of the strike-breaking craft, whose influence is to lower the life of the community."[95]

In addition to being skeptical about industrial education, members of the BCLU were disinclined to cooperate with state and city officials. Organized labor supported Julia Duff, an outspoken Irish Catholic schoolteacher, in her campaigns for school committee membership between 1900 and 1907 to represent Boston's working-class families.[96] Duff's chief rival was James Jackson Storrow, a Harvard-educated Republican investment banker who helped organize a bloc within the Boston School Committee opposed to growing Catholic representation. In 1905, Storrow led a successful effort to reduce the school committee from twenty-four district representatives to five members elected at large, which was seen by organized labor and the Democratic Party as an attack on the working men and women of the city.[97] Although Governor Douglas was a Democrat, Republican leaders dominated the state government through the 1920s, coming into increasing conflict with Democrats at the local level.

These conflicts heightened the skepticism with which organized labor viewed public industrial education. In response to the new Douglas Commission, Frank Foster clarified the stance of organized labor on state-funded industrial schools. He noted that, based on his experience with trade schools in the past, they had primarily been used as "recruiting stations" for strikebreakers and as seedbeds of anti-union indoctrination. However, he said, if "it is the intention of the state to assist workingmen to a higher understanding of their trade, to give them an opportunity to improve themselves in its practical workings, they should not oppose it." Foster expressed his hope that a public institution, as distinguished from those controlled by employers, would serve the interest of working people.[98]

Between September and December 1905, the Douglas Commission, which included one labor representative and claimed to be "heartily in accord with the declaration of the BCLU," conducted twenty public hearings around the state in order to gather input on the new state initiative. The report on these proceedings was published in 1906. The commission appointees presented their conclusions: the problem afflicting American industry was a lack of training, and this problem could be solved by increasing industrial education and hence the supply of skilled workers. They pointed to the success of European industrial schools, especially those of Germany, which had made possible "a most remarkable advance of scientific knowledge and industry." They recommended the creation of a commission on industrial education, independent of the state board of education, to administer a separate set of industrial schools that would be funded equally by the state and by local governments. Paul Hanus, a Prussian-born mathematics teacher and Harvard professor who helped organize the university's new division of education, was appointed chair of the commission. Robert Woods, who considered Germany "our greatest rival" whose "superiority in international commerce rests almost wholly on [its] superior school system," called industrial education the "salvation" of Massachusetts and the commission "the most important educational departure that has been made in the United States in the last decade."[99]

The Douglas Commission officers reassured the public that several union-friendly restrictions would be incorporated into the new industrial programming. Planned industrial courses for youth would be preparation for, not replacement of, apprenticeships.[100] Evening industrial education would be restricted to those already in the trades.[101] In response to labor demands, the governor also made a commitment that a "bona fide active labor man" would be appointed to the new state commission.[102]

As a separate entity, the new Commission on Industrial Education was short-lived. Jurisdictional conflict with the state board of education led in just three years to the commission's dissolution. State funding for industrial education was placed under control of the state board of education, now under the leadership of David Snedden.[103] Organized labor was likely relieved. Unions trusted that if overseen by the academic educational establishment, industrial education would be less likely to serve as a replacement of union-controlled craft training.

NEGOTIATING CRAFT RESTRICTIONS IN THE PUBLIC SCHOOLS, 1908–1918

By 1908, Boston was already ahead of many other cities in Massachusetts in its industrial offerings, but it quickly moved to take advantage of new state funding. An evening industrial school was established that year using the facilities of the Mechanic Arts High School and later several other branch high schools, supplementing the work of students employed in machine shops, the offices of architects, builders, designers, illustrators, or decorators, and those preparing to enter technical institutes. In 1909, the Boston School Committee, with the enthusiastic support of the new school superintendent and loyal friend of James Storrow, Stratton Brooks, converted several city initiatives into half state-funded industrial schools. These included a trade school for girls teaching needle trades and "preapprenticeship" schools, which received union approval in 1910, offering preliminary training for students who signed an agreement to become apprentice bookbinders, printers, and sheet metal workers. By this date, with municipal funding, the school committee also launched afternoon classes for high school students in electrical manufacturing, commercial designing, and jewelry making and silversmithing.[104]

Even though these initial public industrial offerings had union-friendly restrictions, they faced challenges. The preapprenticeship bookbinding and printing schools attracted very few students and were folded into prevocational courses in regular elementary schools. The electrical manufacturing course was discontinued within a year because "the equipment in the school was planned for woodwork alone" and "the making of interchangeable parts was thereby rendered impossible." The commercial design course was also discontinued within a year due to "decreased attendance." The preapprenticeship school for sheet metal workers never opened at all.[105]

After 1912, the chief architect of industrial education in the Boston city school system was Frank Thompson. Before becoming superintendent, Thompson had earned a reputation as a successful coordinator between employers and the public schools as principal of Boston's new High School of Commerce in 1906. Working with the Merchants Association, the Associated Board of Trade, and the Boston Chamber of Commerce, he had created an advisory committee of businessmen to make recommendations to the school committee. Like many educational leaders in the state, Thompson was inspired by German educational practices that drew schools and industry closer together, including such advisory boards as well as industrial, commercial, and continuation schools, which he observed firsthand on a European tour in 1906. When Franklin Dyer became superintendent of Boston schools in 1912, he expanded the scope of Thompson's work to include the coordination of all state-aided work, including industrial education. Now, Thompson's job description included the challenging task of coordinating between both employers and labor unions.[106]

The former math teacher championed industrial education as a means of broadening instruction because, as he put it, "democracy of educational opportunity means that there shall be many varieties of educational opportunity."[107] But unions already had reason to be skeptical of Thompson's approach. The BCLU saw his cooperation with the chamber of commerce as a threat. At a January 1911 meeting, the BCLU voted to form its own twenty-five-member advisory committee to attend school board meetings and voice its concerns.[108] One of the strongest advocates of the creation of this advisory committee was an activist schoolteacher, Mrs. Page. In an address to the BCLU, Page called the entire system of vocational education in the public schools a "deliberate plan to 'peasantize' the children of working classes and provide cheap workmen with but a smattering of a trade." As she explained, "If a strike occurs, well, you can't expect the school to shut down or to ask the employers to cease employing these pupils or training them under their agreement with the school board. Certainly not. What is the result? Strike breakers, nothing else."[109] Over the next year, in addition to creating the advisory committee, the BCLU voted to investigate the vocational work in the Boston public schools, increase labor representation on the school committee, return the school committee to twenty-four members, and ensure stricter oversight of the industrial schools.[110]

Thompson sought to accommodate union demands. Under his supervision in 1912, the first daytime public industrial school, the Boys Industrial School, was approved by the state board of education with half-state, half-city funding and opened in a school building in the South End. The one-to-two-year course of study consisted of both shop work and academic work. Unions were skeptical of providing daytime instruction to students who were not already employed, but Thompson stressed in his public reports that the school was "not incompatible" with union apprenticeship, as the school would only give boys knowledge of the "elements" of work to prepare them to begin apprenticeships at the age of 16. This reassurance, as well as sufficient funding, helped make this industrial school more successful than earlier public efforts. By 1914, about 400 students applied for 200 spots, and in 1916, the renamed Boston Trade School moved to a larger building in Roxbury that could accommodate 400 to 600 students per year.[111]

Thompson also oversaw the implementation of part-time continuation schools and cooperative courses, in which students split time between school and a partnered company. While unions supported continuation schools that enrolled workers who were already employed, they viewed cooperative instruction, which tended to serve older high school students, with more suspicion.[112] In 1914, the Hyde Park High School became the first high school to offer a cooperative course in machine-shop work, and sixty-five boys enrolled. In this industrial neighborhood with many machine shops, recently annexed by the city of Boston in 1912, firms including American Tool and Machine, B. F. Sturtevant Company, and the New York, New Haven, and Hartford Railroad agreed to partner with the school system. Cooperative students received school instruction in shop mathematics, shop science, drawing, and English, designed to "help [student-workers] in their particular trade." Shop instructors also visited students while they were at work and consulted with their foremen. Cooperative courses were expanded to additional neighborhood high schools over the next years.[113]

While these cooperative arrangements were made under the supervision of advisory councils of both labor and employers, the companies involved were typically members of strongly anti-union employers' associations.[114] The B. F. Sturtevant Company, whose representatives attended meetings of the American Foundrymen Association, was one example.[115] This producer of fans and ventilation systems was one of the largest manufacturing companies in Boston, employing 1,500 workers in 1919. The company had moved from a smaller factory in Jamaica Plain to Hyde Park in 1903, under the leadership of Sturtevant's son-in-law and future governor of Massachusetts, Eugene Foss. Although Foss began his political career as a Republican, he supported some Democratic policies, including free trade with Canada, where he planned to move part of his company's production. He defected to the Democratic Party and was elected governor in 1910. As governor, Foss took aggressive antilabor positions, including sending the Massachusetts militia to crush the Lawrence textile workers' strike in 1912. In 1913, when B. F. Sturtevant did move part of its operations to Canada, craftworkers at the Hyde Park plant went on strike. By 1914, Foss had alienated the labor wing of the Democratic Party and left politics to return to business. It was during this year that the cooperative arrangement with the public schools was established.[116]

The relationship between organized labor and advocates of industrial education remained tense through the 1910s. One indication of union power was that public school officials felt obligated to attend BCLU meetings to explain new public school initiatives and answer questions.[117] Union members were also not afraid to criticize school leaders and oppose them on the issue of industrial education. In 1918, a faction of the BCLU unsuccessfully mobilized against Thompson when he sought election as school superintendent, evidently because he had failed to gain their trust. The same year, labor organizer Henry Abrahams was elected to the Boston School Committee after the BCLU had spent nearly a decade seeking labor representation.[118]

Craft unions in Boston achieved significant success in shaping the landscape of both private and public industrial training. In the private sector, they were able to limit some instruction in craft skills by private trade schools. In the public sector, they established the precedent that in decision-making about industrial education, administrators and employers would heed the demands of labor. They were able to limit public instruction in specific craft skills to workers who were already employed and, for those who were not, to push public industrial education toward rudimentary or academic instruction. Industrial education, as a result, never became a viable substitute for a union apprenticeship. In response, employers pushed aggressively to take back control of training and the shop floor.

THE OPEN-SHOP MOVEMENT AND THE DECLINE OF CRAFT UNIONS

The World War I–driven surge in production heightened conflict over training, particularly in the metal trades that produced war machinery and munitions. Immigration restriction and male conscription severely limited the supply of labor, and a coordinated wartime industry and full employment gave labor unions new strength. Nationally, companies sought new sources of inexpensive labor, including African Americans and women, and pursued mechanization and restructuring processes that favored dependence on machine operators who could be trained on the job quickly.[119] Wartime employers experimented with "vestibule schools" that trained new labor recruits with little prior knowledge of industry in record time, from three days to three months. As described in the *Open Shop Review* in 1919, these training programs were "applicable in some form in every shop and [went] far toward solving the problem of the shortage of skilled labor."[120]

After the war, these short-term training programs became a key part of an anti-union drive dubbed the "American plan." The Lunkenheimer Company in Cincinnati developed a two-week training program to replace striking workers in 1921; once it was in place, the company trained enough workers to supply a 100 percent turnover.[121] In Massachusetts, colleges and universities, including Harvard and MIT, developed short courses to train their students to operate railcars in order to serve as strikebreakers during a threatened railroad strike in 1921.[122] Nationally, short training courses made possible the surge in the export of American mass-standardized machinery and transportation equipment. These new forms of training also significantly weakened metal trade unions in the postwar period.

While not as dramatic as the 442 percent growth of foundry and machine-shop production in the Midwest from 1899 to 1923, New England production grew nearly 300 percent over this period.[123] Boston still retained a high proportion of small-batch machine shops. The average number of employees in Boston's machine and metal works grew from under fifteen in 1880 to about sixty in 1920. However, while small firms such as the Special Tool and Machine Company in South Boston with twenty-five employees persisted, other Boston firms exemplified the new trend of large-scale production. For example, Walworth, the pipe and valve firm, grew over 600 percent in the span of four decades to employ 5,000 workers by 1929. Edison Electric Illuminating Company grew to 3,500 employees.[124]

Reflecting the national trend, union membership in the metal and machinery trades in Massachusetts declined in the 1920s, as shown in Figure 3.1. As the training time for new workers decreased, so did the power of unions to wield the threat of withdrawing craft labor. In 1924 the Boston Chamber of Commerce claimed, "Less than twenty per cent of the employees in [foundry and machine shops] are organized. . . . The factor of organized labor may be considered comparatively unimportant." The chamber also marginalized the prior importance of metal trade unions by claiming that "there have been no industrial disturbances of any importance in New England in the history of the industry."[125] Erased from employers' historical memory for the time being, organized labor in the metal industry would only begin to climb again during the Great Depression and World War II, in many cases led by unions on an industry-wide rather than craft basis.

The building trades, as shown in Figure 3.1, were the only trades that experienced rising rates of union membership in the 1920s. Despite a fierce anti-union drive, they successfully maintained their power and training regulations. One open-shop supporter complained in 1921 that "The building trades of Boston are to all intents and purposes 100% unionized. I mean by that, that . . . it would be a practical impossibility to build any large building today—without employing union men."[126] Democratic leadership in the city remained a strong ally to the building trades in these years. During his mayoralty starting in 1914, James Curley launched major public transit projects that employed union labor, pushed prolabor legislation, and further raised the salaries of municipal workers. In 1922, when Curley was reelected, he helped the United Building Trades

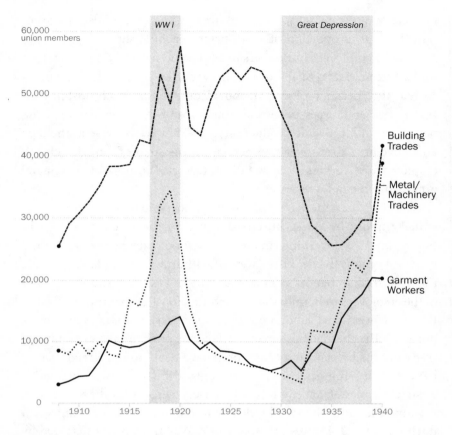

FIGURE 3.1: Union membership in Massachusetts, by industry, 1908–1940.

DATA SOURCES: "Labor Organizations," in *BSL* (Boston: Wright & Potter, 1908–1916); "Statistics of Labor Organizations in Massachusetts," in *BSL* (Boston: Wright & Potter, 1917–1925); "Annual Directory of Labor Organizations in Massachusetts," in *BSL, LB,* nos. 176–182 (1936–1940). © Cristina Groeger.

NOTE: The Massachusetts Bureau of Statistics of Labor collected total union membership by industry for the state, not the percentage of unionized employees in each industry or totals for the city. Unionization rates in Boston were typically higher than the state average.

Council, representing thirty-five building-trade locals, to negotiate a new agreement with the Building Trades Employers Association (BTEA). During this period, the building trades upgraded licensing requirements and revised apprenticeship training to keep up with ongoing techno-logical changes. In 1929, building-trade unions reported "long waiting lists of applicants for apprenticeship." Despite a decline during the Great Depression, union membership rose again during World War II.

Well into the twentieth century and, indeed, into the present, the overwhelming majority of US apprenticeships have been in the building trades, and these apprenticeships remain an attractive pathway into a well-paying union job.[127]

Building-trade power, however, remained premised on exclusion. These craft unions often controlled access to apprenticeships and typically granted them to the relatives of union members.[128] A St. Louis contractor claimed in 1928 that "a boy has as good a chance to get into West Point as into the building trades unless his father or his uncle is a building craftsman."[129] This control significantly restricted entry along racial, ethnic, and gender lines. Throughout the 1940s, eastern and southern Europeans and African Americans in Boston were almost entirely barred from entry.[130] In 1937, only three women were listed as belonging to a building-trade union in Boston, compared to over 27,000 men.[131] One of the legacies of craft power was restricted and often discriminatory access to these trades.

For the majority of Boston's trades, industrial transformation entailed decreasing reliance on craftworkers and the virtual elimination of union apprenticeship as a pathway into industrial jobs. As a percentage of Boston's male labor force between 1920 and 1940, craftworkers dropped by nearly one-third. Managerial strategies of control also relied on a new hierarchy of workers with different training backgrounds. A small group of engineers and managers with the most authority, who had received training in engineering institutes and universities, rose to the top. At the bottom of the production ladder were factory operatives, who by and large did not receive specialized industrial training in a school or a workplace, but basic literacy, numeracy, and acculturation in public schools.

THE ABSENCE OF CRAFT CONTROL IN THE GARMENT INDUSTRY

Boston's needle trades offer an example of how the absence of craft union power shaped both the outcome of industrial development and the landscape of training. The transition from custom-made dresses and suits to ready-made garments illustrates the rapid transformation from artisanal craftwork to low-wage piecework. The weakness of craft unions in this sector meant that there was little conflict over training, and some trade schools thrived as pathways into the remunerative positions available. It also meant that craftworkers had little power to counter the reorganization of industry that eventually reduced interest in specialized training for these jobs.

In the late nineteenth century, men's clothing was the first needle trade industry to be significantly reorganized. Through extensive division of labor, the small tailor shop gave way to factories of mostly German Jewish clothing manufacturers employing hundreds of sewing machine operators producing ready-made garments. Due to the influx of new immigrant workers in the 1880s, clothing manufacturers expanded the contract system, in which portions of work were contracted out to predominantly Russian Jewish tailors. The burdens of seasonal variation and capital investment were thereby foisted onto these contractors. Jewish contractors subdivided even further, giving work to Jewish and Italian women who worked in their tenement homes, known as the sweating system. In 1892, a majority of the men's clothing traded in Boston was produced either wholly or in part via contracted labor, a significant proportion of which was made with the sweating system.[132] In 1900, Russian Jewish women were the most overrepresented ethnic group among Boston tailors, but by 1920, Italian women had replaced them as the dominant ethnic group.[133]

Small dressmaking and millinery shops making one-of-a-kind dresses and hats were less subject to piecework and the sweating system, but these shops were also declining relative to factories producing ready-made garments.[134] In 1880, nearly 13 percent of the women's workforce worked as dressmakers and seamstresses outside of factories, but by 1920 this percentage had fallen to 4 percent, and by 1930 it had fallen to under 2 percent. Correspondingly, the proportion of women garment factory operatives in this industry rose. The demographics also changed: while early-twentieth-century dressmakers (outside of factories) were disproportionately the sons and daughters of American and Canadian-born parents, by 1920, Russian Jewish and Italian women were overrepresented.[135]

Amid this transformation, workers in the needle trades formed unions. The largest craft union was the United Garment Workers, founded in 1891, with locals in Boston for clothing cutters and trimmers, overalls and shirt makers, tailors, vestmakers, and pants makers. This union advocated for wage increases, shorter working days, and against the "the tenement house sweat-shop evils."[136] Although the union did win some contracts, and the state legislature passed new sweatshop regulations in the 1890s, subcontracted labor could still undermine the power of craftworkers in a shop, and it fueled a gender division between predominantly male unionists and women pieceworkers. Women garment workers also organized their own locals with the support of wealthier women reformers and the Women's Trade Union League (WTUL), formed in Boston in 1903 with Mary Kehew as its first president. Despite the AFL's formal endorsement of the WTUL, in practice women's unions received little direct support. Hostility to women members from male union members and leadership, internal ethnic divisions, and mistrust between native-born women allies and rank-and-file immigrant workers stymied many of the earliest efforts to organize women in the needle trades.[137] The Consumers League of Massachusetts formed in 1898 to promote goods made under fair working conditions, but this women-led organization also had a difficult relationship with union leadership.[138]

Craft unions in the needle trades struggled to control the training process. A few, such as the Clothing Cutters and Trimmers Union, tried to regulate apprenticeship. In 1893, this union considered "complaints that the clothing trimmers were being reduced in their wages through the apprentice system as operated by the employers of Boston."[139] However, many immigrants brought fine needle skills with them from abroad, and women learned such skills informally in the home, making the control of craft skills next to impossible.

The limits of craft control in the needle trades had a significant impact on the development of industrial education in this sector. The weakness of craft control allowed some trade schools for dressmaking and sewing to thrive from the 1890s through World War I while there was demand for entry into positions as custom dressmakers, tailors, milliners, and seamstresses. Training in needlework, compared to trades such as the metal trades, required less expensive equipment and was easier to provide in a school setting. Philanthropic organizations including the YWCA, the Women's Educational and Industrial Union, the North Bennet Street Industrial School, and the Hebrew Industrial School offered classes in dressmaking, millinery, and sewing. Other schools aimed to make a profit. The national chain of McDowell Dressmaking and Millinery Schools opened first in New York and Chicago in 1891 before opening in Boston by 1900. McDowell Schools offered day and evening classes for novices as well as craftworkers who sought advanced training in cutting, fitting, and dressmaking. In 1898, a "Ladies Tailor, Dressmaking, and Millinery College" took out an ad in the "Female Help Wanted" section of the *Boston Globe,* advertising itself as the "largest dressmaking and millinery college in this country," with "spring positions" waiting. Some "colleges" like these were likely housed within stores themselves, making it very easy for them to promise or even guarantee positions, and effectively served as unregulated apprenticeship programs.[140]

In July 1904, several women settlement house leaders, including Mary Kehew, opened the Boston Trade School for Girls in the South End. This school ultimately proved to be one of the most successful institutions serving needleworkers.[141] It offered courses in dressmaking, millinery, sewing machine operating, design, and domestic science. At the outset, it seems to have offered working-class students a successful pathway into some of the remaining opportunities for well-paying garment work. As the director of the trade school noted, "A girl whose parents were in very poor circumstances, and who was about to enter a candy factory, where she could contribute her wages of three or four dollars a week to the family support, was influenced by a friend to attend the school for a few months. . . . At the end of 6 months [she was] placed in a millinery establishment, and last week . . . earned nine dollars on piece work." The majority of students had completed eighth grade. Most were Irish, but between 1904 and 1909 about 10 percent of students were Jewish, and another 10 percent were Black. After a period of four months to one year of training, the school helped place these students into positions in dressmaking and millinery shops, department stores, and as sewing machine operators. Black women were also placed, although compared to their 10 percent representation in the school, they made up about 5 percent of successful placements.[142]

In 1909, with new state funding for industrial education, the Boston School Committee took over the private Boston Trade School for Girls. Public school officials had long treated women's industrial education as training for homemaking rather than wage employment. Women's trade education was imagined to steer women away from urban temptations and vices, and sewing was deemed particularly appropriate because women could perform it in their own homes and use it in their future lives as homemakers.[143] Rather than another failed school of housekeeping, however, the new public Trade School for Girls did provide some women useful training that they used to enter the needle trades. The superintendent reported in 1913, "It is a common occurrence for a Trade School graduate to come in and say: 'Miss A or Mr. B is going to promote me and wants another girl to take my place,' or a telephone call will come: 'The girl you sent me Saturday is fine; send me two more just like her.'"[144] According to a 1916 survey, nearly 30 percent of Boston milliners learned their trade in the Boston Trade School for Girls, while 60 percent learned through apprenticeship (in this context, a non-union-regulated apprenticeship). By comparison, in Philadelphia, which was not home to a comparable trade school, over 90 percent of milliners had been apprenticed, and most shops trained their own milliners.[145]

The Boston Trade School for Girls was similar to the public High School of Practical Arts (HSPA), which was founded as a sister school to the boys-only Mechanic Arts High in 1907. The HSPA, however, was located in the outskirts of Dorchester, in contrast to the central location of the boys' school in the Back Bay.[146] The HSPA was devoted above all to the preparation of women for the "practical arts of the household," with the acknowledgment that some women may choose or need to "earn a livelihood in industrial pursuits."[147] In spite of this domestic orientation, the school developed a popular dressmaking program that helped its students access paid work outside the home. In 1912, one of its graduates,

Mary T. Hogan, noted that her dressmaking training had enabled her to work as an independent dressmaker, and that she was now making 40 percent more than she had in her previous job in the waist-making rooms of a specialty women's clothing store.[148]

In an unregulated field, some needle-trade schools may have been little more than an experienced dressmaker seeking to use young learners as cheap labor. Other schools, such as the Trade School for Girls, became effective channels for women into dressmaking and millinery positions. The opportunities for well-paying jobs in the needle trades, however, were quickly diminishing. With little craft power to influence the development of this industry, expansion and restructuring further shifted the occupational structure toward low-paid operatives. By 1914, 80 to 90 percent of women employed in the needle trades worked as sewing machine operators in large workrooms.[149] Schools like the Trade School for Girls repeatedly shifted their offerings to match new labor market needs for sewing machine operators, but in 1916, the average woman "power machine operator" and dressmaker alike earned less than a living wage.[150] Industrial education for the needle trades was only as popular as the jobs into which it could lead. In the next years, training in this sector would join the path of training for other trades. Employers, less reliant on craftworkers with specific craft skills, would come to prefer rank-and-file workers with a public school elementary education, while industrial education would suffer from declining enrollment and reputation.

The weakness of craft unionism in the garment industry had another important implication: it opened up a space for women and immigrant garment workers to pioneer industrial models of union organizing. In 1914, at a convention of the AFL-affiliated United Garment Workers, delegates from Boston and New York split to form a new industrial union, the Amalgamated Clothing Workers Union (Amalgamated), open to women and immigrants across skill levels. By 1920, this union had won contracts covering 6,500 Boston clothing workers representing a majority of all clothing factory workers in Boston.[151] As depicted in Figure 3.1, the garment industry contributed to the surge of union strength at the end of World War I. The Amalgamated had the support of the

International Ladies Garment Workers Union (ILGWU), an AFL-affiliated union whose militant leaders, mostly Jewish immigrant women, broke ranks with official leadership in the 1910s and embraced an industrial union model.[152] While suffering defeats in the 1920s, these unions pioneered organizing strategies that made possible significant union growth in the mid-twentieth century.

These early industrial unions also began the first union-run schools devoted to labor education. Labor union schools became a counterpoint to employer-sponsored private trade schools, the paternalism of many philanthropic and public initiatives, and the male dominance of the labor movement. Labor activist Fannia Cohn secured funding for the ILGWU Education Department in 1916, which organized a Workers University in New York in 1918, and by 1922 had organized classes in five cities, including Boston. As historian Annelise Orleck describes, Cohn's model of workers' education reflected her industrial feminist vision of giving workers the knowledge, confidence, and community they needed to effectively build working-class power and bring forward the "reconstruction of society." At a time when union leadership was overwhelmingly male, this form of education also cultivated rank-and-file women workers to become new leaders of the labor movement. The ILGWU partnered with local public schools to provide space and supplies for its classes, and subjects were decided upon democratically by students, instructors, and union leaders. While history and social science courses dominated the curriculum, these schools also offered arts and humanities classes, as well as social and recreational activities, which Cohn believed were essential to fulfill the human need for "play, joy, and happiness." Courses were offered in multiple languages, including Yiddish, Russian, and Italian. Cohn helped organize the Workers Education Bureau in 1921, which became a central network of labor colleges across the country. While many worker colleges faced funding challenges and, in the case of the ILGWU, clashes between Cohn and male union leaders over the priority of labor education, these schools offered an alternative model for the role of education in reshaping the economy: one premised not on gaining job-related skills, but providing workers with tools to organize collectively.[153]

FROM APPRENTICESHIP TO ACADEMIC EDUCATION

The majority of workers in industry would never attend a labor college, but they did attend school in greater numbers. Employers came to favor school-based education instead of long periods of on-the-job training. The most successful technical institutes catered to those who would become engineers, foremen, or managers. MIT, which maintained the highest enrollment among technical schools and colleges in Boston throughout this period, forged new connections to local industry by expanding applied scientific research and continuing to channel graduates to leading firms.[154] While MIT graduates cornered the market for most elite research jobs, alumni of other institutions filled the niche for technicians and lower-level engineers. Existing private trade schools either closed or remade themselves into collegiate institutions.

The MCMA Trade School was among those institutions forced to close. As a result of financial strain, the institution was shuttered during World War I.[155] Three other trade schools became academic colleges, authorized by the state legislature to grant bachelor's degrees. The YMCA Polytechnic Evening Institute, founded in 1904 at the YMCA's Huntington Avenue location by the Fenway, became the daytime Cooperative Engineering School and Evening School of Engineering of Northeastern College, incorporated in 1916. The Cooperative Engineering School was authorized to grant bachelor of engineering degrees in 1920, and in 1923 the college became Northeastern University, gaining general degree-granting power with the exception of the traditional bachelor of arts, bachelor of science, and medical degrees.[156] Franklin Union struggled financially through the 1920s and 1930s but rebounded with enrollment growth in new wartime training programs during World War II, and in 1953 it was authorized the power to grant associate, bachelor, and master of science degrees in its new capacity as the Franklin Technical Institute.[157] Even Wentworth quickly transformed from a trade school in the 1910s to an advanced technical school by World War I. In a 1914 address, the principal of Wentworth, MIT graduate Arthur Williston, drew a distinction between trade schools and schools like Wentworth that trained the "non-commissioned officers of industry," or foremen and supervisors.[158] By sending graduates into management positions, schools like Wentworth could more easily build their institutional profile and increase alumni contributions. Wentworth also pursued degree-granting authority, which it gained in 1956.[159]

Employers initiated practices in their firms that suggest the high value they placed on academic education for employees they hoped to promote to leadership roles. In the 1920s, Dennison Manufacturing Company began an "Education Committee" headed by education manager J. W. Riegel. He helped develop personalized training programs specifically intended for "our most promising employees." Riegel rejected the notion that "liberal subjects" were beyond the proper field of corporation training, as they could improve employee's "powers of attention and analysis," as well as imagination and resourcefulness.[160] R. F. McDonald, a machine operator with a grammar school education who started at Dennison in 1921, was one such employee. Riegel encouraged McDonald to enroll in a two-year public high school evening course, which provided instruction in English, arithmetic, and penmanship. McDonald subsequently took three more years of in-house English courses offered at Dennison. In 1927, when he became acting foreman, he enrolled in a "report writing" course and was provided with regular written feedback from Riegel himself, who also urged him to pursue the study of leadership problems. McDonald enrolled in a foremanship course the subsequent year.[161]

While verbal and written communication skills were deemed essential for future foremen or supervisors, they were also deemed valuable for rank-and-file factory operatives. While only one-fifth of Boston operatives who grew up at the turn of the century reported having more than an eighth-grade education, in 1940 two-thirds of operatives age 30 or younger reported the same.[162] These employees, unlike craftworkers, did not require specialized craft skills. Rather, basic literacy and numeracy, as well as some scientific knowledge, could help them use complex machinery. In addition to basic academic training, employers also valued the cultural and behavioral qualities instilled by the public schools in their factory workers. The completion of elementary school, or a year or two of high school, served as a proxy for the desirable qualities of self-discipline and ambition.[163] Employers also believed that civic education taught in public schools would instill the proper political attitudes that would subdue radicalism. Once completed, this public school education could be easily supplemented by a short period of on-the-job training in the industrial workplace.[164]

THE MARGINALIZATION OF INDUSTRIAL EDUCATION

The growing preference among employers for academic schooling coincided with the devaluation of school-based industrial education. In a pattern repeated in cities across the United States, specialized industrial education never became a primary channel into industrial employment, and students who received it did not tend to have an advantage in the labor market. The passage of the 1917 Smith-Hughes Vocational Education Act, which provided federal subsidies for the salaries of teachers in vocational programs, was a vindication for its champions and is regarded by scholars as a high point for industrial education. However, federal funding represented only a small fraction of total funding toward industrial education, and at the local level, political conflicts had already helped undermine these initiatives. Industrial education programs across the country faced ongoing obstacles, such as the cost of equipment, the difficulty of securing qualified teachers, and low enrollments. The distribution of public vocational funds and cooperative part-time instruction repeatedly provoked the ire of trade unions.[165]

The marginalization of industrial education occurred despite the efforts of advocates such as Frank Thompson, who had posited, in principle, that all school programs were equally valuable. Thompson worked with the philanthropic Vocation Bureau of Boston, founded in 1908, to place "vocational counselors" in every school by 1910, and he oversaw the creation of a new department of vocational guidance in 1915 that helped students to choose between programs with nominally equal standing and worth.[166] However, already in 1910, young boys in Boston's Quincy School were selected for an industrial class in iron work because, among other reasons, "their conduct and interest in school was unsatisfactory."[167] In 1922, the assistant superintendent in charge of Boston's manual and domestic arts programs, John C. Brodhead, lamented that "there is a tendency on the part of some teachers and principals to place [manual arts] on a lower level than the purely academic subjects."[168]

As with training for household workers, educational reformers could not raise the status of industrial education, or the jobs it supposedly led to, by willing it so. The fate of industrial education was tied up with the transformation of the industrial workplace. With employers' growing reliance on machine operators as opposed to craftworkers, they did not use industrial education in schools to fulfill their training needs, and often preferred students with academic training. The divide between students in industrial courses and their academically successful peers in general or college-preparatory courses reproduced racial and class-based hierarchies. This gave employers even further reason to turn away from industrial students, as employers associated industrial students with behavioral problems. As one employers' association journal warned, the "problem child . . . can be no more successful in these industrial occupations than he is in school."[169] Public industrial education never became the channel into employment that its advocates had hoped.

As the changing industrial landscape rendered industrial occupations less and less attractive, young people sought academic education. To be sure, industrial education in Boston's public schools did not disappear. By 1920 most Boston high schools offered part-time industrial cooperative courses, and many who completed these courses entered specific trades with local employers.[170] The Boston Trade School, which had from the start included both academic and shop training, maintained enrollment equivalent to a neighborhood high school through the 1940s, as did the Trade School for Girls. However, throughout this period, less than an estimated 22 percent of men and 12 percent of women high school students pursued industrial or domestic arts courses of study.[171] In the wake of the Great Depression, limited prospects for employment led many youth to stay in school longer. Overwhelmingly, young men and women chose academic and commercial education.

CONCLUSION

The 1930s marked a shift in organized labor and the politics of training in Boston. With the exception of the building trades, weakened craft unions and the reorganization of production reduced the number of high-paying craftworker positions but opened up employment opportunities to new groups of workers. In the metal trades, throughout the 1940s, the percentage of English and Scandinavian machinists declined as more Irish workers entered this occupation. By the 1930s, due to economic necessity and choice, women entered the metal industry as electrical and machine operatives.[172]

While craft unions also expanded in the mid-twentieth century, new industrial unions organized entire industries across skill level, race, and gender and became the most successful strategy for workers to gain influence and power at work. After the 1920s open-shop drive reduced membership substantially, in 1935 the leadership of several industrial unions, including the ILGWU and the Amalgamated, organized the Congress of Industrial Organizations (CIO), leading to a new wave of successful union organizing.[173] The percentage of Boston employees in unions rose from just over 20 percent in 1930 to nearly 60 percent by 1950, as depicted in Figure 3.2. In Massachusetts, women made up 6 percent of union members in 1908, but this proportion grew to nearly 30 percent by 1951.[174]

These organizing efforts were led and won by a new industrial workforce very different from the craftworkers of 1880. By 1940, a new pattern of industrial training had been forged. Across the United States, the failure of coordination between employers, organized labor, and the state to implement training programs limited the appeal of custom and small-batch production industries. Instead, employers reorganized their production processes to minimize the need for craftworkers.

Industrial education promoters such as William Douglas, Robert Woods, and Frank Thompson had pointed to the technical and industrial training schools of Europe, and Germany in particular, as models for the United States to copy. However, these promoters failed to adequately consider the different political economies of these countries that affected the prospects for industrial education. Other scholars have documented the historical development of the German model, in which "handwerker" artisans had tight legal control of the training necessary to enter employment in different shops.[175] In the twentieth century, German employers and social democratic unions forged an alliance to replace the handwerker monopoly with standardized, industry-wide training through a new state-regulated system. Compared to countries

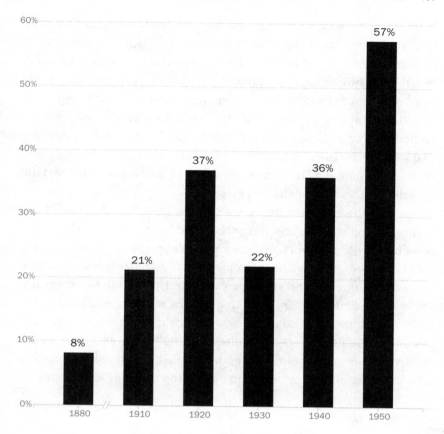

FIGURE 3.2: Percentage of the Boston workforce in unions, 1880–1950.

DATA SOURCES: "Workingmen in Politics," *BG*, August 3, 1881, 3; "Annual Report on Labor Organizations," in *BSL 1911* (Boston: Wright & Potter, 1910), 105; "Statistics of Labor Organizations," in *BSL 1921* (Boston: Wright & Potter, 1921), 18; "Annual Directory of Labor Organizations," in *BSL 1936, LB*, no. 174, 91; "Annual Directory of Labor Organizations," in *BSL 1940, LB*, no. 182, 99; U.S. Census Office, "Table 36," in *Tenth Census of the United States 1880*, vol. 1, *Statistics of the Population* (Washington, DC: GPO, 1883), 864; U.S. Bureau of the Census, "Table 3," in *Thirteenth Census Reports 1910*, vol. 4, *Population: Occupation Statistics* (Washington, DC: GPO, 1914), 152; U.S. Bureau of the Census, "Table 16," in *Fourteenth Census of the United States 1920*, vol. 4, *Population, Occupations* (Washington, DC: GPO, 1923), 128; U.S. Bureau of the Census, "Table 20," in *Fifteenth Census of the United States 1930, Population*, vol. 3, *Reports by States*, part 1, *Alabama–Missouri* (Washington, DC: GPO, 1932), 1103; U.S. Bureau of the Census, "Table A-41," in *Sixteenth Census of the United States 1940, Population*, vol. 2, *Characteristics of the Population*, part 3 (Washington, DC: GPO, 1943), 674; U.S. Bureau of the Census, "Table 79," in *Seventeenth Decennial Census of the United States, Census of Population: 1950*, vol. 2, *Characteristics of the Population*, part 21 (Washington, DC: GPO, 1952), 251. © Cristina Groeger.

NOTE: For more details, see note 174.

like Germany, the US training landscape for the trades was decentralized and unregulated. This fostered worker efforts to maintain power through control of narrow, craft-specific skills, fueling fierce conflict between craft unions and employers. An alliance between unions and employers never emerged, foreclosing the possibility of a state-regulated industrial training regime. The most salient difference between the United States and Germany lay in the political and economic interests that shaped who stood to gain and lose from control of the training process. Simply copying German-style schools in an American context did not address these larger challenges.

The early twentieth-century shift in the United States away from highly trained craftworkers was encouraged by the repeated challenges of industrial training, but it was made possible by a range of other factors. One key factor was the ability of employers to find other types of workers, trained in a different and less expensive way. In addition to factory operatives with a rudimentary schooling and engineers trained in technical institutes, employers also relied on a ready supply of school-educated clerical and sales workers. To understand the role of education in the reconstruction of the political economy in this period, we also need to turn to the parallel transformation of training for white-collar work.

FOUR

Becoming Pink Collar

In his 1906 inaugural address, Mayor John F. Fitzgerald called on Boston to "take its stand in the forefront of progress commercially, industrially, and intellectually." The place to begin, he claimed, was "in the schoolroom." As had industrial education advocates before him, he drew on the example of European schools for inspiration. But rather than focus on industrial education, Fitzgerald highlighted the need for schools of business and commerce that would train youth "to become eminently useful in the business world." To the new mayor, education for business was a public priority, and he "earnestly urged" the "immediate establishment of a [public] Commercial High School" within Boston's school system.[1]

Unlike training for the trades, by this date, cities such as Boston had already witnessed an unprecedented proliferation of schools offering business instruction. This instruction, however, was predominantly offered by market-oriented proprietary "commercial" or "business" schools. After paying a small fee to enroll for a few months or a year in courses on penmanship, bookkeeping, accounting, shorthand, or salesmanship, students obtained jobs as clerks, bookkeepers, accountants, stenographers, secretaries, and sales personnel in Boston's offices, retail shops, and department stores. Proprietary commercial schools offered relatively inexpensive training to students who lacked social ties to established practitioners, especially women and second-generation immigrants. Elected officials such as Fitzgerald, however, along with public school administrators and university presidents, observed the growth of this unregulated sector uneasily. Fitzgerald used the opportunity of his inaugural address to criticize the proliferation of proprietary schools, observing that "Boston is filled with private so-called business colleges, which are supported mainly by Boston students of school age, who have to pay for this special instruction."[2] Reformers hoped the expansion of public high schools would undercut the market for proprietary, fee-charging schools. In a 1918 report on commercial education in New York City, education researcher Bertha Stevens observed that "nothing adequate will ever be accomplished until the public school offers a course of training which sets up an effective rivalry to that now offered by private commercial schools."[3] Many Boston reformers would have agreed.

Fitzgerald and Stevens' vision of public instruction for business jobs soon came to fruition across urban America. Unlike industrial education, which was marked by conflicts between organized interests, school-based instruction for white-collar employment was extremely popular across the political spectrum. The competitive race between rival schools in the private and public sector drove the rapid spread of institutions offering training and credentials relevant to this work.[4] By the turn of the century, widespread support for free public alternatives led to a surge in public high schools of a magnitude unique to the United States.[5] In Boston, the 8 percent of 14–17-year-olds who attended public high schools in 1880 grew to over 50 percent by 1940.[6] Public high schools nationwide eclipsed proprietary schools as the dominant sites of training for white-collar work, and this form of education became an expected public service. This expansion was dramatic on the East Coast; it was even more pronounced in western states, which channeled the highest percentage of their workforce into office and sales work.[7]

This business training revolution was a quiet one that has left only a faint mark in historical scholarship.[8] The lack of controversy it generated at the time, and the fact that the chief constituents of commercial instruction were women, perhaps have made it easy to overlook. Arguably, however, this revolution made possible the corporate restructuring of the economy, the growth of the nascent American welfare state, and the rise of a new middle class. If "vocational" is defined as schooling that prepares students for specific types of work, then we can say that public high schools were immensely successful vocational schools for white-collar jobs. The vast expansion of training for this sector quietly allowed employers to reconfigure industrial hierarchies, gave Americans new expectations of the role of government, and helped to consolidate an ideology of social mobility through education. This training revolution can also help explain the origins of some forms of gender equity in liberal market economies like the United States, which recent studies have connected to the prevalence of school-based training as opposed to on-the-job training regimes.[9]

The women and second-generation immigrants who used formal education to enter white-collar jobs at the turn of the twentieth century were at the heart of this transformation. Boston male clerical workers outnumbered women clerical workers 8 to 1 in 1880; by 1920, women outnumbered men.[10] Still-classic scholarly portrayals of white-collar work such as C. Wright Mills's *White Collar* neglect the role of women and downplay the sense of achievement of many who were able to access this work.[11] For these students, formal education opened up opportunities for social advancement. For example, Dorothy Pierce, a graduate of Boston's Girls' High School in 1915, worked for an insurance company immediately after graduation. She "thoroughly enjoyed" her work compiling vital statistics. Reflecting on her formal education, she noted that the "Girls' High School . . . instilled in me a thirst for knowledge."[12] Esther Zarkin, a Russian Jewish immigrant and daughter of a dressmaker, took all the bookkeeping courses offered at Dorchester High School and, in 1926, answered a newspaper ad to become a bookkeeper at a Boston raincoat manufacturing company.[13] While the "vocationalization" of the high school curriculum in this time period has been characterized as a top-down reform by administrative progressives seeking social efficiency, we can only explain the incredible surge in enrollment in business-related courses by taking into account the bottom-up pressure for these vocational opportunities among students themselves.[14]

As firms hired employees with more formal education, a positive feedback loop strengthened the importance of schools as a pathway into this sector. This educational advantage was not only based on the acquisition of technical skills and knowledge, but also on exposure to preferred cultural, gendered, and class-based behavioral norms, as well as social contacts in the form of administrators, teachers, and classmates. Accounts of the positive experience of social advancement may, however, obscure some of the less publicized features of the shift from work-based to school-based training in this sector. Schooling for office and sales work ultimately helped to enhance managerial control. Employers' eagerness to hire office and sales workers correlated with their efforts to reduce the influence of craft unions. The abundance of a pool of educated workers was an important precondition for the shift from small-scale firms reliant on craftworkers to large bureaucratized companies with hundreds or even thousands of white-collar staff.

Formal education opened up opportunities for some, but not all. Employers continued to discriminate based on racial, ethnic, and gender-based prejudices. Despite its role in shrinking the wage gap between men and women, this new feminized pink-collar sector was also characterized by high levels of wage discrimination (wage differences that cannot be explained through education or training level), especially for highly educated women.[15] The growth of this sector also changed the status of white-collar work itself. The competitive race between schools shaped a steep hierarchy of educational institutions that matched emerging rungs on the white-collar ladder. As corporate bureaucracies grew larger, the typical white-collar job shifted from that of a merchant's apprentice with, if not guaranteed, at least a good chance of becoming a successful proprietor, to a young female stenographer permanently subordinate to her male superiors. The relative economic advantage of entering a clerical or sales job as opposed to a manufacturing job declined for both men and women in this period. As a form of building power in the workplace, unions were weak in a sector shaped by a culture of managerial aspirations.[16]

Both practitioners and reformers pursued "professionalizing projects" for white-collar jobs. New professional associations of clerks, accountants, stenographers, and retail workers sought to emulate the success of other leading professions through setting standards for membership, hosting conferences and social gatherings, and lobbying for state regulations. As in other sectors, educational reformers hoped that special-

ized instruction could help "elevate" the status of clerical and sales occupations. Like craft unions, this professional strategy was premised on
the ability to restrict entry into coveted occupations, but with rapidly
expanding training opportunities, restriction was almost impossible.[17]
Professional projects were most successful at the very top of the corporate hierarchy, where elite educational credentials could be used to control entry. By the 1930s, college-educated men dominated a small managerial class and supervised a vast number of high school–educated
women employed in contingent clerical and retail jobs.

This chapter first surveys broad changes in white-collar workplaces,
including early efforts to organize unions and professional associations.
It then turns to training: first in the form of proprietary schools, followed
by the mass expansion of public evening and daytime high schools. I show
how public high schools and degree-granting colleges and universities
became the dominant institutional types, pressuring proprietary
schools to conform or close. Next, I analyze the specific ways in which
school-based training for white-collar work benefited students in the
labor market. I conclude with a discussion of this sector's shift from
white-collar to pink-collar jobs, and new but limited organizing efforts
among these employees to build their collective power.

THE WHITE-COLLAR WORKPLACE

In 1880s Boston, the sector that would later be called "white collar" was
made up of male clerks and bookkeepers of predominantly New England
parentage who learned in the stores or counting rooms of merchants
and manufacturers. Small shops, between five and fifty employees, were
typically family enterprises in which owners made all the financial and
personnel decisions. In the next decades, especially in cities in the northeastern and midwestern United States, large manufacturing and tele-
communications corporations, chain and department stores, financial
service companies in banking and insurance, and state bureaucracies
expanded spectacularly. Boston had among the highest per capita retail
sales in the country in 1920s, and its many department stores selling
clothing, jewelry, and novelty items were concentrated in its central

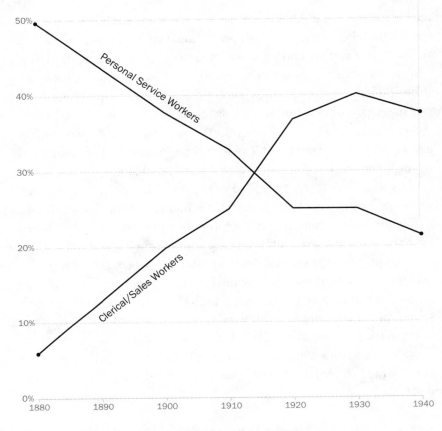

FIGURE 4.1: Largest sectors of the women's workforce, Boston, 1880–1940.

DATA SOURCE: IPUMS 1880–1940, 1890 estimated. © Cristina Groeger.

business district downtown. Boston's large insurance companies, such as John Hancock and New England Mutual, as well as medical and financial service companies erected tall office buildings in the Back Bay.[18] Clerical and sales jobs were the fastest-growing sector of pre–World War II employment in the United States, expanding from about half a million workers to nearly 6.5 million nationally.[19] These jobs transformed the occupational structure, especially for women. In Boston, office and sales jobs grew from 6 percent of women wage earners in 1880 to a peak of 40 percent of women wage earners in 1930, and grew from 15 to 20 percent of men wage earners, as depicted respectively in Figures 4.1 and 4.2.[20]

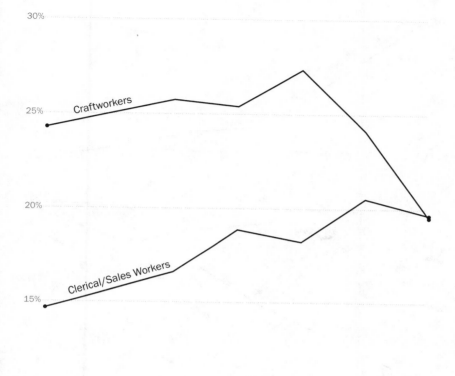

FIGURE 4.2: Largest sectors of the men's workforce, Boston, 1880–1940.
DATA SOURCE: IPUMS 1880–1940, 1890 estimated. © Cristina Groeger.

The already stratified office became further differentiated in these years. A "typewriter" was someone who transcribed documents before it became the name of a machine, and the new occupation of typist exploded with this technological innovation.[21] Stenographers, whose occupation was first included in the published census in 1890, took dictation using shorthand and managed correspondence. Secretaries, who often occupied the highest position obtainable by women in business settings, provided a wide and often undefined range of individual services for their employers. As one secretary for an auto insurance company explained in 1925, "I wait on my two bosses hand and foot and do everything I possibly can to relieve them of details. I try to be a mind-reader."[22]

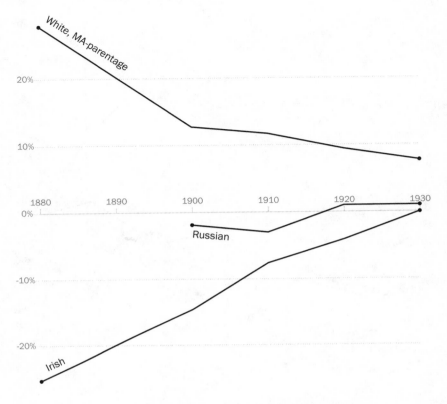

FIGURE 4.3: Overrepresentation by ethnicity of women clerical workers, Boston, 1880–1930.

DATA SOURCE: IPUMS 1880–1930, 1890 estimated. © Cristina Groeger.

NOTE: "Overrepresentation" compares representation in a specific occupation to representation in the work-force. Boston's Russian population was very small prior to 1900, so the representation data begins at this date.

The demographic composition of office work also changed over time. Although men and women from New England made up the largest share of clerical workers through the 1930s, those of Irish heritage made up about one-third of the male and one-quarter of the female clerical work-force by 1900. By 1930, Russian Jewish women like Esther Zarkin made up 8 percent of women clerical workers, surpassing their 7 percent repre-sentation in the women's workforce as a whole. Figures 4.3 and 4.4 show the declining representation of those with Massachusetts parentage and the rising representation of first- and second-generation immigrants in Boston's men and women's clerical workforce.

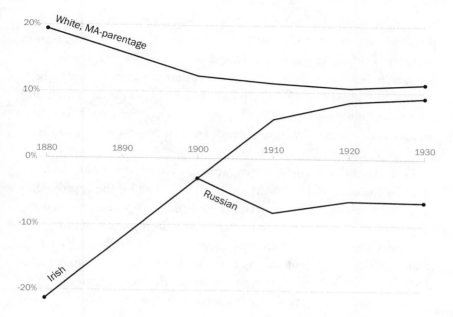

FIGURE 4.4: Overrepresentation by ethnicity of men clerical workers, Boston, 1880–1930.
DATA SOURCE: IPUMS 1880–1930, 1890 estimated. © Cristina Groeger.

Sales work was a lower-status field than clerical work, and census reports distinguished between "clerks in stores" and their more prestigious counterparts in offices.[23] Before the cash register became ubiqui-
tous after World War I, "cash" and "bundle" girls and boys carried
money and goods to a centralized office, "bundled" them, and then carried change and wrapped packages back to customers. Inspectors, examiners, checkers, and cashiers handled money and corrected errors,
and floor managers supervised saleswomen and salesmen.[24] These occupations were the outgrowth of the industrial transformation of the
needle trades into the ready-made garment industry. In the late nineteenth century, the German Jewish immigrants who owned department stores, including Boston's Filene's Sons Company, employed vast
numbers of sales personnel and facilitated the entry of Russian Jewish
men and women into this sector. By 1930, Russian employees were significantly overrepresented in sales work, at about 20 percent each of the
male and female sales workforces.[25]

A range of new white-collar positions emerged in new communications industries such as telegraph and telephone exchanges. Most Boston operators worked for the New England Telephone and Telegraph Company, a "Bell System" subsidiary of the American Telephone and Telegraph Company (AT&T).[26] Telephone operating was faster paced and even more highly regulated than typing.[27] This new field was almost immediately dominated by Irish women, who made up a majority of Boston's telephone operators by 1900.[28]

As white-collar occupations expanded, they became feminized. Already by the turn of the century, cultural tropes about the appropriateness of women in office jobs—comparing piano keys and typewriting, for instance—were normalized.[29] Nationally, in 1870, women made up less than 5 percent of all bookkeepers and stenographers; by 1930, women made up over 50 percent and 95 percent of these occupations, respectively.[30] Boston mirrored national trends. The rising proportion of women stenographers, typists, bookkeepers, and sales workers is shown in Figure 4.5.

For many working-class families, a son or daughter entering clerical or sales employment marked a significant step into the middle class. As craft traditions were eroded, the families of craftworkers sent their children into clerical work as a form of what historian Ileen DeVault calls "conspicuous employment." Because work in an office or store, compared to many other jobs, was cleaner and less physically taxing, required proper dress, and necessitated skills acquired through formal education, having a daughter working as a stenographer or son as a bookkeeper was a sign of respectability. At a time when the opportunity cost of each additional year of schooling for working-class families was high, the extension of training was an important indicator of status. Conspicuous employment also enabled ethnic distinction, as native-born populations sought to differentiate themselves from Irish or eastern and southern European immigrants.[31] In 1880 Boston, women clerical workers were disproportionately of Massachusetts parentage compared to their male counterparts (as shown in Figures 4.3 and 4.4), reflecting the role of ethnic distinction in clerical work for women in particular. While Irish employees were overrepresented among male clerical workers by 1910, they remained underrepresented among women clerical workers until

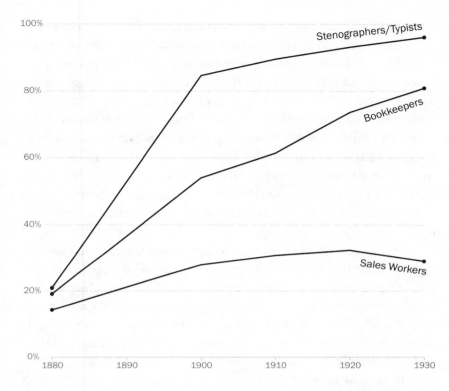

FIGURE 4.5: The feminization of white-collar work: women as a percentage of white-collar workers in Boston, 1880–1930.

DATA SOURCE: IPUMS 1880–1930, 1890 estimated. © Cristina Groeger.

1930. The higher status of clerical workers compared to retail workers, disproportionately Russian Jewish, also reflected an ethnic hierarchy.

White-collar jobs held out the promise of social mobility for both men and women, in distinct ways. For men, as industrial change made the trades less appealing, white-collar work offered more stable employment and healthier working conditions. Although most men who began entry-level clerical work would stay in the lower-middle ranks of management, ascending to an executive position was an attractive possibility.[32] For women, white-collar work similarly offered job stability, a healthier work environment, and shorter hours than domestic service and factory work.[33] As secretaries or saleswomen, women could earn higher wages than teachers, the other comparable high-status occupation open to them. Importantly, most women expected to work temporarily before getting married and leaving the paid workforce.[34] Although employers tended to enforce a strict code of behavior to maintain the "respectability" of mixed-gender spaces, offices and stores were some of the few workplaces in which women might, as one secretary put it, "[come] into contact with well educated, broad-minded men."[35] Such interactions increased women's chances of gaining upward mobility through marriage.[36] In a study of Pittsburgh office workers, over half of women who worked for a time in clerical or sales jobs married workers like themselves.[37] In Boston, Esther Zarkin was introduced to her boss's brother-in-law at her bookkeeping job, and the two were married several years later.[38]

These jobs also offered newfound independence, especially for women. Compared to living in their employers' homes as domestic workers, young office and sales workers enjoyed the "freedom when work is over."[39] Among workers who were not domestic servants, about one-quarter each of working men and women in 1900 lived independently as boarders or lodgers.[40] The neighborhoods of Boston's South and West Ends contained a high concentration of boarding and lodging houses, close to jobs downtown.[41] Clerical and sales workers, who tended to have more disposable income than their counterparts in factory or service work, took advantage of a growing number of eateries, cafés, and theaters in the neighborhood. Office and sales workers were also overwhelmingly young: the majority of male white-collar workers in the early twentieth century were below the age of 30, and women were mostly under 25. These workers participated in a shared youth culture of the streets, parks, and restaurants of the city.[42]

Due to these many attractions, youth interest in white-collar occupations surged. Studies of vocational aspirations in the 1920s suggested that 40 to 50 percent of girls in public junior high and high schools aspired to clerical or sales work.[43] Of male high school graduates in Boston in 1920, 46 percent aspired to positions in business, surpassing the 40 percent with aspirations to enter the professions.[44] Based on a national survey of secretaries in 1925, the majority of respondents enjoyed their jobs, citing their relative freedom and the frequent opportunities for contact with interesting people. One stenographer expressed a sense of satisfaction due to the "realization that your initiative may bring success to your firm" and the "unspoken respect from your fellow employees."[45] A department store saleswoman described her personal fulfillment in her work with customers as follows: "I was the person who connected them with their dreams, their special saleslady."[46]

Despite the many benefits of white-collar employment, the average job in this field yielded fewer benefits as the sector expanded and became feminized. By 1910, new colloquialisms, such as the "six-dollar girl" appeared in magazines as a derogatory term for the low-paid stenographer. Many upper-class observers suspected that poorly paid women, especially "shop girls" tempted by luxurious consumer goods, would resort to prostitution. These concerns peaked in the 1910s during a wave of anti-vice activism and the "white slavery" scare over women purportedly abducted or enticed into sexual labor. While paternalistic concerns can be understood as a response to the changing economic position of women as well as changing norms of sexuality, they also reflected the reality of women workers' meager wages.[47] In 1934, one researcher observed that many "office jobs are routine in nature, afford little training and few leads for advancement, and belong to the blind-alley class."[48]

As white-collar work feminized and became pink-collar work, its gendered power imbalance became more apparent. Employers often preferred hiring young women immediately upon leaving school, as these women accepted lower wages than experienced older women and were invariably paid less than their male counterparts. Male office workers policed the boundaries of their own clerical and managerial positions as distinct from the feminized occupational titles of secretary and stenographer. Young women clerks could be harassed and abused by their male superiors but would often not complain for fear of losing their jobs.[49] Most companies fiercely resisted any union organizing efforts, especially among women and part-time employees, whose value lay precisely in their low cost and the contingent nature of their employment.[50] As clerical and sales jobs grew from one-eighth to one-quarter of the total Boston workforce, the economy shifted toward jobs with little organized worker power.

A few white-collar workers organized unions. The Retail Clerks International Protective Association (RCIPA), founded in 1890, offered benefits for sickness, death, and unemployment. It advocated for early closing times, a ten-hour workday, Sundays off, a minimum wage, compensation for overtime, paid vacations, and equal pay for men and women. At the height of its national power in 1903, the RCIPA had organized 10 percent of retail clerks.[51] Some white-collar worker unions even sought to control entry into their jobs by limiting schools. In Chicago, for example, the National Union of Stenographers decried the so-called scab schools that were "turning out swarms of rats" and depressing salaries.[52]

Overall, union organizing in this sector remained limited for several reasons. The RCIPA drew much of its strength from predominantly male drug clerks and grocery clerks, many of whom sought to prevent the feminization of their sector.[53] The cultural norms of professionalism inhibited organizing strategies that were associated with lower-prestige craftworkers.[54] Even as these workers pursued their own forms of mutual organization, many embraced a laissez-faire faith in the market. According to one Connecticut stenographer in 1886, "The really competent man will always receive good pay," and unions only impeded "the natural order of things."[55] Even those who did not share this faith faced many impediments to organizing. As in the industrial workplace, gender and ethnic divisions were intensified by fine-grained workplace hierarchies. In addition, with little job security, those on the lower rungs of white-collar work could be easily replaced and were reluctant to risk their positions.

Professional associations for white-collar workers, which proliferated after the 1880s, provided another means of attaining some workplace control as well as prestige. Unlike craft unions that battled employers, professional associations were traditionally groups of independent practitioners who sought to self-regulate their occupations through limiting membership and lobbying for state regulations and licensing laws, as well as promoting education and training standards. White-collar employees, even though very few were independent practitioners, aspired to this professional status. Some white-collar occupations in key positions of the corporate economy, like public accountants, successfully pursued regulation through state-level examinations.[56] Similarly, state employees such as court reporters raised standards through civil service reform.[57] However, the fastest-growing occupations in the private sector—secretaries, stenographers, clerks, and retail workers—had little success in regulating entry into their occupation. Instead, professional associations primarily provided social and cultural benefits to their members. For example, the Boston Shorthand Club, organized in 1891 for both men and women who could pass a speed test of ninety words per minute, sponsored an employment bureau as well as lavish balls, artistic performances, banquets, and even a literary and dramatic club.[58] These organizations offered women spaces in which to assert their identities as competent professionals while also maintaining feminine refinement and respectability. But associations also marked distinctions within occupations, especially along gender lines. Even though both required a speed test of 150 words per minute, the regional New England Shorthand Reporters' Association was made up of 40 percent women in 1900, while the more exclusive National Shorthand Reporters' Association had only 9 percent women in 1904.[59]

Although professional associations of clerical and sales workers could dictate terms of entry into their own associations, they were not sufficiently powerful to regulate entrance into the white-collar workforce. Widespread demand for white-collar jobs led to a surge of competing training schools that multiplied across the northern United States at the turn of the twentieth century.

NINETEENTH-CENTURY BUSINESS TRAINING

Already in the 1880s, the rise of larger and less personalized firms began to make the process of learning business practices on the job less viable. Aspiring practitioners and employers alike looked to alternatives. Unlike industrial education, commercial instruction had a low start-up cost, and classrooms could be easily adapted for teaching business subjects. Moreover, as opposed to the craft skills that might vary from firm to firm in the industrial sector, the skills of shorthand or bookkeeping were transferable across companies, increasing the field of potential employment as well as instructors. A wide range of programs quickly emerged to meet demand.

Philanthropic and religious institutions offered some courses as part of their expanding commitment to vocational instruction. The Boston YMCA organized classes for young men in penmanship and bookkeeping in the early 1870s, later adding banking, commercial arithmetic, shorthand, telegraphy, and typewriting based on popularity.[60] Some settlement houses offered courses in arithmetic and other grammar school subjects.[61] Catholic high schools such as Boston College High School offered a commercial course including typewriting, stenography, and bookkeeping in 1889. The parochial school system, however, still primarily catered to elementary school students and was fairly marginal in the provision of commercial education.[62]

The bulk of provision of business instruction was provided by proprietary schools—occasionally calling themselves "colleges," although none could grant degrees—as educational entrepreneurs moved in to take advantage of a profitable market. While a few proprietary commercial schools dotted the educational landscape of New England before the Civil War, a wave of new schools opened across the country in the late nineteenth century. By 1890, Boston's daytime commercial schools enrolled 1,600 students, at a time when total public high school enrollment was about 2,700.[63] Some of these schools in New England had been established as women's seminaries, private academies, or denominational colleges that chose to add commercial subjects to their curriculum to boost enrollment.[64]

One of Boston's earliest commercial schools was Comer's Commercial College, founded in 1840 by an accountant, George Nixon Comer. Frustrated with the inefficient practice of keeping "journals," Comer wrote *Bookkeeping Rationalized,* which became the textbook used in his school.[65] Comer initially faced skepticism from a business world not used to commercial instruction. "Many are still unwilling to believe that Book-Keeping can be taught," he wrote.[66] His school offered individualized instruction in penmanship, correspondence, bookkeeping, arithmetic, English, navigation, and advanced mathematics. In 1848, the school opened a "Ladies Department" that prepared women for work as "Book-keepers, Cashiers, Saleswomen, &c., in wholesale and retail stores, Banks, Insurance Offices, Registries of Deeds, Post Offices."[67] Students could choose to enroll in a flexible combination of day or evening classes for as little as a week or as long as six months. The school regularly updated its offerings, adding courses in banking, shorthand, and business economics by the 1890s.[68]

Comer's had no educational prerequisites and accepted many students directly from grammar school. Yet to its founder, this was a professional school for business, "affording to [students] the same advantages of learning business that persons who are preparing a profession have at medical, divinity, or law schools." In 1890, Comer's enrolled about 500 students per year, one-third of whom were women. The school charged $140 for a full year of instruction, comparable to the tuition of local degree-granting colleges, but only $40 for a ten-week course that would have been accessible to the children of Boston's shopkeepers and craftworkers.[69]

At least forty new private commercial and business schools were founded in Boston between 1890 and 1920. In addition to large establishments like Comer's, dozens of smaller schools sprung up, many consisting of no more than a single bookkeeper or stenographer who tutored young acolytes for a price.[70] Boston newspapers regularly advertised these schools: "Bookkeeping taught; accountants' private school will receive pupils day or evening," or "Shorthand, Typewriting, Day or Eve, private teacher, $1 a week; speed, dictation. Miss Herman."[71] While bookkeeping and penmanship were the primary focus of early commercial schools, the transformation of office technology by the turn of the century quickly made shorthand and typing the most popular subjects.

At a time when public high schools and private colleges in Boston tended to cater to men entering the learned professions, these commercial schools took advantage of an educational market among working-class immigrant communities and women. In 1897, two brothers, Myron C. Fisher and Edmund H. Fisher, moved from the Midwest to teach business classes at the Burdett College of Business and Shorthand in Boston. Noticing a demand among inhabitants of their own immigrant neighborhood in Somerville, they opened the Winter Hill Business College in 1903, offering individualized courses to students. At this school and elsewhere, women made up the majority of students by the early twentieth century. Comer's became majority female by 1906.[72]

To attract students, proprietary schools competed with each other, relying on extensive advertising to market their own educational offerings. By 1900, about 5 percent of the ads of one of the largest national advertising companies were taken out by proprietary schools.[73] These schools' chief selling strategy was to tout the employment opportunities that would be opened to their students upon the completion of their studies. In 1882, Bryant & Stratton Commercial School, which by this date was an extensive chain with fifty locations in cities nationwide and a large building in downtown Boston, advertised the "frequent application of merchants and others for students of this school to fill positions in their counting rooms and offices."[74] A 1912 bulletin featuring testimonials from Burdett announced that "Burdett College Guarantees a Satisfactory Situation to Every Graduate."[75]

In addition to advertising, one of the novel innovations of commercial schools was the internal employment bureau. These bureaus offered assistance to students by actively forging relationships to local employers, strengthened over time through alumni networks. In 1900, Bryant & Stratton publicized the fact that its "Employment Department" had received "nearly twelve hundred direct applications for graduates to take positions in business."[76] By 1923, the employment bureau of Burdett College was sending bulletins to local employers with graduates' photos, interests, and personal characteristics, under a headline reading, "If any man here interests you, get in touch with Burdett College at once, because the number becomes fewer each week."[77] According to one study of office workers in 1914, these bureaus were perhaps the primary reason students enrolled, since graduation purportedly guaranteed lifetime access to employment assistance.[78]

In their promotional materials, commercial schools aggressively promoted a human capital understanding of education: instruction in their school would directly lead to higher wages. Despite the fact that these schools touted their employment bureaus offering assistance, recommendations, and even guarantees of employment, they attributed any advantage in the labor market to a student's superior training. "The better education one has the higher up in the ranks he can go," noted the 1900 catalogue of Miss Pierce's Shorthand School. As the author, presumably Miss Pierce, explained, "Some are deterred from taking up the study [of shorthand] by the cry that the market is flooded. It is flooded, but with incompetents. A skilled workman in any line of business is always in demand."[79] Many also promoted an individualist notion of market success that placed failure squarely on the shoulders of the employee: "Too many young men are simply plodders; working day by day with little or no ambition. . . . Promotion is the result of exceptional work, and that exceptional work is the direct result of training."[80] These schools marketed themselves as the key to achieving economic reward. The 1893 Burdett College catalogue was titled, in gold letters, "How to Achieve Success."[81] Bryant & Stratton issued a 1926 pamphlet titled *How to Make More Money $,* and in 1930 advertised its school as "Your Next Step toward Securing a Position, Gaining a Competence, and Amassing a Fortune."[82]

As evidence from alumni testimonials suggests, many students used commercial schools to obtain desirable jobs. Around the turn of the century, Jennie M. Ogston, who worked as a stenographer in the State-Street Exchange Building in Boston, expressed gratitude for the help of Miss Pierce's Shorthand School in securing her new job. She wrote that "[Miss Pierce] obtained the position I now have so that I did not have to wait even a day for one, and I feel that without her aid I should not have been able to find such a position."[83] Arthur F. Adams, a student who completed a four-month course at Burdett College, thanked the school for obtaining his present position "in the National Bank of Redemption of Boston, which I like very much."[84] One secretary commented in 1925 that "the backing of a business college in obtaining satisfactory positions is helpful if not absolutely necessary nowadays."[85]

Others, however, reported less positive experiences and results. Bertha Stevens's study of New York private commercial schools revealed a significant degree of dissatisfaction among students, likely shared by many in Boston. One student, Lena S., claimed of her commercial school, "They skin you something fierce; they make girls stay on week after week by telling them that they did not pass the examinations." Frances L. described how her school "makes too much profit on stationery and supplies; and that if one does not 'watch out' there are likely to be mistakes in the monthly bills to the student's disadvantage." In a transcribed interview, one student's mother was reported to have exclaimed, "All dat money, all dat money, and no help from de school! What dey do for you? Nothing."[86] These complaints suggest an unregulated field of for-profit schools rife with opportunities for exploitation.

REGULATING PROPRIETARY SCHOOLS

In an 1899 address at the National Export Exposition, Charles Eliot accused commercial schools of low standards and challenged their claim to professional status when they "seldom train anybody for service above that of a clerk."[87] Eliot likely agreed with the editors of the *Boston Herald,* who criticized the "multitude of humbugs . . . seeking nothing but immediate financial returns" that "outrageously abused the name 'college' to which none of them had any right."[88] This disdain was also likely informed by gender and ethnic prejudice, as proprietary schools served a higher proportion of women, Irish, and Jewish students than did private colleges and universities. Their use of the term "college" also threatened the educational niche of traditional degree-granting institutions. Established institutions were undoubtedly the chief mobilizers behind the passage of a 1893 Massachusetts law to "Protect the Name and Credit of Certain Educational Institutions," which made it a punishable offense of up to one year in prison or a fine of up to $1,000 to falsely grant degrees without authorization from the state, or make "false and fraudulent" statements of behalf of an educational institution.[89] Not all commercial "colleges" were moneymaking rackets, and several had strong reputations locally. University officials and many public school allies, however, were determined to investigate, expose, and regulate their proprietary competitors.

A coalition of educational reformers, philanthropists, and business leaders came together in Boston in 1911 to address what they believed to be the growing problem of the "exploitation of boys and girls in 'private schools for profit' in our city and state." The meeting included Massachusetts commissioner of education David Snedden, assistant superintendent of schools Frank Thompson, and members of the Boston Chamber of Commerce. The authors of the subsequent report established three different categories of schools, depending on the use of particular egregious practices. One such practice was the use of solicitors, which might "prejudice parents against the public schools" or "cause pupils to drop out of [public] high school." The practice of guaranteeing employment was identified as a misleading form of advertising. The lack of educational prerequisites also indicated a lower grade of school: those schools that did not require at least a grammar school education were placed in the bottom category. Few made the first-grade cut; Comer's was placed into the third grade. The members of the Boston committee hoped that publicizing their rankings would make low-grade schools "feel the need of a high standard."[90]

This Boston investigation was one of many. In 1909, University of Chicago sociologist George Herbert Mead chaired an investigation of industrial and commercial schools in over ten cities. Bertha Stevens had undertaken extensive research on commercial training and work in Cleveland before her study of New York.[91] The criticisms of private commercials schools that filled these reports closely matched those of Boston's.

Legal means were also used to crack down on the abuses of proprietary schools. The School of Successful Salesmanship, Inc., founded in Boston in 1905 and attended by nearly 300 students who paid $80 in annual tuition, was accused in 1917 of having made "fraudulent representations" of the school leading students to believe that employment was guaranteed, violating the 1893 act. Forrest O. Copithorne, the president of the school, was found guilty of using mail to defraud students and sentenced to eight months in the House of Correction in Plymouth, Massachusetts.[92]

The most frequently propounded solution to limit exploitation, however, was to expand public alternatives. Bertha Stevens, George Mead, and the authors of the Boston investigation all championed this solution in their reports. Indeed, it was the growth of free, public alternatives that proved to be the most effective means of undercutting the market position of proprietary schools.

PUBLIC HIGH SCHOOLS, 1869–1940

Public education for white-collar employment was the most successful form of vocational education in the early twentieth century. Employers supported the free public provision of basic literacy and numeracy in addition to bookkeeping, stenography, and salesmanship courses, and families and students sought the advantages that this form of training could offer in the labor market. Philanthropists and educators believed that public commercial education would expand opportunities for youth, elevate the status of lower-end white-collar occupations, and limit the exploitation of proprietary schools. Politicians of both parties pointed to the state-funded technical and commercial schools of Europe to argue for the necessity of public training in not only industrial skills but those of commerce and salesmanship. By 1901, the *Boston Herald* editors called the expansion of public commercial education a "foregone conclusion, for its practical importance is self-evident."[93]

Some commercial subjects, including bookkeeping, had been offered in Boston's public schools since the early nineteenth century. Commercial offerings were greatly expanded in 1869 with the opening of Boston's Evening High School in the South End as a "commercial school."[94] Courses were revised regularly based on student interest, and students could take whatever courses they chose in an elective system. The most popular courses were those in English composition, bookkeeping, arithmetic, and penmanship, and, by 1907, shorthand and typewriting.[95] Many students saw a clear relationship between their training and employment. In 1886, a group of women told the headmaster of the Evening High School what had motivated them: "It is simply a matter of dollars and cents. We are worth more to our employers, and we come here for the money we can get out of it."[96]

Demand for evening commercial courses emerged from both working-class immigrant neighborhoods and wealthier suburban districts, and the school committee responded to this demand by creating new branch evening high schools. The North End Evening Commercial High School opened in 1911 in response to a petition presented to the school committee by 200 predominantly second-generation immigrant graduates of the Eliot Elementary School. The cost of carfare to attend the nearest evening high school in the South End was prohibitive to them, and they demanded a local option. The same year, parents and students in suburban Dorchester submitted "repeated petitions" for an evening high school in their neighborhood, which opened in 1911 to 1,026 students.[97] These schools served a range of constituencies, from older stenographers who took a "speed course" to keep up their practice, to younger women working in factories or domestic service who wished to find an entry-level office job. Some women who performed unpaid labor in their own homes during the day came to enjoy the companionship of other classmates. While students from different backgrounds enrolled, the vast majority of evening high school students across the city were working-class, second-generation immigrants who had just an elementary school education and were already employed in the lower ends of office and sales work. Of women evening high school students in 1915, two-thirds had fathers who were manual workers, 70 percent had foreign-born parents, especially Russian Jewish, and 20 percent were foreign-born themselves.[98]

While Boston's Central Evening High School included both academic and commercial courses, all neighborhood branches became "commercial high schools" after 1910. Through the mid-twentieth century, Boston's evening high schools were effectively commercial schools, as illustrated by the enrollment numbers depicted in Figures 4.6 and 4.7.[99] Even among those taking academic courses, the director in 1920 wrote, "most of them are taking academic subjects with a strictly vocational end in view."[100]

In addition to evening high schools, public daytime high schools experienced a spectacular boom across the northern United States in the early twentieth century. Complaints about the overcrowding of high schools became commonplace, and their popularity allowed the Boston School Committee to lobby successfully for greater tax appropriation power for the maintenance of the school system. Adjusting for inflation, the annual taxes appropriated by the school committee more than tripled between 1897 and 1929.[101] In addition to expanding state capacity, schools also made up an increasing proportion of city budgets. In 1880, school expenditures made up 12 percent of Boston's total city budget; in 1926, it reached 24 percent. By comparison, expenditures on police remained about 6.5 percent.[102] Public high schools made up a significant proportion of this expenditure.

School officials attributed the growth of daytime high school enrollment to the variety of nonacademic courses offered, the majority of which were commercial subjects.[103] Frank Thompson's work in establishing commercial training programs rivaled in importance his work on

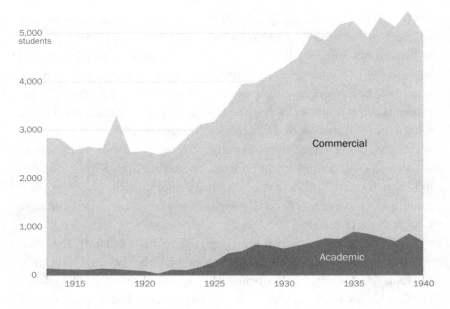

FIGURE 4.6: Women's evening public high school enrollment by course type, Boston, 1913–1940.

DATA SOURCE: *AS 1913–1940* (Boston: Printing Department, 1913–1940). © Cristina Groeger.

NOTE: Based on reported registration data.

education for immigrants and industrial education. In his 1915 book *Commercial Education in Public Secondary Schools,* Thompson reflected that "commercial education was perhaps the first subject to be generally adopted by the high school as a concession to the public desire that the school should furnish preparation for vocations."[104] A two-year commercial course of study was first introduced into six day high schools in 1897, including shorthand, typewriting, penmanship, commercial arithmetic, bookkeeping, and commercial geography. Enrollment at the Girls' High School was the highest. Within two years, stenography and typewriting were offered in seven day high schools.[105] In 1900, Superintendent Seaver argued that a flexible curriculum was the best way to ensure that students remained in school as long as possible. The following year the day high schools adopted the elective system pioneered in the evening high schools, allowing students to substitute commercial subjects for other requirements.[106]

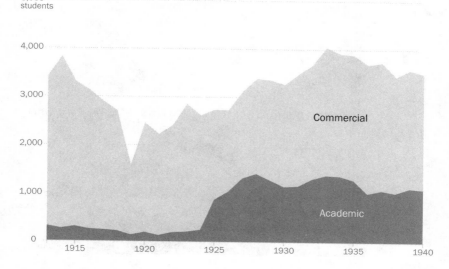

FIGURE 4.7: Men's evening public high school enrollment by course type, Boston, 1913–1940.

DATA SOURCE: *AS 1913–1940* (Boston: Printing Department, 1913–1940). © Cristina Groeger.

NOTE: Based on reported registration data. The jump in academic courses around 1924 likely reflects a change in how enrollments were tallied; see note 99.

These programs explain much of the public day high school enrollment surge in the first decades of the twentieth century, illustrated in Figures 4.8 and 4.9.[107] Besides a dip during World War I when voluntary enlistment, conscription, and war industry jobs drew men and women away from school, enrollment grew impressively, swelling by a factor of seventeen between 1880 and 1940. The majority of female students and a large proportion of male students pursued a commercial course of study, typically within a commercial department of their high school. Far fewer students enrolled in college-preparatory or industrial courses.

Relative to their counterparts pursuing other curricular tracks, "commercial" students in day high schools were more likely to be working class and have immigrant parents. In 1914, over 80 percent of female students in the high schools of Charlestown and East Boston—both heavily Irish working-class neighborhoods—enrolled in commercial subjects, whereas only half of women students did so in the wealthier

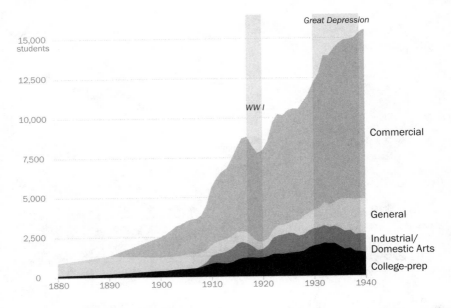

FIGURE 4.8: Women's day public high school attendance by course type, Boston, 1880–1940.

DATA SOURCES: *Semi-AS 1880–1897* (Boston: Rockwell & Churchill, 1881–1898); *Semi-AS 1898–1907* (Boston: Municipal Printing Office, 1898–1907); *Semi-AS 1908* (Boston: E. W. Doyle, 1908); *Semi-AS 1909* (Boston: Printing Department, 1909); *AS 1910–1940* (Boston: Printing Department, 1910–1940); *ARS 1913* (Boston: Printing Department, 1913), 94; *ARS 1914* (Boston: Printing Department, 1914), 48–49, 92; *ARS 1920* (Boston: Printing Department, 1920), 301; *ARS 1921* (Boston: Printing Department, 1921), 192; *ARS 1928* (Boston: Printing Department, 1928), 49–50; *ARS 1931* (Boston: Printing Department, 1931), 24; *ARS 1938* (Boston: Printing Department, 1938), 50–78, 122–124; May Allinson, *The Public Schools and Women in Office Service* (Boston: WEIU, 1914), 13, 25–32; Helen Rich Norton, *Department-Store Education* (Washington, DC: GPO, 1917), 60; Frank Victor Thompson, *Commercial Education in Public Secondary Schools* (Yonkers-on-Hudson, NY: World Book Co., 1915), 6; *RCE 1900–1901*, vol. 2 (Washington, DC: GPO, 1902), 2032–2033; *RCE 1905*, vol. 2 (Washington, DC: GPO, 1907), 948–949; *RCE 1906*, vol. 2 (Washington, DC: GPO, 1908), 818–820. © Cristina Groeger.

NOTE: Figures 4.8 and 4.9 are based on reported attendance data and estimates of curricular pursuits based on references in annual school reports. For more details, see note 107.

suburbs of Hyde Park and West Roxbury. A higher proportion of commercial students had fathers in manufacturing and personal service than did their counterparts in academic courses. While many students, both commercial and academic, left high school after a few years without graduating, commercial students did so at a higher rate.[108] These commercial students effectively used high school training as the equivalent of a "short course" at a proprietary commercial school before entering employment.

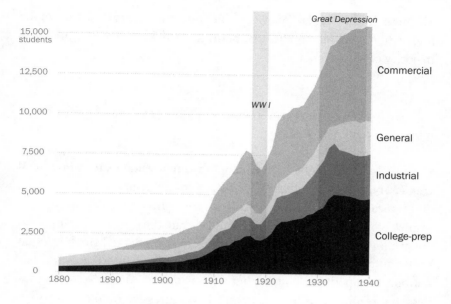

FIGURE 4.9: Men's day public high school attendance by course type, Boston, 1880–1940.
DATA SOURCES AND NOTE: See Figure 4.8. © Cristina Groeger.

It was not only students in commercial courses who pursued employment in business. A college-preparatory or general course effectively served as training for white-collar jobs as well. Business occupations were by far the most popular choice of men and women who graduated from high school, regardless of their curricular track. In 1927, over half of all male high school graduates in Boston who entered the paid workforce did so via business jobs, and 95 percent of all female graduates who went to work after graduation did so in jobs at offices or stores.[109] In 1938, of those who entered employment a year after graduating, roughly 60 percent each of male and female graduates pursued office or sales work.[110] Like its proprietary competitors, the Boston School Committee offered employment services through a new placement bureau organized in 1912 to help students find work.[111] One Roxbury High graduate who worked as a stenographer in 1925 described getting her position through this placement bureau, to which "all Boston high school graduates seeking employment are referred automatically."[112]

Through its curricular offerings and placement services, the public high school became an effective pathway into white-collar work for a majority of its students.

GENDERED PRIORITIES IN PUBLIC COMMERCIAL EDUCATION, 1906–1925

Despite the much higher enrollment of women students in commercial courses, public school officials prioritized commercial education for men and typically spoke of it in masculine terms. This priority reflected administrators' belief that training could elevate the status of business occupations threatened by feminization. It also reflected the hope that well-trained businessmen could promote American interests over international competitors, embodying the virtues of Anglo-Saxon manliness that reached new heights in an era of aggressive US imperialism.[113] Frank Thompson played a leading role in shaping local policies that reflected these priorities. In 1907, after returning from his tour of European schools, he warned that "the Germans are forging ahead in the advanced fields of commercial activity, solely because of . . . their superior educational advantages," and that Bostonians urgently needed to pay attention to the "keen competition which is coming."[114] Thompson argued that a high school of commerce solely for men, offering instruction in foreign languages and international business customs, would allow for the expansion of American goods into foreign markets.[115]

For officials like Thompson, the well-rounded education of a true business leader would not consist merely of technical training in stenography or bookkeeping, but courses in economic history, commercial geography, and applied physics and chemistry. The distinction between clerical workers and businessmen, commonly made in editorials at the time, was increasingly a gendered one, as women filled the lower ranks of office work.[116] As Thompson envisioned, using gendered language, a high school of commerce would prepare men for the "competitive, or active, side of business," as opposed to preparation offered by most commercial instruction for the "passive side of business."[117] Thompson was especially concerned with the field of salesmanship. Sales work, as we have seen, was at the bottom of the white-collar hierarchy, and the poorly compensated shop girl was a popular object of both pity and concern.[118] Thompson hoped to turn the field of "buying and selling" into a central component of commercial instruction in the public schools.[119] As principal of the Bigelow evening school in 1905, he arranged a salesmanship class for men employees of cooperating firms at the city's expense.[120] Similarly, in collaboration with several retail stores, Thompson launched part-time voluntary "continuation" classes for 75 sales employees in the spring of 1910.[121]

Bipartisan support for men's commercial education played an important role in Boston's electoral contests in the first decade of the twentieth century. Irish Democrat John F. Fitzgerald was among the most vocal champions of commercial education, and made the men's High School of Commerce a central feature of his 1905 mayoral campaign for a "bigger, better, and busier" Boston.[122] Across the aisle, Republicans also embraced commercial training for men. James Storrow, who ran against Fitzgerald for mayor and became his fiercest political opponent, did not distance himself from the commercial high school but in fact claimed credit for the school himself during his time as chairman of the school committee.[123] Boston's men-only High School of Commerce was opened in 1906 with Thompson as its first principal, embodying his vision of a well-rounded education for the "active" side of business. By 1915, the school was second only to the English High School in men's enrollment.[124]

The lower priority placed on women's trajectories is visible in the parallel development of women-only public instruction in salesmanship and clerical work. About the same time that the school committee was promoting new opportunities for men's commercial education, a new school for women's salesmanship was developed in the private sector. In 1905, Lucinda Prince, a Wellesley graduate and member of the Women's Educational and Industrial Union (WEIU), launched a cooperative School of Salesmanship for women employees of Boston department stores. Like Thompson, and like the WEIU's prior approach to domestic workers, Prince believed that education for business occupations "would result in greater efficiency and better wages." The root of the problem of the "shop girl," according to Prince, was that her lack of training prevented her from seeing "the possibilities in [her] work."

Saleswomen, "like nurses, teachers, and doctors, would profit by training for their special vocation."[125]

Compared to WEIU's School of Housekeeping, there was high demand for Prince's School of Salesmanship. After enrollment grew from eight girls in 1906 to over 100 by 1912, Prince urged the public schools to take over salesmanship instruction. At a meeting held in conjunction with business leaders and public school officials in 1912, the Girls' High School headmaster agreed that advanced training in salesmanship would help the hundreds of women students currently taking commercial classes to find higher-paying jobs. While not organized into a separate school like the men's High School of Commerce, in 1913, courses in salesmanship for women were initiated in Boston high schools in partnership with local department stores. Beginning the following year, salesmanship training for women was also offered in compulsory continuation schools for students aged 14–16 working in stores.[126]

The incorporation of popular commercial and salesmanship courses into the public schools is evidence of the responsiveness of the Boston School Committee to student interest and demand, including that of women students. But resources were disproportionately channeled to men's training. After four years of complaints about the overcrowding of commercial courses open to women in Boston's high schools, the school committee opened a specialized Boston Clerical School for women in 1914. The funding disparity between the men's High School of Commerce and the women's Clerical School were evident from the outset. The Clerical School operated as a specialized track for office service in the Roxbury High School building, an already crowded women's high school far from the central business districts. In the meantime, an impressive new High School of Commerce building opened in downtown Boston in 1915 to accommodate 1,800 young men. This was, according to the school committee, "the most expensive high school yet constructed."[127] In 1925, parents of Clerical School students petitioned for expansion, drawing a contrast between its cramped and unhealthy quarters and those of the new men's school. Their petition was ignored.[128] The school committee's responsiveness to the local demand for women's instruction, particularly when it came to investment of resources, only extended so far.

The difference between a brand-new, well-furnished school of commerce downtown and a specialized track within a crowded high school in a suburban district likely shaped the relative advantages offered by each school. To be sure, specialized commercial instruction did not "elevate" the status of the jobs their graduates entered, either for men as Thompson hoped or women as Prince anticipated. Although in this sector, unlike low-wage work, there was high demand for training, the notion that vocational education could leverage an occupation into a higher-status position in the economy was not the correct analysis for either. Nonetheless, the degree of designated resources as well as the gendered curriculum in men's and women's public commercial education likely helped reinforce gender segregation in the white-collar workforce. If schools could not elevate the status of an occupation, they could help delineate distinctions within it.

PAROCHIAL SCHOOLS, 1907–1930

In contrast to other cities with a substantial Catholic population, parochial schools in Boston never became a primary provider of commercial instruction.[129] The dominance of Irish Catholics in Boston led most Catholic students to attend public rather than parochial schools, especially at the secondary level. After 1907, when Boston's new archbishop, William O'Connell, espoused a separatist mode of building Catholic power, the parochial school system did grow: while 10 percent of Boston students attended parochial schools in 1880, about 18 percent did so throughout the 1920s. O'Connell promoted the ethnic diversity within Boston's Catholic community, encouraging Italian, Lithuanian, French, and Polish Catholics to organize their own parishes and schools, and he defended foreign-language parochial schools against state intrusion. Yet of all students attending secondary schools in the 1920s, only about 5 percent attended parochial high schools. Parochial high schools in Boston were almost entirely for women: through the 1920s, no parochial secondary school with over 100 students catered to men. Ensuring opportunities for Catholic women's secondary education likely reflected the preference for single-sex education and more conservative gender norms of the Catholic Church.[130] Boston's female academies, or "convent schools," which typically spanned primary through high school, offered a religious-based, classical course. The Boston Academy of Notre Dame, located in the Fenway, trained women to embody the "perfect ideal of Christian Womanhood," with particular attention to "correct deportment, gracious manner, and the formation of habits of order and punctuality." This academy briefly offered a one-to-two-year secretarial course in 1923, but this course only admitted high school graduates, and at $150 annually it was more expensive than the standard academy rate of $100. By 1927, the secretarial course had been discontinued, and the school only offered an "exclusively classical course," or college-preparatory course that included Latin.[131] Catholic secondary schools thus seem to have catered to a more affluent group of Catholic women seeking a classical education in an environment of other Catholic women. Working-class Catholics, if they did attend high school, overwhelmingly chose to take commercial courses in public schools.

FROM PROPRIETARY SCHOOL TO DEGREE-GRANTING COLLEGE, 1910–1940

The rapid growth of public high schools in the 1910s and 1920s compelled proprietary commercial schools to respond. Some were forced to close. Despite its status as the oldest commercial school in Boston, Comer's College shut its doors in 1925.[132] Others launched renewed advertising campaigns, pitching themselves as postsecondary, and even postcollegiate, professional schools for those who sought a practical, short course of instruction before entering the workforce.[133] The most successful became degree-granting colleges. Winter Hill Business College, renamed Fisher College in 1910, first petitioned for degree-granting power from the Massachusetts legislature during the Great Depression. As part of its bid, it began to adopt characteristic collegiate features, including liberal arts courses, selective enrollment, new campus buildings and dormitories, and it stopped advertising a "guarantee" of positions. At long last in 1957, Fisher received the authority to grant associate of science degrees.[134]

In 1913, after successfully offloading basic sales training onto the public schools, Lucinda Prince's School of Salesmanship was absorbed into Simmons College, adding store management to existing professional programs in household economics, secretarial studies, and library science. These new collegiate programs catered to a much more limited demographic of students, who were training not to become saleswomen but educational managers in department stores or teachers of salesmanship in public schools.[135] Like the trajectory of domestic service, reformers may have hoped that eventually salesmanship would be elevated through the development of specialized fields of knowledge. In the meantime, they created new occupations for more affluent women.

Traditional degree-granting colleges also responded to a changing educational landscape and the heightened demand for business training. Some marketed a bachelor of arts degree as a desirable credential for future managers and executives, while others launched new collegiate business degree programs of their own.[136] By 1910, public high schools and degree-granting colleges and universities had marginalized proprietary schools in the provision of commercial instruction, as shown in Figure 4.10.[137] While the eclipse of proprietary schools in Boston occurred about a decade earlier than the national average, the creation of free, mass public alternatives effectively halted the expansion of the for-profit sector.[138] At the same time, the new dominant institutional types formed a new educational hierarchy that matched the occupational ladder. Irish Catholic and Russian Jewish women received their training in public schools and filled the lower rungs of office and sales work, while a small number of college-educated white, Protestant, male managers filled positions at the top.

THE EDUCATIONAL ADVANTAGE

Among office and sales workers who reached their twenties by the turn of the century, not even half had over an eighth-grade education. By 1940, 85 percent reported having this amount.[139] The success of schools in attracting enrollment and the success of their graduates in finding

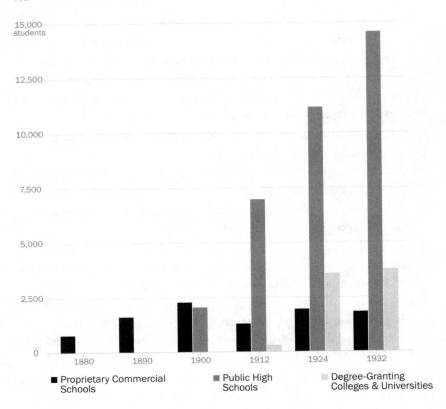

FIGURE 4.10: Enrollment in day business/commercial courses by school type, Boston, 1880–1932.

DATA SOURCES: *Semi-AS 1880–1897* (Boston: Rockwell & Churchill, 1881–1898); *Semi-AS 1898–1907* (Boston: Municipal Printing Office, 1898–1907); *Semi-AS 1908* (Boston: E. W. Doyle, 1908); *Semi-AS 1909* (Boston: Printing Department, 1909); *AS 1910–1932* (Boston: Printing Department, 1910–1932); *RCE 1880* (Washington, DC: GPO, 1882), 482; *RCE 1890–1891*, vol. 2 (Washington, DC: GPO, 1894), 1462–1463; *RCE 1901*, vol. 2 (Washington, DC: GPO, 1902), 2282–2283; *RCE 1913*, vol. 2 (Washington, DC: GPO, 1914), 221–222, 587–588; *BSE 1918–1920, Statistics* (Washington, DC: GPO, 1923), 337–338; *BSE 1930–1932* (Washington, DC: GPO, 1932), 141–142, 201–202; *BSE 1932–1934*, chapter 7 (Washington, DC: GPO, 1937), 25–26; *Annual Register of Comer's Commercial College 1874* (Boston: Rand, Avery & Co., 1875), 27; Scott Adams Fisher, "The Development and Recession of the Private Junior College Including Fisher Junior College: A Case Study" (PhD diss., Harvard Graduate School of Education, Harvard University, 1983), 81; *Catalogue of the Day School 1912–13* (Boston: Boston YMCA Institute, 1912), 61–62; *The Year Book, 1923–1925*, Boston University Bulletin, vol. 13, no. 32 (Boston: University Council, 1924), 95; Eleanor Rust Collier, *The Boston University College of Business Administration, 1913–1958* (Boston: Boston University, 1959); *The Day School of Business Administration 1925–26* (Boston: Northeastern University, 1926), 55–59; *Northeastern Day Division School of Business Administration 1934–35* (Boston: Northeastern University, 1935), 20. © Cristina Groeger.

office and sales jobs helped to solidify the importance of formal education in the white-collar labor market. Higher educational attainment
translated into positions with higher status and pay. A 1914 study of
young women office workers found that while only 8 percent of those
with a grammar school education earned eight dollars a week or more,
51 percent of women high school graduates did. Grammar school graduates became clerks and copyists, while high school graduates (or those
who supplemented their public school education with a short course at
a commercial school) rose to the level of stenographers and secretaries.
Many reports of the period agreed with this study's conclusion: "Education seems to be the most important determining factor in advancement in office service."[140]

Students themselves understood this connection and often attributed
their success to education. One graduate of Somerville High School in
1907 wrote that her course had provided ample preparation for her current position as a secretary.[141] Nanette Calver, a graduate of Boston's
Girls' High School in 1915 who worked for the Treasury (likely of the city
of Boston) before managing her late husband's manufacturing business
wrote, "Whatever success I have had in life had its foundation largely in
my training in that school."[142]

Education offered white-collar workers a range of advantages. Some
forms of specialized knowledge, such as the operation of typewriters,
cash registers, or telephone switchboards, could be learned in a few weeks
or months in a commercial school. Subjects learned through a high school
curriculum—writing, reading, public speaking, and mathematics—were
also essential skills for white-collar occupations. These seemingly academic skills were often laden with specific cultural norms and the pro-
prieties of "office etiquette." As vocational studies and guide books at
the time detailed, formal business correspondence required knowledge of how to properly format, address, date, and sign a letter, employ
a broad vocabulary, spell flawlessly, and use a "gracious and dignified"
tone. For those who worked in stores and spoke regularly to upper-class
customers, employees were expected to know "correct usage [of En-
glish] and what may be termed good taste or judgment in the selection
of words."[143] Appropriate speech was essential for telephone operators,
whose sole impression was made through their voice. Women who had

foreign accents were eliminated entirely from the labor pool, as were women with "harsh or displeasing voices." Telephone operators were instructed to be "courteous and ladylike" and use "the cheery tones of a Pollyanna."[144]

Other behavioral traits and social skills that may have been learned in schools were also essential, and strongly gendered. Men had to possess "good character," which implied collegiality, good manners, loyalty to the firm, and ethical standards.[145] Because secretaries were often trusted with confidential information, discretion was an indispensable quality. One secretary noted the informal "code of secretarial ethics": to "hear much and say little."[146] Contemporary descriptions of women's requirements focused extensively on personal presentation, including "courteous manners, dainty personal habits . . . and a sympathetic disposition." Women were to avoid being "quarrelsome," having "irritating manners," chewing gum, and, one of the most common complaints of saleswomen, talking too much. Physical appearance and dress were also crucial. A study of store work training explained, "The public buys most willingly from young, good-looking, neatly dressed women," and women had to walk the fine line of "cultivating a pleasing but not particularly striking personal appearance."[147] These norms of femininity also served as a means of ethnic and class distinction, as working-class eastern and southern European women were often characterized as untidy or unrefined.[148] When office workers themselves were surveyed about the most important qualifications for their jobs, the most common responses after "accuracy" were "tact," "ability to get along with people," and, as one secretary put it, "chronic cheerfulness."[149]

Schools also opened up new social networks that were extremely useful in securing jobs. Formal education did not replace the family and personal ties that characterized pathways to work in the nineteenth century, but rather helped broaden their reach. In 1914, one study of women office workers in Boston found that while 12 percent of them found their position with the help of their school's placement bureau, nearly 40 percent secured their positions through a relative or friend.[150] Many friends were likely classmates. The new social environment and youth culture within high schools not only cultivated social skills but also opened new paths into employment.

These school-based social networks also expanded opportunities for social mobility through marriage. While a majority of women high school students entered employment immediately after leaving school, most would eventually marry, and when they did, they tended to marry those with a similar education level. At the turn of the century, two-thirds of men and women who reported having some high school education married spouses with at least some high school education as well. By 1940, the correlation among high school students had grown stronger: 77 percent of men and 74 percent of women who reported having some high school education married spouses with the same or higher level of schooling.[151]

Gender continued to structure pay differentials. Based on the findings of a 1926 study of Boston office workers, nearly 90 percent of women made less than $30 per week, while 60 percent of men made $30 per week or more.[152] While entry-level clerical positions for men and women paid comparable amounts, wage differentials increased higher up the white-collar ladder, and women's promotional opportunities were heavily restricted.[153] Employers and personnel managers would often only hire workers of their own race or ethnicity, creating a segregated workforce. Operators for the New England Telephone Company (NETC) were almost entirely Irish Catholic. Mary E. Harrington, in charge of hiring and training, stopped advertising positions in newspapers because ads attracted "foreigners, illiterate and untidy." Instead, personal referrals from school officials, she believed, secured "young ladies of refinement."[154] Schools were thus used as an initial screen to complement Harrington's selection process based on her ethnic preferences.

No level of educational attainment could overcome explicit policies of exclusion. The NETC rejected Jewish applicants until the 1940s. Alice O'Meara, an agent of the WEIU's appointment bureau, complained in 1921 of the difficulty of placing Catholic stenographers and bookkeepers, even those "of the best type," because many employers requested Protestant girls only.[155] Despite the historically high levels of educational attainment among Boston's Black youth, almost no companies hired African Americans, other than a few Black-owned businesses.[156] In Massachusetts in 1920, 0.7 percent of all clerks and 0.2 percent of all sales personnel were Black.[157] Employers, it seems, had a large enough pool of workers to choose from to simply reject applications based on their own prejudices. Educational attainment had little effect on these discriminatory practices.

FROM WHITE COLLAR TO PINK COLLAR, 1914–1930

As clerical and sales work expanded and became feminized, the nature of these jobs changed. While nineteenth-century clerks in small firms had assisted with a wide range of business operations and often contributed to business decisions, the majority of new copyists, typists, and stenographers worked among dozens or hundreds of employees who mediated between higher-level managers and clients. Low wages for women in office and sales work were endemic. In 1914, 25 percent of women clerks and 60 percent of department-store saleswomen in Boston earned less than eight dollars per week, below the calculated living wage of nine dollars per week. At this date, on average, saleswomen earned less than needleworkers in store workrooms.[158]

White-collar workers were among the first to benefit from the wave of "welfare work" undertaken by large firms around the turn of the century such as Filene's Sons Company in Boston.[159] Founded in 1881 by German-Jewish immigrant William Filene, the department store was turned over to his sons, Abraham Lincoln Filene and Edward Filene, in 1901. The Filene brothers developed a heightened interest in labor relations after the 1893 depression and created a novel system of employee representation in 1903 with the assistance and encouragement of attorney Louis Brandeis.[160] The Filene's Cooperative Association (FCA) sponsored activities and worker benefits, and also gave employees the power to amend company rules ("except policies of the business") and elect members to an arbitration board that would mediate worker grievances. Employees used the FCA to settle hundreds of grievances and to challenge store policies such as closing hours, holiday schedules, and dress codes.[161]

Despite the benefits offered by some of the largest companies, white-collar workplaces exhibited extreme power imbalances between employees and employers. Testimonies before the US Commission on Industrial Relations in 1916 revealed a wide range of grievances and employer abuses among retail workers. Store employees were regularly compelled to work overtime without pay, or were forbidden from sitting down, despite legislation restricting working hours and mandating seating. Employer associations could easily blacklist employees for trivial offenses.[162] Among Boston office workers in 1914, 15 percent left a position because they were dissatisfied with working conditions, most commonly long hours and low wages. In addition, about 10 percent of office workers complained of eyestrain and 7 percent of poor ventilation.[163] Employers resisted union-organizing efforts among their staff. Silvia Shulman was fired from A. I. Namm & Sons in 1916 after being employed as a sales clerk for four years because she "dared to belong" to the retail clerks union.[164] Even the enlightened Edward Filene dismissed labor "agitators" as merely interested in "petty privileges."[165]

World War I and its aftermath revealed the limited bargaining position of white-collar workers compared to their organized industrial counterparts. Nationally, wages for the average industrial worker increased 20 percent during the war, but they fell 14 percent for white-collar employees.[166] As one industrial relations advisor observed, "In many a corporation the unlearned toiler in mine or factory receives a wage greater than that of the clerk, and enjoys, moreover, superior facilities for bringing his wants to the attention of the management."[167] Wartime production also encouraged employers to adopt new management practices and labor-saving technologies such as the cash register that further reduced the bargaining power of office and sales workers.[168] The term "white collar" first came into popular usage at the close of the war, especially pejoratively as part of the phrase "white-collar slave." *The Adding Machine,* a play by Elmer L. Rice first staged in 1923, exemplified the plight of the white-collar slave. The main character, a frustrated bookkeeper named Mr. Zero, worked adding accounts for twenty-five years before he was fired unexpectedly when a new adding machine was acquired on the advice of an "efficiency expert."[169] Many office and sales workers faced a similar precarity of employment.

A minority of white-collar workers channeled this discontent into wartime-era labor activism, which peaked in a wave of national strikes in 1919. Despite the obstacles to entering male-dominated labor organizations, some women white-collar workers were able to use labor unions for their own purposes. One of the most successful unions, active between 1912 and 1923, was made up of young, high school–educated Irish Catholic telephone operators. Frustrated with wage reductions, split work schedules dubbed the "split trick," night work, unpaid overtime, and a harsh penalty system, operators of the NETC worked with the Women's Trade Union League (WTUL) in 1912 to gain a charter from the AFL-affiliated International Brotherhood of Electrical Workers (IBEW) as the Boston Telephone Operators' Union. One member of the union remembered, "The organization came easy because conditions were so bad it was practically spontaneous. . . . As soon as [each exchange] heard . . . they came in from everywhere to join the union."[170]

By 1919, over 70 percent of all telephone operators in Massachusetts were union members. In the spring of that year, the women-led Telephone Operators' Union of the IBEW led a strike of nearly 8,000 telephone operators in New England, paralyzing telephone services in five states. As in other local strikes, Harvard and Massachusetts Institute of Technology students were brought in as strikebreakers. Class antagonism broke out between strikebreakers and working-class Irish unionists, who taunted the students for their wealth (the "snobveracy of Harvard and Tech") as well as the feminized roles they were taking by replacing telephone operators ("twenty Lizzies from Harvard," "rah rah sissies," "powder puff boys"). Collegians' attempts at strikebreaking proved unsuccessful. After just five days, the telephone operators won wage increases and the recognition of their right to collectively bargain with management.[171]

Multiple unique factors allowed the operators to achieve success. Their occupation had been women dominated from the start and did not compete directly with traditionally male jobs. Irish women were the daughters and sisters of many Irish trade unionists, which facilitated their entry into organized labor. They also belonged to the same ethnic networks of Irish police officers (before the police strike several months later that led to the dismissal of many of those officers), which curbed law enforcement intervention in their strike. Unlike the experience of Italian or Jewish workers in earlier Boston strikes, not a single telephone operator was arrested over the course of the strike. There was only one employer controlling telephone service in New England, which fell under enormous pressure to resolve labor disputes with its workers. WTUL leaders also helped garner public support by influencing the media portrayal of women unionists as respectable young ladies. However, like other unions in the aftermath of World War I, the Telephone Operators' Union faced an aggressive open-shop drive, and union membership dropped through the 1920s.[172] Only in the mid-twentieth century would white-collar unions gain significant strength.

Employees did find ways to exert power without unions. Sales workers collectively enforced "the stint," an informal quota of sales per day, among their coworkers, which thwarted the management tactic of incentive payment schemes to increase worker productivity.[173] Many won temporary improvements through the threat of unionization.[174] However, office and sales workers remained insecure. According to one commentator in the early 1920s, "Every clerk and every employer knows that . . . the places of the lower orders of clerical workers can be filled more readily than can those of almost any other industrial class."[175] Even a strong "work culture" could not protect workers from the arbitrary decisions of management.[176]

By 1930, clerical and sales employees had become a feminized pink-collar sector. The abundance of educational opportunities meant that unions and professional associations were limited in their ability to regulate entry and set the terms of employment for these jobs. But far from discrediting the importance of education, the ability of workers to access these jobs through their training in schools verified it. Even with limited power in the workplace, these positions still held out higher wages, better conditions, and more status than alternatives, especially for women. In the white-collar workplace, educational attainment increasingly matched occupational status and pay. For many employees, observing the match between education level and managerial rank would have confirmed their faith in schooling as the best means of achieving social advancement.

CONCLUSION

The American corporate economy of the early twentieth century was made possible by the immense growth of private and public schools offering business training. Students, parents, educators, administrators, philanthropists, politicians, and employers agreed that instruction for white-collar work was desirable. Young men and women, especially working-class, second-generation immigrant women, used schools to learn technical and cultural skills, access valuable social networks, and enter preferable fields of office and sales work. The early surge of proprietary commercial schools indicates their historical role in providing forms of training that were otherwise unavailable in the educational landscape. While some of these schools used misleading advertising and false promises to take advantage of students, others offered accessible, vocationally relevant education to groups that were not the priority of existing schools.

This history reveals how the public school system was shaped in reaction to the private sector, and why we must understand the competitive relationship between them in order to understand the development of either. Educational reformers saw expanding public commercial training as the best way to undercut the market for potentially unscrupulous proprietary schools. Grassroots demand and bipartisan support pushed forward the provision of this training as a public, rather than a private, good. Municipalities took on the responsibility of educating students for office and sales jobs, enormously expanding state capacity and helping to establish education as the chief public policy to address problems of work and employment. This history also provides insight into how we might limit the exploitative practices of the for-profit sector in the present. Rather than restrict these institutions through regulation, the most effective approach in the early twentieth century was to offer free, public alternatives.

In many education histories, and in common understandings of education that still persist today, "liberal" and "academic" education is usually contrasted with "vocational" education. But this dichotomy is ill-suited to explain the history of education through much of the nineteenth and twentieth centuries. Academic education in high schools played an extremely important vocational role for their students. It was not only students pursuing a commercial course of study but those pursuing academic subjects who overwhelmingly used their education to enter the white-collar workforce.

The employment of a sizeable pool of contingent pink-collar employees made possible sweeping changes to the industrial workplace and a dramatic reorganization of corporate bureaucracies. The fact that the majority of these workers were women is a crucial corrective to popular perceptions of the man in the gray flannel suit as the face of business and economic change in this period.[177] Male managers depended on a foundation of office and retail work performed by thousands of female employees. The feminization of the sector of white-collar work should also be understood as one of the primary instigators of new educational strategies among elites to maintain their professional and managerial positions at the top. In response to rising high school enrollment and the expansion of school-based credentials, affluent Bostonians pursued professional strategies that transformed the top of both the educational and occupational ladder. These practitioners in central positions of the corporate economy developed powerful professional associations and forged relationships with degree-granting universities, successfully using exclusive educational credentials to control entry into the top professional and managerial jobs. If the American faith in education and its economic benefits was bolstered through the vast expansion of high schools, it was consolidated through the use of higher education by an emerging professional class. This class provided the most obvious evidence that advanced education was key to scaling the economic ladder. In the process, elite professionals forged new definitions of educational merit imbued with cultural meanings that legitimized and reproduced long-standing class-based, racial, ethnic, and gender inequalities. They also used the legitimacy of their own positions to further secure managerial power over the majority of employees.

FIVE

Professional Ladders

Gleason Archer, founder of a proprietary evening law school in Boston in 1906, spent his career fighting against what he dubbed the "Educational Octopus": Harvard University. As he wrote in 1915,

> The Great Octopus is there with its crimson tentacles reaching from Committee Room to Committee Room, from the halls of legislation to the Governor's office, playing its pawns in the great game of legislation. And the searchlight plays not only upon the heights of Beacon Hill; but over the State itself and discloses who controls ... all things educational in Massachusetts, to the furtherance of class distinctions that even now threaten the life of the Republic.[1]

For Archer, efforts to restrict professional schools like his own were salvos in the war of elites against the sons and daughters of Boston's working class. While Archer had a penchant for dramatic rhetoric, his analysis reflects the intensity of early twentieth-century conflicts over pathways into professions like law. In this period, competition between schools offering professional training reshaped the top rungs of the occupational ladder. This competition also turned advanced educational credentials into key tools in the reproduction of inequality. While reformers pursued a wide array of professionalizing projects in this period, it was practitioners in strategic areas of the new corporate economy that successfully used credentials to control entry into their jobs and enhance their status. This chapter explores the transformation of two of the oldest professions, education and law; Chapter 6 examines the profession of business.

The differences between the professions of education and law were stark. The teaching profession was feminized in the early nineteenth century and remained a lower-status "semi-profession."[2] Law, meanwhile, was and continued to be the most exclusively male profession in Boston and a model of prestige to which other professions aspired. Yet similarities in the process of professionalization stand out. In both, rather than an internally driven quest for higher standards, professionalization was to a significant degree a reaction to larger economic, demographic, and educational changes. In the late nineteenth century, the number of practitioners in each profession rose. Growing school systems opened up positions for teachers and educational administrators, and the expansion of corporate and state bureaucracies generated opportunities for legal specialists. Heightened demand led to enrollment growth in public professional schools such as Boston's Normal School for teacher training and the founding of proprietary schools such as Gleason Archer's Suffolk Law School. These schools, which found local allies within the Democratic Party, provided working-class men and women with opportunities to acquire the skills and social networks needed to enter these professions.

As the increasing representation of immigrants and women threatened existing practitioners, and new schools threatened traditional degree-granting institutions, Boston elites sought new strategies to maintain their status.[3] They organized professional associations whose membership included alumni of select schools and worked with university leadership to develop new standards and requirements for professional degree programs. The politically influential leaders of private universities used their power to regulate the landscape of higher education. They opposed the movement to give degree-granting power to the Normal School, stymied repeated efforts to open a public university in Boston, and, while unable to shut them down, derided proprietary schools as inferior to collegiate education. They promoted college degrees as the preferred credential to enter professional schools and professional careers, with the bachelor of arts setting the highest standard of prestige. As Democratic control of the city grew stronger, leading universities and professional associations found allies at the Republican-dominated state level. While they could not completely restrict access to professions, they shaped internal hierarchies that matched the class, ethnic, and gender characteristics of practitioners.[4]

Boston's unusually high number of private colleges and universities played a central role in national elite formation in this era. The outsized influence of private universities distinguished American higher education from the state universities of France and Germany, and private institutions and foundations played a substantial role in regional and national accreditation in the United States.[5] Administrators and alumni of Harvard and the Massachusetts Institute of Technology (MIT) facilitated emerging professional networks that established criteria for professional standards across the country. Elite schools used selective admissions to shape their preferred student body and actively built relationships with leading employers. In restructuring the channels into the most well-paying jobs, these institutions further elevated the importance of educational credentials for reaching peak positions in the economy. This in turn instigated competitor schools to launch new degree-granting programs to emulate the markers of elite status and prompted higher demand from students seeking these ever more vital credentials. Many professional leaders strongly believed that extended training in new bodies of scientific knowledge would place their field on a more "scientific" basis and enable practitioners to better serve the public good. At the same time, professionalizing projects provoked political battles between rival interpretations of that public good, and ultimately preserved traditional hierarchies of power, now reproduced in and through schools.

By 1940 census calculations, Boston's professional class had expanded in numerous ways. As a percentage of the total Boston workforce, those listed as professionals grew from about 4 percent to 8 percent of the men's workforce, and 5 percent to 16 percent of the women's workforce. By 1920, Russian Jewish men were overrepresented in the legal profession, and Irish teachers and lawyers rose to reflect their proportion in the workforce by 1930. By 1940, first- and second-generation immigrants became a majority of Boston's proprietors and managers.[6]

But not all "professionals" were equal. The process of professionalization, in Boston as in other cities, fortified steep internal ladders.[7] Not only did the educational requirements to enter the professions lengthen, but different educational institutions channeled graduates into positions with vastly different status and pay. Women's colleges, public institutions, and proprietary schools sent their graduates into positions as teachers, trial lawyers, and small business owners. The male graduates of elite universities had a virtual monopoly on the most lucrative positions as educational administrators, corporate lawyers, and executives. Russian Jewish and Irish Catholic professionals tended to enter the lower ranks of the profession, while white Protestants dominated the top. Some groups, despite their educational achievements, were virtually barred from the professional ranks: African Americans made up less than 1 percent of teachers or lawyers in Boston as late as 1940.[8] These forms of discrimination would seem to disprove the notion that higher professional status was premised solely on one's advanced knowledge and expertise. However, the professional success of some helped cement an ideological commitment to the meritocratic hierarchy of education.

This chapter first turns to the profession of education, examining debates over Boston's Normal School for teacher training and private opposition to public higher education in the city. It explores the pioneering Boston Trade Union College, a labor college open to Boston's working class, and early efforts by teachers to organize through both clubs and unions. Despite significant opposition, private universities became the dominant institutions for the training of both teachers and educational administrators. Next, the chapter turns to law, exploring the growth of law schools and the differentiation among practicing attorneys. I describe the outsized role of Harvard University in shaping legal standards, particularly on display in Suffolk Law School's battle for degree-granting authority. I also explore how the legal profession marginalized women's legal practices and kept the law an almost entirely male realm. Finally, I discuss national regulation led by professional associations, which consolidated the role of universities in shaping access to the law.

In both education and law, the struggle over training dramatically reconfigured access into the professions and created a new educational scaffolding for their internal hierarchies.

EDUCATION AS A PROFESSION

The Normal School and Ethnic Politics, 1880–1902

Boston's rapidly expanding school system required staffing by hundreds of new teachers. Between 1870 and 1902, Boston's public school teaching force grew from 950 to 2,364.[9] Boston's Normal School became the primary avenue for women to access a respected occupation as an elementary school teacher. In 1899, 60 percent of yearly public primary and grammar school appointments in Boston were Normal School graduates.[10] Although Irish women were never overrepresented as teachers, their representation grew dramatically, as shown in Figure 5.1. The Normal School's graduating class of 1878 included only nine Irish women out of fifty-eight; by the turn of the century, half of Normal School graduates were of Irish heritage.[11]

The rising proportion of Irish Catholic teachers was a cause for concern among public school administrators. Superintendents and grammar school masters defended the Normal School as a key institution for elevating the teaching profession and supported an 1888 regulation giving preference to Normal School graduates.[12] However, they were concerned by the way in which student demographics were shaping its reputation. Over his long tenure as superintendent from 1880 to 1904, Edwin Seaver voiced these concerns. In his 1899 annual report, he claimed that the need for the "best teachers" far outweighed the claims of Normal School graduates to receive appointments. Seaver based his preference for "outsiders" on the premise that "staff that is recruited all from one source inevitably becomes narrow, conceited and unprogressive." Seaver noted that many grammar school masters were disinclined to take local women fresh from the Normal School. Instead, they preferred teachers with more experience who came from outside Boston or women graduates of local private colleges. These "outsiders" were also typically wealthier, native-born, and Protestant.[13] Seaver also hoped to

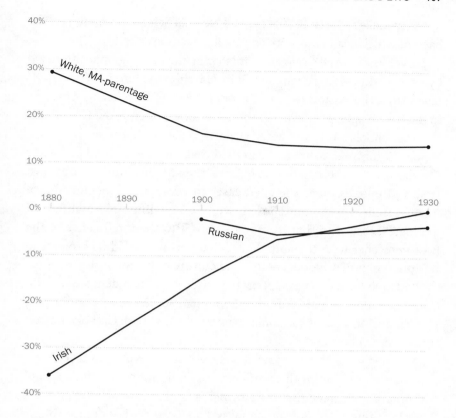

FIGURE 5.1: Overrepresentation by ethnicity of women teachers in Boston, 1880–1930.
DATA SOURCE: IPUMS 1880–1930, 1890 estimated. © Cristina Groeger.

attract more men, who made up 15 percent of Boston's total teaching force in 1900 and tended to be concentrated in private schools.[14]

Among those who shared Seaver's views was Abbott Lawrence Lowell, the future president of Harvard, who served on the Boston School Committee from 1896 to 1899. Lowell, a descendent of one of Boston's most established First Families, was a fierce immigration restrictionist who favored ethnic homogeneity. In his campaign for school committee, he ran on a platform to reform the appointment and promotion of teachers, claiming the process was subject to corrupt political influence. Once elected, he worked with Seaver to shift the power to appoint teachers from the school committee to the superintendent, and in 1898 he helped to put in place a "merit list" of ranked Normal School graduates, on the basis of which graduates were chosen for positions.[15]

Seaver and Lowell's reforms came up against strong opposition, led by Irish working-class champion, Julia Harrington Duff. Duff had graduated from the Boston Normal School in 1878 and worked as a teacher in the Irish neighborhood of Charlestown for fourteen years. Her slogan, "Boston schools for Boston girls," effectively won her a seat on the Boston School Committee in 1901. She argued that the criteria used by Seaver to judge the "best" teachers were in fact a cover for discrimination against Irish Catholic women. She cited cases in which incompetent "out of town" teachers had been chosen over well-qualified Normal School graduates, asserting that it was "an affront to the intelligence of the Boston teacher to ever imply that such a person should be brought to Boston to give new blood, energy, and culture to Boston girls." By 1904, she had mobilized enough support to replace Superintendent Seaver with George Conley. A native of Lowell who had served as a school supervisor in Boston since 1886, Conley became the first Irish Catholic Boston superintendent of schools.[16]

Duff's bigger fight, however, was with private degree-granting colleges and their allies. For all their differences, Duff and most public school administrators agreed that the Normal School should be strengthened as the keystone of the Boston school system. Over the last decades of the nineteenth century, the school committee raised the admissions age to the Normal School from 17 to 18, increased the amount of practice teaching, lengthened training from one to two years, and added course offerings to match new curricular innovations.[17] Twice in the 1890s, Duff helped lead a coalition of local teachers and administrators to successfully defeat proposals that would have shifted the Boston Normal School from city to state control.[18] Teachers and administrators also lobbied, unsuccessfully until 1907, to move the Normal School out of the cramped two floors of a South End grammar school without laboratories or a library into a fully equipped building.[19]

Duff and local school administrators, including Seaver, advocated turning the Normal School into a degree-granting teachers college. Enrollment in Boston's private colleges was rapidly rising in the years after 1880, in liberal arts subjects as well as more specialized business, engi-

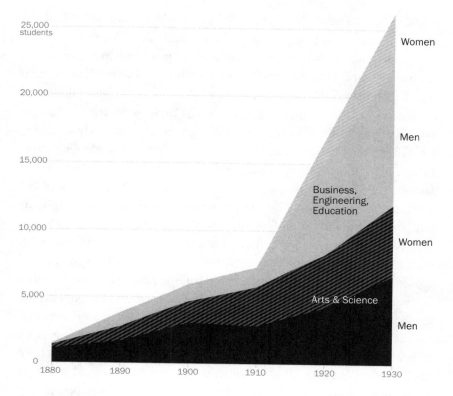

FIGURE 5.2: Men's and women's enrollment in Boston-area colleges by bachelor-degree type, 1880–1930.

DATA SOURCES: *RCE 1880* (Washington, DC: GPO, 1882), 626, 656, 678; *RCE 1890–91*, vol. 2 (Washington, DC: GPO, 1894), 1404, 1414, 1443–1444; *RCE 1901*, vol. 2 (Washington, DC: GPO, 1902), 1660–1661, 1708–1709, 1720–1721; *RCE 1910*, vol. 2 (Washington, DC: GPO, 1911), 890–891, 914, 962; *BSE 1918–1920, Statistics* (Washington, DC: GPO, 1923), 337–338; *BSE 1928–1930*, vol. 2 (Washington, DC: GPO, 1932), 442–444. © Cristina Groeger.

neering, and educational bachelor's degrees, depicted in Figure 5.2. As a percentage of 18–24-year-olds, college attendance grew to over 30 percent of men and nearly 20 percent of women in Boston by 1930.[20] Many women college graduates entered teaching positions in Boston's elementary schools, and made up the entire women's high school teaching force, where a college degree was required.[21] While high school teaching was a predominantly male domain in the mid-nineteenth century, women had risen to half of high school teachers by 1880.[22] As positions as headmasters and principals of schools were effectively closed to women until 1902, private colleges thus maintained a monopoly on training women for the highest public school positions available to them.[23] For Duff, degree-granting power would allow Normal graduates to compete fairly with college graduates for positions in primary and grammar schools, and it would open up high school positions to them for the first time. Many public school administrators and educators, committed to fortifying the boundaries of their own profession, supported a plan to develop teacher training as a separate body of expertise within the public school system, distinct from an academic education in private institutions controlled by university administrators and faculty.[24] Degree-granting authority would elevate the standing of the Normal School as an institution that even college graduates might attend in order to obtain professional training in education.

Private degree-granting colleges and their allies, including male high school teachers and political opponents of Julia Duff on the school committee, rejected the new teachers college plan. Male high school teachers, nearly all alumni of private colleges, were concerned with the feminization of their own vocation. They hoped to develop professional educational courses within traditional private colleges and universities rather than the Normal School. Privately educated women high school teachers, mostly upper class and of New England parentage, also sought to distinguish themselves from the heavily Irish, working-class teaching force in the lower grades.[25] Private universities, for their part, had long been hostile to public higher education. Charles Eliot had opposed the founding of the Massachusetts Agricultural College in the 1870s on the grounds that it would make the school a "perpetual pensioner of the state." He resisted policies of free tuition because "the habit of being helped by the government . . . is a most insidious and irresistible enemy of republicanism; for the very essence of republicanism is self-reliance."[26] While Eliot tempered his laissez-faire position in the next decades, his belief that public institutions were subject to the corrupting influence of partisan politics was likely shared by many private university leaders. In addition, while Harvard may not have feared direct competition from a new state-funded institution, other local private colleges had more reason to be concerned.

A select group of high school educators and college administrators, including Eliot and Wellesley president Alice Freeman, formed the

New England Association of Colleges and Preparatory Schools in 1885. This group was devoted to closer "articulation" between secondary schools and private colleges through standardized admissions requirements and teacher qualifications. Over the next few decades it consolidated its role as the primary regional accreditation body for secondary and higher education in New England.[27] Through numerous professional associations and foundations, private university leaders sought to shift educational authority from lay school boards and toward educational experts.[28] Eliot, who by the 1880s had come to realize that cooperation with public high schools was necessary to supply sufficient enrollment to Harvard, chaired the National Education Association's 1892 Committee of Ten Report, which did not so much offer up new ideas as it gave university experts a national stage to promote their vision of national uniformity in modern secondary school subjects, teaching standards, and college admissions.[29] Charles Eliot and Columbia University president Nicholas Butler helped found the College Entrance Examination Board in 1900, later the College Board, which promoted uniform admissions standards.[30] Initiatives to standardize secondary and higher education received additional strength from the Carnegie Foundation for the Advancement of Teaching in 1906 under the leadership of former MIT president Henry Pritchett. Such efforts included the promotion of the "Carnegie unit" metric, which became an influential school credit standard across the country.[31]

Given their interest in shaping the public schools, Eliot and his allies on the Boston School Committee worked together to develop professional training for teachers under private university, rather than public sector, auspices. In 1891, in part to preempt a new collegiate-level state normal course considered by the state legislature, Harvard launched a one-year "Normal course" for Harvard graduates. In 1892 Harvard began offering afternoon, Saturday, and summer courses taught by its professors to local teachers. In 1896, the Boston School Committee required one year of teaching experience as a prerequisite for the high school teacher's examination. Eliot negotiated an exception to this requirement specifically for Harvard College graduates who had taken education courses.[32]

The coalition of university leaders, college-educated high school teachers, and allies on the school committee was strengthened by their shared reaction to the changing political landscape. The school committee was one of the first sites of the political struggle between Boston Brahmins and Irish Catholics over the future of the city. In 1897, opponents of the growing number of women and Irish representatives on the school committee formed the Public School Association (PSA), using the campaign slogan "Keep the schools out of politics."[33] In addition to its leader, James Storrow, the PSA included his friends and Harvard classmates: Robert Woods, Abbott Lawrence Lowell, banker John Farwell Moors, educational reformer Joseph Lee, and Robert Treat Paine Jr., president of the Boston Associated Charities; all were also founding or active members of the Immigration Restriction League. Some Jewish allies, such as Louis Brandeis and Lincoln Filene, believed in the value of ostensibly enlightened, nonpartisan leadership for the city, and they aligned with the Brahmins against Irish Democratic ward bosses. This powerful bloc of "administrative progressives," who viewed the corporate board as a model for school organization and favored centralized power in the hands of experts, exemplified the leading ideology of school reform sweeping across the country.[34]

The 1901–1902 debate over the teachers college exposed deep class, ethnic, and gendered fault lines that shaped teacher training in Boston. Duff and her allies had succeeded in securing widespread support for the proposal from figures including Republican governor Winthrop Crane, Democratic mayor Patrick Collins, and a wide range of state and city public school officials. In December 1901, the school committee unanimously voted to petition the state legislature for the establishment of the teachers college. However, PSA members gained strength on the school committee in that year's election, and in 1902 an opponent of the Normal School was appointed to author a report on the matter, along with several PSA allies, including James Storrow.[35]

The subsequent report ordered the withdrawal of the school committee's petition for a new teachers college. Its authors argued that a teachers college would unfairly benefit a special class only and that drawing teachers solely from Boston would hurt the caliber and quality of the teaching force. The report also argued that it was unnecessary to duplicate efforts already provided for "admirably" in private colleges and universities, although they did not openly state their own conflict of interest as advisors and investors in these institutions. Finally, the authors argued that the Normal School had yet to prove itself worthy of degree-granting authority.[36]

Duff submitted her own minority report that countered each one of these arguments. She pointed out that state and municipal law required children to be taught in schools, and that, as such, Boston had a responsibility to train its own teachers. The concern with "caliber and quality" reflected the prejudices of supervisors against Irish women. In Duff's view, the argument that private universities already offered teacher training programs revealed their elitism, as "only the children of the wealthy . . . can afford to attend the universities." Boston, she argued, needed to provide similar instruction for those who could not. Duff defended the high standards of the Normal School, quoting the school's head assistant, who claimed that the level of work done was already equivalent to that of a degree-granting college. She concluded by declaring that the history of education in Massachusetts recounted a war waged by the propertied class against the plebian and working-class women of Boston. The attempt to thwart the teachers college was, in her view, only the most recent battle.[37]

The teachers college proposal was defeated. Within one year of the defeat, the proportion of annual public school appointments offered to Normal School graduates fell by 6 percent. Normal School graduates continued to be barred from teaching in Boston's high schools, as private colleges channeled their own graduates into the highest-paid public school positions open to women.[38]

Teachers against the School Committee, 1903–1919

Duff did not overcome the strength of PSA members on the school committee in her campaign for a teachers college, but her efforts did win her a strong public following and likely inspired new forms of organizing among teachers. Since the founding of the Lady Teachers' Organization in 1875, Boston teachers had organized a wide range of clubs and associations by gender and subject matter. While outside of the male-dominated labor movement, these groups played an important role in winning salary increases in 1896 and a retirement fund for teachers by

1900.[39] The Boston Teachers' Club, founded in 1898 and open to all public and private school teachers in Boston, led the effort to unify teacher clubs toward further collective action. In 1903, Emma S. Gulliver, president of the Boston Teachers' Club, organized a vote of its membership to create a new "federation of Boston teachers' clubs" to "secure for the teachers of the public schools of Boston all the rights and benefits to which they are professionally entitled." These rights and benefits included reducing class sizes from sixty to thirty-five students, teacher autonomy over curriculum, and better retirement funding. These teacher activists likely provided an important base of support for George Conley's superintendency appointment in 1904.[40]

In response to the growing influence of Duff and women teachers in school committee affairs, Storrow and his PSA allies mobilized to pass legislation in 1905 that reduced the twenty-four-member school committee, elected by district, to five committee members elected at large. Although Storrow promoted this plan as a means of taking school governance out of the hands of corrupt politicians, it had the effect of limiting Irish working-class representation.[41] The school committee plan was drawn up by Frank Thompson, who, before becoming headmaster of the High School of Commerce, took graduate courses at Harvard's new Division of Education. In drafting this plan, Thompson had the assistance of Henry Holmes, then a fellow graduate student and head of the English department of the High School of Commerce. In another year, Holmes would join the Harvard Education faculty and later become dean of the Harvard Graduate School of Education.[42] Thompson, while sympathetic to working-class demands, shared with Storrow a preference for expert rule over volatile district-level politics.

Conley's superintendency was cut short by his death in 1905, and the following year, Storrow helped ensure the election of his own protégé, Stratton Brooks, as the new superintendent. A University of Michigan graduate and assistant professor of education at the University of Illinois, Brooks faced opposition from many Bostonians who wanted someone local with actual experience running a school system, not an academic researcher appointed by a "master, millionaire politician, Chairman James J. Storrow."[43] Brooks was appointed anyway, and in his first report as superintendent in 1906, he heralded the new reduced school committee of five. "It may be said," Brooks wrote, "that on Jan 1, 1906, the schools of Boston ceased to be governed by a board having a provincial attitude, and came under the control of a board having a national attitude towards the schools." Brooks did give in to several teacher demands: class sizes were reduced to forty-four students, and salaries for elementary school teachers increased by $100 annually. But Brooks also adopted a "civil service" system of teacher appointments that incorporated ratings of "personal characteristics" and eliminated the preference given to Normal School graduates.[44] Julia Duff, who ran for a position on the five-person school committee in 1907, sharply criticized these reforms. She accused Brooks of using the merit list unfairly, citing the case of a teacher from Dedham who was number twenty on the list but was bumped ahead of a local teacher at the top of the list.[45] Duff lost this election bid, and the PSA bloc dominated the school board for the next decade.[46]

Under PSA control, the school committee developed new arrangements with local private colleges for teacher training. In 1907, a Committee on College Credit was organized to collaborate with local colleges offering teachers part-time and summer courses toward a college degree. Boston University (BU), Simmons College, Wellesley, Tufts, Harvard, and MIT each developed an outline of requirements, transfer credits, and fees for teachers to gain a college degree. Based on the recommendation of this committee, college credit could be substituted for a promotional exam and could move a teacher higher in the merit ranking.[47] By 1919, the Boston School Committee had reached agreements with Harvard, BU, and Boston College (BC) that graduate-level courses leading to a master of education degree would be counted as the equivalent of two or three years of teaching experience.[48] In this way, private colleges and universities, rather than the public Normal School, gained increasing prominence and influence over the field of teacher training and promotion.

Private Challenges to a Public University, 1913–1924

Private institutions continued to stymie efforts to grant degree-granting status to a public institution in the city of Boston. Support for accessible avenues through which working-class women could obtain high school teaching positions was one reason among many that a broad coalition of Bostonians supported public higher education. Organized labor, which had long championed free public higher education, became a powerful proponent. As one electrical worker stated in 1905 at a BCLU meeting, "Organized labor will have its own university of labor before long—one not dependent on false-natured philanthropists, such as Carnegie and Rockefeller."[49] Boston's Irish Catholic working class and organized labor were strongly aligned, and after 1907 Boston's conservative Archbishop O'Connell also helped reinforce the partisan divisions of the city along religious lines.[50] In 1910, the Irish-dominated Democratic Party, with the key support of Boston's unions, began a fifteen-year period of mayoral control of the city, and the political fault line between the city of Boston and the Republican-dominated state legislature grew more prominent.

In 1913, the Boston Central Labor Union led a legislative initiative to establish a state university in the city of Boston.[51] The BCLU and allies successfully pressured the state legislature to pass a resolution in 1914 that directed the state board of education to report a "bill embodying a plan for the establishment of a state university" in Boston. The final conclusions of the subsequent report, however, recommended against its implementation. Notably, while Boston superintendent Jeremiah Burke was a member of the committee that drafted this report, the committee also included Frederick W. Hamilton, former president of Tufts University, who had played a key role in blocking a 1909 public college bill, and Paul Hanus, representing Harvard's Division of Education. The committee included several bankers and manufacturers, but no labor representative. The chief argument presented against the state university was cost. Private universities, the report concluded, already served the needs of college-goers, so instead of a costly duplication of efforts, the school board should cooperate with existing institutions.[52]

World War I gave renewed strength to organized labor in Boston, which shaped the landscape of education in several important ways. The repeated setbacks to public higher education led the BCLU to found its own Boston Trade Union College (BTUC) in the spring of 1919, among the first trade union colleges in the emerging national movement for workers' education.[53] Quoting an AFL statement on education, the school aimed to "awaken the mind to the application of natural laws and to a conception of independence and progress."[54] Operating out of the High School of Practical Arts school building, the BTUC offered free evening courses to AFL members and members of their families; in 1921 access was broadened to include any wage worker or family member. Despite the conservatism of their university administrations, many Harvard graduates and faculty members were sympathetic to labor and offered courses at BTUC, including professor of literature Henry Dana, professor of philosophy Horace Kallen, political theorist Harold Laski, and dean of Harvard Law School Roscoe Pound. Like the ILGWU school, BTUC classes were decided upon democratically by a committee of students, instructors, and union members, and students also voted on whether or not to keep a faculty member. Women unionists, especially members of the Telephone Operator's Union, participated in BTUC classes.[55] The school joined the Workers Education Bureau at its first meeting, connecting BTUC to ILGWU and Amalgamated-sponsored labor colleges, as well as worker colleges in New York, Washington, DC, Philadelphia, Pittsburgh, and Rochester.[56] The BTUC catered primarily to labor activists and was never intended as a mass training institution, but until its closure in 1931 it was a counterweight to the landscape of private colleges and universities in Boston.[57] As one BTUC student, Frank Fenton, explained, "I first believed that college was a step too high for one who left school at fourteen to enter the coal industry . . . but I have been gladly disillusioned." His professors had taught him that "education should not be the property of the few, but the right of all who wish to acquire it."[58]

In the spring of 1919, several faculty members of the BTUC were also involved in the formation of the first teachers' labor union in Boston. These faculty included Dana and Kallen, both on the executive committee of the campus-based Intercollegiate Socialist Society, as well as Laski, who had caused a dispute over academic freedom by defending striking police officers against Harvard's support for strikebreakers.[59] These instructors, along with two local high school teachers, received a charter from the American Federation of Teachers (AFT) to form the Greater Boston Federation of Teachers, Local No. 66, which was open to teachers in public schools, college, and universities in the Boston area. This "one big union" encountered some support from local public school teachers, including the new president of the Boston Teachers' Club, Cora E. Bigelow, whose organization now included over 1,000 women high school, elementary, kindergarten, and vocational teachers. Unionization encountered resistance, however, from male high school teachers opposed to the AFT's equal pay for equal work clause, as well as from women teachers skeptical of Harvard professors with socialist ties and the male-dominated labor movement. Three small gender-segregated teacher union locals were formed in the summer of 1919, but all three withdrew their charters by 1925.[60] For the next decade, Boston's teacher clubs continued to serve as the primary vehicle for collective action to improve teacher working conditions.

The militancy of 1919 gave new life to the struggle for a state university, although this postwar effort failed once again. In 1919, Superintendent Frank Thompson declared that "the day has come in Massachusetts to agitate" for a public state university in Boston, arguing that Massachusetts was falling behind western states that had already made college a guaranteed "democratic right" for all young people.[61] In 1922 the state of Massachusetts launched another commission to investigate the matter of establishing a state university, and this time the commission included a representative of organized labor. However, private university leadership, including the chair of the commission, BU president Lemuel H. Murlin, successfully opposed the effort. In public discussions of the bill, private school leaders repeated the argument that a state university would be subject to corrupt political control.[62] Despite the strong support from public officials, labor leaders, and Boston's working-class community, existing private institutions were instrumental in blocking a state university in Boston until the mid-twentieth century.[63]

While not a public state university, the Boston Normal School finally won authority in 1922 to grant bachelor of education and bachelor of science in education degrees. The traditional bachelor of arts degree, which only the oldest private colleges in Boston had authority to grant, was still off-limits. In 1924, the Normal School was renamed the Teachers College of the City of Boston.[64] By this date, private universities such as Harvard and BU had expanded their own education degree programs and had consolidated their role in the training of teachers. They also helped create and differentiate new administrative fields within the profession of education with far more power than teachers themselves.

University Training and Professional Differentiation, 1906–1940

Private colleges and universities took advantage of a growing market for collegiate teacher training. As high school enrollment surged in the first decades of the twentieth century, so did the number of women students who attended college in order to become high school teachers. Universities reacted to the influx of women students with policies that turned universities into key arenas for gendered professional stratification.

BU, the only co-ed university in Boston, saw a rapid increase of women students in its College of Liberal Arts: from 40 percent of the student body in 1880, women made up 76 percent by 1900. The vast majority of these students intended to become secondary school teachers. BU expanded its teacher programming, which had the effect of channeling women students away from its liberal arts college. In 1906, BU launched Saturday and afternoon courses for teachers, and in 1914, students intending to become teachers took six hours of education courses with a newly appointed education professor, Arthur Wilde. Wilde became dean of a new separate two-year school of education in 1918, offering bachelor of education degrees to aspiring teachers. This school quickly became the city's leading institution for teacher training: after starting with 170 students, less than the annual enrollment of the Normal School, this school was attracting over 2,500 students annually by 1930. The creation of a separate school of education helped tilt the gender balance of BU's liberal arts college back toward men.[65] At BC, women were first admitted in 1923 as students pursuing education degrees, while the liberal arts college remained closed to them until the 1970s.[66] In this way, these schools preserved the prestigious bachelor of arts degree for men, while expanding opportunities for women to obtain education degrees.

The evolution of Harvard's school of education best exemplifies professional differentiation along gendered lines through both educational credentials as well as professional subspecializations. The PSA alliance

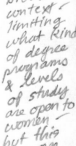

This also has a broader context — limiting what kind of degree programs & levels of study are open to women — but this is more subtle when ostensibly voluntary

directly shaped Harvard's professional educational offerings. Storrow, who had served on Harvard's Board of Overseers since 1897, helped to create an official "visiting committee" for Harvard's educational program in 1901, on which he served as a member and, later, chair, alongside other PSA members, including Joseph Lee, John Farwell Moors, and Lincoln Filene. Paul Hanus had been appointed as the first assistant professor of the "history and art of teaching" in 1891. Hanus worked closely with Storrow and the visiting committee to develop the mission and implementation of education courses at Harvard. His first three courses attracted only four male teachers. Due to this lack of interest, in 1892 education courses were opened to men college undergraduates, and in 1897, still facing low demand, they were opened to women Radcliffe undergraduates. Enrollment, especially among undergraduate women, grew, justifying the establishment of an independent Division of Education within the Faculty of Arts and Sciences in 1906.[67]

By 1917, women undergraduates made up 45 percent of enrollment in the Division of Education, while graduate-level courses were 94 percent men. The new dean of the division, Henry Holmes, believed that the reputation of the school was "directly proportional" to its male enrollment and was worried about its feminization, as were many of his colleagues. After a successful fundraising drive, Holmes converted the Division of Education into the Harvard Graduate School of Education (HGSE) in 1920, cutting all undergraduate courses and only offering a doctorate and a master's in education. This move immediately eliminated almost all women students. When women graduate student enrollment, primarily in the one-year master's program, caught up, reaching nearly 50 percent of enrollment by 1924, Holmes replaced it with a two-year master's degree program. His efforts to deter women from enrolling through additional credentials, however, were repeatedly outpaced by women. In 1929, women's enrollment at HGSE surpassed men's enrollment, at 206 to 178.[68]

By this date, HGSE had shifted its focus from training future teachers to training educational administrators and experts. This shift reinforced a gendered distinction within the education profession between teachers and administrators. While administrative positions such as principals and superintendents had long existed, universities played new roles in structuring pathways into each. Eliot had created a University Appointment Committee to help place male Harvard College graduates into teaching and faculty positions in 1897. However, given the low interest in teaching, Eliot and Hanus drew on their connections to public school systems to place male graduates into positions as principals and super-intendents around the Northeast. These efforts were incredibly successful. The *New England Journal of Education* reported in 1900, "Several important selections of superintendents and high school principals this season have established beyond question the efficacy of the department of education at Harvard University. . . . The man who takes that course and wins the respect and confidence of President Eliot and Professor Hanus is as sure of a good position as any man can be of anything." In 1917, the Division of Education launched its own Committee on Appointments, which became a placement office within the new HGSE. This office placed dozens of graduates annually. By 1929, while the majority of HGSE women graduates entered public school teaching positions, the majority of male graduates entered college faculty and administrative positions.[69]

Aligned with the PSA, university administrators also sought to carve out separate professional spaces for experts in the school system to further the goals of school and municipal reform, as well as to recruit more men. Emerging subfields of educational administration, many with links to managerial innovations in industry, institutionalized new services within school systems and also strengthened the power of predominantly male experts over a female teaching force. One subfield that developed in this context was vocational guidance. The director of the philanthropic Vocation Bureau of Boston, Meyer Bloomfield, had been working with the Boston Public Schools to train and appoint vocational counselors, while also working with business managers to develop the industry-centered personnel management movement. In 1918, when Bloomfield shifted to personnel management full-time, the Vocation Bureau was transferred to Harvard's Division of Education as the Bureau of Vocational Guidance.[70] By this date, Lincoln Filene had persuaded Pauline Shaw, both close associates of Bloomfield, to endow a faculty position in educational guidance at Harvard. In 1919 this position was given to John Brewer, a graduate of Harvard's Division of Education, who was also appointed as the new director of the Bureau of Vocational

Guidance. Brewer oversaw extensive research and helped build up a new administrative field of vocational guidance counseling.[71]

Another reform movement and professional specialization was educational measurement. In 1911, two years after becoming president of Harvard, Lowell tried to lure Edward Thorndike, a behaviorist scientist who had helped to develop the field of intelligence testing, away from Columbia University's Teachers College in New York. When he declined, Lowell appointed Thorndike's protégé, Walter Dearborn, who later launched a psycho-educational clinic to study mental testing at Harvard.[72] The mental testing craze among social scientists and the general public in the years around World War I helped popularize the link between occupation and innate ability. Harvard economist Frank Taussig, an avowed eugenicist, drew on the idea of innate intelligence to explain the higher salaries paid to business executives.[73] Mental testing was just one application of a broadly conceived field of educational measurement. The Boston School Committee opened a Department of Educational Investigation and Measurement (DEIM) in 1914, directed by Frank Ballou, a student at Columbia University's Teachers College and research fellow at Harvard. Ballou's research, under the direction of Paul Hanus, had focused on merit-based schemes for teacher appointment and promotion, the same issue that had repeatedly provoked Julia Duff's ire. In Ballou's view, the jurisdiction of his department was "the investigation of any educational problem which the school authorities have to solve."[74]

Not surprisingly, as one of its first projects within this astonishingly vast scope, the DEIM was tasked with reforming the merit list on which Boston teacher promotions were based. In addition, under the leadership of this department in 1921, Boston Public Schools became one of the first school systems to administer intelligence tests, and the 15,448 tests taken represented "the largest number of elementary school children which has been tested in any school system." The DEIM was staffed with college-educated researchers, helping to create a selective and prestigious tier of experts within the public schools.[75]

Teachers themselves were skeptical of the proliferation of educational experts. In her graduation oration for the Normal School class of 1917,

Dorothy M. O'Brien satirized the Department of Educational Investigation and Measurement:

> What do they investigate? Everything—even our most secret thoughts, words, and actions. . . . What do they measure? . . . Everything that can possibly be measured is measured. . . . My friends in the profession no longer eat at noon, for they must save time. One munches a bar of chocolate as she works; another needs only a glass of water and a date to keep alive the spark of life. . . . Just think what we are coming to! Beware that you do not become a pompous five-foot measuring stick. I am a healthy-looking specimen now, but I feel that I am not for long in this sphere. Efficiency takes hold of me.[76]

O'Brien's ridicule hints at teachers' resentment of the administrative experts who reshaped their everyday work experience and had significantly more power than they did within the school system. While powerful advocates within Boston's Irish working-class community defended institutions like the Normal School, private universities reshaped the training landscape through their new collegiate and graduate programs that awarded advanced credentials. Graduates of Harvard's Graduate School of Education monopolized the most prestigious leadership positions in school administration, while graduates of women's colleges and the Normal School became public school teachers.

As universities set the highest standard of prestige, Boston's Normal School, like other normal schools across the country, was pressured to conform to the norm of offering bachelor's degrees. Even among bachelor's degrees, however, a hierarchy existed: a bachelor of arts degree was more prestigious than a bachelor of education degree. This put Boston's Teachers College at a disadvantage, and ultimately it could not compete. After nearly shutting during the Great Depression due to lack of funding, in 1952 the college was absorbed into the state system as the State Teachers College at Boston. In 1960, it became Boston State College—the first public institution in Boston authorized to grant a bachelor of arts degree, but one no longer dedicated to the training of teachers.[77] Private schools of education in Boston would continue to dominate access to professional positions in education.

Educational Differentiation

The profession of education was and remains plagued by lower status than many of its professional counterparts. The early feminization of teaching reduced its status in the eyes of male educators and administrators, and the standing of public elementary schools where most teachers taught did not place it in a high-ranking position in the new corporate economy. As an occupation with one of the longest traditions of school-based training, teaching reveals the limits of educational credentials alone to elevate the status of an occupation. Its history also dramatically illustrates the creation of an internal ladder matching the class, ethnicity, and gender of its practitioners. Male, mostly Protestant, high school teachers sought to align with more prestigious private universities against public school–educated, mostly Catholic, women elementary school teachers. This same division emerged between the working-class support for a public university against the powerful interests of private universities and state officials. Institutions like the Normal School felt immense pressure to achieve degree-granting power to place their own graduates on equal footing with the graduates of private universities. But private universities, which were in the meantime expanding their own teacher-training programs, had significant control of state legislatures, and by the time the Normal School was granted degree-granting authority, it was no longer a significant threat to established private institutions.

Universities pursued new strategies to differentiate positions within the profession of education, largely on gendered lines. Universities played a new role as channels into administrative positions and created new professional subfields based on educational research, promoted to male students. Working with leading school reformers, university officials supported efforts to reorganize school committees and centralize power away from working-class representatives and women teachers. Despite early movements toward teacher organizing, in their new roles at the top of the professional ranks, male university graduates maintained authority over women professionals.

THE LEGAL PROFESSION

Practicing Law in Late Nineteenth-Century Boston

If Julia Duff was Boston's working-class teachers' champion, Gleason Archer was her counterpart in the profession of law. Archer founded his own evening law school in 1906 and mobilized both his students and Boston's Democratic political establishment against the "Educational Octopus" of Harvard University. Unlike Duff, Archer faced a profession dominated by male practitioners, and the school he championed was not an established fixture of Boston's public school landscape but a proprietary school he started out of his own living room. Despite these differences, the professionalization of law in Boston was shaped by similar class, ethnic, and gender-based conflicts that, as the site of training moved into elite schools, created an even more stratified profession.

Before the 1880s, law schools only played a marginal role in the formation of new lawyers. Less than 40 percent of notable lawyers listed in *Who's Who in America* in 1899 were law school graduates. Schools such as Harvard Law School (HLS) were primarily a means of developing contacts with established lawyers in preparation for a legal apprenticeship. After the Civil War, the expansion of large corporate and government bureaucracies created new legal specializations—tax law, government regulation, corporate and patent law, trust and estate planning—increasingly offered by larger law firms. Attempts to learn the basics of law in larger specialized offices became more difficult, and aspiring practitioners sought alternative forms of instruction.[78]

Legal practice also expanded in ways that created opportunities for attorneys from modest backgrounds. The growing political power of Irish Bostonians opened up lower municipal and police courts and judgeships to first- and second-generation immigrant practitioners. Rising work and transportation accidents created a market for personal injury lawyers, debt and wage disputes for civil suits, and growing urban policing and incarceration systems for criminal defense attorneys. These legal services were provided by a growing number of solo practitioners who advertised their assistance to working-class clients of their own ethnic backgrounds.[79] The growing number of Bostonians who aspired to become lawyers threatened the control of the profession by the traditional nineteenth-century legal elite. These attorneys lamented the "overcrowding" of their field by the sons of immigrants and called for the creation of bar associations. In 1876, thirty-seven leading attorneys formed the Boston Bar Association (BBA), whose ranks included well-connected politicians and an exceptionally credentialed group: 86 percent had attended college, three-quarters of them at Harvard. Exercising political leverage at the state level, the BBA helped create a new Board of Bar Examiners to administer the bar exam, staffed by its own members.[80]

The creation of this exclusive professional association corresponded with changes in university legal education. In 1870, as one of his first efforts to extend the public influence of universities by upgrading professional education, Charles Eliot appointed Christopher Columbus Langdell, a former Harvard College and HLS student, as dean of the law school. Langdell initiated a series of reforms intended to place university legal education on a "scientific" foundation. He hired law professors on a full-time basis and instituted the use of the case method of instruction, which quickly became the dominant form of pedagogy in law schools across the country.[81] By 1877 Harvard had changed its bachelor of laws (LLB) program from two to three years, and in 1893 it instituted a college degree requirement to enter as an LLB candidate. Despite these increased requirements, or perhaps because of them, enrollments grew rapidly in the 1880s and 1890s.[82]

Langdell's reforms took place amid a changing educational landscape. Beginning in the 1880s, part-time law schools emerged, and by 1900 their enrollment across cities in the United States had already surpassed enrollment in full-time day law schools. New law schools catered to a growing pool of aspiring lawyers who had experienced difficulty in securing apprenticeships. Many new law "schools" did not offer degrees; they were staffed by entrepreneurial practitioners who offered part-time study in the evenings to prepare students for the bar exam.[83]

The differentiation among professional schools came to reflect internal distinctions within the legal profession. A closer look at the implementation of the case method reveals the increasing divergence in legal skills within the legal hierarchy. Previous law instruction in schools had been based on studying local and state law and practicing oratory as preparation for arguing cases in court. Langdell's case method, however, entailed deriving broader legal principles from specific appellate cases. The case method marked a movement away from instruction in the content of the law toward instruction in legal reasoning, which could be applied to further research and investigation. While the case method was justified philosophically as the best form of training for a legal mind, it also met very practical demands. It allowed for a higher faculty-student ratio to accommodate rapidly growing enrollments, it replaced tedious recitations with more exciting cold-call quizzing (dignified as the "Socratic method") in large lecture halls, and, most importantly, it mirrored the skills required for the members of the most lucrative sectors of legal practice. Many HLS graduates entered the ranks of judges and state attorneys who wrote briefs and opinions, which required greater knowledge of the theory behind legal decisions than did the arguments of trial lawyers.[84]

The skills learned through the case method were also applicable to the emerging field of corporate law. While most nineteenth-century legal disputes had been over small sums of money, new corporations faced the threat of potentially high-risk lawsuits. Corporations hired lawyers, often retained on a long-term basis, to draw up contracts and arrange the firm's affairs in advance to prevent future challenges. Rather than the court advocate, the lawyer became the "office counselor," for whom mastery in theoretical legal knowledge and writing technical legal language was essential.[85] In the 1880s, Louis Brandeis, one of the pioneers of the modern law firm, hired almost entirely HLS graduates, trained in the case method and with the highest rankings in their classes, to work as salaried assistants and then partners.[86] Critics of the case method claimed that it was "in the bad sense, a schoolman's concept" that would not train court advocates in the "alertness and nimblemindedness of the active practitioner."[87] These criticisms were correct, but they missed the larger point. The new training reflected the divergence in the way that the courtroom lawyer and the office counselor practiced law.

The links forged between HLS and the corporate world were not merely pedagogical. HLS actively cultivated its ties to leading law firms through its far-reaching alumni network.[88] While HLS did not establish a formal placement office until the 1940s, professors before then regularly received information about openings in top law firms and recommended students. The office of the secretary also provided students with alumni contacts in cities such as New York and Chicago, where local alumni clubs functioned as informal employment bureaus.[89] Among Harvard College graduates through the 1920s, law was second only to business as a career path.[90] Harvard produced legal professionals who were overwhelmingly male, white, Protestant, and from upper-class backgrounds. The university's reputation depended on what Marcia Synott has termed "academic nativism," which entailed discriminatory admissions policies against Jewish students, Catholic school graduates, and women.[91]

Many graduates of HLS also joined the BBA, and this professional association helped draw a boundary around the most prestigious tier of legal practitioners. At the turn of the century, nearly 40 percent of Boston lawyers were immigrants or descendants of immigrants, half of them Irish. The BBA included half of all Boston's practicing lawyers in 1900, but only 3 percent of its members were Irish. While a few African Americans had been practicing lawyers since the 1840s, the BBA admitted its first African American member in 1915. BBA attorneys continued to advocate for raising entrance standards to the bar and strengthening links between their members, the corporate world, and select universities.[92]

Regulating Legal Education in Boston, 1893–1919

Harvard Law School played a central role in the standardization of training for the legal profession, both locally and nationally. The model of HLS—featuring the case method, a three-year program, full-time professors, and a carefully selected student body—quickly spread nationwide.[93] Because it was the standard bearer for institutional prestige, its admissions criteria had important consequences for surrounding institutions. In 1893, HLS adopted a new policy that as of 1895–1896, only those graduates of select, "respectable" colleges from a list printed in its annual catalog were to be admitted without examination. The list did not include a single Catholic college, despite the fact that a steady stream of Catholic college graduates had been attending HLS for years. In response to an outcry from Boston's Catholic press, Charles Eliot denied any anti-Catholic prejudice but also derided Jesuit education as being "retrograde" in its lack of attention to "modern" subjects such as science and foreign languages. Catholic college leaders, such as BC president Father W. G. Reed Mullan, countered that their classical curriculum was the best preparation for legal study.[94]

Harvard's list of respectable colleges was repeatedly used to disadvantage Catholic schools. After adding four Catholic colleges, including BC, to its list, new dean James Barr Ames decided to remove BC and Holy Cross in 1897. These were the only two institutions ever removed after being placed on the list. In 1904, after continued bad publicity, HLS simply ceased publishing its list. Applicants were directed to send inquiries to the secretary about the status of their school. BC's enrollment declined between 1898 and 1904, which historians have attributed to Harvard's discriminatory policies. BC would only launch its own law school in 1929.[95]

Harvard Law School also played a primary role in efforts to regulate part-time and evening law schools. Harvard had a cooperative relationship with the evening law school of the Boston YMCA, founded by HLS graduates in 1898, which frequently hosted HLS professors as lecturers. The YMCA was a central institution in the Protestant philanthropic community of Boston's leading families. Its law school catered to students who were otherwise excluded from the legal profession, such as Forrest Anderson, an African American waiter, union president of Local 183, and subsequent practicing lawyer in Kansas.[96] With the backing of both Harvard and the Massachusetts Board of Bar Examiners, the YMCA Law School was awarded the power to grant LLB degrees by the state legislature in 1904.[97]

Most schools, however, did not receive Harvard's blessing, including Gleason Archer's law school. Archer was the son of a Maine logger who, with the sponsorship of a Boston corset manufacturer, became a student at BU Law School.[98] As a second-year law student in 1905, he was approached by a colleague who wanted to pass the bar exam. By the fall of 1906, Archer had recruited nine students (including a second cousin) to "Archer's Evening Law School" in his home in Roxbury, holding classes four days a week for two hours. Over the next several years, Archer changed the school's name to "Suffolk," financed the school through student fees as well as the publication of several law textbooks, and moved the school to a suite of offices downtown.[99]

Archer repeatedly touted the humble origins of his school and students. Most Suffolk Law School attendees were small proprietors, low-level managers, salesmen, and local or state politicians, who were using legal training to upgrade their jobs. In a 1928 survey of Suffolk alumni, most had opened solo or joint legal partnerships with other Suffolk graduates, in general or specialized practice in insurance, probate, tax, real estate, and domestic and family law. Many found work in local politics or government agencies, some taught law themselves, and others pursued nonlegal work in the insurance and banking industries. No Suffolk graduates were employed in the State Street corporate firms of Boston's legal elite.[100]

By 1911, Suffolk Law School had grown in size, but so had the stigma attached to "evening law" students. Archer established a day department for his school, not because of demand, but so that Suffolk could be advertised as a higher-status day school. More importantly, he believed, the creation of a day department would increase his chances to win degree-granting power from the state legislature. While law degrees played a minor role in the preparation for legal practice in the nineteenth century, by 1911 they had become an important marker of standing. Archer considered degree-granting power "necessary if the school were ever to become a success."[101]

Suffolk Law School's petition for degree-granting authority encountered fierce resistance from the legal and educational establishment of Massachusetts. As Archer put it, Harvard viewed "with alarm the prospect of Suffolk graduates . . . coming into competition with the spineless aristocrats who form so large a proportion of Harvard Law School graduates." In reality, HLS and Suffolk Law School catered to very different demographics and were not in direct competition. However, Suffolk Law was in direct competition with the Harvard-sponsored YMCA Law School and also threatened to siphon students away from BU's school of law. Archer's bill faced opposition from all of Boston's law schools, the local and state bar associations, and the state board of education. In the first hearing on Suffolk's petition, President Lowell of Harvard argued against conferring degree-granting authority without a state board of education investigation. Frank Speare, dean of the YMCA Law School, also spoke in opposition, although his position was undercut when he admitted that he himself had never studied law. Lowell was backed into a corner when he admitted that if Suffolk could prove to be equal to the YMCA Law School, the school should be given degree-granting authority. In the meantime, the dean of BU Law School sent a letter to each member of the state legislature urging defeat of Suffolk's bill.[102]

Archer garnered political support for his school among a sizeable number of Democratic legislators. Suffolk's lawyers, many of whom worked in the local and state court systems, had ties to Massachusetts Democratic politicians or held elected office themselves. Archer managed to pull together a board of trustees for his school that included former Democratic candidates for governor and former congressmen, and with these endorsements, he "lined up the whole Democratic vote of the House and Senate." During the hearings, Democratic ward boss Martin Lomasney also emerged to defend the bill, exclaiming, "Don't let the lawyers of this body make a trust of legal education in Massachusetts." Here, the growing fault lines between the city of Boston and the state of Massachusetts again emerged.[103]

Despite having "the support of every Democratic Senator and of eighty percent of the Democrats in the House," the Suffolk Law School bill was vetoed by Governor Foss, first in 1912 and a second time in 1913. Foss, the antilabor Republican turned Democrat, aligned against his nominal party and with the legal and educational establishment of Massachusetts. Foss himself was a trustee of the YMCA Law School, and before the first veto Foss had privately consulted with the state commissioner of education, David Snedden, who hastily prepared a negative report about Suffolk Law School.[104] In addition, in between the first and second veto, the state legislature passed an act that mandated any petition for degree-granting authority would first be referred to the state board of education, which would then submit its recommendation to the legislature. This act thus strengthened the state board's authority over degree-granting power.[105]

Archer, however, did not give up his fight. By the time Foss vetoed his bill a second time, Archer had gained not only widespread media attention but additional support from powerful Democratic constituencies, including labor unions, who were furious that Foss would twice veto a bill against a majority of his own party. The controversy over Suffolk Law School contributed to Foss' loss in the 1913 gubernatorial election. His successor, Democrat David Walsh, became the first Irish governor of Massachusetts. Archer's bill was signed into law in March 1914.[106] In the next decade, Suffolk's enrollment boomed, surpassing that of HLS, as illustrated in Figure 5.3.

Suffolk's success points to the limits of elite practitioners' control through legislative means. However, the state educational establishment would continue to consolidate control of degree-granting power. In 1919, the state legislature further strengthened the power of the state board of education with an act that required a petition for degree-granting power to first obtain approval from the state board, effectively turning the state board into a gatekeeper. The act also made usage of the term "college" or "university" by an institution that did not have the authority to grant degrees an offense punishable by a fine of $1,000.[107] These legal regulations helped cement the dominance of the most wealthy and established institutions in the educational landscape. The graduates of distinct schools entered different rungs on the professional ladder. As each school consolidated its niche along this ladder, the distance between rungs grew greater.

Gender and the Professionalization of Law

The fact that law remained the most exclusively male profession in Boston through this period, at 93 percent men practitioners in 1940, was no accident.[108] Rather, it was the outcome of an active campaign by male attorneys against women's legal practices. The history of legal aid exemplifies the ways in which professional strategies were used to keep women out of law.

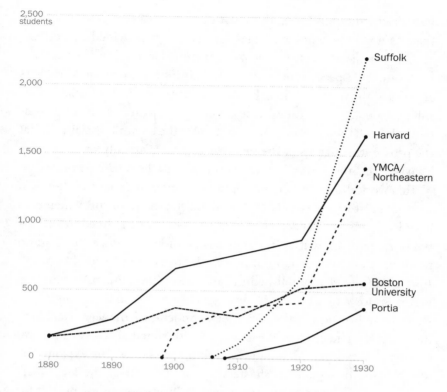

FIGURE 5.3: Enrollment in Boston-area law schools, 1880–1930.

DATA SOURCES: *RCE 1880* (Washington, DC: GPO, 1882), 656, 702; *RCE 1890–91*, vol. 2 (Washington, DC: GPO, 1894), 1404, 1440; *RCE 1901*, vol. 2 (Washington, DC: GPO, 1902), 1660–1661, 1762–1763; *RCE 1910*, vol. 2 (Washington, DC: GPO, 1911), 890–891, 1054; *BSE 1918–1920, Statistics* (Washington, DC: GPO, 1923), 337–338; *BSE 1928–1930*, vol. 2 (Washington, DC: GPO, 1932), 442–444. © Cristina Groeger.

Although in some states women would have to wait until the Nineteenth Amendment in 1920 to be admitted to the bar, a few women in Massachusetts broke this barrier in the late nineteenth century. Since its founding in 1872, BU Law School had been open to women, and several attended every year, including Lelia Robinson, who in 1882 became the first woman to gain admission to practice law in the state.[109] Women also provided an array of legal services even without passing the bar exam. In the 1870s, upper-class women had organized protective agencies offering legal assistance to working-class and immigrant women in major cities, including the Women's Educational and

Industrial Union (WEIU). The most common type of case was wage theft of domestic workers. Legal services were provided by college-educated women volunteers, most of whom had learned law through the trial and error process of on-the-job training, as many male lawyers also did at the time. While WEIU's protective committee initially consulted male attorneys on all cases, within four years, women staff settled half of all their cases themselves. In 1882 the committee claimed that the prosecuting agents of the department "have already attained such legal skill that the Boston bar could properly call them *sisters-in-law*."[110]

This work did not meet the approval of male attorneys of the BBA, who sought to "professionalize" legal aid for the poor. BBA members founded the Boston Legal Aid Society in 1900, which aimed to address the stark class disparities in the provision of legal services but had no room for women who had not passed the bar exam. Reginald Smith's *Justice and the Poor*, published in 1919, exemplified this new reformist vision. Smith, a 1914 Harvard Law graduate who began his career on the staff of the Boston Legal Aid Society, condemned the legal establishment for their neglect of the poor.[111] Smith noted that instead of receiving quality legal aid, poor and working-class men were exploited by fee-charging disreputable "shysters" at the bottom of the legal hierarchy. "Shysters" and "ambulance chasers" were common epithets for immigrant Jewish and Irish lawyers, most of whom trained in evening law schools.[112] Smith's critique also encompassed women practitioners. Smith lumped women's legal work and the emerging field of social work into the category of unscientific and sentimental "charity," which was not up to the appropriate professional standards of legal aid. He also argued that women's legal work disproportionately aided women clients, which skewed legal aid away from its proper focus on male breadwinners. In the 1920s, the National Association of Legal Aid Organizations received support from the American Bar Association (ABA), founded in 1878, to help increase the "correct" type of legal aid by local bar associations across the country. This professionalizing process restricted the legal work of women and immigrant attorneys and limited the access of working-class women to legal services.[113]

While women continued to be excluded from leading law schools and professional associations (the BBA admitted its first woman in 1916, the

ABA in 1918), part-time law schools opened some doors.[114] In 1908, the partner of Gleason Archer, Arthur W. MacLean, founded Portia Law School, the first women-only law school in the country. MacLean was not motivated by a political commitment to women's rights, but like his partner he saw an untapped market. After 1919 when Portia successfully won a state charter to grant LLB degrees, enrollment grew to hundreds per year, including the former president of the Boston Teachers' Club, Cora Bigelow, who attended law school and passed the bar in 1922 while continuing to teach during the day.[115] The YMCA Law School began to admit women when it became part of Northeastern University in 1923.[116]

In navigating the professional landscape, women's law schools and women lawyers faced severe restrictions and often a gendered double standard. In 1929, MacLean petitioned the state board of education to make Portia Law School co-ed by admitting male students. That year, Portia's women graduates passed the bar at a rate of 65 percent, compared to the average pass rate of 40 percent. MacLean's petition was refused, however, on the grounds that the standards of Portia Law School were "not high enough."[117] Women lawyers did carve out some spaces within the legal profession, including domestic relations and juvenile cases. Professional demarcation into "masculine" and "feminine" specialties was the predictable result of exclusive practices by the male legal elite.[118]

National Regulation of Legal Training, 1920–1940

Ultimately, the tentacles of the Educational Octopus proved to be of insufficient reach to prevent new schools like Suffolk and Portia from granting degrees and the bar from admitting a more diverse range of attorneys. Undeterred, the legal elite of Massachusetts allied with national legal professional associations and persisted in their efforts to raise national standards of the profession through forms of accreditation. This project faced many challenges. The ABA only included 3 percent of lawyers among its members by 1910, compared to 50 percent of doctors in the American Medical Association.[119] The American Association of Law Schools (AALS), founded in 1900 by leading law schools including

Harvard, was an even more exclusive national group of deans and law professors. The AALS and the committee on Legal Education and Admission to the Bar within the ABA were inspired by the 1910 Flexner report for the medical profession, sponsored by the Carnegie Foundation. The Flexner report legitimized the closing of many "sub-par" proprietary medical schools around the country, including some of the few run by and catering to African Americans.[120]

The ABA and AALS solicited the Carnegie Foundation to produce an equivalent report for the legal profession. Henry Pritchett commissioned Columbia PhD Alfred Reed to write a report, which was published in 1921 as *Training for the Public Profession of the Law*. Upon its publication, AALS legal professionals were disappointed. While Reed noted the problem of unregulated and exploitative law schools, he argued that shutting down evening and part-time law schools would deprive "Lincoln's plain people" of access to the practice of law as well as access to most legal services. Against the concept of a "unitary bar," or a universal set of standards for legal practices, Reed argued for the value of different types of schools, catering to distinct populations, for a range of legal services.[121]

AALS members redirected their efforts to raising the admissions standards of their own professional association. Law school members were required to have a full-time faculty, a large library, a three-year length of study, and to practice the case method. Harvard Law School, unsurprisingly, was the gold standard. The AALS focused in particular on the provision that law schools should require two years of college as an admissions requirement, and that only graduates of those law schools should be allowed admission to the ABA. This requisite was strongly opposed by evening law school leaders such as Gleason Archer, who feared that it would create a "college monopoly" on legal education.[122]

Although many ABA members shared Archer's views, the AALS worked to influence the policies of the ABA by strategically packing a 1920 meeting to ensure their own nominee, Elihu Root, would be placed in charge of a new ABA committee on legal education. In 1921, the same year the Reed report was published, the ABA committee on legal education brought forward Root's recommendations and passed the two-year college requirement through the ABA. These and future membership requirements helped pressure schools to conform, although their reach was still limited. Because state law, rather than the ABA, governed the requirements to pass the bar and practice law, many schools and lawyers continued to operate without meeting their recommendations. In 1927, only about half of law schools met ABA standards, and only one-third of law schools belonged to the AALS.[123]

The Great Depression spawned a long sought-after wave of legislative action that narrowed training pathways into law. As the income of lawyers fell, many left the profession, and struggling proprietary evening schools, facing enrollment declines, were forced to close. Remaining practitioners were more amenable to the argument that stricter requirements for practice should be imposed on an "overcrowded" profession. In 1934, Massachusetts adopted the "college monopoly" prerequisite: applicants to the bar had to have two years of college study and have completed law school. Whereas in 1932 only seventeen states had adopted the two-year college requirement, in 1938 forty states had. Nationally the percentage of students in ABA-approved schools increased from 32 percent in 1928 to 64 percent in 1938.[124] Even Archer himself was pressured to conform: the same year that the two-year college requirement became law, he launched a new college of liberal arts alongside his law school to capture students who might otherwise obtain their college study elsewhere prior to entering law school.[125]

By 1940, 77 percent of all practicing Boston attorneys reported having at least four years of higher education. In the meantime, the demographic composition of lawyers had shifted significantly, as depicted in Figure 5.4. In 1930, Russian Jewish practitioners were significantly overrepresented and made up one-quarter of all Boston attorneys. Women, however, made up less than 7 percent of lawyers in 1940, and African Americans made up 0.8 percent.[126] As late as 1967, there were only sixty practicing Black lawyers in the entire state of Massachusetts, and only two integrated firms in Boston.[127] Indeed, despite the expansion of diverse practitioners and law schools, law remained an exceptionally restricted profession.

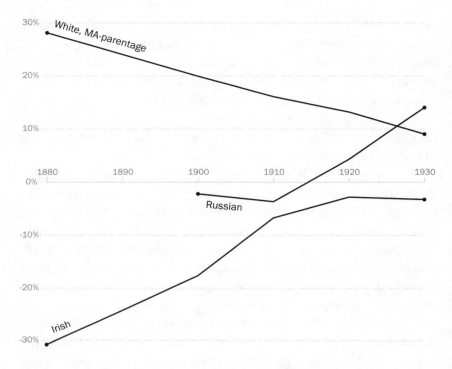

FIGURE 5.4: Overrepresentation by ethnicity of male lawyers in Boston, 1880–1930.
DATA SOURCE: IPUMS 1880–1930, 1890 estimated. © Cristina Groeger.

CONCLUSION

As schools and universities restructured pathways into the professions, old hierarchies persisted. Public and proprietary schools helped working-class students acquire marketable skills as well as access to social networks that facilitated their entry into the professions of education and law. Concerns about a changing educational and demographic landscape led established practitioners to seek to raise standards and place their profession on a "scientific" basis. By establishing professional associations, forging ties with universities, and working with the state, elite lawyers and educational administrators could monitor, regulate, and set the gold standard for professional training.

The battle over degree-granting authority between the educational establishment and schools such as Boston Normal School and Suffolk

Law School laid bare the gender, ethnic, and class divisions of Massachusetts politics. Irish women, the Democratic Party, organized labor, and the city of Boston lined up against the Protestant, Republican-dominated male leadership of the state. In both cases, the champions of the working class won the degree-granting power they had hoped for, but by that point each profession was already steeply differentiated. Boston's Teachers College and Suffolk Law School graduates entered the bottom of the professional hierarchy, while Harvard-educated administrators and corporate lawyers entered the highest ranks of the profession. Women made up the majority of the teaching force but few reached the ranks of administration; in the case of law, women practitioners were relegated to a feminized sliver of the profession, if not pushed out entirely. The boundaries erected around the most remunerative and high-powered professional specializations were legitimated on the basis of their connection to some of the oldest Boston Brahmin institutions. Despite the transformation of the professions in this period, the top of the professional ladder looked strikingly familiar.

If law and education exemplify the remaking of long-established professions, the transformation of business offers an even more dramatic illustration of the changing significance of a college credential in the making of a new profession. Boston's traditional universities and financial elite mutually constructed a new corporate workplace and culture. In the process, schools became the institutional basis for reproducing long-standing hierarchies redefined as educational merit, and consolidated significant economic power for themselves and their graduates.

SIX

Placement in Corporate America

In 1935, Robert C. Hosmer, vice president and general manager of the Excelsior Insurance Company of New York, was looking to hire a new insurance salesman. He sent an inquiry to the director of the Harvard University Alumni Placement Service, James F. Dwinell, whom he knew from years of correspondence about prospective employees. An Excelsior salesman needed to be a "good mixer" and a "gentleman" with a "good personality."[1] Dwinell replied to Hosmer on March 11, 1935, with a description of "a possibility for you":

> Dear Bob . . . Burns graduated in '28 and is now 31 years old. While in college he was pretty active in extra-curricular affairs. He played on the baseball team three years, being Captain in his Senior Year, was on the track team three years, and was on the football team his Senior Year. He was a member of the Hasty Pudding, the Institute, and the Varsity Club. . . . He [strikes] me as being a bright, energetic, rather attractive young man. His father was a Nova Scotian and the family are Protestants.[2]

This exchange was one of thousands that occurred between employers and the Harvard placement office in the years between 1897 and 1940. During these years, the college degree became a coveted credential in the world of business. According to one national survey, in 1900 fewer than one-fifth of American business leaders were college graduates. Of those who assumed leadership positions between 1921 and 1940, over half had secured this credential.[3] During this period, small family enterprises were overshadowed by large manufacturing corporations, chain stores, and financial services companies staffed by vast bureaucracies and led by college-educated managers and executives.

While recent studies of the corporatization of American universities have focused on developments after World War II, the modern university and corporate economy were already inextricably linked in the early twentieth century.[4] Major industrialists made enormous donations to universities, providing much of the capital for this expanding sector.[5] Scientific knowledge circulated between the academic and industrial worlds, fueling new research disciplines and management techniques.[6] Universities also became the chief training ground for a new cohort of business managers and executives.

Like education and law, the professionalization of business during this period should be understood as a reaction by traditional economic elites and university officials to broad political and economic changes. Boston Brahmins looked on as wealthy industrialists accumulated vast fortunes, and the legitimacy of corporate management was threatened by industrial disputes and populist revolts. They saw immigrants rising as a proportion of Boston's proprietors and managers, and while most were small shopkeepers, an increasing number of them entered midlevel managerial roles and executive positions.[7] They witnessed the dramatic feminization of white-collar jobs and the swift expansion of competitor schools. As public high schools displaced proprietary schools in this expanding market, some proprietary schools refashioned themselves as postsecondary collegiate institutions, directly competing with Boston's established colleges.

In the face of these trends, elite Bostonians with close ties to degree-granting institutions adopted new strategies to maintain their position in a rapidly changing social order. Leading colleges and universities became key spaces for acculturation and the forging of networks between the children of leading Bostonians and wealthy newcomers, as these institutions strategically shaped their student bodies through selective and often discriminatory admissions policies and degree requirements.[8] Business leaders saw the benefit of aligning with the cultural prestige and scientific legitimacy of universities to buttress their own managerial authority.[9] While the roles of admissions policies and socialization strategies in elite formation have been well documented, the ties that facilitated the placement of graduates into employment have not been as carefully scrutinized. These included the direct mediation of college placement services, in which universities used alumni networks to develop personal relationships with firms to place selected graduates.[10] Not all students used these services, but the letters between university officials and employers, including those between Dwinell and Hosmer, document the transformation of the college degree (and subsequently the MBA) into a coveted credential that facilitated entry into the higher ranks of business.

In forging employment pathways for their graduates, universities and employers defined the meaning of educational merit. The immense bodies of correspondence between their representatives reveal that technical knowledge was but one component of a broad range of criteria, which included personality traits, social activities, mastery of cultural norms, physique, gender, religion, race, and ethnicity. Universities developed placement services not only to help their graduates find high-paying jobs, but also to cultivate an institutional reputation based on the qualities and characteristics of their graduates. By assisting or hindering their graduates' employment options, universities shaped the composition of the upper class beyond their walls, and employers found a reliable service to deliver the type of "college man" they preferred into their offices and boardrooms.

The professionalization of business can thus be understood historically as the successful construction and deployment of educational credentials by elite practitioners to reserve the most lucrative executive positions for individuals like themselves. Financial and business elites made up less than 1 percent of the entire male workforce in Boston and, through the 1930s, remained overwhelmingly native-born white men with long roots in the Northeast.[11] A 1917 study of 200 CEOs of leading US firms found that less than 1 percent were Catholic and less than 0.5 percent were Jewish. Over one-third had parents who were also company executives and less than 1 percent had fathers who were manual workers.[12] While Jewish businessmen did enter the top ranks of the corporate world, they did not surpass 10 percent of business leaders in the Northeast before 1950 and, even after that point, remained segregated socially. African Americans, Asian Americans, and women were almost entirely barred from entry.[13]

Women's liberal arts colleges, like their male counterparts, similarly aligned themselves with the business world in the early twentieth century. While Boston's private women's colleges continued to place the majority of their graduates into teaching positions, they developed alumni networks and placement bureaus to place predominantly white women into high-status positions as secretaries and office or store managers, albeit subordinate to male leadership.

By 1940, colleges and universities had become the chief pathway for positions at the top of the corporate hierarchy. While informal personal networks continued to operate, they often did so through social networks developed on college campuses. For larger firms that could no longer rely solely on a small network of trusted relatives or personal connections for their hiring needs, select schools came to serve as a "surrogate family."[14] As college enrollments and degree-programs expanded, an educational hierarchy of degree-granting institutions grew steeper.[15] Harvard University continued to set the standard of prestige to which many colleges and universities aspired, even as they found their own niche in the higher education landscape. Upper-class families increasingly turned to the most elite universities as the primary way to secure their class position and status. The marriage of university credentials and corporate leadership in this period laid the foundation for the present-day role of elite institutions in channeling their graduates into business positions with immense economic power.[16]

This chapter begins with the uneasy relationship between businessmen and higher education before turning to the rapid transformation of the business world and the reorientation of Brahmin institutions to it. I examine in detail the role of placement services in facilitating the entry of college graduates into business jobs, the criteria on which placement was based, and how the entry of collegians reshaped the corporate workplace and corporate culture. I then turn to the proliferation of business degree programs before examining the limits of college credentials, exemplified by their distinct significance for women entering business. The rewards of advanced educational credentials came to symbolize, and reinforce, a faith of academic merit in leveling the economic playing field. However, this faith obscured its meaning in practice and legitimized its unequal rewards.

THE PATRICIAN VERSUS THE BUSINESSMAN

In the late nineteenth century, the relationship between business and traditional colleges was fraught. Although many sons of Boston Brahmins were educated in the classical curriculum of Harvard College, the primary orientation of the college was still to the learned professions, not business. Most businessmen were ambivalent about the "college man," whom they considered to be condescending and impractical. Henry Dennison, a Harvard graduate in 1899 who became president of the paper company founded by his grandfather, described the "typical slang" businessmen used to refer to college graduates: "He knows it all," "He hasn't got his feet on the earth," "He isn't willing to get his hands dirty," "He expects good things passed to him on a silver platter."[17] Many professors, such as economist Thorstein Veblen, were eager to distinguish their emerging scientific enterprises from the vulgar world of profit-seeking and, correspondingly, disdained vocational subjects like business.[18]

But the city of Boston was undergoing a rapid transformation. Immigrant establishments, largely catering to ethnic clienteles, had long been a central route to economic advancement in Boston, and their success led to a declining share of proprietors with Massachusetts parentage, depicted in Figure 6.1. Russian Jewish immigrants were already overrepresented among small proprietors by 1900 and occupied 25 percent of these positions by 1930. For example, the father of Esther Zarkin first found a job sewing caps through a family contact when he arrived in Boston in 1900 before launching his own cap-making company. His business grew from a handful of employees to fifty employees by 1920. The majority of those whom he hired on the production and business side of the company were relatives or other Russian Jewish im-

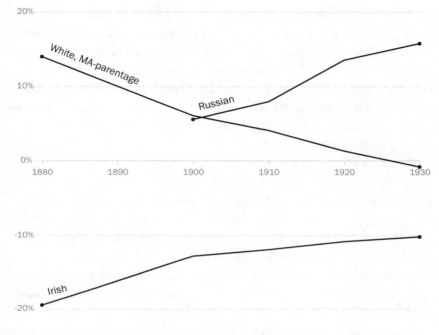

FIGURE 6.1: Overrepresentation by ethnicity of male owners and managers in Boston, 1880–1930.
DATA SOURCE: IPUMS 1880–1930, 1890 estimated. © Cristina Groeger.

migrants.[19] Although Irish immigrants were never overrepresented among proprietors, they made up an increasing percentage of them. Boston's small Chinese community developed strategies of shared pools of credit and regulated competition that allowed Chinese entrepreneurs to dominate the laundry business. African Americans were the exception to this story. Southern-born African Americans in Boston were three times more likely to establish businesses than the Irish in 1880, but over half of Black businesses between 1880 and 1890 failed, whereas the comparative rate for Irish businesses was under 30 percent.[20] Compounding discriminatory practices, this failure rate further lowered African American credit ratings and access to capital.

Small immigrant establishments represented more of a cultural than an economic threat to Boston Brahmins, as they did not directly compete with the large firms whose managerial and executive positions were reserved almost entirely for men of New England heritage. The greater threat to Brahmin authority was an emerging national elite. While still maintaining a strong presence in finance and corporate law, Boston's economic leaders were losing their class position relative to financiers, executives, and industrialists in other cities profiting from railroads, oil, and mass-production industries. While Boston patricians may have looked down upon the "flashiest profiteers," they needed to forge ties with those in key economic positions in order to become integrated into this national upper class.[21]

Brahmin institutions such as Harvard, which increasingly sought to attract students from outside of New England, stood to gain from a new orientation to business. In this period, Harvard was more interested in recruiting students than excluding them: as late as 1940, Harvard College admitted 90 percent of applicants.[22] By recruiting from a national pool, colleges and universities gained access to new alumni donors and extended their cultural influence over the industrial world. In turn, these institutions offered sons of the nouveau riche social refinement as well as access to eastern financial networks. Many wealthy sons attended private secondary schools, from which Harvard drew over half of its students in 1908. Such schools and colleges facilitated a mutually beneficial marriage between an old and new upper class.[23]

The groundwork for Harvard's institutional shift toward the world of business had already begun with the reforms of Charles Eliot. While earning the scorn of some classical educators who held "vocational" training in contempt, Eliot believed any subject was worthy of study at its highest levels: "We would have them all, and at their best."[24] "All" fields included the emerging field of business management. An outspoken critic of proprietary commercial schools, Eliot instead supported what he called an "upper commercial school" that would be "parallel with a college or scientific school." These institutions would train a middle tier of businessmen for occupations such as public accountants, merchants, managers, and foreign consuls. For aspiring "captains of industry," however, Eliot believed that a liberal arts college education was the best preparation.[25] The Harvard curriculum of his design included an elective system, in which students could specialize in natural sciences, social sciences, humanities, or foreign languages. In any of these subjects, Eliot believed, a collegian "develops and increases his own powers, and gains command of those powers." The mental training and discipline offered by a college education was what made it appropriate for entering the business world, according to Eliot.[26] He supported the organization of business-related courses for Harvard undergraduates, such as principles of accounting, which was first offered in 1900.[27]

The benefits of Harvard's turn to business were quickly apparent. Enrollment remained high: as men's enrollment in Boston's degree-granting institutions doubled nearly every decade between 1880 and 1930, Harvard College consistently made up about one-third of that enrollment, higher than any other institution. Its students increasingly pursued business jobs. With remarkable speed, the minority of Harvard College graduates who entered business grew into a majority. In 1897, 15 to 20 percent of graduates obtained positions in business; by 1908, a full 50 percent did.[28] Business retained its popularity over succeeding decades, and pathways into these positions were aided by the careful cultivation of relationships between university officials and company representatives.[29]

COLLEGIATE PLACEMENT SERVICES, 1897–1940

College graduates had long relied on informal connections through their classmates or professors to secure employment. Universities pursued numerous strategies to formalize these ties, including strategies similar to those used by proprietary schools, such as the internal employment bureau. The purpose of Harvard's Appointment Committee when it was founded in 1897 was to place professors and teachers, but a branch of this committee coordinated with the Harvard Alumni Association, an organization dating back to 1842, for students seeking business positions. By 1908, teaching placement and business placement services had been split in two.[30] While male staff officially directed placement into business positions, the bulk of the work was carried out by an "appointment secretary"—a college graduate named Ruth Mork—who served in this capacity for twenty-two years.[31] In these decades, the Alumni Appointment Office placed 100 to 200 graduates each year in business-related positions. With around 400 students in each graduating college class between 1900 and 1917, these placements represented a substantial proportion of Harvard graduates.[32]

At the turn of the century, established institutions like Harvard had the advantage of a large alumni network. Harvard's Alumni Appointment Office developed relationships with hundreds of employers, coordinating with Harvard alumni clubs across the United States. While the heaviest concentration of employer contacts was in New England, where over half of all graduates in the 1920s stayed, the office made a concerted effort to "nationalize" its placement service after 1925.[33] The crash of 1929 prompted an infusion of resources to placement services for students entering a depressed labor market. From a staff of one secretary and stenographer in 1898, the office was expanded into the "Alumni Placement Service" in 1929, which included three male supervisors, two male directors, and two female staff.[34]

The Alumni Placement Service adopted another marketing practice first pioneered by proprietary schools that proved crucial to its success. This was the publication of a special bulletin sent to employers nationwide advertising registered candidates and highlighting their academic records, extracurricular activities, and personal attributes.[35] This type of national outreach facilitated the disproportionate impact of Harvard and other well-resourced universities on the emerging corporate scene.

New professional associations helped facilitate the connections between college placement officers and company personnel departments. While the National Association of Appointment Secretaries (NAAS) was founded in 1924 by women serving in these roles, including Harvard's own Ruth Mork, this organization was ignored by an expanding cohort of male administrators. Walter Daly, a Harvard alum and administrator in charge of student employment, coordinated with other male placement officers at the Massachusetts Institute of Technology (MIT), Boston University (BU), and Massachusetts Agricultural College to form the Associated College Employment Officers in 1926. When a placement officer and "Advisor of Women" for the Harvard Graduate School of Education, Miriam Carpenter, inquired about the relationship between this organization and the NAAS, Daly admitted he had no familiarity with the latter association, and to distinguish his organization further, he changed its name to the Eastern College Personnel Officers (ECPO).[36]

In the reorganization and expansion of the office several years later, these aspiring male professionals, all Harvard alumni, transferred Ruth Mork's nearly 1,000 employer contacts, developed over two decades, to her new male superiors.[37]

ECPO gatherings became an important site for networking between colleges and employers. Although representatives from women's colleges attended, the focus was overwhelmingly on placing male college graduates into business.[38] Over time, representation in ECPO expanded geographically, and placement officers and employment managers across the country formed close professional and personal ties.[39] When the employment manager of Ohio-based Procter & Gamble Company left his firm in September 1940, he made sure to introduce his replacement, David Watt, to the directors of Harvard's placement office.[40] A few weeks later Watt wrote to the assistant director, Donald Moyer, noting how much he had enjoyed meeting him and how much he looked forward to getting better acquainted when he visited Cambridge.[41]

These ties were further reinforced as personnel circulated between universities and firms. Paul Viets, one of the founding members of ECPO from Massachusetts Agricultural College, left his academic post in 1927 to take up a job as industrial relations manager of the Plymouth Cordage Company.[42] James Dwinell, who graduated from Harvard in 1902, had been an employment manager at the New England Telephone and Telegraph Company before becoming the director of Harvard's Alumni Placement Service in the reorganization of 1929.[43] Other colleges and universities saw the benefits that these services could provide for their own institutions and their alumni. In 1925, 44 percent of large universities in the United States had organized placement offices.[44] By the 1940s, most colleges and universities had joined one of a growing number of regional and national placement associations that vied for professional dominance.[45]

THE MEANING OF ACADEMIC MERIT

The records of the Harvard placement office between the 1920s and 1940s have preserved the frank correspondence between school officials and employers about qualities valued in prospective employees. Employers based their decisions on a mix of technical knowledge, social and cultural skills, personal characteristics, and assumptions about what particular activities and pursuits revealed about college graduates. Specialized technical knowledge was essential for certain jobs, especially engineers and scientists. The Walworth Company called for "experienced metallurgists"; Lever Brothers in Cambridge was "eager to see promising young chemists at any time" for "general industrial chemistry work."[46] The placement office compiled lists of students who had taken courses in physics, math, and advanced economics.[47]

Technical knowledge, however, was a necessary but not sufficient condition for employment in engineering and scientific research positions. Social skills and cultural norms were also valued. Kendall Mills, a textile company headquartered in Boston, wanted scientists who had the "ability to get along with others"; it preferred to hire a chemist with an "advanced degree and industrial experience, though personality and adaptability come first."[48] Firms also distinguished between prospective technicians and those whom they wanted to groom into executives. For the latter group, cultural knowledge and social skills were of particular importance.

The parallel development of Harvard and MIT illustrates the distinction between these two types of college graduates. Among a growing field of private technical schools, MIT actively cultivated a reputation for training the best engineers and industrial researchers. Before 1916, MIT was known as "Boston Tech," and it had a solid reputation as an institute that prepared future technicians. Chemistry professor William H. Walker and engineering consultant Arthur D. Little promoted a new vision of MIT with close ties to industry and at the forefront of applied science. In 1908 Walker established the Research Laboratory of Applied Chemistry, funded by industrial firms and employers' associations. Richard C. Maclaurin, president of MIT between 1909 and 1920, fostered these connections, and funding from donors such as George Eastman and T. Coleman du Pont made possible MIT's move in 1916 across the Charles River to Kendall Square, a center of manufacturing in Cambridge. Taking advantage of the proximity of multiple factories, Walker established the cooperative School of Chemical Engineering

Practice, in which MIT undergrads spent part of their time in school and part in industrial plants.[49] Walker's efforts culminated in the 1920 "Technology Plan," which aimed, through industrial cooperation, to "maintain a steady stream of trained men constantly flowing into industry with the best preparation for scientific work," which would in turn "swell the store of knowledge on which the scientific progress of the community, as a whole, depends." Firms paid a fee to MIT in exchange for the technical and consulting services of MIT graduates. Like a labor bureau, MIT was contractually obliged to "maintain a record of the qualifications, experience and special knowledge of its alumni," and to share this information with cooperating companies.[50] MIT first organized an employment bureau in 1902 that coordinated with designated faculty in each department to place graduates, and placement services greatly expanded over the next two decades.[51] Between 1910 and 1920, undergraduate enrollment at MIT almost doubled from under 1,500 to over 2,700 students.[52] Department chairs, especially in engineering fields, reported regular requests for technically trained men, often more than they could supply.[53]

MIT's success in placing engineers and scientists shaped a distinctive reputation for its graduates relative to those of Harvard, apparent in the debate over a potential Harvard-MIT merger. The success of MIT as an engineering institute, as well as financial concerns, led to repeated merger attempts by the leadership of Harvard and MIT between 1869 and 1912. The overwhelming majority of MIT alumni believed that a merger would destroy MIT's independence as a technical institute as opposed to a liberal arts college.[54] There were also strong demographic differences between the two institutions: a greater proportion of MIT students came from working-class backgrounds, nearly 30 percent of students were international, and women attended MIT in small numbers.[55] Critics of the merger such as Francis Walker, president of MIT from 1881 to 1897, contrasted the hard-working MIT student with the Harvard undergraduate who could be seen "loafing in academic groves" and "browsing around among the varied foliage and herbage of a great university."[56] There was some truth to this caricature. Harvard undergraduates at the turn of the twentieth century were overwhelmingly the sons of wealthy New Englanders, and the social tone was set by "club men" who were catered to by a small army of "uniformed servants" and who lived in luxurious private dormitories that recalled "the splendor of a Venetian palace."[57]

These divergent reputations had an impact on their graduates' employment prospects. John Ripley Freeman, an MIT alum who headed a successful hydraulic engineering consulting firm, supported the merger plan in 1904.[58] Freeman argued that MIT only trained the corporals of industry, while Harvard trained the captains. What MIT students lacked was the general education of a liberal arts college, which would propel its graduates into higher positions in the corporate hierarchy. Employers reaffirmed this distinction. In the 1920s, Howard Coonley, president of the Walworth Company, said, "If I want to obtain engineers I go to an institution which specializes in training engineers of a certain type, but if I want an engineer executive I always seek a man who has had a general course of engineering training."[59] An executive was expected to have a "general" training in addition to their technical specialization.

While the MIT–Harvard merger plan ultimately failed due to a legal technicality, MIT began to expand humanities and social science requirements in ways that reflected Freeman's and Coonley's observations, as well as a broader shift in elite engineering education.[60] MIT economist Davis Rich Dewey (the brother of philosopher John Dewey) was instrumental in launching Course XV in engineering administration in 1914. The course was designed "to fit men for administrative positions" and included classes in law, history, economics, and scientific management.[61] With funding from Alfred Sloan, an alumnus of MIT and president of the General Motors Company, Course XV eventually became MIT's Sloan School of Management in 1965.[62] As other engineering schools in Boston expanded, MIT graduates were groomed to enter higher managerial and executive positions. A 1910 survey of MIT alumni found that 9 percent were in executive positions; by 1939, 20 percent were.[63] The cultivation acquired through a liberal arts education was an increasingly important prerequisite for future executives.

Over one-quarter of Harvard College students who entered business after graduating in the 1920s went into finance and banking, among the most remunerative business positions. While this proportion dropped to 8 percent at the height of the Great Depression, it was still among the most popular pathways for Harvard graduates.[64] For these exclusive positions, academic knowledge was important primarily as an indicator of ingenuity and problem-solving abilities. In 1936, the Boston investment bank Kidder, Peabody and Company, whose partners included several "Harvard men," reached out to the Harvard placement office for "promising Seniors with 'spark.'" Among the requisites, partner Chandler Hovey wrote, was "outstanding records scholastically, as such records indicate brains." As Hovey elaborated, "We are not looking for clerks; we have plenty of those. We are looking for the type of young men who have enough imagination and intelligence to work up into responsible positions." The magical combination of "brains" plus "spark" was something intangible but identifiable. Hovey admitted that he himself had never attended college, but, he said, "I remember distinctly when I was at school that there were always some scholars who were head and shoulders above the others."[65] Employers often possessed a vision of the brilliant "college man"—a vision that encompassed many implicit qualities beyond measurable academic performance.

CRITERIA BEYOND ACADEMICS

In addition to attributes nominally based on academic training, a wide variety of social, cultural, and personal qualities were also the subject of extensive correspondence between Harvard placement officers and employers. Marketing and sales jobs, which made up nearly one-third of business job placements of Harvard graduates in the 1920s and 1930s, placed a high premium on personal appearance and an affable yet aggressive personality.[66] Procter & Gamble sought a man for its sales department who was of the "dominant type" with an "impressive appearance."[67] In its request for salesmen, the Dennison Manufacturing Company specified that the candidate "must be a diplomat, good sales type. No timid souls."[68] Unmarried men were preferable, especially in sales, since salesmen were expected to travel frequently.[69]

James Dwinell regularly included information about extracurricular participation in his letters to employers. Evidence suggests employers believed extracurriculars demonstrated important leadership qualities and interpersonal skills. Procter & Gamble representative David Watt wrote to the Harvard placement office of his interest in men who "have demonstrated qualities of leadership and managerial ability in their campus activities."[70] Membership in fashionable fraternities or social clubs could also serve as a proxy for desirable employees, as these clubs selected out a wealthy, Protestant "aristocracy among students" within an increasingly diverse student body.[71] By the early twentieth century, campus activities had become, for many Harvard students, more important than academics. According to alumnus George Biddle, in 1910 "by the measure of undergraduate and graduate prestige—college activities far outweighed scholarship; athletics outweighed undergraduate activities; social standing—the importance of club life—outweighed them all."[72] Employers were interested in these informal student hierarchies, as reflected in their attention to a student's "standing" and popularity. In a letter to the American Steel & Wire Company, Dwinell wrote that one prospective employee was "reasonably active in athletics, and is very popular socially."[73] To Kidder, Peabody, and Co., he wrote of another student, "Although his scholastic achievements have not been outstanding, his extra-curricular activities provide testimony to his personal characteristics and are evidence of his standing among his classmates. He is a member of the varsity hockey squad, secretary of the Lampoon, a member of the Hasty Pudding-Institute of 1770 and the D.U. Club."[74]

The latter club was among Harvard's "final" clubs, which mainly admitted those who had attended select private boarding schools.[75] Before 1940, many Northeastern private boarding schools were much more selective than Harvard College, overwhelmingly enrolling the children of Boston Brahmins plus a small number of the children of wealthy outsiders.[76] The path from elite boarding school, to membership in Harvard's final clubs, to jobs in finance, was a well-worn channel by the first decade of the twentieth century. Between 1906 and 1912, all but one of the members of the two most exclusive final clubs (the Porcellian and the A.D.) came from an eastern prep school, and in 1926 all members of the Porcellian came from three schools: Groton, St. Mark's, and St. Paul's.[77] Of graduating members of the Porcellian and the A.D. between 1880 and 1930, over 50 percent went into banking and finance.[78] According to a 1912 observer, it was "a fact known and traded on among the undergraduates themselves" that these clubs served as an "open sesame" into the top business positions.[79] Harvard administrators tolerated these clubs because they fostered intense club loyalties that translated into alumni donations.[80] Without the mediation of a placement office, these clubs thus created a privileged internal track within the already rarified environment of Harvard College.

Intercollegiate athletics had been an essential component of college life since the late nineteenth century. They were a centerpiece of student campus culture and school spirit, and participation was promoted by administrators as a means to foster the personal qualities valuable in the workplace.[81] In praise of athletic contests in 1881, Charles Eliot commented that "the perseverance, resolution and self-denial necessary to success in athletic sports turn out to be qualities valuable in business and other active occupations."[82] A fine-grained hierarchy also existed among sports teams. George Biddle, himself a graduate of Groton School, considered football and rowing the most prestigious teams, followed by track, tennis, golf, and soccer. Beyond that, he said, "very few Grotties went in for baseball. . . . One hardly knew the fellows who played lacrosse or basketball . . . and never, never, never, the members of the wrestling or debating teams," as these students "were probably Jews."[83] Intercollegiate athletic leagues, including the "Ivy League," first referred to as such in the 1930s, became important "status clubs."[84] For Boston collegians who did not participate in the top tier of campus activities, there were rapidly growing opportunities in less exclusive fraternities and sororities, campus journalism and student publications, student government, literary and debating teams, and music and drama clubs.[85] Because these student organizations tended to maintain strong ties with their alumni, who often helped fund extracurricular organizations, participation in these groups opened up valuable social networks and could provide employment opportunities after graduation.[86]

The Harvard placement office, while aiding a broader cross section of students than those who belonged to sports teams and social clubs, did seek to provide employers with employees who matched their own understanding of a "college man." Many descriptors that placement officers used to describe candidates were proxies for other characteristics, particularly class. Lower-class graduates were usually described as "chaps," with adjectives that connoted roughness and resilience. For example, the son of a packing-house foreman and mechanical engineer by training was "a substantial chap"; a Catholic student recommended for production work was described as a "small but very husky sort of chap"; the son of a mining engineer recommended for production in a foundry was "a rugged, self-reliant chap who knows how to take it." Students from lower-class backgrounds typically had attended public high school, were the recipients of scholarships, and worked part-time during college and over summers. This personal history was made known to potential employers, which likely factored into their hiring decisions and exacerbated class disparities.[87]

Some companies asked directly for information about religion, race, and ethnicity. Procter & Gamble desired "men of good ability and personality, not in last quarter of class, and Christians preferred."[88] Kendall Mills requested Protestants.[89] The International Business Machines Corporation in New York asked for photos of students and information about "what [his] father does," because the company believed that "family background [was] important in estimating [a] boy's capacity and interest."[90]

Because there were so few candidates who were not white Protestants, the Harvard placement officers tended to note exceptions. In correspondence about a prospective employee for Kendall Mills, Dwinell wrote, "He is good-natured, cheerful, and does not betray too forcibly in his appearance that he is of Levantine origin."[91] Regarding another student, Dwinell wrote to a Connecticut manufacturing company, Landers, Frary & Clark, "It has, of course, occurred to me that you may not react favorably to Woodhouse's record on account of his race. I realize that it is difficult to imagine a native of India being particularly successful in working with New Englanders. I want to reassure you, however. . . . Woodhouse is extremely attractive and has made good with all kinds of people around here."[92] Over the next few years, Landers, Frary & Clark would continue to ask for detailed information about "pedigree" and would follow up about "peculiar" names to confirm that students were of desirable nationalities.[93] When the American Telephone and Telegraph Company (AT&T) in New York sought a statistician and Moyer recommended a Jewish student, he reassured the personnel manager that "although Bernstone is Jewish, he is one of the most popular men in the department."[94] These were instances in which Harvard placement officers chose to recommend students despite their racial and religious characteristics. It is not knowable how many were passed over entirely.[95]

Jewish students were of particular concern to Harvard administrators. From less than 1 percent of the college student body in 1881, Jewish students made up more than 20 percent by 1922.[96] President Lowell responded by attempting to implement a 15 percent Jewish admissions cap the same year. When this blatant form of discrimination failed, he led changes to admissions criteria by 1926 to include selection based on "character and fitness," a passport-sized photo, and questions about religion and ethnicity. He also appointed climatology professor and cofounder of the Immigration Restriction League, Robert DeCourcy Ward, to the Harvard admissions committee. Needless to say, these efforts effectively achieved the same result as a quota.[97] Once on campus, Jewish students were socially ostracized. In 1922, less than 4 percent of Jewish students belonged to social clubs, and between 1912 and 1918 none belonged to the five most prestigious final clubs. Harvard freshman dormitories, a project of President Lowell to reduce class divisions among college students, became another arena of racial and ethnic discrimination. Housing allocations were made on a caste system that included a "Category X" for Jewish students, and Black students were excluded entirely.[98] Even as Harvard admitted students who were outside of the Boston Brahmin caste, administrators and classmates found new methods of enforcing social boundaries.

The placement office became an important tool to delineate these boundaries as well. While the Harvard placement office promoted itself as a service to aid all students, its officers openly admitted among alumni circles that they did not help everyone who registered. Addressing the Harvard Associated Clubs in 1930, Dwinell explained that graduates could be classified into three categories. About 10 percent of each class consisted of successful men who were eagerly sought by employers and were thus easy to place. A much larger second group encompassed men "of capacity, but whose personalities do not so clearly reveal that capacity." Dwinell offered an example:

> I have one man whose case concerns me very much. He is grad-
> uating from College at the age of 26, and he worked four years
> between the grammar and high schools. . . . He came to Har-
> vard and majored in English Literature with a better than av-
> erage standard, but he still speaks the language of the small
> town machine-shop. Harvard may have deepened his under-
> standing of English literature, but superficially he is just what
> he was four years ago. In no outward respect is he a college man.
> He has sought four opportunities [through placement] unsuc-
> cessfully. . . . It is the men in this group that constitute the real
> placement problem. They are not the type of men the average
> employer has in mind when he says he wants college men.[99]

Academic achievements notwithstanding, this was a working-class
student who would never be a "college man." A third category of men,
according to Dwinell, was made up of low-achieving students whom the
placement office would simply not help, students who really "should have
gone to work directly after leaving high school and never gone to college at all." Dwinell implied that a college education had been wasted
on these students. The placement office should not assist them, he explained, because the office "is finally going to be sold, not by advertising,
but by the men placed."[100]

In correspondence with employers, placement officers would often
state that they did not have anyone who fit the bill. In 1936, Dwinell wrote
to the Excelsior Insurance Company, "While we have one hundred or
so men registered [in that geographic area], frankly there is not one of
them whom I care to suggest to you."[101] The Harvard placement office
was careful to help leading firms find exactly who they wanted with respect to class, race, ethnicity, and any other attributes that employers desired. In this way, deferring to the preferences of large employers, the
Harvard placement office exerted significant power over the meaning
of a college credential for different students. Even a Harvard degree did
not offer the same benefits to everyone.[102] College policies and informal
campus organizations, as well as placement practices, served as mechanisms through which a select few could be culled even from within a
larger institution.

THE CREDENTIALED CORPORATE WORKPLACE

The pathways from leading universities to leading firms strengthened over time. Once alumni moved into executive positions, they often favored those from their own alma mater. Between 1896 and 1939, AT&T and its subsidiaries hired between one and fourteen Harvard graduates per year and became one of the largest employers of college graduates in the United States by the 1920s.[103] Henry Dennison was partial to other Harvard alumni for new hires at his manufacturing company.[104] In 1930, general agent Frank Bobst of the John Hancock Mutual Life Insurance Company in Boston wrote to the Harvard placement office to express the firm's continued interest in alumni: "In view of the fact that a number of Harvard graduates have been and are now members of the sales staff of this Agency . . . we will be most interested to interview others who might qualify for work of this sort."[105] In this way, employers used academic credentials as an initial screen, selecting from a pool that was likely to share certain qualities with existing staff. As the hiring needs of larger firms exceeded the capacity of personal networks to secure trusted employees, membership within a community of alumni—of an elite college, or even a social club within a college—served as a substitute.

The entry of college graduates into business significantly shaped the corporate occupational structure. Employers benefited from easy access to a supply of employees with desired characteristics as well as the prestige and social networks that college graduates brought to their firms. At the same time, most graduates had very little experience in the actual operation, let alone management, of business. Large firms restructured their internal training procedures to accommodate this lack of experience. Many created distinct "tracks" and training programs for college graduates, who started at the bottom and would rotate through departments before being promoted to managerial roles. At Lever Brothers, college graduates started as "messengers" before advancing to administrative positions.[106] In the early 1930s, Procter & Gamble developed a yearlong salesmanship training course for future division managers as well as a preforemanship training course to groom collegians into factory superintendents.[107] Because firms usually hired college graduates in order to promote them to management, these graduates quickly surpassed less-educated employees in the race to attain executive positions.[108]

The common practice of starting college graduates at the bottom was evocative of an apprenticeship that taught novices the ins-and-outs of the firm at a low cost.[109] This policy also had the effect, however, of weeding out students from lower-class backgrounds who could not afford to live in a city like Boston on such a small income. In correspondence with Filene's Sons Company, Moyer noted that one prospective employee "questions whether he can afford to accept employment in Boston for as little as you are prepared to offer him"; two other candidates, said Moyer, "are local boys and I assume are interested."[110] Based on data from vocational surveys of graduates in the 1920s and 1930s, a large proportion of Harvard graduates lived at home with parents immediately after college.[111] Boston consulting firm Lichtner Associates expected a new hire to be "able to support himself for a time," which reflected an assumption that he would have access to assistance from parents or significant financial savings.[112] As with prestigious unpaid internships in the present, being able to forgo a livable income for a time was the cost of entry into the most desirable firms.

Employers pitched a low starting salary as a meritocratic means of proving oneself as a dedicated, worthy employee. The Employers Group, an insurance company, explained, "We are willing to start them in on what we call a livable wage and from there on it's up to the man himself."[113] Waldo Adler, a Harvard alum and Philadelphia-based real estate executive, preferred to hire "entirely green" graduates as salesmen, who would serve a six-to-seven-year-long apprenticeship on a commission basis before earning a salary. Adler was one of many employers who specified that they did not want graduates who had previously worked for competitors, which was likely to ensure that new employees did not have conflicting loyalties.[114] Some firms, such as Procter & Gamble, developed summer internship programs for college juniors and seniors as a way to cultivate loyal recruits fresh from college.[115] In these ways, college graduates were habituated to become dependable, devoted corporate employees.

The influx of college graduates into business also shaped a new corporate culture. In the upper echelons of the business world, alumni were increasingly surrounded by other collegians. An actuarial clerk for the State Mutual Life Assurance Company in Worcester, Massachusetts, remarked in an alumni survey that "at the neighboring desk is a Yale grad—behind me is a New Hampshire man with a year's graduate work in Math at Brown; my 'boss' is a Yale man, and the Actuary himself is a University of Toronto graduate."[116] One Harvard graduate started as a messenger at Lever Brothers with six colleagues from his Harvard class. Alumni enjoyed working with fellow college graduates and described their associates as "high grade" men who made work more "pleasant" and "attractive."[117] If not living at home, college graduates often boarded and socialized together.[118] These associations spilled over into their professional life, especially in the context of investment and marketing jobs, in which lunching or playing golf with clients was part of day-to-day work.[119]

Alumni also took to heart the superiority of college-educated men. These attitudes are expressed most clearly in their descriptions of non-college-educated associates. One Harvard alum who worked among "high school graduates . . . of both sexes" in the classified ad department of a Cleveland newspaper described his coworkers this way: "For the most part a fine lot, but many of them little children as far as ideas and social development is concerned."[120] Another accountant for the New Jersey Bell Telephone Company was surrounded by "clerks drawn from the lower middle class" and claimed that they were all "of indifferent intelligence and small education."[121]

Because college graduates often experienced rapid promotion, a common way to refer to less-educated associates was to suggest their limited promotion prospects. "My associates were mostly high school or less products without the desire to accomplish anything more advanced than what they were doing," stated one New York *Daily News* clerk. Another AT&T accounting clerk wrote, "Only a few were college grads. . . . Majority were of the type that would never receive much advancement."[122] The failure of a college graduate to receive rapid promotion was, in turn, a major blow to his own self-worth as a collegian. One

Harvard graduate working at Dennison Manufacturing claimed that his clerical job was one "any elementary high school pupil could do," and added, "I feel quite useless, and it is a 'deflating' thought to think that if I left the company I would not be missed one iota."[123]

These attitudes of entitlement and superiority were racialized and gendered. One insurance agent of the Harvard class of 1920 complained that he dealt with "petty Jewish types principally. Unprepossessing, uninteresting and for the most part unintelligent."[124] Many college graduates had women working for them as secretaries and stenographers. These women were commonly referred to as "girls," and some male collegians expressed annoyance with the "petty office politics" of women employees.[125] Some college graduates especially resented having superiors that subverted the racial and gender hierarchy. A sales employee of Godfrey L. Cabot Inc., a Boston-headquartered chemical company, wrote, "The person immediately over me was a Jewess who had been working there five years. She was most ignorant and domineering."[126] As male college graduates increasingly filled the higher ranks of management, they internalized an occupational ladder that conflated an elite college credential with intelligence, job proficiency, ethnic background, and gender.

UNIVERSITY DEGREES AND THEIR LIMITS

The rising number of college graduates in business prompted changes in the institutional landscape of business-training institutions. Harvard University leaders supported a professional school of business open only to college graduates. If put on a scientific basis and guided by the ethical ideal of service, business could become the "newest and possibly the greatest profession," claimed Henry Dennison.[127] Many educators and businessmen would have agreed. Ongoing labor strife and cyclical recessions threatened managerial power and highlighted management's potential as a tool for social reform in the eyes of progressive businessmen including Edward Filene, Henry Dennison, and Louis Brandeis.[128] At the turn of the century, economist Frank Taussig and then–professor of government Abbot Lawrence Lowell drafted the plan for a new professional business school at Harvard. In 1908, the Harvard Graduate School of Business Administration (HBS) opened, offering a two-year master's in business administration, with courses including accounting, commercial contracts, banking, and finance.[129] The core of the curriculum was scientific management, drawing on the ideas of Frederick Taylor, who lectured annually between 1908 and 1914.[130] By 1929, the school had grown to over 1,000 students annually, and over 40 percent of that year's graduating class entered positions in banking and finance, the majority as investment bankers.[131] The HBS placement office, founded in 1923, only aided those students deemed most worthy of its assistance.[132] Even with this selective policy, by the mid-1920s the HBS placement office was placing a majority of registered graduates.[133] While half of HBS students were Harvard College graduates when the school first opened, in 1926 Harvard graduates only made up 15 percent, while the rest of the students came from 203 other colleges around the country and internationally.[134] In the 1930s, HBS placement officers made in-person trips to promote alumni to leading businessmen across the United States, helping to turn the MBA into a coveted credential nationally.[135]

While Harvard dominated the niche of bachelor of arts and graduate degrees, other Boston colleges and universities began to offer tailored bachelor's degrees in business subjects. In 1911, the YMCA won degree-granting power for a male-only evening School of Commerce and Finance, which offered bachelor's and master's degrees in commercial science. Enrolling nearly 700 annually, it became one of the largest schools of the newly incorporated Northeastern College in 1916; by 1920 it was the primary training institution for certified public accountants in the state.[136] In 1913, BU founded an evening (and subsequently daytime) College of Business Administration (CBA), which offered a bachelor's degree in business administration. By 1925, the CBA enrolled over 4,000 students per year, which far outpaced all of BU's other schools.[137] Never one to forgo an educational opportunity, Gleason Archer launched his own college of business administration in 1937, incorporated (with his law school and liberal arts college) into Suffolk University the same year.[138] Boston College (BC), which in 1913 had relocated to Chestnut Hill in suburban Newton, opened a male-only school of business administration in

1938 at its new "Intown Center" on Newberry Street in Boston, offering bachelor of science degrees in business administration.[139]

Across the country, programs of "higher commercial education" multiplied.[140] Compared to the traditional bachelor of arts degrees, these degrees typically required one or two years of study and were often attainable via evening classes, which made them attractive and accessible to working adults. As these programs multiplied, non-degree granting proprietary schools faced more pressure to seek degree-granting power for themselves. Private university leaders and the educational associations they led continued to play an outsize role in shaping standards for what institutions could grant degrees and call themselves "colleges." The Carnegie Foundation adopted a four-year secondary school prerequisite as a college standard in 1906, and in 1920 the New England Association of Colleges and Secondary Schools made a minimum income from sources other than student fees (such as an endowment or large donations) a college standard, which effectively excluded many small proprietary schools.[141]

The race to open new collegiate business programs may be partly understood as a response to the feminization of white-collar work and the surge of women students in proprietary schools, public high schools, and colleges. Advanced business education was a way of elevating men above "dead-end" feminized clerical jobs. As with the separation of BU's school of education from its liberal arts college, BU's CBA was also designed to combat the reputation of its liberal arts college as a "girl's college." BU alumni organized a "More Men Movement" promoting a new, evening, collegiate business school to tilt the gender balance toward men. Upon opening in 1913, BU's CBA initially counted 234 men and forty women among its students, and for a time it did have the desired effect on BU's gender balance. However, the number of women in the school quickly rose. This prompted, in 1917, the creation of a women-only secretarial science department, which became a separate College of Secretarial Science (CSS) in 1919. This school had the desired effect of siphoning off a significant proportion of women business administration students. By 1925, the CSS enrolled 900 women, and the CBA enrolled another 900 women but also over 3,000 men.[142] BC's business school explicitly aimed to train "upright and God-fearing ... Christian gentlemen" for "the various fields of business activity."[143] Often driven by the demands of their alums, institutions like BU and BC used their degree-granting authority to differentiate men's and women's credentials and launch their preferred male graduates into the upper levels of business employment.

Despite these efforts, women attained college degrees in increasing numbers, outpacing each new credentialed hurdle. The meaning of a woman's credential, however, was distinct from that of her male counterparts. In the 1870s, women collegians had been considered "social rebels"; by the turn of the century, many upper-class families chose to send their daughters to college. Popular magazines contrasted the studious woman collegian with the man who attended "because his father or his grandfather went there" or because he wanted to join the football or crew team. Boston-area women's colleges also developed an elaborate array of extracurricular activities, including literary and debating societies, sororities, and athletic teams such as rowing, tennis, golf, and basketball.[144] For more affluent Catholics, Boston's Catholic college network expanded with the addition of two new Catholic colleges for women: Emmanuel College, which opened in the Fenway in 1919, followed by Regis College in the Boston suburb of Weston in 1927. Both of these colleges granted the bachelor of arts degree and featured a similar array of extracurriculars.[145]

Like high schools, colleges offered social mobility not only through potential job opportunities after graduation but also through marriage. While affluent women like Marian Peabody had attended social functions in Boston organized outside of schools in 1880, by the turn of the century college campuses had become popular settings for co-ed interaction. At the largest co-ed institution in Boston, BU, one student recalled, "People come here [for] an A.B. degree and go away more often with a marriage certificate." Although most of Boston's colleges were gender segregated, this did not hinder co-ed social interaction: the largest women's college in a Boston suburb, Wellesley College, regularly hosted formal dinners and dances attended by men from "brother colleges," including Harvard, Yale, and Amherst.[146] Colleges thus became important settings for "assortative mating," in which elite men and women picked partners with similar educational levels, maintaining their status and financial standing through intermarriage.[147] At the turn of the century, about half of women college graduates and one-third of male college graduates married spouses with at least some college education; by 1940 these percentages had grown to over two-thirds of women college graduates and 40 percent of male college graduates.[148]

Even if most women college graduates would eventually leave the paid labor market for marriage, the majority worked for a time after graduation, and a growing minority pursued a career in addition to marriage. Teaching was still the most popular career path for women college graduates, but a larger number began to pursue business work, which could offer higher pay and greater opportunities to interact with men.[149] After giving up its Domestic Reform League in 1910, the Women's Educational and Industrial Union's (WEIU) women's appointment bureau became a placement service for women college graduates. The bureau's director, Laura Drake Gill, was also president of the Association of Collegiate Alumnae that represented women college graduates across the country. Under her leadership, the WEIU bureau focused on placing college women into "non-teaching" professions, which primarily meant business jobs. It developed extensive connections to firms more than a decade before placement networks for male college graduates, through professional associations like ECPO, achieved the same level of coordination.[150]

While the WEIU bureau aspired to promote new professions for women, the pathways into employment were restricted. It was the rare female college graduate who became a top manager or executive herself.[151] More commonly, in large firms, women tended to reach the position of stenographer, secretary, or midlevel manager (typically managing other women), while remaining subordinate to male executives.[152] Many women were content with their positions. However, according to one 1926 national survey, 20 percent of secretaries hoped to use their job as a "stepping stone" into higher managerial or professional positions, and some complained about the limits of advancement and salary.[153] Specialized college degree programs—such as BU's College of Secretarial Science or Simmons's secretarial studies program—aspired to elevate but, in practice, demarcated the feminized positions of secretaries, stenographers, and office and department store managers.[154] Credentials and placement services ran up against the limits of the corporate hierarchy set by those with the most power.

CONCLUSION

By 1940, colleges and universities structured pathways into the top of the corporate world. The changing composition of the upper class, the influx of women and immigrants into business, and the expansion of business-training schools provoked a reaction among traditional elites and university leaders seeking to maintain their prestige and power. Business leaders and the most well-connected universities—increasingly linked on a national scale—mutually strengthened their control of corporate leadership. As the history of placement services demonstrates, universities did not merely reflect the organization of the corporate world but, through their administrators and alumni, actively forged its composition and culture.

A close historical reconstruction of the nexus between elite universities and American business leaders allows us to observe the process through which administrators and employers defined the criteria that defined one's value in the modern corporate economy. While technical skill and scientific expertise may have been the external justification for a new hire, the historical record reveals many other factors at work. Employers looked not only for knowledge and skill but also proper socialization and status, based on a particular range of gendered, racial, ethnic, and class traits. These criteria had long operated to reproduce inequalities; now they operated within the structure of colleges and universities, partially disguised under notions of academic merit and supposedly neutral credentials. As graduates entered the business world, rose through the ranks, and recruited graduates similar to themselves, they replicated the forms of knowledge and personal traits that typified those from their own alma maters or even narrow social networks within these institutions.

Based on the success of the alumni they promoted, elite universities helped set the standards of prestige to which other students, and institutions, aspired. Surrounding degree-granting colleges and universities developed business programs and placement services to establish niches in this competitive landscape. Competition between institutions fueled the proliferation of a variety of business degrees and credentials, the holders of which entered distinct rungs on the corporate ladder.

Through the creation of an upper echelon of college-educated corporate managers and executives, private universities played a central role in transforming business into a profession. These business professionals would lead the implementation of new managerial practices that enhanced the power of management over employees and helped consolidate the corporate restructuring of the American economy. By 1929, this restructuring had created an economy with one of the highest levels of social inequality in US history. In 1880, colleges and universities had served as one among many cultural institutions through which economic advantage could be reproduced. By 1940, the most exclusive of these institutions had become key markers of elite status and primary institutional bases through which upper-class families could secure their economic power.

Conclusion

Schools, Inequality, and Worker Power

The expansion of education, on the face of it, appears to be an unqualified good. What could be the downside of broadening opportunities for inquiry, discovery, and self-realization? As resolved by the American Federation of Labor in 1919, education promised to "awaken the mind . . . to a conception of independence and progress."[1] Before the establishment of a public university, Boston's Trade Union College was premised on the ideal that education, including advanced knowledge, should not be the exclusive domain of a wealthy elite, but open to all. Learning was a source of power to which, in a democracy, everyone could lay claim.

Schools also provided many students with access to good jobs. It would be misguided to discount the economic benefits that education provided to a large number of those who attended. For a Bostonian like Esther Zarkin, education offered not only knowledge and personal fulfillment, but also a way to find a respected and remunerative occupation as a bookkeeper. Today, despite repeated laments about students' careerism and the vocationalization of the educational system, the economic role of education should not be dismissed. For students who have been promised the chance of a better life through education, using school to find employment can be a source of pride and often a means of survival.

Yet the history of education in the United States reveals that education has always been embedded in a broader political and economic context. New educational opportunities, therefore, cannot be added without changing the environment around them. In the United States, schools were shaped by conflict and coalitions between a wide range of organized interests, with winners and losers. The expansion of schooling relevant to each sector of the economy was shaped by, and in turn shaped, the balance of power between workers and employers. Our modern school system and the inequalities of our modern corporate economy grew up hand in hand.

In the years between 1880 and 1940, workplace training gave way to school-based training for the majority of occupations. Philanthropists, public officials, employers, teachers, families, and students from different class, racial, and ethnic backgrounds supported the expansion of educational opportunities, with different understandings of what this expansion would accomplish. By the end of this period, a strong faith in education as a solution to social ills was solidified. Far from being a mere ideology, this faith was based on the lived experience of many students able to achieve social advancement through their schooling. In particular, white women and working-class, second-generation immigrants were able to use schools to access preferable employment in office and sales work. Some were able to use advanced educational credentials to enter emerging professions in key nodes of the corporate economy.

At the same time, a narrow focus on the experiences of success may obscure the full consequences of this transformation for the occupational structure as a whole. For one thing, such a focus neglects the ways in which educational expansion allowed employers to undercut evolving forms of worker power and shift the bulk of their workforce to low-paid operatives and contingent staff. Furthermore, in response to rising school enrollments, professionals used college and university credentials as tools of exclusion. Enduring forms of discrimination increasingly operated *within* the structure of formal education, hidden behind seemingly objective assessments of merit. Ironically, thus, at the same time that education became and was increasingly lauded as a means of achieving the American dream, schools became a new foundation for the reproduction of social inequality.

Many educational projects were attempted; most failed. By taking a broad view of the economy as a whole while distinguishing between different economic sectors, we can more easily identify patterns of school success and failure in the restructuring of pathways into employment. Educational failures were nowhere more obvious than in the case of low-wage and industrial work. A key idea animating reforms of the Progressive Era, and indeed many in the present, was that training could not only help an individual obtain better employment, but could also help elevate the status and working conditions of an occupation. In Boston, as in other cities across the urban North, reformers embarked on wide-ranging professionalizing projects: elevating domestic service through schools of housekeeping, restoring the status of traditional crafts through industrial education, and turning sales into a profession through schools of salesmanship. The limits of these efforts reveal that education alone was not the only, or even the most important, factor in the making of a high-status, well-paid occupation. Rather, successful professionalization depended upon the structural position of a particular occupation in the economy and whether access to that occupation could be controlled and restricted. Advanced education or training alone could not a profession make.

The failure of industrial education in the early twentieth century also offers an instructive counternarrative to a popular contemporary understanding of vocational education in the United States. Many scholars and commentators look to the robust vocational training systems of continental Europe and suggest that if the United States expanded similar opportunities, the average American would have better access to a well-paying middle-class job.[2] In these analyses, the lack of training opportunities for jobs in the middle of the occupational distribution contributes to the "polarization" of skills and income, and thus, social inequality.[3]

Continued calls for a pivot to industrial training on the model of Germany or Scandinavia today echo those made in the late nineteenth century. But efforts to reshape the economy simply by providing training does not acknowledge the larger structural reasons that have led to their failure in the United States. These include the long history of conflict between employers and craft unions and lack of state coordination that ultimately contributed to US employers' shift away from a reliance on highly trained craftworkers. Tellingly, jobs in the building trades are often held up as evidence that remunerative craft jobs still exist and could proliferate if only the state would invest in expanding apprenticeship opportunities.[4] Yet these are precisely the jobs in which, presently, craft unions retain tight control over the training process despite efforts by both employers and the state to provide additional forms of instruction. Local endeavors to coordinate industrial training apprenticeships with willing firms may achieve limited success, but they do not address the deeper sources of conflict that have led to the marginalization of these efforts in the American economy as a whole. They also do not address the late-twentieth century shift of the US economy away from well-paid unionized manufacturing jobs, or the unequal balance of power between employers and workers that contributes to the further polarization of the labor market. Any program of vocational education today cannot afford to ignore this larger historical context.

While industrial education largely failed, many localities in the United States did successfully develop a program of vocational education for white-collar work. In an unregulated educational system, the most successful "vocational" schools, from the late nineteenth century onward, prepared students for the fastest-growing sector of white-collar jobs— clerks, stenographers, sales workers, secretaries, and managers—with little organized opposition.

The history of schooling for white-collar work presented here challenges a popular decline narrative about American education from a "liberal" past to a "vocational" present.[5] Likely because of the high status of the jobs its graduates obtained, liberal arts education has not typically been considered vocational. But dating back to the nineteenth century, "liberal" education has often been the most vocational instruction: in a landscape with few formal paths to work, it provided students with one of the most structured pathways into white-collar and professional employment. The mutually constitutive growth of the US educational system and the corporate economy suggests that this vocational function was deeply embedded from the start. Critics of vocationalism will need to take this economic role of the educational system seriously if they are interested in changing it in the present. This history suggests that in order to make space in our educational system for broader social or intellectual goals that go beyond economic subsistence, the need for secure and well-paid employment must be met first. Failing to acknowledge the role of our educational system in the distribution of economic benefits will hinder efforts to liberate education for the pursuit of nonvocational ends.

Recognizing the specific vocational functions of "liberal" education also challenges a common dichotomy in economic and political science research between "general" skills, often associated with "high" academic skills that are transferable between jobs, and "specific" skills, associated with "low," narrow, firm-specific skills learned through apprenticeship or vocational training.[6] This general / specific dichotomy can have the odd implication that specialized skills among the most highly educated professions—legal expertise, academic disciplines, medical knowledge—are considered "general." In addition, this dichotomy erases the historical roots of the general / specific divide when it had the opposite meaning: nineteenth-century craftworkers contrasted their own highly specific skills with the low, unspecialized "general" skills of low-wage workers. The ways that social scientists refer to and categorize "skills" often reproduce very historically specific understandings of these terms, as well as historically specific ideas about their status and worth. To avoid unwittingly replicating these assumptions in contemporary scholarship, skills should be interpreted historically with attention to the power dynamics that have shaped not only their specificity and transferability but also their relative value in the labor market.[7]

Within the crowded landscape of schools, the history of white-collar training also offers another insight for educational policy today. Proprietary schools were among the first forms of training for new vocational subjects and were open to constituencies—women, immigrants, and working-class students—not well served by the public sector. They adopted aggressive promotional tactics still observable in the advertisements of for-profit schools today.[8] However, to prevent these schools from taking advantage of students, rather than restrict them through regulation, the most effective strategy in the early twentieth century was the vast expansion of public high schools that undercut their student base. Today, to challenge the sector with the most egregious record of defaulted student debt and deceptive claims about job prospects, a promising strategy would be to offer free, public alternatives.

At the same time, it is necessary to stress the limits of mass educational expansion as a self-sufficient policy solution to the problem of inequality. In the early twentieth century, the restructuring of paths to work made schools vastly more important across the occupational structure, especially at the top. Particularly striking are the ways that schools were used as tools not to empower workers but to undermine that power. Industrial employers used private trade schools to undermine craft unions and used the graduates of commercial schools and public high schools to increase the proportion of their nonunionized staff. Professional elites used universities to control access to the most coveted positions. Schooling on its own is not inherently equalizing, and the history recounted in this book demonstrates the many different ways that schools have been used to entrench and magnify inequality.

This book also details what exactly education meant to those making hiring decisions, in jobs from low-status domestic work to highly paid investment banking. The academic skill and knowledge offered by education was only part of an expansive set of criteria based on social behavior, personality traits, gender norms, social class, religious faith, and racial and ethnic identity. Schools—through the credentials they offered, the personal networks they facilitated, and for some the direct aid of placement services—became useful mediators between individuals and jobs, and employers came to rely on these institutions to aid in their hiring decisions. While a student's advantage in the labor market was legitimated externally as the reward for higher skill, internally we can observe a process of selection on the basis of a wide range of preferences and prejudices. This selection process preserved the most lucrative jobs for elite graduates and relegated other groups to the least desirable and lowest-paid jobs, despite educational achievement. The fact that many students themselves understood the advantages of education in terms of skills and knowledge has clouded our historical understanding of the ways that employers used schools in practice.

Just as secondary education became a majority youth experience by the 1930s, investment in public education in the middle of the twentieth century led college education to become a majority aspiration, if not quite yet experience, by the 1970s. In a booming postwar economy, many students used public higher education to access employment. However, the history of the early twentieth century would suggest that expanding education was a partial but not the principal contributor to the decline in inequality in this period. Rather, the history recounted in this book requires us to turn our attention to the collective power of workers in the economy. Beginning in the 1930s, workers successfully organized powerful industrial unions and won social protections through the federal welfare state, shifting the balance of power to themselves. These gains set the stage for many (but not all) workers, veterans, and students to use education to enter well-paying industrial and white-collar jobs from the 1940s to the 1970s.

In the 1970s, the power of workers and social protections began to erode. Well-paying jobs declined as the occupational structure became increasingly polarized between a low-wage, largely immigrant, feminized service sector on the one hand, and the professional elites of the "knowledge economy" on the other. Recent studies continue to confirm the importance of education in accessing work, even as the number of well-paid jobs has shrunk as a proportion of the workforce.[9] Cuts to public education and rising tuition costs have erected new barriers for working-class students seeking to scale the educational ladder. While there are many differences between our current conditions and those of the early twentieth century, there are some striking similarities. Elites, once again, are using higher educational credentials from exclusive universities to control access to the top of the economic hierarchy, especially in the fields of financial services, management consulting, corporate law, and specialized medicine.[10] Today these credentials are increasingly at the postgraduate level; half of college graduates have not experienced wage growth since 2000, and a college degree is not a guarantee of a stable, well-paying job.[11]

The early twentieth century offers insights into how we might think about the relationship between education and worker power. Attempting to break the power of the elite by providing everyone else with additional education—even tuition- and debt-free—will not be sufficient. Rather, the history of worker organizing in this period shows how workers themselves can lead efforts to shift the balance of economic and political power. Craft unions and professional associations were (and are) guild-like organizations that derive their power in large part from their ability to exclude. More promising is the inclusive model of industrial unions, based on mass organizing of workers across skill level, gender, and race. These unions were pioneered in cities such as Boston by women and immigrant service workers, laborers, and garment workers in the early twentieth century. During the mid-twentieth century, powerful industrial unions in the manufacturing sector significantly increased the power of workers in the economy, as private-sector unionization rates grew nationally to a peak of 36 percent.[12] This power translated into more secure and highly paid employment, the expansion of a wide range of public services and safety nets, and the progressive, redistributive taxes necessary to fund these programs.

Today, growing social inequality has matched the sharp decline of labor union membership, which encompassed only 6 percent of private sector employees in 2019. However, the fastest-growing service-sector occupations at present—those of health care workers, teachers, and private household workers—are leading new organizing efforts to rebuild workers' collective power. These workers are also at the core of local community organizing and political mobilization efforts across the country.[13]

Keeping the balance of worker power front and center will be essential for debates about the future of work, whether considering the impact of technological change and automation or responses to mass unemployment in the wake of public health crises. Commentators and politicians continue to call for renewed investment in education and retraining programs to help individuals retool for a changing economy.[14] The evidence from this book suggests an educational approach to jobs and unemployment will be insufficient. By locating the burden of reform on the individual, these approaches naturalize the labor market as an inevitable reflection of technological change or unavoidable natural causes, rather than the product of political choices. In periods of drastic economic reorganization, the ways in which human beings achieve a livelihood and thrive will require not only new approaches but new forms of worker organizing within workplaces and communities to build the power necessary to implement them.

For those concerned with social inequality, redirecting attention from a narrow focus on education to broader labor and political solutions is an essential step. Many educators have already witnessed the "education-alizing" of larger social problems firsthand, as unrealistic burdens and expectations have been heaped onto schools even in the face of budget cuts.[15] Educators thus have a role to play in reframing inequality debates away from a student's perceived lack of skills, or parents' lack of commitment to their child's education, and toward the role of power in politics and the economy. Indeed, educators are already leading the fight not only for labor rights but also for the rights of the disinvested communities in which they teach.[16]

Educators also have an important role to play in dismantling the ideology that upholds and legitimizes our unequal economy. The belief that educational merit shapes the occupational hierarchy has widespread implications. The perception that one's worth is measured by the labor market, and that higher earners deserve what they earn because they have scaled the educational ladder, has become a dominant outlook, in part because of the history recounted in this book. Understanding the historical origins of this faith allows us to see how labor markets are products of conflict between powerful interests. This should challenge us to rethink whether "market value" captures the true value of human labor, and to be conscious of hierarchies of work that too often translate into a hierarchy of human beings.

The meritocratic faith in education is also deeply ingrained in our political system. Progressive-era professional elites with ties to leading universities amassed a strong hold on political decision-making. As criticized by working-class fighters such as Julia Duff, elites like James Storrow used this power to limit rather than expand access to democratic governance and legitimated their positions through appeals to expertise. The history of our institutional and ideological faith in education should encourage us to be critical of technocratic approaches to politics, or the notion that one's educational level should determine one's influence in a democracy. Without diminishing the value of experts that can contribute to society in lifesaving ways, the linked histories of elite formation and exclusive credentials suggest that in the political realm, those affected by decisions require a seat at the table if decisions are not to be made at their expense.

The academy itself plays a central role in upholding and perpetuating the ideology of meritocracy, institutionally through the students it trains, as well as the ideas it produces. In particular, the human capital framework of neoclassical economics provides an intellectual apparatus that reinforces the notion that one's compensation in the labor market reflects one's merit. This book suggests that a nuanced historical understanding, attentive to the ways in which organized interests have wielded their power and individuals have navigated their circumstances, may help us better explain how we have come to live in a society with abundant educational access and high social inequality. By revealing how the shift to an economy based on the labor of school-trained workers created a new institutional foundation for social inequality, this history shows how seemingly indisputable policy wisdom—that education can reduce inequality—may obscure and intensify the very problem it aims to reduce. By offering a new way of thinking about the mixed legacy of American education, this book can help us to break the implicit equation between schooling and worth, and help us think anew about what it will take to create a more egalitarian society.

Abbreviations

ARS	*Annual Report of the Superintendent of Schools of the City of Boston*
ARSC	*Annual Report of the School Committee of the City of Boston*
AS	*Annual Statistics of the Boston Public Schools*
BCC	Boston Chamber of Commerce Records, 1842–1949, Special Collections, Baker Library, Harvard Business School, Boston
BG	*Boston Daily Globe*
BH	*Boston Herald*
BP	*Boston Post*
BSE	US Department of the Interior, Bureau (Office) of Education, *Biennial Survey of Education*
BSL	*Annual Report of the Bureau of Statistics of Labor* (Massachusetts)
BVI	Bureau of Vocational Information Records, 1908–1932, Schlesinger Library, Radcliffe Institute, Harvard University, Cambridge, MA
DMC	Dennison Manufacturing Company Records, 1815–1990, Special Collections, Baker Library, Harvard Business School, Boston
LB	*Labor Bulletin of the Commonwealth of Massachusetts*
NBSIS	North Bennet Street Industrial School Records, 1880–1973, Schlesinger Library, Radcliffe Institute, Harvard University, Cambridge, MA

OCS   Records of the Office of Career Services, 1913–1958, Harvard
        University Archives, Harvard University, Cambridge, MA
RCE   US Department of the Interior, Bureau of Education, *Report
        of the Commissioner of Education*

Notes

Introduction

Details about quantitative data sources, as well as a complete bibliography, can be accessed at tinagroeger.com/educationtrap.

1. Horace Mann, *Twelfth Annual Report of the Secretary of the Board of Education 1848* (Boston: Dutton and Wentworth, 1849), 59.

2. White House, Office of the Press Secretary, "Remarks by the President in State of the Union Address," January 27, 2010, https://obamawhitehouse .archives.gov/the-press-office/remarks-president-state-union-address.

3. Thomas Piketty, *Capital in the Twenty-First Century* (Cambridge, MA: Harvard University Press, 2014), 313.

4. "Mean Years in Schooling," *Our World in Data,* accessed August 22, 2020, https://ourworldindata.org/grapher/mean-years-of-schooling-1?tab=chart &country; "Share of the Population with Completed Tertiary Education 1970– 2010," *Our World in Data,* accessed August 22, 2020, https://ourworldindata.org /grapher/share-of-the-population-with-completed-tertiary-education?tab =chart.

5. "Mean Years in Schooling."

6. Marius R. Busemeyer, *Skills and Inequality: Partisan Politics and the Political Economy of Education Reforms in Western Welfare States* (Cambridge: Cambridge University Press, 2015), 182–185; Miles Corak, "Income Inequality, Equality of Opportunity, and Intergenerational Mobility," *Journal of Economic Perspectives* 27, no. 3 (August 2013): 79–102.

7. Katie Brockman, "Most Americans Are Living Paycheck to Paycheck," *USA Today,* August 14, 2019, https://www.usatoday.com/story/money/2019/08

/14/paycheck-to-paycheck-most-americans-struggle-financially-survey-says
/39940123/; Hillary Hoffower, "We Did the Math," *Business Insider,* January 9, 2019, https://www.businessinsider.com/what-amazon-ceo-jeff-bezos-makes-every-day-hour-minute-2018-10.

8. Joseph E. Stiglitz, *The Price of Inequality: How Today's Divided Society Endangers Our Future* (New York: W. W. Norton, 2012); Richard V. Reeves, *Dream Hoarders: How the American Upper Middle Class Is Leaving Everyone Else in the Dust, Why That Is a Problem, and What to Do about It* (Washington, DC: Brookings Institution Press, 2017); Larry M. Bartels, *Unequal Democracy: The Political Economy of the New Gilded Age* (New York: Russell Sage Foundation, 2008).

9. Jon C. Teaford, *The Unheralded Triumph: City Government in America, 1870–1900* (Baltimore: Johns Hopkins University Press, 1984); Richardson Dilworth, ed., *The City in American Political Development* (New York: Routledge, 2009), 1–5.

10. David A. Gamson, *The Importance of Being Urban: Designing the Progressive School District, 1890–1940* (Chicago: University of Chicago Press, 2019).

11. Charles H. Trout, *Boston, the Great Depression, and the New Deal* (New York: Oxford University Press, 1977), xi.

12. The subject of groundbreaking historical studies of economic, immigration, educational, and women and gender history, Boston offers a wealth of data to construct a new interpretation of the relationship between education and the economy. To name just a few works: Stephan Thernstrom, *The Other Bostonians: Poverty and Progress in the American Metropolis, 1880–1870* (Cambridge, MA: Harvard University Press, 1973); Elizabeth Hafkin Pleck, *Black Migration and Poverty: Boston 1865–1900* (New York: Academic Press, 1979); Oscar Handlin, *Boston's Immigrants, 1790–1880: A Study in Acculturation* (Cambridge, MA: Harvard University Press, 1959); Marvin Lazerson, *Origins of the Urban School: Public Education in Massachusetts, 1870–1915* (Cambridge, MA: Harvard University Press, 1971); Nancy F. Cott, *The Bonds of Womanhood: "Woman's Sphere" in New England, 1780–1835* (New Haven, CT: Yale University Press, 1977).

13. Gary Stanley Becker, *Human Capital: A Theoretical and Empirical Analysis, with Special Reference to Education* (Chicago: University of Chicago Press, 1964).

14. Peter F. Drucker, *The Age of Discontinuity: Guidelines to Our Changing Society* (London: William Heinemann, 1969), 247–356.

15. The link between human capital and social inequality is made explicitly in Claudia Goldin and Lawrence F. Katz, *The Race between Education and Technology* (Cambridge, MA: Harvard University Press, 2008); James J. Heckman

and Alan B. Krueger, *Inequality in America: What Role for Human Capital Policies?*, ed. Benjamin M. Friedman (Cambridge, MA: MIT Press, 2003). Some economists have pointed to the limits of educational interventions for improving mobility or reducing inequality. Jesse Rothstein, "Inequality of Educational Opportunity? Schools as Mediators of the Intergenerational Transmission of Income," IRLE Working Paper no. 105-17 (April 1, 2017), 66; Brad Hershbein, Melissa S. Kearney, and Lawrence H. Summers, "Increasing Education: What It Will and Will Not Do for Earnings and Earnings Inequality," The Hamilton Project, March 30, 2015, http://larrysummers.com/wp-content/uploads/2015/03/impact_of_edu_earnings_inequality_hershbein_kearney_summers.pdf.

16. A challenge to human-capital theory from within economics considers education to be a "screen" or "signal" to employers that a person is highly productive, whether or not that productivity is related to the skills the person learned in school. These theories bear some resemblance to sociological "credentialist" theories. Other economists have highlighted the frictions in the labor market that give employers wage-setting power, or "monopsony" power, challenging the assumption that wages reflect skill. These challenges open up more space for considering the role of factors other than skill level, including power, in shaping returns to education in the labor market. Michael Spence, "Job Market Signaling," *Quarterly Journal of Economics* 87, no. 3 (August 1973): 355; Lester C. Thurow, *Generating Inequality: Mechanisms of Distribution in the U.S. Economy* (New York: Basic Books, 1975); Andrew Weiss, "Human Capital vs. Signalling Explanations of Wages," *Journal of Economic Perspectives* 9, no. 4 (November 1995): 133–154; Sydnee Caldwell and Suresh Naidu, "Wage and Employment Implications of U.S. Labor Market Monopsony and Possible Policy Solutions," in *Vision 2020: Evidence for a Stronger Economy* (Washington, DC: Washington Center for Equitable Growth, 2020), 33–43.

17. Paul Attewell, "What Is Skill?," *Work and Occupations* 17, no. 4 (November 1, 1990): 429–435.

18. Wolfgang Streeck, "Skills and Politics: General and Specific," Discussion Paper 11/1 (Cologne, Germany: MPIfG, 2011).

19. David P. Baker, *The Schooled Society: The Educational Transformation of Global Culture* (Stanford, CA: Stanford University Press, 2014), 125–155; John W. Meyer, "The Effects of Education as an Institution," *American Journal of Sociology* 83, no. 1 (July 1977): 55–77.

20. Kathleen Thelen, *How Institutions Evolve: The Political Economy of Skills in Germany, Britain, the United States, and Japan* (Cambridge: Cambridge University Press, 2004); Marius R. Busemeyer and Christine Trampusch, eds., *The Political Economy of Collective Skill Formation* (Oxford: Oxford University Press, 2012); Peter A. Hall and David Soskice, eds., *Varieties of Capitalism:*

The Institutional Foundations of Comparative Advantage (Oxford: Oxford University Press, 2001).

21. Margarita Estévez-Abe, "Gender Bias in Skills and Social Policies: The Varieties of Capitalism Perspective on Sex Segregation," *Social Politics: International Studies in Gender, State and Society* 12, no. 2 (2005): 180–215.

22. Pierre Bourdieu, *Distinction: A Social Critique of the Judgement of Taste*, trans. Richard Price (Cambridge, MA: Harvard University Press, 1984).

23. Samuel Bowles and Herbert Gintis, *Schooling in Capitalist America: Educational Reform and the Contradictions of Economic Life* (New York: Basic Books, 1976); Michael B. Katz, *The Irony of Early School Reform: Educational Innovation in Mid-Nineteenth Century Massachusetts* (New York: Teachers College Press, 1968).

24. Randall Collins, *The Credential Society: An Historical Sociology of Education and Stratification* (1979; repr., New York: Columbia University Press, 2019); Ivar Berg, *Education and Jobs: The Great Training Robbery* (New York: Praeger, 1970); David F. Labaree, *The Making of an American High School: The Credentials Market and the Central High School of Philadelphia, 1838–1939* (New Haven, CT: Yale University Press, 1988).

25. Lauren A. Rivera, *Pedigree: How Elite Students Get Elite Jobs* (Princeton, NJ: Princeton University Press, 2015); Amy J. Binder, Daniel B. Davis, and Nick Bloom, "Career Funneling: How Elite Students Learn to Define and Desire 'Prestigious' Jobs," *Sociology of Education* 89, no. 1 (January 2016): 20–39.

26. Collins, *The Credential Society*, 172; David F. Labaree, *Someone Has to Fail: The Zero-Sum Game of Public Schooling* (Cambridge, MA: Harvard University Press, 2010), 195–221. In this regard, I build on the work of scholars such as Samuel Bowles and Herbert Gintis, who analyze the specific work-related skills and behaviors cultivated within school, and the work of David Brown, who reformulates skills such as collegiate-level literacy not merely as technical knowhow but as a wide set of social and cultural behaviors relevant to the professional workplace. Bowles and Gintis, *Schooling in Capitalist America*, 125–151; David K. Brown, *Degrees of Control: A Sociology of Educational Expansion and Occupational Credentialism* (New York: Teachers College Press, 1995), 59–72. A helpful survey of "job assignment" theories is David B. Bills, "Credentials, Signals, and Screens: Explaining the Relationship between Schooling and Job Assignment," *Review of Educational Research* 73, no. 4 (December 1, 2003): 441–449.

27. Collins, *The Credential Society*, 148; Bowles and Gintis, *Schooling in Capitalist America*, 180–201.

28. Studies that pay scant attention to education include Gary Gerstle, *Liberty and Coercion: The Paradox of American Government from the Founding to*

the Present (Princeton, NJ: Princeton University Press, 2015); Brian Balogh, *The Associational State: American Governance in the Twentieth Century* (Philadelphia: University of Pennsylvania Press, 2015); Nell Irvin Painter, *Standing at Armageddon: A Grassroots History of the Progressive Era* (1987; repr., New York: W. W. Norton, 2008); Richard Franklin Bensel, *The Political Economy of American Industrialization, 1877–1900* (Cambridge: Cambridge University Press, 2000); Alfred D. Chandler Jr., *The Visible Hand: The Managerial Revolution in American Business* (Cambridge, MA: Harvard University Press, 1977).

29. Tracy L. Steffes, *School, Society, and State: A New Education to Govern Modern America, 1890–1940* (Chicago: University of Chicago Press, 2012), 7; Peter H. Lindert, *Growing Public: Social Spending and Economic Growth since the Eighteenth Century* (Cambridge: Cambridge University Press, 2004), 87–126; Michael B. Katz, "Public Education as Welfare," *Dissent* 57, no. 3 (2010): 52–56; Miriam Cohen, "Reconsidering Schools and the American Welfare State," *History of Education Quarterly* 45, no. 4 (December 1, 2005): 511–537.

30. Recent works that explore the deepening of inequalities during the Progressive Era include Khalil Gibran Muhammad, *The Condemnation of Blackness: Race, Crime, and the Making of Modern Urban America* (Cambridge, MA: Harvard University Press, 2010); Thomas C. Leonard, *Illiberal Reformers: Race, Eugenics, and American Economics in the Progressive Era* (Princeton, NJ: Princeton University Press, 2016); David Huyssen, *Progressive Inequality: Rich and Poor in New York, 1890–1920* (Cambridge, MA: Harvard University Press, 2014). A focus on the consolidation of power by elites as well as the expansion of public services in these years suggests that the Gilded Age, the Progressive Era, and the decade of the 1920s exhibit more continuity than discontinuity. Rebecca Edwards, "Politics, Social Movements, and the Periodization of U.S. History," *Journal of the Gilded Age and Progressive Era* 8, no. 4 (2009): 463–473.

31. Thomas Piketty and Emmanuel Saez, "Income Inequality in the United States, 1913–1998," *Quarterly Journal of Economics* 118, no. 1 (February 2003): 11–24; Piketty, *Capital in the Twenty-First Century*, 24; Eli Cook, "Why We Might Just Be Living in a Second 'Progressive' Era," *Journal of the Gilded Age and Progressive Era*, 19, no. 2 (2020): 1–11; Peter H. Lindert, *Unequal Gains: American Growth and Inequality since 1700* (Princeton, NJ: Princeton University Press, 2016), 173.

32. Elizabeth Faue, "Retooling the Class Factory: United States Labour History after Marx, Montgomery, and Postmodernism," *Labour History*, no. 82 (2002): 109; L. Fink, "The Great Escape: How a Field Survived Hard Times," *Labor: Studies in Working-Class History of the Americas* 8, no. 1 (March 2011): 109–115; J. Sklansky, "Labor, Money, and the Financial Turn in the History of

Capitalism," *Labor Studies in Working-Class History of the Americas* 11, no. 1 (March 2014): 23–46.

33. The meaning of "equal opportunity" in economic and educational contexts also has a long, and contested, history. See Claire Goldstene, *The Struggle for America's Promise: Equal Opportunity at the Dawn of Corporate Capital* (Jackson: University Press of Mississippi, 2014); Frank Dobbin, *Inventing Equal Opportunity* (Princeton, NJ: Princeton University Press, 2009); Leah N. Gordon, "If Opportunity Is Not Enough: Coleman and His Critics in the Era of Equality of Results," *History of Education Quarterly* 57, no. 4 (November 2017): 601–615.

34. Jefferson Cowie, for example, presents this ideology as an "individualist ethos so deeply embedded in . . . America's public culture." Jefferson Cowie, *The Great Exception: The New Deal and the Limits of American Politics* (Princeton, NJ: Princeton University Press, 2016), 26.

35. Joseph F. Kett, *Merit: The History of a Founding Ideal from the American Revolution to the Twenty-First Century* (Ithaca, NY: Cornell University Press, 2013), 68–126, 159–191.

36. Henry J. Perkinson, *The Imperfect Panacea: American Faith in Education, 1865–1976* (New York: Random House, 1977); David F. Labaree, "The Winning Ways of a Losing Strategy: Educationalizing Social Problems in the United States," *Educational Theory* 58, no. 4 (November 2008): 447–460; Harvey Kantor and Robert Lowe, "Educationalizing the Welfare State and Privatizing Education: The Evolution of Social Policy since the New Deal," in *Closing the Opportunity Gap: What America Must Do to Give Every Child an Even Chance*, ed. Prudence L. Carter and Kevin G. Welner (Oxford: Oxford University Press, 2013), 25–39.

37. Michael B. Katz, *In the Shadow of the Poorhouse: A Social History of Welfare in America*, 10th anniversary ed. (New York: Basic Books, 1996); Leah Gordon, *From Power to Prejudice: The Rise of Racial Individualism in Midcentury America* (Chicago: University of Chicago Press, 2015); Elizabeth Hinton, *From the War on Poverty to the War on Crime: The Making of Mass Incarceration in America* (Cambridge, MA: Harvard University Press, 2016).

38. Daniel Markovits, *The Meritocracy Trap: How America's Foundational Myth Feeds Inequality, Dismantles the Middle Class, and Devours the Elite* (New York: Penguin Press, 2019); Anthony P. Carnevale, Peter Schmidt, and Jeff Strohl, *The Merit Myth: How Our Colleges Favor the Rich and Divide America* (New York: New Press, 2020); Lani Guinier, *The Tyranny of the Meritocracy: Democratizing Higher Education in America* (Boston: Beacon Press, 2015).

39. Kett, *Merit*, 10–13; Michael Young, *The Rise of the Meritocracy* (1958; repr., New Brunswick, NJ: Transaction Books, 1994), xiii–xiv.

40. Joseph F. Kett, "'Theory Run Mad': John Dewey and 'Real' Vocational Education," *Journal of the Gilded Age and Progressive Era* 16, no. 4 (October 2017): 500–514; David F. Labaree, "Public Goods, Private Goods: The American Struggle over Educational Goals," *American Educational Research Journal* 34, no. 1 (1997): 44; W. Norton Grubb and Marvin Lazerson, *The Education Gospel: The Economic Power of Schooling* (Cambridge, MA: Harvard University Press, 2004).

41. Michael Fabricant and Stephen Brier, *Austerity Blues: Fighting for the Soul of Public Higher Education* (Baltimore: Johns Hopkins University Press, 2016); Sarah Knopp and Jeff Bale, *Education and Capitalism: Struggles for Learning and Liberation* (Chicago: Haymarket Books, 2012).

42. Historians of education have called for the breaking down of these silos since at least Bernard Bailyn, *Education in the Forming of American Society: Needs and Opportunities for Study* (Chapel Hill: University of North Carolina Press, 1960); Christine A. Ogren points out their persistence in "Sites, Students, Scholarship, and Structures: The Historiography of American Higher Education in the Post-Revisionist Era," in *Rethinking the History of American Education,* ed. William J. Reese and John L. Rury (New York: Palgrave Macmillan, 2008), 196. Many works helpfully challenge these divisions; a few in particular that I build on are Nancy Beadie, *Education and the Creation of Capital in the Early American Republic* (Cambridge: Cambridge University Press, 2010); Marc A. VanOverbeke, *The Standardization of American Schooling: Linking Secondary and Higher Education, 1870–1910* (New York: Palgrave Macmillan, 2008); Robert N. Gross, *Public vs. Private: The Early History of School Choice in America* (New York: Oxford University Press, 2018); Joseph F. Kett, *The Pursuit of Knowledge under Difficulties: From Self-Improvement to Adult Education in America, 1750–1990* (Stanford, CA: Stanford University Press, 1994).

43. The public-private nature of the American welfare state is explored in Balogh, *The Associational State;* William J. Novak, "The Myth of the 'Weak' American State," *American Historical Review* 113, no. 3 (2008): 752–772; Jennifer Klein, *For All These Rights: Business, Labor, and the Shaping of America's Public-Private Welfare State* (Princeton, NJ: Princeton University Press, 2003); Jacob S. Hacker, *The Divided Welfare State: The Battle over Public and Private Social Benefits in the United States* (New York: Cambridge University Press, 2002); M. B. Katz, *The Price of Citizenship: Redefining the American Welfare State* (New York: Metropolitan Books, 2001).

44. Studies that primarily focus on industrial education include Herbert M. Kliebard, *Schooled to Work: Vocationalism and the American Curriculum, 1876–1946* (New York: Teachers College Press, 1999); Harvey A. Kantor, *Learning to Earn: School, Work, and Vocational Reform in California, 1880–1930* (Madison: University of Wisconsin Press, 1988). Studies with more attention to women's

white-collar work include John L. Rury, *Education and Women's Work: Female Schooling and the Division of Labor in Urban America, 1870–1930* (Albany: State University of New York Press, 1991); Ileen A. DeVault, *Sons and Daughters of Labor: Class and Clerical Work in Turn-of-the-Century Pittsburgh* (Ithaca, NY: Cornell University Press, 1990); Carol Srole, *Transcribing Class and Gender: Masculinity and Femininity in Nineteenth-Century Courts and Offices* (Ann Arbor: University of Michigan Press, 2010).

45. An old argument made by many theorists of education including John Dewey, "Labor and Leisure," in *Democracy and Education: An Introduction to the Philosophy of Education* (New York: Free Press, 1916), 250–276.

46. William Whyte, *The Organization Man* (New York: Simon & Shuster, 1956).

47. David B. Tyack, Robert Lowe, and Elisabeth Hansot, *Public Schools in Hard Times: The Great Depression and Recent Years* (Cambridge, MA: Harvard University Press, 1984), 124–126; David L. Angus and Jeffrey Mirel, *The Failed Promise of the American High School, 1890–1995* (New York: Teachers College Press, 1999), 78–79.

48. The deep institutionalization of schooling, as David Baker puts it, "transformed the currency of stratification to all things educational." David P. Baker, "Forward and Backward, Horizontal and Vertical: Transformation of Occupational Credentialing in the Schooled Society," *Research in Social Stratification and Mobility* 29, no. 1 (January 2011): 5–29.

49. Claudia Goldin and Robert A. Margo, "The Great Compression: The Wage Structure in the United States at Mid-Century," working paper no. 3817 (Cambridge, MA: National Bureau of Economic Research, August 1991).

50. Claudia Goldin and Lawrence F. Katz, *The Race between Education and Technology* (Cambridge, MA: Harvard University Press, 2008).

51. Cowie, *The Great Exception;* Frank Levy and Peter Temin, "Inequality and Institutions in 20th Century America," working paper no. 13106 (Cambridge, MA: National Bureau of Economic Research, May 2007); Thomas Piketty and Emmanuel Saez, "Income Inequality in the United States, 1913–1998," *Quarterly Journal of Economics* 118, no. 1 (February 2003): 39; Leonard Burman, "Taxes and Inequality," *Tax Law Review* 66, no. 4 (Summer 2013): 563–592; Ellora Derenoncourt and Claire Montialoux, "Minimum Wages and Racial Inequality," Washington Center for Equitable Growth, January 2020, https://equitablegrowth.org/working-papers/minimum-wages-and-racial-inequality/; Michael Reich, "The Ups and Downs of Minimum Wage Policy: The Fair Labor Standards Act in Historical Perspective," *Industrial Relations: A Journal of Economy and Society* 54, no. 4 (October 2015): 538–546; Richard B. Freeman and James L. Medoff, *What Do Unions Do?* (New York: Basic Books, 1984); Henry Farber et al., "Unions and

Inequality over the Twentieth Century: New Evidence from Survey Data," working paper no. 24587 (Cambridge, MA: National Bureau of Economic Research, May 2018).

52. David Autor, "The Polarization of Job Opportunities in the U.S. Labor Market: Implications for Employment and Earnings," Center for American Progress and the Hamilton Project (Washington, DC: Center for American Progress, April 2010), 1–40.

53. Paul Osterman, "The Promise, Performance, and Policies of Community Colleges," in *Reinventing Higher Education: The Promise of Innovation,* ed. Ben Wildavsky, Andrew P. Kelly, and Kevin Carey (Cambridge, MA: Harvard Education Press, 2011), 129.

54. David H. Autor, "Skills, Education, and the Rise of Earnings Inequality among the 'Other 99 Percent,'" *Science* 344, no. 6186 (May 23, 2014): 849; Piketty, *Capital in the Twenty-First Century,* 314.

55. Jonathan Rothwell, "Myths of the 1 Percent: What Puts People at the Top," *New York Times,* November 17, 2017; Florencia Torche, "Is a College Degree Still the Great Equalizer? Intergenerational Mobility across Levels of Schooling in the United States," *American Journal of Sociology* 117, no. 3 (November 2011): 794–797; Dirk Witteveen and Paul Attewell, "Reconsidering the 'Meritocratic Power of a College Degree,'" *Research in Social Stratification and Mobility* 66 (April 2020): 100479.

1. Nineteenth-Century Networks

1. Calculated by dividing the total high school attendance figures reported by the Boston Public Schools by the population of 14–17-year-olds in Boston in 1880. *ARSC 1880* (Boston: Rockwell & Churchill, 1881), 85; U.S. Census Office, "Table 9: Population, As Native and Foreign-Born, of Cities, Etc.: 1880 and 1870," in *Tenth Census of the United States 1880,* vol. 1, *Statistics of the Population of the United States* (Washington, DC: GPO, 1883), 450. To examine Boston's demographic, educational, and occupational composition in 1880, I used the statistical software STATA to analyze IPUMS USA (digitized individual-level data samples of the US decennial census) 100 percent sample from 1880, hereafter referred to as IPUMS 1880. Steven Ruggles, Sarah Flood, Ronald Goeken, Josiah Grover, Erin Meyer, Jose Pacas, and Matthew Sobek, IPUMS USA: Version 10.0 [dataset] (Minneapolis: IPUMS, 2020), https://doi.org/10.18128/D010.V10.0.

2. Randall Collins, *The Credential Society: An Historical Sociology of Education and Stratification* (1979; repr., New York: Columbia University Press, 2019), 4–5.

3. I do not use the term "middle class" in my characterization of these worlds, a term that does not helpfully distinguish between, on the one hand, small proprietors, clerks, and craftworkers, and, on the other, large employers, managers, and the chief beneficiaries of the new industrial economy. The latter I refer to as "upper class" or "elite." For an exploration of this elusive term historically, see Burton J. Bledstein and Robert D. Johnston, *The Middling Sorts: Explorations in the History of the American Middle Class* (New York: Routledge, 2001).

4. Cleveland Amory, *The Proper Bostonians* (New York: E. P. Dutton, 1947), 40.

5. The classification of occupations is itself historically and politically contested: see Margo Anderson's excellent discussion in *The United States Census and Labor Force Change: A History of Occupation Statistics, 1870–1940* (Ann Arbor: UMI Research Press, 1980). For occupational data in this book, I used the IPUMS occ1950 variable, recoded directly from the original manuscript census entries, consistent throughout the 1880–1940 time period. In addition to the occ1950 code, I also cross-referenced my results with the "occ" variable specific to 1880 and looked up samples of workers in key occupations in the manuscript census to gain useful context about class position, accessed through Ancestry.com and the Church of Jesus Christ of Latter-day Saints, *1880 United States Federal Census* [database online] (Provo, UT: Ancestry.com Operations, 2010). The categories used in Figure 1.1 are based on the IPUMS occ1950 classification scheme, with some exceptions. Two are to correct for the common downgrading of women's occupations based on gendered assumptions about skill. "Dressmakers and seamstresses, except factory" and "milliners" were originally grouped with "operatives," a low-wage category, but I grouped them with "craftworkers" to better reflect their position as a trade. I also moved "boarding and lodging housekeepers," predominantly women, from "service" workers (another low-wage category) to "small proprietors." Finally, I moved "hucksters and peddlers" from "sales workers" to "low-wage workers" to better reflect their world of work. For more about my use of IPUMS data and historical occupational statistics, see my website, tinagroeger.com/educationtrap.

6. Katie Kenneally, Anne Millet, and Susan Wick, *Hyde Park* (Boston: Boston 200 Corporation, 1976), 10.

7. Sari Roboff and Katie Kenneally, *The North End* (Boston: Boston 200 Corporation, 1975), 15.

8. L. F. Lyne, "Shop Kinks: Running Lines and Putting Up Shafting," *The American Machinist* 4, no. 38 (September 17, 1881): 2.

9. *BSL 1884* (Boston: Wright & Potter, 1884), 77; *BSL 1879* (Boston: Rand, Avery & Co., 1879), 70; Horace G. Wadlin, "Hours of Labor in Domestic Service," *LB*, no. 8 (October 1898): 2.

10. Thomas H. O'Connor, *Civil War Boston: Home Front and Battlefield* (Boston: Northeastern University Press, 1997), 235–236; Edwin Monroe Bacon, *The Book of Boston: Fifty Years' Recollections of the New England Metropolis* (Boston: Book of Boston Co., 1916), 61–76.

11. Elizabeth Hafkin Pleck, *Black Migration and Poverty: Boston 1865–1900* (New York: Academic Press, 1979), 31; Walter Irving Firey, *Land Use in Central Boston* (Cambridge, MA: Harvard University Press, 1947), 88–89.

12. IPUMS 1880.

13. *BSL 1879*, 67–77; National Bureau of Economic Research, Index of the General Price Level for United States [M04051USM324NNBR], retrieved from FRED, Federal Reserve Bank of St. Louis, https://fred.stlouisfed.org/series /M04051USM324NNBR, June 15, 2020; CPI Inflation Calculator, https://www .bls.gov/data/inflation_calculator.htm.

14. Katie Kenneally, *South Boston* (Boston: Boston 200 Corporation, 1976), 13.

15. IPUMS 1880; Thomas H. O'Connor, *The Boston Irish: A Political History* (Boston: Northeastern University Press, 1995), 121.

16. IPUMS 1880.

17. Year: *1880;* Census Place: *Boston, Suffolk, Massachusetts;* Roll: *556;* Family History Film: *1254556;* Page: *391B;* Enumeration District: *676;* Image: *0445.*

18. *BSL 1879*, 67–77.

19. Sarah Scovill Whittelsey, *Massachusetts Labor Legislation: An Historical and Critical Study* (Philadelphia: American Academy of Political and Social Science, 1900), 25; James R. Green and Hugh Carter Donahue, *Boston's Workers: A Labor History* (Boston: Boston Public Library, 1979), 35–36.

20. IPUMS 1880; Katie Kenneally, *The South End* (Boston: Boston 200 Corporation, 1975), 9; "Record of Families Connected with No. Bennet Day Nursery, 1883," MC269, Series II, Box 101, Biv. 45, North Bennet Street Industrial School Records 1880–1973, Schlesinger Library, Radcliffe Institute, Harvard University, Cambridge, MA.

21. IPUMS 1880; Year: *1880;* Census Place: *Boston, Suffolk, Massachusetts;* Roll: *556;* Family History Film: *1254556;* Page: *322A;* Enumeration District: *673;* Image: *0306.*

22. Ileen Devault, "Family Wages: The Roles of Wives and Mothers in U.S. Working-Class Survival Strategies, 1880–1930," *Labor History* 54, no. 1 (2013): 1–20; *BSL 1879*, 6. See also Alice Kessler-Harris, *Out to Work: A History of Wage-Earning Women in the United States* (New York: Oxford University Press, 1982); Eileen Boris, *Home to Work: Motherhood and the Politics of Industrial Homework in the United States* (Cambridge: Cambridge University Press, 1994).

23. *BSL 1871* (Boston: Wright & Potter, 1871), 525–528; *BSL 1875* (Boston: Wright & Potter, 1875), 278.

24. IPUMS 1880; "Social Conditions in Domestic Service," *LB*, no. 13 (February 1900): 1–16; *BSL 1884*, 76; *LB*, no. 8 (October 1898): 23.

25. Timothy J. Gilfoyle, *City of Eros: New York City, Prostitution, and the Commercialization of Sex, 1790–1920* (New York: W. W. Norton, 1992), 59–66; Barbara Meil Hobson, *Uneasy Virtue: The Politics of Prostitution and the American Reform Tradition* (Chicago: University of Chicago Press, 1990), 90; Walter Elmore Fernald, *Report of the Commission for the Investigation of the White Slave Traffic, So Called* (Boston: Wright & Potter, 1914), 31; *BSL 1884*, 124–126.

26. Ruth Rosen, *The Lost Sisterhood: Prostitution in America, 1900–1918* (Baltimore: Johns Hopkins University Press, 1982), 3–11; Howard Brown Woolston, *Prostitution in the United States*, vol. 1 (New York: Century Co., 1921), 22–30; Perry Duis, *The Saloon: Public Drinking in Chicago and Boston, 1880–1920* (Urbana: University of Illinois Press, 1999), 235–236; Fernald, *White Slave Traffic*, 9, 51; Hobson, *Uneasy Virtue*, 98–107.

27. Katie Kenneally, *Dorchester* (Boston: Boston 200 Corporation, 1976), 16.

28. Roboff and Kenneally, *The North End*, 5.

29. Pleck, *Black Migration*, 73–75.

30. Roboff and Kenneally, *The North End*, 15.

31. Suzanne Model, "Work and Family: Blacks and Immigrants from South and East Europe," in *Immigration Reconsidered: History, Sociology, and Politics*, ed. Virginia Yans-McLaughlin (Oxford: Oxford University Press, 1990), 133–141.

32. Kenneally, *South Boston*, 20–21.

33. Peleg Whitman Chandler, *The Charter and Ordinances of the City of Boston* (Boston: J. H. Eastburn, 1850), 249.

34. *BSL 1894* (Boston: Wright & Potter, 1894), 81–107.

35. "Intelligence Offices," *BG*, January 13, 1879, 2.

36. Chauncey Mitchell Depew, *One Hundred Years of American Commerce*, vol. 1 (New York: D. O. Haynes, 1895), 78.

37. "Male Help," *BH*, February 11, 1879, 3; "Male Help," *BH*, June 23, 1879, 3; "Female Help" and "Male Help," *BH*, May 30, 1879, 3.

38. "Female Help," *BH*, October 29, 1881, 5; "Female Help," *BH*, March 19, 1879, 3.

39. "Female Help," *BH*, March 19, 1879, 3; "Male Help," *BH*, October 29, 1881, 5.

40. "Male Help," *BH*, October 29, 1881, 5; "Female Help," *BH*, January 8, 1879.

41. Carl F. Kaestle, *Pillars of the Republic: Common Schools and American Society, 1780–1860* (New York: Macmillan, 1983), 75–103; Joseph F. Kett, *Merit:*

The History of a Founding Ideal from the American Revolution to the Twenty-First Century (Ithaca, NY: Cornell University Press, 2013), 93–114.

42. Davison Douglas, *Jim Crow Moves North: The Battle over Northern School Segregation, 1865–1954* (New York: Cambridge University Press, 2005), 58–60; Bryn Upton, "Black Sisyphus: Boston Schools and the Black Community, 1790–2000" (PhD diss., Brandeis University, 2003), 118–187.

43. The decentralized and unregulated landscape of US schools also allowed for large regional variation, including the exclusion of African Americans from most schools in the South and overall low levels of public expenditure on southern schools for either white or Black youth. Pamela B. Walters and Philip J. O'Connell, "The Family Economy, Work, and Educational Participation in the United States, 1890–1940," *American Journal of Sociology* 93, no. 5 (1988): 1116–1152; John W. Meyer et al., "Public Education as Nation-Building in America: Enrollments and Bureaucratization in the American States, 1870–1930," *American Journal of Sociology* 85, no. 3 (November 1979): 591–613.

44. Kaestle, *Pillars of the Republic,* 153–156.

45. Grammar schools were among the first public schools established in Massachusetts in the colonial period, but they did not provide rudimentary literacy. Free primary schools were authorized to do so in 1818. After common-school reforms to create a graded school system, Boston's primary schools covered the first three years of school, and grammar schools the next six. In 1906, these school types were merged into elementary schools, and the total course length was reduced from nine to eight years. *ARSC 1906* (Boston: Municipal Printing Office, 1906), 35. Kaestle, *Pillars of the Republic,* 132; Alan DiGaetano, "The Longue Durée of School Governance in Boston," *Journal of Urban History* 45, no. 4 (July 2019): 718–720.

46. In the reported rate of school attendance for all 14–17-year-olds, Boston matched the national average of 43 percent. IPUMS 1880; Thomas D. Snyder, *120 Years of American Education: A Statistical Portrait* (Washington, DC: National Center for Education Statistics, 1993), 26–27. See a discussion of sources for school enrollment statistics in Claudia Goldin, "America's Graduation from High School: The Evolution and Spread of Secondary Schooling in the Twentieth Century," *Journal of Economic History* 58 (1998): 345–374.

47. Donna Merwick, *Boston Priests, 1848–1910: A Study of Social and Intellectual Change* (Cambridge, MA: Harvard University Press, 1973), 68–73, 111–115; James W. Sanders, *Irish vs. Yankees: A Social History of the Boston Schools* (Oxford: Oxford University Press, 2018), 102–125.

48. *Report of the Commissioner of Education 1880* (Washington, DC: GPO, 1882), 416; IPUMS 1880. Other cities with significant Catholic populations

experienced intense competition between public and parochial systems: see Robert N. Gross, *Public vs. Private: The Early History of School Choice in America* (New York: Oxford University Press, 2018), 26–45.

49. IPUMS 1880.

50. Appendix, *ARSC 1880*, 240; Robert L. Osgood, *For "Children Who Vary from the Normal Type": Special Education in Boston, 1838–1930* (Washington, DC: Gallaudet University Press, 2000), 28–29.

51. IPUMS 1880; Douglas, *Jim Crow Moves North*, 186.

52. *BSL 1879*, 115, 125.

53. IPUMS 1880; Sam Bass Warner, *Streetcar Suburbs: The Process of Growth in Boston, 1870–1900* (Cambridge, MA: Harvard University Press, 1962); Lloyd Rodwin, *Housing and Economic Progress: A Study of the Housing Experiences of Boston's Middle-Income Families* (Cambridge, MA: Harvard University Press, 1961), 85–107.

54. David B. Tyack, *The One Best System: A History of American Urban Education* (Cambridge, MA: Harvard University Press, 1974), 57–59.

55. *BSL 1875* (Boston: Wright & Potter, 1875), 224; *BSL 1879*, 69–75.

56. Warner, *Streetcar Suburbs*, 117–152.

57. Year: *1880*; Census Place: *Boston, Suffolk, Massachusetts*; Roll: *556*; Family History Film: *1254556*; Page: *181C*; Enumeration District: *666*; Image: *0023*.

58. Monte A. Calvert, *The Mechanical Engineer in America, 1830–1910: Professional Cultures in Conflict* (Baltimore: Johns Hopkins University Press, 1967).

59. *Leading Manufacturers and Merchants of the City of Boston: And a Review of the Prominent Exchanges* (Boston: International Publishing Co., 1885), 276.

60. *BSL 1879*, 67–77.

61. Richard Herndon, *Men of Progress: One Thousand Biographical Sketches and Portraits of Leaders in Business and Professional Life in the Commonwealth of Massachusetts*, ed. Edwin Monroe Bacon (Boston: New England Magazine, 1896), 188; Bacon, *The Book of Boston*, 383.

62. Rosara Lucy Passero, "Ethnicity in the Men's Ready-Made Clothing Industry, 1880–1950: The Italian Experience in Philadelphia" (PhD diss., University of Pennsylvania, 1978), 125, 140–142; IPUMS 1880; *BSL 1879*, 69–71.

63. Wendy Gamber, *The Female Economy: The Millinery and Dressmaking Trades, 1860–1930* (Urbana: University of Illinois Press, 1997), 31–32, 55–95; IPUMS 1880; *BSL 1884*, 79; *BSL 1879*, 71.

64. Based on a sample of apprentices that were traced back into the 1880 manuscript census. IPUMS 1880.

65. Joshua L. Rosenbloom, *Looking for Work, Searching for Workers: American Labor Markets during Industrialization* (Cambridge: Cambridge University Press, 2002), 80–114.

66. Kathleen Thelen, *How Institutions Evolve: The Political Economy of Skills in Germany, Britain, the United States, and Japan* (Cambridge: Cambridge University Press, 2004), 21; Paul Howard Douglas, *American Apprenticeship and Industrial Education* (New York: Columbia University, 1921), 19–63.

67. The Railroad Labor Act (1926) provided some of these protections to railroad workers; the National Industrial Recovery Act (1933) and National Labor Relations Act (1935) extended these protections to many more private-sector employees but still excluded independent contractors, domestic workers, and agricultural workers. Michael Wallace, Beth A. Rubin, and Brian T. Smith, "American Labor Law: Its Impact on Working-Class Militancy, 1901–1980," *Social Science History* 12, no. 1 (Spring 1988): 3–7; NLRA, 29 U.S.C. §§ 151–169.

68. Sari Roboff, *Boston's Labor Movement: An Oral History of Work and Union Organizing* (Boston: Boston 200 Corporation, 1977), 11; Green and Donahue, *Boston's Workers*, 36; "Boston Knights," *BG*, March 7, 1886, 1.

69. Mark Schneider, *Boston Confronts Jim Crow, 1890–1920* (Boston: Northeastern University Press, 1997), 9, 23; Green and Donahue, *Boston's Workers*, 38–39.

70. Douglas, *American Apprenticeship and Industrial Education*, 62–73.

71. William Thomas Ham, "Employment Relations in the Construction Industry of Boston" (PhD diss., Harvard University, 1926), 179–200; Frank Tenney Stockton, *The Closed Shop in American Trade Unions* (Lancaster, PA: New Era Printing Co., 1911), 60–61, 69, 81–97; Nathaniel Ruggles Whitney, *Jurisdiction in American Building-Trades Unions* (Lancaster, PA: New Era Printing Co., 1914), 12.

72. Geoffrey T. Blodgett, "Josiah Quincy, Brahmin Democrat," *New England Quarterly* 38, no. 4 (December 1965): 15–19; Roboff, *Boston's Labor Movement*, 15–19.

73. *An Act Relative to the Inspection and Construction of Buildings in the City of Boston*, 1885 MA Acts Chap. 374; *An Act Relative to the Licensing of Plumbers and the Supervision of the Business of Plumbing*, 1893 MA Acts Chap. 477.

74. Hal Hansen, "Caps and Gowns: Historical Reflections on the Institutions That Shaped Learning for and at Work, 1800–1945" (PhD diss., University of Wisconsin-Madison, 1997), 56–64, 41–103; Douglas, *American Apprenticeship and Industrial Education*, 60; Lorinda Perry, *The Millinery Trade in Boston and*

Philadelphia: A Study of Women in Industry (Binghamton, NY: Vail-Ballou Co., 1916), 105–115.

75. "Male Help," *BH,* November 7, 1881; "Female Help," *BH,* September 27, 1879.

76. Mark Erlich, *With Our Hands: The Story of Carpenters in Massachusetts* (Philadelphia: Temple University Press, 1986), 4; Hansen, "Caps and Gowns," 234–238.

77. L. D. Burlingame, "The Importance of an Apprentice System," *The Open Shop* 5, no. 1 (January 1906): 16–21; "Position of Unskilled Labor" and "What Are the Boys to Do?," in *The American Machinist* 4, no. 47 (November 19, 1881): 8; "Industrial Education," *The Carpenter* 2, no. 10 (October 1882): 3.

78. Bogman and Vinal letter, September 19, 1881, Box 2, Folder 3, Margaret Urann Collection, Boston Athenaeum, Boston.

79. *BSL 1875,* 43–44; Charles Felton Pidgin, *History of the Bureau of Statistics of Labor of Massachusetts* (Boston: Wright & Potter, 1876), 41.

80. Spencer Miller Jr., *Labor and Education* (Washington DC: American Federation of Labor, 1939), 8.

81. "The Interests of Labor," *BH,* July 30, 1888, 2.

82. "Letters from Practical Men: An Apprentice Plan," *The American Machinist* 4, no. 13 (March 26, 1881): 5.

83. "Apprentices," *The Carpenter* 1, no. 3 (July 1881): 1.

84. *ARSC 1858* (Boston: Geo. C. Rand & Avery, 1859), 121, 142; *Semi-ARS 1874* (Boston: Rockwell & Churchill, 1874), 44–47, 89; *ARSC 1870* (Boston: Alfred Mudge & Sons, 1871), 359.

85. Bacon, *The Book of Boston,* 72–74.

86. IPUMS 1880.

87. Jocelyn Wills, "Respectable Mediocrity: The Everyday Life of an Ordinary American Striver, 1876–1890," *Journal of Social History* 37, no. 2 (2003): 323–349. See also Michael Zakim, *Accounting for Capitalism: The World the Clerk Made* (Chicago: University of Chicago Press, 2018).

88. Carole Srole, "'A Position That God Has Not Particularly Assigned to Men': The Feminization of Clerical Work, Boston 1860–1915" (PhD diss., University of California, Los Angeles, 1984), 118–122, 174–194, 641.

89. *BSL 1884,* 77; Olivier Zunz, *Making America Corporate, 1870–1920* (Chicago: University of Chicago Press, 1990), 176; IPUMS 1880.

90. Augustus D. Ayling Papers, 1971.028. Diary, 1867, Box 1, Envelope 1, New Hampshire Historical Society, Concord, NH (hereafter Ayling Papers); R. P. Hall & Co., *A Treatise on the Hair* (Nashua, NH: R. P. Hall & Co., 1866).

91. January 29, 1867, Ayling Papers.

92. May 9, 1867, Ayling Papers.

93. March 22, 1867, Ayling Papers.

94. October 25, 1867, Ayling Papers; emphasis in original.

95. September 18, 1867, Ayling Papers.

96. "Male Help," *BH,* August 4, 1881, 3.

97. "Male Help," *BH,* November 7, 1881, 3.

98. "Female Help," *BH,* January 8, 1879, 3.

99. Male Help," *BH,* April 24, 1879, 3.

100. "Male Help," *BH,* August 4, 1881, 3.

101. Brian P. Luskey, "'What Is My Prospects?' The Contours of Mercantile Apprenticeship, Ambition, and Advancement in the Early American Economy," *Business History Review* 78, no. 4 (Winter 2004): 699.

102. *ARSC 1858,* 150.

103. George A. Moore, *Commemorating the Fiftieth Anniversary of the Class of 1888 English High School* (Boston: George A. Moore, 1941).

104. *ARSC 1876* (Boston: Rockwell & Churchill, 1877), 283; *ARSC 1888* (Boston: Rockwell & Churchill, 1889), 45–57.

105. George Cary Eggleston, *How to Educate Yourself: With or without Masters* (New York: G. P. Putnam & Sons, 1872), 2.

106. Bacon, *The Book of Boston,* 161.

107. Dennis P. Ryan, "Beyond the Ballot Box: A Social History of the Boston Irish, 1845–1917" (PhD diss., University of Massachusetts Amherst, 1978), 140.

108. Bacon, *The Book of Boston,* 122.

109. Merwick, *Boston Priests, 1848–1910,* 74, 214.

110. Thomas Lester, "The Birth of the Catholic Union of Boston," *Boston Pilot,* September 29, 2017; Ryan, "Beyond the Ballot Box," 141.

111. Firey, *Land Use,* 87–113, 262–274; Amory, *Proper Bostonians,* 11.

112. *Leading Manufacturers,* 186, 255; Orra Laville Stone, *History of Massachusetts Industries: Their Inception, Growth, and Success* (Chicago: S. J. Clarke Publishing Co., 1930), 1245. Salary estimates are based on comparable salaries for finance-related positions in city government: *City of Boston 1879 Revised Salary Bill,* Document 55 (Boston: Rockwell and Churchill, 1879), 15.

113. *Leading Manufacturers,* 145.

114. Herndon, *Men of Progress,* 490, 751.

115. Zunz, *Making America Corporate,* 61–64.

116. Herndon, *Men of Progress,* 188.

117. Herndon, *Men of Progress,* 992–993. The sample is taken from those listed in this book.

118. Nationally in 1880, only about half of students who enrolled in an institution of higher education actually earned a degree. Snyder, *120 Years,* 75.

119. "The Chambers Humbug," *Manufacturer and Builder* 12, no. 2 (February 1880): 26–27.

120. *How to Manage a Retail Shoe Store* (Boston: Boot and Shoe Recorder, 1888), 53.

121. Roger L. Geiger, *The History of American Higher Education: Learning and Culture from the Founding to World War II* (Princeton, NJ: Princeton University Press, 2014), 7; *ARSC 1858*, 151, 156.

122. IPUMS 1880; Gerard W. Gawalt, "The Impact of Industrialization on the Legal Profession in Massachusetts, 1870–1900," in *The New High Priests: Lawyers in Post-Civil War America*, ed. Gerard W. Gawalt (Westport, CT: Greenwood Press, 1984), 99.

123. Douglas Lamar Jones, *Discovering the Public Interest: A History of the Boston Bar Association* (Canoga Park, CA: Boston Bar Association and CCA Publications, 1993), 20, 31–32, 37–39, 41; William R. Johnson, *Schooled Lawyers: A Study in the Clash of Professional Cultures* (New York: New York University Press, 1978), 24–25.

124. Felice Batlan, *Women and Justice for the Poor: A History of Legal Aid, 1863–1945* (New York: Cambridge University Press, 2015), 125; Stephen Kendrick and Paul Kendrick, *Sarah's Long Walk: The Free Blacks of Boston and How Their Struggle for Equality Changed America* (Boston: Beacon Press, 2004), 154; Jones, *Discovering the Public Interest*, 55, 85; Johnson, *Schooled Lawyers*, 171.

125. Jones, *Discovering the Public Interest*, 41–43; Johnson, *Schooled Lawyers*, 24–25, 42–54.

126. *ARSC 1858*, 121; *ARS 1884* (Boston: Rockwell & Churchill, 1885), 37.

127. *ARSC 1858*, 151, 156.

128. IPUMS 1880.

129. Horace Mann, *A Few Thoughts on the Powers and Duties of Woman: Two Lectures* (Syracuse, NY: Hall, Mills, and Co., 1853), 82.

130. Karen Mastrobattista Curran, *Her Greatness Proclaim: The History of Girls' Latin School, Boston, Massachusetts, 1878–1976* (Amesbury, MA: Vern Associates, 2014), 2–39.

131. *ARS 1903* (Boston: Municipal Printing Office, 1903), 61; *ARS 1907* (Boston: Municipal Printing Office, 1907), 12–13.

132. Appendix, *ARSC 1858*, 145; *AS 1911* (Boston: Printing Department, 1911), 33; *ARSC 1880*, 24; Kaestle, *Pillars of the Republic*, 123–125.

133. Kathleen Murphy, "Boston Teachers Organize, 1919–65" (Ed.D. diss., Harvard Graduate School of Education, Harvard University, 1981), 14.

134. Karen Leroux, "'Lady Teachers' and the Genteel Roots of Teacher Organization in Gilded Age Cities," *History of Education Quarterly* 46, no. 2 (2006): 187–188.

135. *Annual Report of the Board of Education of Massachusetts* (Boston: Wright & Potter, 1907), 320–330; Lucile Eaves, *Old-Age Support of Women Teachers* (Boston: Spartan Press, 1921), 25, 43; *ARSC 1902* (Boston: Municipal Printing Office, 1902), 42.

136. This data is based on tracking thirty-three out of forty students of the 1880 Normal School entering class through the manuscript census. Boston Normal School Records, 1872–1942; Admissions, 1872–1906, Series 1, Vol. 1, Healey Library and Archives, University of Massachusetts, Boston.

137. *Rules of the School Committee* (Boston: Municipal Printing Office, 1906), 44. These policies were not always enforceable, and some teachers were married, including 2 percent of women teachers in Boston in 1880. Geraldine J. Clifford, *Those Good Gertrudes: A Social History of Women Teachers in America* (Baltimore: Johns Hopkins University Press, 2014), 128–134; IPUMS 1880.

138. Firey, *Land Use,* 106–107. Year: *1880;* Census Place: *Boston, Suffolk, Massachusetts;* Roll: *555;* Family History Film: *1254555;* Page: *311C;* Enumeration District: *642;* Image: *0003.*

139. Oscar Handlin, *Boston's Immigrants, 1790–1880: A Study in Acculturation* (Cambridge, MA: Harvard University Press, 1959), 3–12.

140. Henry Cabot Lodge, *Boston* (New York: Longmans, Green, and Co., 1891), 205.

141. Ronald Story, *The Forging of an Aristocracy: Harvard and the Boston Upper Class, 1800–1870* (Middletown, CT: Wesleyan University Press, 1980), 7.

142. Story, *The Forging of an Aristocracy,* 7, 92.

143. Oliver Wendell Holmes, "The Brahmin Caste of New England," *Atlantic Monthly* 5, no. 27 (1860).

144. Noam Maggor, *Brahmin Capitalism: Frontiers of Wealth and Populism in America's First Gilded Age* (Cambridge, MA: Harvard University Press, 2017), 21–22, 96–99.

145. Charles Francis Adams, *Charles Francis Adams, 1835–1915: An Autobiography* (Boston: Houghton Mifflin, 1916), 190.

146. Lodge, *Boston,* 198–199.

147. Geoffrey T. Blodgett, "Yankee Leadership in a Divided City, 1860–1910," in *Boston, 1700–1980: The Evolution of Urban Politics,* ed. Ronald P. Formisano and Constance Burns (Westport, CT: Greenwood Press, 1984), 92–100; Story, *The Forging of an Aristocracy,* 172.

148. Polly Welts Kaufman, *Boston Women and City School Politics, 1872–1905* (New York: Garland, 1994), 28–178; Constance Burns, "The Irony of Progressive Reform, 1898–1910," in Formisano and Burns, *Boston, 1700–1980,* 137–144.

149. Paul Dimaggio, "Cultural Entrepreneurship in Nineteenth-Century Boston: The Creation of an Organizational Base for High Culture in America," *Media, Culture, & Society* 4, no. 1 (January 1982): 33–50.

150. Amory, *Proper Bostonians*, 167–187.

151. Records of the Saturday Morning Club, 1871–1983, Schlesinger Library, Radcliffe Institute, Harvard University, Cambridge, MA.

152. Bacon, *The Book of Boston*, 120–122.

153. Steven B. Levine, "The Rise of American Boarding Schools and the Development of a National Upper Class," *Social Problems* 28, no. 1 (October 1980): 74.

154. *RCE 1880* (Washington, DC: GPO, 1882), 626, 634, 656, 668, 678, 697, 702.

155. Samuel Eliot Morison, *Three Centuries of Harvard, 1636–1936* (Cambridge, MA: Harvard University Press, 1936), 409; William Bruce Leslie, *Gentlemen and Scholars: College and Community in the "Age of the University," 1865–1917* (University Park: Pennsylvania State University Press, 1992), 187–209; Jerome Karabel, *The Chosen: The Hidden History of Admission and Exclusion at Harvard, Yale, and Princeton* (Boston: Houghton Mifflin, 2006), 42; Clifford Putney, *Muscular Christianity: Manhood and Sports in Protestant America, 1880–1920* (Cambridge, MA: Harvard University Press, 2009).

156. Marian Lawrence Peabody, *To Be Young Was Very Heaven* (Boston: Houghton Mifflin, 1967), 119.

157. Veritas, "A Catholic View of Education," *Boston Pilot*, January 17, 1880, 6.

158. Henry Fitch Jenks, "Historical Sketch," in *Catalogue of the Boston Public Latin School* (Boston: Boston Latin School Association, 1886), 5–6, 41, 75.

159. George Washington Copp Noble, *Classical School. Mr. G. W. C. Noble Will Open a Classical School, in Boston . . .* (Boston: s.n., 1866); J. Evarts Greene, "The Roxbury Latin School: An Outline of Its History," *Proceedings of the American Antiquarian Society* 4, no. 4 (December 1887): 349.

160. *Chauncy Hall School Catalog, 1879–1880* (Boston: David Clapp & Son, 1880), 21–42; Edward H. Cole, *A School and a Man* (Newtonville, MA: Oakwood Press, 1951), 1.

161. Levine, "American Boarding Schools," 64–68.

162. *RCE 1880*, 538, 614; *ARSC 1879* (Boston: Rockwell & Churchill, 1879), 28; *Catalogue and Circular of Gannett Institute for Young Ladies, 1879* (Boston, 1879), 4–7; *Miss Caroline C. Johnson's School for Young Ladies*, June 1876; *The Boston Academy of Notre Dame* (Boston, 1923), 3, in Gutman Special Collections, Gutman Library, Harvard University, Cambridge, MA; Kaufman, *Boston Women*, 75; Curran, *Her Greatness Proclaim*, 44–46; "To Leave South End," *BG*, March 11, 1907, 16.

163. Student Register for H. Williams' Private School (Mss C 5646), R. Stanton Avery Special Collections Department, New England Historic Genealogical Society, Boston; "Intelligence and Miscellany," *The Massachusetts Teacher,* April 1956, 195.

164. Boston college attendance was higher than the national average for 18–24-year-olds, which was slightly over 1 percent in 1880. Snyder, *120 Years,* 64; IPUMS 1880; U.S. Census Office, "Table 9: Population, as Native and Foreign-Born, of Cities, Etc.: 1880 and 1870," in *Tenth Census of the United States 1880,* vol. 1, *Statistics of the Population of the United States* (Washington, DC: GPO, 1883), 450; *RCE 1880,* 626, 656.

165. Richard Freeland, *Academia's Golden Age: Universities in Massachusetts, 1945–1970* (Oxford: Oxford University Press, 1992), 18–40; Julie A. Reuben, *The Making of the Modern University: Intellectual Transformation and the Marginalization of Morality* (Chicago: University of Chicago Press, 1996), 61–87.

166. Kett, *Merit,* 161n299.

167. Geiger, *The History of American Higher Education,* 1–7; Story, *The Forging of an Aristocracy,* 93; National Bureau of Economic Research, Index of the General Price Level for United States; CPI Inflation Calculator.

168. Charles Eliot, "The New Education," *Atlantic Monthly,* February 1869.

169. Hugh Hawkins, *Between Harvard and America: The Educational Leadership of Charles W. Eliot* (New York: Oxford University Press, 1972), 146–148, 167, 180–193.

170. *RCE 1880,* 656, 668.

171. Schneider, *Boston Confronts Jim Crow,* 110–111; David Levering Lewis, *W. E. B. Du Bois, 1868–1919: Biography of a Race* (New York: Henry Holt, 1994), 79–116. See also Adelaide M. Cromwell, *The Other Brahmins: Boston's Black Upper Class, 1750–1950* (Fayetteville: University of Arkansas Press, 1994).

172. Karabel, *The Chosen,* 14–15; Amory, *Proper Bostonians,* 291–311.

173. *RCE 1880,* 678, 682; Julius Adams Stratton and Loretta H. Mannix, *Mind and Hand: The Birth of MIT* (Cambridge, MA: MIT Press, 2005), xvii–xviii.

174. *RCE 1880,* 656, 668; Kathleen Kilgore, *Transformations: A History of Boston University* (Boston: Boston University, 1991), ix, 31; David J. Loftus, *Boston College High School, 1863–1983* (Boston: Addison C. Getchell, 1984), 1; Charles Francis Donovan, *History of Boston College: From the Beginnings to 1990* (Chestnut Hill, MA: University Press of Boston College, 1990), 59.

175. Helen Leah Read, "The Home: Radcliffe College," *The Outlook,* October 6, 1984, 547; *Reports of the President and Treasurer of Harvard College 1893–1894* (Cambridge, MA: Harvard University, 1895), 237; *Reports of the President and Treasurer of Harvard College 1894–1895* (Cambridge, MA: Harvard University, 1896), 250; *RCE 1880,* 626; *RCE 1901,* vol. 2 (Washington, DC:

GPO, 1902), 1709; Nancy Weiss Malkiel, *"Keep the Damned Women Out": The Struggle for Coeducation* (Princeton, NJ: Princeton University Press, 2018), 34–35.

176. Peabody, *To Be Young Was Very Heaven*, 31.

177. Peabody, *To Be Young Was Very Heaven*, 31, 34, 57.

2. Uplifting the "Unskilled"

1. Sari Roboff and Katie Kenneally, *The North End* (Boston: Boston 200 Corporation, 1975), 23.

2. Edwin Monroe Bacon, *The Book of Boston: Fifty Years' Recollections of the New England Metropolis* (Boston: Book of Boston Company, 1916), 90.

3. Asha Weinstein, "Congestion as a Cultural Construct: The 'Congestion Evil' in Boston in the 1890s and 1920s," *Journal of Transport History* 27, no. 2 (September 2006): 103–104.

4. Orra Laville Stone, *History of Massachusetts Industries: Their Inception, Growth, and Success* (Chicago: S. J. Clarke Publishing Co., 1930), 1236.

5. Year: *1880*; Census Place: *Boston, Suffolk, Massachusetts*; Roll: *554*; Family History Film: *1254554*; Page: *429C*; Enumeration District: *624*; Image: *0143*; Ancestry.com. *Massachusetts, Marriage Records, 1840–1915* (online database). Year: *1900*; Census Place: *Boston Ward 6, Suffolk, Massachusetts*; Roll: *677*; Page: *9B*; Enumeration District: *1219*; FHL microfilm: *1240677*; Year: *1910*; Census Place: *Boston Ward 6, Suffolk, Massachusetts*; Roll: *T624_615*; Page: *6B*; Enumeration District: *1324*; FHL microfilm: *1374628*; Year: *1920*; Census Place: *Boston Ward 18, Suffolk, Massachusetts*; Roll: *T625_737*; Page: *5B*; Enumeration District: *452*; Image: *832*; Year: *1930*; Census Place: *Boston, Suffolk, Massachusetts*; Roll: *953*; Page: *10B*; Enumeration District: *0433*; Image: *564.0*; FHL microfilm: *2340688*; Year: *1940*; Census Place: *Boston, Suffolk, Massachusetts*; Roll: *T627_1674*; Page: *19A*; Enumeration District: *15-535*; Samuel Nathaniel Behrman, *The Worcester Account* (New York: Random House, 1954), 33; Sam Bass Warner Jr., *Streetcar Suburbs: The Process of Growth in Boston, 1870–1900* (Cambridge, MA: Harvard University Press, 1962), 57, 201n11.

6. Stephan Thernstrom, *The Other Bostonians: Poverty and Progress in the American Metropolis, 1880–1870* (Cambridge, MA: Harvard University Press, 1973), 89–93.

7. Mary Antin, *The Promised Land* (Boston: Houghton, Mifflin and Company, 1912); Peter Randolph, *From Slave Cabin to the Pulpit: The Autobiography of Rev. Peter Randolph* (Boston: J. H. Earle, 1893).

8. Joshua L. Rosenbloom, *Looking for Work, Searching for Workers: American Labor Markets during Industrialization* (Cambridge: Cambridge University Press, 2002), 88; Christine E. Bose, Philip L. Bereano, and Mary Malloy, "House-

hold Technology and the Social Construction of Housework," *Technology and Culture* 25, no. 1 (January 1984): 65–66.

9. This chapter uses IPUMS USA (digitized individual-level data samples of the US decennial census) 100 percent samples from 1880, 1900, 1910, 1920, 1930, and 1940, in addition to the 5 percent sample for 1900, which includes a school enrollment variable, hereafter referred to as IPUMS plus the sample year (e.g., IPUMS 1880–1940, IPUMS 1900, etc.). The original manuscript census of 1890 was destroyed in a fire, so the data points for this year are estimates. This chapter focuses on laborers and service workers as representative low-wage workers; factory operatives will be described in Chapter 3 on the industrial workplace. Steven Ruggles, Sarah Flood, Ronald Goeken, Josiah Grover, Erin Meyer, Jose Pacas, and Matthew Sobek, IPUMS USA: Version 10.0 [dataset] (Minneapolis: IPUMS, 2020), https://doi.org/10.18128/D010.V10.0.

10. Annette D. Bernhardt, *The Gloves-off Economy: Workplace Standards at the Bottom of America's Labor Market* (Urbana-Champaign: University of Illinois, 2008).

11. Nancy Foner, "The Uses and Abuses of History: Understanding Contemporary U.S. Immigration," *Journal of Ethnic and Migration Studies* 45, no. 1 (2018): 2; U.S. Census Office, "Table 9: Population, as Native and Foreign-Born, of Cities, Etc.: 1880 and 1870," in *Tenth Census of the United States 1880*, vol. 1, *Statistics of the Population of the United States* (Washington, DC: GPO, 1883), 450; U.S. Bureau of the Census, "Table 8: Age, for Cities and Towns of 10,000 or More: 1920," in *Fourteenth Census of the United States 1920*, vol. 3, *Population, Composition and Characteristics of the Population by States* (Washington, DC: GPO, 1922), 438.

12. Suzanne W. Model, "Italian and Jewish Intergenerational Mobility: New York, 1910," *Social Science History* 12, no. 1 (1988): 31.

13. Walter Irving Firey, *Land Use in Central Boston* (Cambridge, MA: Harvard University Press, 1947), 170–197; IPUMS 1880–1940.

14. Katie Kenneally, *The South End* (Boston: Boston 200 Corporation, 1975), 7–9.

15. Katie Kenneally, *Chinatown* (Boston: Boston 200 Corporation, 1976), 1–8.

16. Kenneally, *The South End*, 12–15; Elizabeth Hafkin Pleck, *Black Migration and Poverty: Boston 1865–1900* (New York: Academic Press, 1979), 77.

17. Charles H. Trout, *Boston, the Great Depression, and the New Deal* (New York: Oxford University Press, 1977), 30–33; "Organizational History," Overseers of the Public Welfare of the City of Boston, CC 11, Simmons College Archives, Boston.

18. Associated Charities of Boston, *A Directory of the Charitable and Beneficent Organizations of Boston* (Boston: A. Williams & Co., 1880), iv–vii, 17–30,

47–79; Nathan Irvin Huggins, *Protestants against Poverty: Boston's Charities, 1870–1900* (Westport, CT: Greenwood Publishing Corp., 1971), 10, 60–66; Michael B. Katz, *In the Shadow of the Poorhouse: A Social History of Welfare in America,* 10th anniversary ed. (New York: Basic Books, 1996), 41; Michael B. Katz, *The Undeserving Poor: America's Enduring Confrontation with Poverty* (New York: Pantheon Books, 1989), 9–35; Peter C. Holloran, *Boston's Wayward Children: Social Services for Homeless Children, 1830–1930* (Rutherford, NJ: Fairleigh Dickinson University Press, 1989), 63–104, 165; Susan Ebert, "Community and Philanthropy," in *The Jews of Boston,* ed. Jonathan D. Sarna, Ellen Smith, and Scott-Martin Kosofsky (New Haven, CT: Yale University Press, 2005), 221–248.

19. Paul Kleppner, "From Party to Factions: The Dissolution of Boston's Major Party, 1876–1910," in *Boston, 1700–1980: The Evolution of Urban Politics,* ed. Ronald P. Formisano and Constance Burns (Westport, CT: Greenwood Press, 1984).

20. Sarah Deutsch, *Women and the City: Gender, Space, and Power in Boston, 1870–1940* (New York: Oxford University Press, 2000), 136–160; Edward T. James, *Notable American Women, 1607–1950: A Biographical Dictionary,* vol. 2 (Cambridge, MA: Harvard University Press, 1971), 313. See also Karen J. Blair, *Clubwoman as Feminist: True Womanhood Redefined, 1868–1914* (New York: Holmes & Meier, 1980); Gwendolyn Mink, *The Wages of Motherhood: Inequality in the Welfare State, 1917–1942* (Ithaca, NY: Cornell University Press, 1995); Joan Marie Johnson, *Funding Feminism: Monied Women, Philanthropy, and the Women's Movement, 1870–1967* (Chapel Hill: University of North Carolina Press, 2017).

21. Robert Archey Woods, *The Settlement Horizon* (New York: Russell Sage Foundation, 1922), 35, 49, 169–176, 331.

22. "Initial Step for Industrial School," *BH,* December 6, 1906, 9; "To Save Waste of Youthful Years," *BH,* March 30, 1907, 16.

23. Michael B. Katz, *Reconstructing American Education* (Cambridge, MA: Harvard University Press, 1987), 17–23; Katz, *In the Shadow of the Poorhouse,* 3–88; Daniel T. Rodgers, *The Work Ethic in Industrial America, 1850–1920* (Chicago: University of Chicago Press, 2009), 223–226.

24. Alice O'Connor, *Poverty Knowledge: Social Science, Social Policy, and the Poor in Twentieth-Century U.S. History* (Princeton, NJ: Princeton University Press, 2009), 25–54; Robert A. Woods, "Does the Present Trend toward Vocational Education Threaten Liberal Culture?," *The School Review* 19, no. 7 (September 1911): 469.

25. Holloran, *Boston's Wayward Children,* 67; William Alan Braverman, "The Ascent of Boston's Jews, 1630–1918" (PhD diss., Harvard University, 1990), 135; Ebert, "Community and Philanthropy," 225–226.

26. Samuel Haber, *The Quest for Authority and Honor in the American Professions, 1750–1900* (Chicago: University of Chicago Press, 1991), 193–205.

27. Magali Sarfatti Larson, *The Rise of Professionalism: Monopolies of Competence and Sheltered Markets,* new ed. (New Brunswick, NJ: Transaction Publishers, 2013); Joseph F. Kett, "The Adolescence of Vocational Education," in *Work, Youth, and Schooling: Historical Perspectives on Vocationalism in American Education,* ed. Harvey Kantor and David B. Tyack (Stanford, CA: Stanford University Press, 1982), 86–104.

28. Haber, *The Quest for Authority and Honor,* 193–359.

29. Wolfgang Streeck, "Skills and Politics: General and Specific," Discussion Paper 11 / 1 (Cologne, Germany: MPIfG, 2011), 2–3.

30. Ronnie J. Steinberg, "Social Construction of Skill: Gender, Power, and Comparable Worth," *Work and Occupations* 17, no. 4 (November 1990): 449–482; Paul Attewell, "What Is Skill?," *Work and Occupations* 17, no. 4 (November 1990): 429–435.

31. *LB,* no. 8 (October 1898): 28.

32. "Social Statistics of Workingwomen," *LB,* no. 18 (May 1901): 48.

33. Venila S. Burrington, "Negro Domestic Workers in Boston," *Bulletin of the Inter-Municipal Committee on Household Research* 1, no. 7 (May 1905): 12–13; IPUMS 1880–1940.

34. Lucy Maynard Salmon, *Domestic Service* (New York: Macmillan, 1897), 146–147.

35. *WEIU Report 1882* (Boston: No. 157 Tremont Street, 1882), 2.

36. Salmon, *Domestic Service,* 114–115.

37. *Annual Report of the New England Society for the Suppression of Vice 1888–1889* (Boston: Office of the Society, 1889), 13.

38. *WEIU Report 1882,* 52; *WEIU Report 1905* (Boston, 1905), 26.

39. Lara Vapnek, *Breadwinners: Working Women and Economic Independence, 1865–1920* (Urbana: University of Illinois Press, 2009), 102–129; Deutsch, *Women and the City,* 54–78.

40. *WEIU Report 1889* (Boston: No. 98 Boylston Street, 1889), 36; *WEIU Report 1888* (Boston: No. 74 Boylston Street, 1888), 36.

41. *WEIU Report 1890* (Boston: No. 98 Boylston Street, 1890), 33; *WEIU Report 1896* (Cambridge: Cambridge Cooperative Society, 1896), 40.

42. *WEIU Report 1890,* 33; *WEIU Report 1891* (Boston: Geo. E. Crosby & Co., 1891), 12.

43. *WEIU Report 1895* (Boston: The Barta Press, 1895), 33; *WEIU Report 1896,* 39.

44. *WEIU Report 1898* (Cambridge: Co-operative Printing Society, 1898), 49; *WEIU Report 1910* (Boston, 1910), 18–25.

45. Vapnek, *Breadwinners,* 109.

46. *WEIU Report, 1905,* 29; "School of Housekeeping: Course for Employers, 1897," and "School of Housekeeping: Course for Employees, 1899–1900," Box 2, Folder 9, Women's Educational and Industrial Union Records, 1894–1955, Schlesinger Library, Radcliffe Institute, Harvard University, Cambridge, MA.

47. *LB,* no. 18 (May 1901): 48.

48. Vapnek, *Breadwinners,* 118.

49. Sylvester Baxter, "Boston's Fenway as an Educational Center," *New Outlook* 86, no. 17 (August 14, 1907): 895; *WEIU Report 1905,* 28–29; *WEIU Report 1910,* 15–28, 33–35; *WEIU Report 1911* (Boston, 1911), 34–36.

50. *The Work of NBSIS from 1881 to 1887* (Boston: Rand Avery Co., 1887), 4.

51. Class Register and Attendance Book, 1886–1887, MC 269, Carton 1, Series IV, Vol. 1, North Bennet Street Industrial School Records, 1880–1973, Schlesinger Library, Radcliffe Institute, Harvard University, Cambridge, MA (hereafter NBSIS); "Industrial Schools of the Christian Associations," *LB,* no. 38 (December 1905): 292–293.

52. Ebert, "Community and Philanthropy," 225–226.

53. Isabel Eaton, "Robert Gould Shaw House and Its Work," *The Crisis* 6, no. 3 (July 1913): 142; John Daniels, *In Freedom's Birthplace: A Study of the Boston Negroes* (Boston: Houghton Mifflin, 1914), 190, 194; Helen Porter Utterback, "Mrs. Ruffin and the Woman's Era Club of Boston," *Los Angeles Herald Illustrated Magazine* 29, no. 187 (April 6 1902), 7; Craig Doughty, "Black Elitism and Cultural Entrepreneurship in 1920's Boston, Massachusetts: The League of Women for Community Service," *European Journal of American Studies* 14, no. 2 (July 6, 2019): 5; Mark Schneider, *Boston Confronts Jim Crow, 1890–1920* (Boston: Northeastern University Press, 1997), 83–103; See also Elisabeth Lasch-Quinn, *Black Neighbors: Race and the Limits of Reform in the American Settlement House Movement, 1890–1945* (Chapel Hill: University of North Carolina Press, 1993).

54. Laura S. Wilkinson, "Household Economics," in *The Congress of Women: Held in the Woman's Building, World's Columbian Exposition, Chicago, USA, 1893,* ed. Mary Kavanaugh Oldham Eagle (Philadelphia: International Publishing Co., 1895), 233–236.

55. "National Household Economics Association: State Reports Presented at Nashville," *The American Kitchen Magazine* 9, no. 1 (April 1898): 33–34.

56. Ellen H. Richards, *Euthenics, the Science of Controllable Environment* (Boston: Whitcomb & Barrows, 1910); Sarah Stage, "Ellen Richards and the Social Significance of the Home Economics Movement," in *Rethinking Home Economics: Women and the History of a Profession,* ed. Sarah Stage and Virginia B. Vincenti (Ithaca, NY: Cornell University Press, 1997), 17–34.

57. Rima D. Apple, "Liberal Arts or Vocational Training? Home Economics Education for Girls," in Stage and Vincenti, *Rethinking Home Economics,* 87–90.

58. Salmon, *Domestic Service,* 181–186, 261–262.

59. "Project More Unions," *BG,* March 14, 1904, 2; "Labor Notes," *BP,* May 11, 1908, 4; "President of the Culinary Workers," *BP,* April 5, 1910, 15; "Labor Notes," *BP,* June 29, 1908, 4.

60. Carolyn D. McCreesh, *Women in the Campaign to Organize Garment Workers, 1880–1917* (New York: Garland, 1985), 40; Daniels, *In Freedom's Birthplace,* 376–377.

61. "President of the Culinary Workers," *BP,* April 5, 1910, 15; "Union for Domestics," *BP,* October 23, 1911; "Directory of Labor Organizations in Massachusetts," *LB,* no. 83 (September 1911): 14; "Directory of Labor Organizations in Massachusetts," *LB,* no. 93 (August 1912): 14–15.

62. Hotel and Restaurant Employees International Alliance and Bartenders International League of America, *Fifty Years of Progress, 1890–1941* (Cincinnati: American Federation of Labor, 1941), 15–18.

63. J. Clay Smith Jr., *Emancipation: The Making of the Black Lawyer, 1844–1944* (Philadelphia: University of Pennsylvania Press, 1999), 76; L. J. Pettijohn, *Twenty-Second Biennial Report of the Secretary of State of the State of Kansas, 1919–1920* (Topeka: Kansas State Printing Plant, 1920), 75; "Legal Directory," *The Crisis* 46, no. 12 (December 1939): 379; J. J. Boris, ed., *Who's Who in Colored America* (New York: Who's Who in Colored America Corp., 1927), 5.

64. "Boston, Mass.," *The Mixer and Server* 12, no. 6 (June 15, 1903): 41; "Boston, Mass.," *The Mixer and Server* 15, no. 1 (January 15, 1906): 28; "Boston, Mass.," *The Mixer and Server* 16, no. 2 (February 15, 1907): 38.

65. J. E. Laycock, "Boston, MA March 3, 1908," *The Mixer and Server* 17, no. 3 (March 15, 1908): 18; J. E. Laycock, "Lowell, MA Oct. 2, 1908," *The Mixer and Server* 17, no. 10 (October 15, 1908): 16.

66. "Speaking of Boston," *The Mixer and Server* 18, no. 7 (July 15, 1909): 44; "Memorandum of the General Executive Board," *The Mixer and Server* 25, no. 7 (July 15, 1916): 7; "Washington D.C.," *The Mixer and Server* 31, no. 4 (April 15, 1922): 14.

67. IPUMS 1880–1940; "Directory of Labor Organizations in Massachusetts," *LB,* no. 93 (August, 1912): 18; "Directory of Labor Organizations in Massachusetts," *LB,* no. 113 (March 1916): 21.

68. Schneider, *Boston Confronts Jim Crow,* 75.

69. Drew Keeling, *The Business of Transatlantic Migration between Europe and the United States, 1900–1914* (Zurich: Chronos, 2012).

70. William P. Dillingham, "Contract Labor and Induced and Assisted Immigration," in *Abstracts of Reports of the Immigration Commission,* vol. 2 (Washington, DC: GPO, 1911), 371–386.

71. Gunther Peck, *Reinventing Free Labor: Padrones and Immigrant Workers in the North American West, 1880–1930* (Cambridge: Cambridge University Press, 2000), 18; William P. Dillingham, "The Greek Padrone System in the United States," in *Abstracts of Reports of the Immigration Commission*, vol. 2 (Washington, DC: GPO, 1911), 392–406; Dillingham, "Contract Labor and Induced and Assisted Immigration," 383; Roboff and Kenneally, *The North End*, 9.

72. "Project More Unions," *BG*, March 14, 1904, 2.

73. Peck, *Reinventing Free Labor*, 208.

74. *LB*, no. 83 (September, 1911): 15; "Hod Carriers' Union in Outside Hands," *BG*, October 2, 1916, 15; Arch A. Mercey, *The Laborers' Story, 1903–1953: The First Fifty Years of the International Hod Carriers', Building and Common Laborers' Union of America (AFL)* (Washington, DC: Ransdell, 1954), vii; James R. Green and Hugh Carter Donahue, *Boston's Workers: A Labor History* (Boston: Boston Public Library, 1979), 91.

75. "D'Allessandr Is Dead at Quincy," *BG*, September 12, 1926, B4.

76. "Labor Notes," *Boston Post*, June 29, 1908, 4.

77. *BSL 1894* (Boston: Wright & Potter, 1894), 57–82; *BSL 1904* (Boston: Wright & Potter, 1904), 131–214; "Free Public Employment Offices," *LB*, no. 14 (May 1900): 45–55; "Statistical Abstracts," *LB*, no. 25 (February 1903): 50–51; "Free Employment Offices," *LB*, no. 35 (March 1905): 4–11.

78. *BSL 1907* (Boston: Wright & Potter, 1908), 415, 437–447; E. Leroy Sweetser, *Sixteenth Annual Report of the Public Employment Offices, 1922* (Boston: Wright & Potter, 1922), 19.

79. Rosenbloom, *Looking for Work*, 70–79.

80. Charles F. Gettemy, *First Annual Report of the Chief of the Bureau of Statistics of Labor on the State Free Employment Offices, 1907* (Boston: Wright & Potter, 1908), 23.

81. Tracy L. Steffes, *School, Society, and State: A New Education to Govern Modern America, 1890–1940* (Chicago: University of Chicago Press, 2012), 7.

82. *ARS 1921* (Boston: Printing Department, 1921), 24.

83. Daniel Amsterdam, *Roaring Metropolis: Businessmen's Campaign for a Civic Welfare State* (Philadelphia: University of Pennsylvania Press, 2016), 1–13, 83. See also Christina A. Ziegler-McPherson, *Americanization in the States: Immigrant Social Welfare Policy, Citizenship, and National Identity in the United States, 1908–1929* (Gainesville: University Press of Florida, 2010); Clif Stratton, *Education for Empire: American Schools, Race, and the Paths of Good Citizenship* (Oakland: University of California Press, 2016).

84. Steffes, *School, Society, and State*, 15–26; William J. Reese, *Power and the Promise of School Reform: Grassroots Movements during the Progressive Era* (New York: Teachers College Press, 2002), xix–xxiv.

85. "Record of Families Connected with No. Bennet Day Nursery, 1883," MC 269, Series II, Box 101, Biv. 45, NBSIS.

86. Application, 1908–1909, MC 269, Series II, Box 101, Biv. 48, NBSIS.

87. Barbara Beatty, *Preschool Education in America: The Culture of Young Children from the Colonial Era to the Present* (New Haven, CT: Yale University Press, 1995), 102.

88. *Semi-AS 1900* (Boston: Municipal Printing Office, 1900), 98, 116–117; *ARSC 1900* (Boston: Municipal Printing Office, 1900), 44.

89. *ARS 1915* (Boston: Printing Department, 1916), 78; "Schools for New Citizens," *BG*, September 26, 1915, 47.

90. "Will Teach Immigrants," *BG*, November 11, 1915, 16.

91. *ARS 1917* (Boston: Printing Department, 1918), 60.

92. *ARS 1919* (Boston: Printing Department, 1919), 32.

93. *ARS 1904* (Boston: Municipal Printing Office, 1904), 65; *ARS 1907* (Boston: Municipal Printing Office, 1907), 49; *ARS 1915*, 19, 78; "Practical Help to Immigrants," *BG*, March 29, 1914, 52; "Must Learn English," *BG*, September 19, 1915, 46.

94. Barbara Miller Solomon, *Ancestors and Immigrants: A Changing New England Tradition* (Cambridge, MA: Harvard University Press, 1956), 100–140.

95. *ARS 1922* (Boston: Printing Department, 1922), 40–41; Green and Donahue, *Boston's Workers*, 100–103.

96. Frank Victor Thompson, *Schooling of the Immigrant* (New York: Harper & Brothers, 1920), 13, 360–371.

97. "Pointers on the Americanization Plan of the Boston Chamber of Commerce," undated, p. 3, and "Special Committee on Americanization of Immigrants 1916–1917," in Case 5, Folder: "Americanization of Immigrants 1915–1932—General 1," Boston Chamber of Commerce Records, 1872–1949, Special Collections, Baker Library, Harvard Business School, Boston (hereafter BCC).

98. *ARS 1913* (Boston: Printing Department, 1913), 104.

99. "Americanization of Immigrants: A Tentative City Wide Program," circa 1917, Case 5, Folder: "Americanization of Immigrants 1915–1932—The Education of Immigrants," BCC; "Pointers on the Americanization Plan of the Boston Chamber of Commerce," undated, p. 2, and "Committee on Americanization: Purpose, Briefly Stated," Case 5, Folder: "Americanization of Immigrants 1915–1932—General 1," BCC.

100. "Works Manager Report 1923–1924," Box 164, Dennison Manufacturing Company Records, 1815–1990, Special Collections, Baker Library, Harvard Business School, Boston (hereafter DMC).

101. Desmond S. King, *Making Americans: Immigration, Race, and the Origins of the Diverse Democracy* (Cambridge, MA: Harvard University Press, 2000), 99.

102. *AS 1924* (Boston: Printing Department, 1924), 59; *ARS 1924* (Boston: Printing Department, 1924), 73–78.

103. Based on tracking nineteen out of twenty-six graduates, whose names were published in the *Boston Globe,* through the manuscript censuses. "Graduates Number 498," *BG,* March 31, 1916, 16.

104. Thompson, *Schooling of the Immigrant,* 56, 372.

105. *ARSC 1902* (Boston: Municipal Printing Office, 1902), 18.

106. *ARSC 1870* (Boston: Alfred Mudge & Son, 1871), 229; *ARSC 1879* (Boston: Rockwell & Churchill, 1879), 9–10; *ARS 1886* (Boston: Rockwell & Churchill, 1887), 3; *ARS 1902* (Boston: Municipal Printing Office, 1902), 57.

107. *ARS 1900* (Boston: Municipal Printing Office, 1900), 79–89.

108. *ARSC 1912* (Boston: Printing Department, 1912), 27.

109. *ARS 1905* (Boston: Municipal Printing Office, 1905), 84; Joan C. Tonn, *Mary P. Follett: Creating Democracy, Transforming Management* (New Haven, CT: Yale University Press, 2008), 166.

110. *ARSC 1902,* 18–23.

111. *ARSC 1902,* 18–23; *ARS 1908* (Boston: Municipal Printing Office, 1908), 54.

112. Arthur Julius Jones, *The Continuation School in the United States* (Washington, DC: US GPO, 1907), 33–52; *ARS 1909* (Boston: Printing Department, 1909), 41.

113. *ARS 1915,* 79; Boston School Committee, *Household Arts School Misc. Pamphlets,* Gutman Library Special Collections, Harvard University, Cambridge, MA.

114. *ARS 1913,* 110, 173–180.

115. *ARS 1914* (Boston: Printing Department, 1914), 38–39, 147–154, 178–184. Boston's full-time Parental School for Truants, founded in 1895, was replaced with a daytime-only Disciplinary School for truant youth in 1914. Both schools combined manual labor with academics. For the development of disciplinary programs that operated through or in conjunction with Boston public schools, see Robert L. Osgood, *For "Children Who Vary from the Normal Type": Special Education in Boston, 1838–1930* (Washington, DC: Gallaudet University Press, 2000), 118–126; Holloran, *Boston's Wayward Children.* On increasing state compulsion to attend school, see Steffes, *School, Society, and State,* 119–154.

116. "Successful School Men," *American Education* 16, no. 1 (September 1912): 25.

117. *ARS 1914,* 65; *ARS 1915,* 15.

118. *ARS 1914,* 65.

119. *ARS 1913,* 111–112.

120. Franklin J. Keller, *Day Schools for Young Workers: The Organization and Management of Part-Time and Continuation Schools* (New York: The Century Co., 1924), xii.

121. Kenneally, *The South End*, 6.

122. Roboff and Kenneally, *The North End*, 15.

123. *ARS 1915*, 81.

124. *ARS 1922*, 87.

125. *AS 1915–1939* (Boston: Printing Department, 1915–1939); Brian Gratton and Jon Roger Moen, "Immigration, Culture, and Child Labor in the United States, 1880–1920," *Journal of Interdisciplinary History* 34, no. 3 (2004): 355–391; Viviana A. Rotman Zelizer, *Pricing the Priceless Child: The Changing Social Value of Children* (Princeton, NJ: Princeton University Press, 1985), 6, 56–112.

126. *ARSC 1906* (Boston: Municipal Printing Office, 1906), 35.

127. *ARS 1922*, 85–87.

128. *ARS 1922*, 85–86.

129. "Special Syllabus Drawing and Manual Training—Grades IV, V, VI, VII, VII," *School Document No. 6* (Boston: Printing Department, 1920); "Curricula for the General High Schools," *School Document No. 9* (Boston: Printing Department, 1917), 1–20.

130. Walter Elmore Fernald, *Report of the Commission for the Investigation of the White Slave Traffic, So Called* (Boston: Wright & Potter, 1914), 66–67.

131. Carl F. Kaestle, *Pillars of the Republic: Common Schools and American Society, 1780–1860* (New York: Macmillan, 1983), 88–103; Reese, *Power and the Promise of School Reform*, 11–16, 60–62, 209–238; Elizabeth A. Gagen, "Making America Flesh: Physicality and Nationhood in Early Twentieth-Century Physical Education Reform," *Cultural Geographies* 11, no. 4 (October 2004): 417–442; *ARS 1907*, 38–42; *ARS 1910* (Boston: Printing Department, 1910), 32–34.

132. Reed Ueda, *Avenues to Adulthood: The Origins of the High School and Social Mobility in an American Suburb* (Cambridge: Cambridge University Press, 1987), 119–152.

133. IPUMS 1880–1940.

134. "Female Help Wanted," *BG*, March 31, 1920, 19; "Female Help Wanted," *BG*, September 11, 1921, 43; "Male Help Wanted," *BG*, September 13, 1920, 13.

135. Schneider, *Boston Confronts Jim Crow*, 11.

136. IPUMS 1880–1940.

137. Davison Douglas, *Jim Crow Moves North: The Battle over Northern School Segregation, 1865–1954* (New York: Cambridge University Press, 2005), 186.

138. Pleck, *Black Migration*, 84.

139. Daniels, *In Freedom's Birthplace*, 268–269.

140. Douglas, *Jim Crow Moves North*, 134.

141. Douglas, *Jim Crow Moves North*, 176.

142. Schneider, *Boston Confronts Jim Crow*, 5.

143. Douglas, *Jim Crow Moves North*, 176. Residential segregation increased as Boston's Black community expanded in the 1940s and 1950s, creating de facto segregated schools in the mid-twentieth century. Tahi Lani Mottl, "Social Conflict and Social Movements: An Exploratory Study of the Black Community of Boston Attempting to Change the Boston Public Schools" (PhD diss., Brandeis University, 1976), 73. See also Adam R. Nelson, *The Elusive Ideal: Equal Educational Opportunity and the Federal Role in Boston's Public Schools, 1950–1985* (Chicago: University of Chicago Press, 2005).

144. Schneider, *Boston Confronts Jim Crow*, 103.

145. Douglas, *Jim Crow Moves North*, 216.

146. Pleck, *Black Migration*, 142–144; Schneider, *Boston Confronts Jim Crow*, 9, 23.

147. Kazuteru Omori, "Burden of Blackness: Quest for 'Equality' among Black 'Elites' in Late-Nineteenth-Century Boston" (PhD diss., University of Massachusetts Amherst, 2001), 83, 89.

148. Kenneally, *The South End*, 12.

149. Sarah Scovill Whittelsey, *Massachusetts Labor Legislation: An Historical and Critical Study* (Philadelphia: American Academy of Political and Social Science, 1900), 9–34; Vivien Hart, *Bound by Our Constitution: Women, Workers, and the Minimum Wage* (Princeton, NJ: Princeton University Press, 1994), ix, 63–72; Trout, *Boston, the Great Depression, and the New Deal*, 30–33; "Organizational History," Overseers of the Public Welfare of the City of Boston, CC 11, Simmons College Archives, Boston.

150. Trout, *Boston, the Great Depression, and the New Deal*, 73–199; Kenneally, *The South End*, 11; Green and Donahue, *Boston's Workers*, 107–109.

151. *Seventeenth Annual Report of the Civil Service Commissioners of Massachusetts, November 20, 1900* (Boston: Wright & Potter, 1901), 34, https://archives.lib.state.ma.us/handle/2452/799242; *Annual Report of the Commissioner of Civil Service for the Year Ending November 30, 1920*, Public Document no. 53 (Boston: Wright & Potter, 1921), 68, https://archives.lib.state.ma.us/handle/2452/799262; *Annual Report of the Commissioner of Civil Service for the Year Ending November 30, 1930*, Public Document no. 53 (n.p., 1931), 9, https://archives.lib.state.ma.us/handle/2452/799272; U.S. Census Office, "Table 94: Total Persons Ten Years of Age and Over Engaged in Each Specified Occupation . . . ," in *Twelfth Census of the United States 1900*, vol. 2, *Population*, part 2 (Washington, DC: U.S. Census Office, 1902), 554–556; U.S. Bureau of the Census, "Table 16: Number and Proportion of Persons 10 Years of Age and Over Engaged in Gainful Occupations, by Sex, for Cities of 100,000 Inhabitants or More: 1920," in *Fourteenth Census of the United States 1920*, vol. 4, *Population, Occupations* (Washington, DC: GPO, 1923) 128; U.S. Bureau of the Census, "Table 20: Persons 10 Years Old and Over Engaged in Gainful Occupations, by Sex and In-

dustry Groups, for Cities and Urban Places of 25,000 or More," in *Fifteenth Census of the United States 1930, Population,* vol. 3, *Reports by States,* part 1, *Alabama–Missouri* (Washington, DC: GPO, 1932), 1103.

152. *First Annual Report of the Civil Service Commissioners of Massachusetts, Together with the Civil Service Law . . .* (Boston: Wright & Potter, 1885), 32–37.

153. Robert Archey Woods, *Americans in Process: A Settlement Study* (Boston: Houghton Mifflin, 1902), 121.

154. Robert Archey Woods, *The City Wilderness: A Settlement Study* (Boston: Houghton Mifflin, 1898), 88.

155. Sari Roboff, *Boston's Labor Movement: An Oral History of Work and Union Organizing* (Boston: Boston 200 Corporation, 1977), 14; Pleck, *Black Migration,* 130.

156. *Officials and Employees of the City of Boston 1908* (Boston: MPO, 1908), 6–213; Woods, *Americans in Process,* 121.

157. Year: *1910;* Census Place: *Boston Ward 6, Suffolk, Massachusetts;* Roll: *T624_615;* Page: *6B;* Enumeration District: *1324;* FHL microfilm: *1374628;* Year: *1920;* Census Place: *Boston Ward 18, Suffolk, Massachusetts;* Roll: *T625_737;* Page: *5B;* Enumeration District: *452;* Image: *832.*

158. Estimated based on a sample of employee names. *Officials and Employees of the City of Boston,* Doc. 93 (Boston: Printing Dept., 1919), 234–236.

159. Woods, *The City Wilderness,* 88; US Department of Labor, "Table 1: Hours of Work and Wages of Employees," in *November 1896: Bulletin of the Department of Labor* 1, no. 7 (Washington, DC: GPO, 1897), 734.

160. "Labor Organizations of Massachusetts," *LB,* no. 21 (February 1902): 112–115.

161. IPUMS 1900–1940; *WEIU Report 1910,* 26; Vanessa H. May, *Unprotected Labor: Household Workers, Politics, and Middle-Class Reform in New York, 1870–1940* (Chapel Hill: University of North Carolina Press, 2011), 115; Premilla Nadasen, *Household Workers Unite: The Untold Story of African American Women Who Built a Movement* (Boston: Beacon Press, 2015), 14–15.

3. Craft Power in the Industrial Workplace

1. Quoted in "Industrial Education," *The Carpenter* 2, no. 10 (October 1882): 3; Richard Schneirov, *Labor and Urban Politics: Class Conflict and the Origins of Modern Liberalism in Chicago, 1864–97* (Urbana: University of Illinois Press, 1998), 149–150.

2. Sam Bass Warner, *Streetcar Suburbs: The Process of Growth in Boston, 1870–1900* (Cambridge, MA: Harvard University Press, 1962), 126–132; James H. Soltow, "Origins of Small Business Metal Fabricators and Machinery Makers in

New England, 1890–1957," *Transactions of the American Philosophical Society* 55, no. 10 (1965): 1–58.

3. Adjusted for inflation. Carroll D. Wright, *The Census of Massachusetts 1880* (Boston: Wright & Potter, 1883), 579; *Annual Report on the Statistics of Manufactures for the Year 1920* (Boston: Wright & Potter, 1921), xxvi; National Bureau of Economic Research, Index of the General Price Level for United States [M04051USM324NNBR], retrieved from FRED, Federal Reserve Bank of St. Louis, https://fred.stlouisfed.org/series/M04051USM324NNBR, June 15, 2020.

4. Orra Laville Stone, *History of Massachusetts Industries: Their Inception, Growth, and Success* (Chicago: S. J. Clarke Publishing Co., 1930), 1245, 1261–1285, 1318–1392, 1400–1435; Walter Irving Firey, *Land Use in Central Boston* (Cambridge, MA: Harvard University Press, 1947), 84–85.

5. Joshua L. Rosenbloom, *Looking for Work, Searching for Workers: American Labor Markets during Industrialization* (Cambridge: Cambridge University Press, 2002), 86–89.

6. Anthony Ittner, "Apprentices and Trade Schools," *The Open Shop* 5, no. 1 (January 1906): 27.

7. "Apprentices," *The Carpenter* 1, no. 2 (June 1881); "Why Apprenticeships Are Scarce," *The American Machinist* 4, no. 18 (April 30, 1881): 8 John Commons et al., *History of Labour in the United States*, vol. 3 (New York: The Macmillan Company, 1918), 284; Edward W. Bemis, "Relation of Trades-Unions to Apprentices," *Quarterly Journal of Economics* 6, no. 1 (1891): 83.

8. "The Modern Apprentice System," *The Open Shop* 5, no. 1 (January 1906): 25; Hal Hansen, "Caps and Gowns: Historical Reflections on the Institutions That Shaped Learning for and at Work, 1800–1945" (PhD diss., University of Wisconsin-Madison, 1997), 280–282, 551.

9. I use "industrial education," as it was used at the time to encompass instruction for specific trades as well as instruction for work in industrial workplaces more broadly, including factories.

10. John Dewey, "The Need of an Industrial Education in an Industrial Democracy," *Manual Training and Vocational Education* 17, no. 6 (February 1916); Herbert M. Kliebard, *Schooled to Work: Vocationalism and the American Curriculum, 1876–1946* (New York: Teachers College Press, 1999), 124.

11. "Industrial Education," *The Carpenter* 2, no. 10 (October 1882): 3.

12. Ira Katznelson, *Schooling for All: Class, Race, and the Decline of the Democratic Ideal* (New York: Basic Books, 1985), 150–177; J. L. Ketcham, "Education of the Apprentice," *The Bulletin of the NMTA* 3, no. 13 (December 1904): 550; Anthony Ittner, "Apprentices and Trade Schools," *The Open Shop* 5, no. 1 (January 1906): 29; Charles Henry Winslow, *Industrial Education: Report of Committee on Industrial Education of the American Federation of Labor* (Washington, DC: GPO, 1912), 11–21.

13. In the histories of this transformation by historians such as David Montgomery and Harry Braverman, schools are chiefly cited in reference to new forms of scientific knowledge rather than worker training. David Montgomery, *The Fall of the House of Labor: The Workplace, the State, and American Labor Activism, 1865–1925* (New York: Cambridge University Press, 1987); Harry Braverman, *Labor and Monopoly Capital: The Degradation of Work in the Twentieth Century* (New York: Monthly Review Press, 1974).

14. Lawrence F. Katz and Robert A. Margo, "Technical Change and the Relative Demand for Skilled Labor: The United States in Historical Perspective," in *Human Capital in History: The American Record,* ed. Leah Platt Boustan, Carola Frydman, and Robert A. Margo (Chicago: University of Chicago Press, 2014), 15–58; Peter H. Lindert, *Unequal Gains: American Growth and Inequality since 1700* (Princeton, NJ: Princeton University Press, 2016), 177–178.

15. Rosenbloom, *Looking for Work, Searching for Workers,* 173–181; Monica Prasad, *The Land of Too Much: American Abundance and the Paradox of Poverty* (Cambridge, MA: Harvard University Press, 2012), 63–64; Gavin Wright, "The Origins of American Industrial Success, 1879–1940," *American Economic Review* 80, no. 2 (1990): 651–668.

16. IPUMS 1880–1940; Charles H. Trout, *Boston, the Great Depression, and the New Deal* (New York: Oxford University Press, 1977), xi.

17. Joshua L. Rosenbloom, "Union Membership: 1880–1999," Table Ba4783–4791 in *Historical Statistics of the United States, Earliest Times to the Present: Millennial Edition,* ed. Susan B. Carter et al. (New York: Cambridge University Press, 2006).

18. Sari Roboff, *Boston's Labor Movement: An Oral History of Work and Union Organizing* (Boston: Boston 200 Corporation, 1977), 19; *BSL 1908* (Boston: Wright & Potter, 1909), 216.

19. "Annual Report on Labor Organizations 1910–1911," in *BSL 1911* (Boston: Wright & Potter, 1913), 105; U.S. Bureau of the Census, "Table 3: Total Persons 10 Years of Age and Over Engaged in Each Specified Occupation . . . ," in *Thirteenth Census Reports 1910,* vol. 4, *Population: Occupation Statistics* (Washington, DC: GPO, 1914), 152.

20. James R. Green and Hugh Carter Donahue, *Boston's Workers: A Labor History* (Boston: Boston Public Library, 1979), 76–77; Geoffrey T. Blodgett, "Yankee Leadership in a Divided City, 1860–1910," in *Boston, 1700–1980: The Evolution of Urban Politics,* ed. Ronald P. Formisano and Constance Burns (Westport, CT: Greenwood Press, 1984), 101–102.

21. L. D. Burlingame, "The Importance of an Apprentice System," *The Open Shop* 5, no. 1 (January 1906): 16–20.

22. George Q. Thornton, "Proposed Plan for a Training School for Foundry Foremen," *The Bulletin of the NMTA* 3, no. 12 (December 1904): 537–538; *Gould's*

Commercial Register of the City of St. Louis, vol. 28 (St. Louis: Gould's Directory Co., 1900), 660.

23. Monte A. Calvert, *The Mechanical Engineer in America, 1830–1910: Professional Cultures in Conflict* (Baltimore: Johns Hopkins University Press, 1967), 189–192.

24. This chapter uses IPUMS USA (digitized individual-level data samples of the US decennial census) 100 percent samples for the censuses between 1880 and 1940, hereafter referred to as IPUMS plus the sample year (e.g., IPUMS 1880–1940, IPUMS 1900, etc.). Steven Ruggles, Sarah Flood, Ronald Goeken, Josiah Grover, Erin Meyer, Jose Pacas, and Matthew Sobek, IPUMS USA: Version 10.0 [dataset] (Minneapolis: IPUMS, 2020), https://doi.org/10.18128/D010.V10.0.

25. "Industrial Relations: Welfare Work New England, 1913," Carton 48, p. 15, Boston Chamber of Commerce Records, 1872–1949, Special Collections, Baker Library, Harvard Business School, Boston (hereafter BCC); Nikki Mandell, *The Corporation as Family: The Gendering of Corporate Welfare, 1890–1930* (Chapel Hill: University of North Carolina Press, 2002).

26. Calvert, *The Mechanical Engineer in America,* 128, 142.

27. Mark L. Savickas, "Meyer Bloomfield: Organizer of the Vocational Guidance Movement (1907–1917)," *Career Development Quarterly* 57, no. 3 (March 2009): 260–269.

28. Sanford M. Jacoby, *Employing Bureaucracy: Managers, Unions, and the Transformation of Work in American Industry, 1900–1945* (New York: Columbia University Press, 1985), 173.

29. Magnus Alexander, "The Labor Problem Analyzed," *The Open Shop Review* 16, no. 1 (January 1919): 7.

30. "New NFA Commissioner," *The Iron Trade Review* 39, no. 13 (March 29, 1906): 16; "Recognize Merit," *The Review, National Founders Association,* June 1908, 4.

31. "Personnel Chart of Selling Men," January 16, 1917, Box 13, Folder: Sales Personnel 1917, Dennison Manufacturing Company Records, 1815–1990, Special Collections, Baker Library, Harvard Business School, Boston (hereafter DMC); Jacoby, *Employing Bureaucracy,* 92.

32. Hansen, "Caps and Gowns," 267–270; "The Modern Apprentice System," *The Open Shop* 5, no. 1 (January 1906): 25.

33. F. C. Henderschott, *National Association of Corporation Schools* (New York: AIEE, 1913); John Wolcott, "A Handbook of Educational Associations and Foundations in the United States," *Bureau of Education Bulletin No. 16* (Washington, DC: GPO, 1926), 11.

34. Calvert, *Mechanical Engineer,* 74–75.

35. Magnus W. Alexander, "The Labor Problem Analyzed," *The Open Shop Review* 16, no. 2 (February 1919): 77.

36. Samuel Hannaford, "Bricklayers' Trade School and Others," *The Open Shop* 5, no. 8 (August 1906): 387–388.

37. J. C. Hobart, "Employers Associations," *The Open Shop* 4, no. 3 (March 1905): 181; Robert Wuest, "Industrial Betterment Activities of the National Metal Trades Association," *Annals of the American Academy of Political and Social Science* 44 (1912): 85.

38. "Another Big Strike," *Boston Evening Transcript*, June 11, 1901.

39. *The Bulletin of the NMTA* 2, no. 3 (March 1903): front matter; emphasis in original.

40. W. P. Eagan, "The Passing of the "Bulletin," *The Bulletin of the NMTA* 3, no. 12 (December 1904): 529.

41. "Open and Non-Union Foundries," *The Review* (January 1908): 49–52. See also Chad Pearson, *Reform or Repression: Organizing America's Anti-Union Movement* (Philadelphia: University of Pennsylvania Press, 2015).

42. Wuest, "Industrial Betterment Activities," 84.

43. "NMTA Notes," *The Bulletin of the NMTA* 3, no. 9 (September 1904): 394; "One Labor Bureau," *The Open Shop* 4, no. 6 (June 1905): 276–277.

44. "Worcester Labor Bureau," *The Iron Age*, July 9, 1903, 10–11.

45. "NMTA Certificate of Recommendation," *The Bulletin of the NMTA* 3, no. 10 (October 1904): 447–448.

46. "NMTA Notes," *The Bulletin of the NMTA* 3, no. 9 (September 1904): 394.

47. Chad Pearson, "Making the 'City of Prosperity': Engineers, Open-shoppers, Americanizers, and Propagandists in Worcester, Massachusetts, 1900–1925," *Labor History* 45, no. 1 (February 1, 2004): 14.

48. A. E. Corbin, "The New England Districts," *The Bulletin of the NMTA* 3, no. 2 (February 1904): 72–73; "National Metal Trades Association Notes," *The Bulletin of the NMTA* 3, no. 12 (December 1904): 561.

49. A. C. Fischer, "The Employment Department and Its Influence upon a Community," *The Open Shop* 4, no. 1 (January 1905): 46–48.

50. William Thomas Ham, "Employment Relations in the Construction Industry of Boston" (PhD diss., Harvard University, 1926), 324–325.

51. Anthony Ittner, "We Must Educate Our Boys," *The Open Shop* 4, no. 8 (August 1905): 368.

52. Hugh Hawkins, *Between Harvard and America: The Educational Leadership of Charles W. Eliot* (New York: Oxford University Press, 1972), 151, 247.

53. Quoted in Calvert, *The Mechanical Engineer in America*, 232.

54. A. T. Robinson, "Technical Education: The Massachusetts Institute of Technology," *The Open Shop* 4, no. 3 (March 1905): 117–125; Massachusetts

Institute of Technology, *Sixteenth Annual Catalogue of the Officers and Students, 1880–1881* (Boston: Schofield, 1880), 59–71; Stephen H. Norwood, "The Student as Strikebreaker: College Youth and the Crisis of Masculinity in the Early Twentieth Century," *Journal of Social History* 28, no. 2 (December 1994): 341.

55. Marvin Lazerson, *Origins of the Urban School: Public Education in Massachusetts, 1870–1915* (Cambridge, MA: Harvard University Press, 1971), 92–96; James D. Anderson, *The Education of Blacks in the South, 1860–1935* (Chapel Hill: University of North Carolina Press, 1988), 33–79.

56. Kliebard, *Schooled to Work*, 1–88; Lazerson, *Origins of the Urban School*, 74–131.

57. Thomas Davidson, "Teaching the Mechanic Arts," *The Forum*, vol. 6 (New York: Forum Publishing Co., 1888), 390; James Good, "The Value of Thomas Davidson," *Transactions of the Charles S. Peirce Society* 40, no. 2 (Spring 2004): 301–304.

58. *LB*, no. 26 (May 1903): 58–60, 74–75; *The Work of the NBSIS from1881 to 1887* (Boston: Rand Avery Co., 1887), 5.

59. "Industrial Education," *BH Supplement*, January 19, 1884; Josiah Coleman Kent, *Northborough History* (Newton, MA: Garden City Press, 1921), 304.

60. Appendix, *ARSC 1889* (Boston: Wright & Potter, 1889), 165.

61. "Biographical Note," F. Hastings Rindge Collection, Cambridge Historical Commission, Cambridge, MA.

62. *ARSC 1892* (Boston: Wright & Potter, 1892), 5; *ARSC 1893* (Boston: Wright & Potter, 1893), 16.

63. "Manual Training Schools," *The Bulletin of the NMTA* 3, no. 13 (December 1904): 553.

64. J. L. Ketcham, "Education of the Apprentice," *The Bulletin of the NMTA* 3, no. 13 (December 1904): 550.

65. *LB*, no. 26 (May 1903): 58.

66. Student Records, 1885–1886, MIT School of Mechanic Arts Records, 1876–1886, Box 1, AC 499, Institute Archives, MIT, Cambridge, MA.

67. MIT, *Sixteenth Annual Catalogue of the Officers and Students, 1880–1881* (Boston: Schofield, 1880), 62.

68. C. W. Parmenter to George Conley, June 4, 1897, Box 1, Folder: M. A. H. S. Correspondence, 1893–1898, Mechanical Arts H. S. Historical Files, Collection 0420.015, City of Boston Archives, Boston; *Report of the Mechanic Arts High School* (Boston: Municipal Printing Office, 1901) 41–43.

69. "A Brief Historic Sketch of the Massachusetts Charitable Mechanics Association, 1794–1930," 3–14, Box 8, Massachusetts Charitable Mechanic Asso-

ciation Records, Massachusetts Historical Society, Boston (hereafter MCMA Records).

70. Trade School Report, Executive Committee (EC) Meeting, January 15, 1904, MCMA Trade School EC Minutes, 1903–1916, pp. 10–15, Vol. 5, MCMA Records.

71. *MCMA Proceedings 1909* (Boston: C. M. Barrows Co., 1909), 26.

72. *MCMA Proceedings 1908* (Boston: C. M. Barrows Co., 1908), 30; EC Meeting, January 16, 1906, MCMA Trade School EC Minutes, 1903–1916, p. 106, Vol. 5, MCMA Records.

73. EC Meeting, October 6, 1903, MCMA Trade School EC Minutes, 1903–1916, p. 9, Vol. 5, MCMA Records.

74. EC Meeting, October 29, 1908, MCMA Trade School EC Minutes, 1903–1916, p. 100–101, Vol. 5, MCMA Records.

75. EC Meeting, January 11, 1913, MCMA Trade School EC Minutes, 1903–1916, p. 156, Vol. 5, MCMA Records; *MCMA Proceedings 1919* (Boston: C. M. Barrows Company, 1919), 21.

76. Green and Donahue, *Boston's Workers,* 36, 74.

77. Arthur Mann, *Yankee Reformers in the Urban Age* (Cambridge, MA: Belknap Press of Harvard University Press, 1954), 180–200.

78. "Injunctions and Strikes," *BH,* January 21, 1895, 4.

79. "President Eliot on Trial by Labor," *BG,* February 8, 1904, 1; "Frank K. Foster's Reply, Giving Opinions from the Trade Union's Point of View," *BG,* February 23, 1904, 7.

80. Michele R. Costello, *Benjamin Franklin and the Invention of Microfinance* (London: Pickering & Chatto, 2015), 7–11, 84.

81. "Opposed to It," *BG,* December 19, 1904, 9.

82. "Is Opposed to 'Short Cuts,'" *BG,* March 6, 1905, 8.

83. Charles L. Hubbard, "Heating and Ventilating Plant of the Franklin Union, Boston," *Engineering Review* 19, no. 7 (July 1909): 39; EC Meeting, January 16, 1906, MCMA Trade School EC Minutes, 1903–1916, p. 103, Vol. 5, MCMA Records; Franklin Union, *Annual Report of the Director* 1912–1931 (Boston: Berkeley and Appleton Streets, 1912–1931).

84. Ava Baron, *Work Engendered: Toward a New History of American Labor* (Ithaca, NY: Cornell University Press, 1991), 65.

85. "Legatees Agree," *BG,* January 24, 1904, 21; EC Meeting, March 30, 1904, MCMA Trade School EC Minutes, 1903–1916, p. 19, Vol. 5, MCMA Records; Wentworth Institute of MA 1917–1918, School of Printing and the Graphic Arts, p. 2, Wentworth Institute Misc. Publications, Widener Library, Harvard University, Cambridge, MA.

86. "For Industrial Education," *BG*, June 26, 1911, 13.

87. O. M. Wentworth, "Workmen Have Too Much Leisure," *BG*, June 5, 1904, 32.

88. "Taft Pleads for Liberty in Unions," *BG*, June 11, 1915, 5.

89. "Police Union Vote to Go Back," *BG*, September 13, 1919, 2; Drew Pendergrass, "The Boys in Crimson: Boston's Police Strikebreakers," *Harvard Crimson*, November 10, 2016; "There Is No Middle Ground," *Harvard Crimson*, September 26, 1919; "The Institute and the Police Strike," *Technology Review* 21 (1919): 547; Kathleen Kilgore, *Transformations: A History of Boston University* (Boston: Boston University, 1991), 124.

90. This demographic profile is based on tracking nineteen out of twenty-one students through the manuscript censuses from 1870 to 1940; this profile also matches a description provided in features on the school. "First Wentworth Class Graduated," *Christian Science Monitor*, January 14, 1912, 7; "Worth of Wentworth School," *BG*, January 28, 1912, SM8.

91. Anthony Ittner, "Apprentices and Trade Schools," *The Open Shop* 5, no. 1 (January 1906): 29.

92. "Inaugural Address of William L. Douglas," *Acts and Resolves Passed by the General Court of Massachusetts* (Boston: Wright & Potter, 1905), 581.

93. Lazerson, *Origins of the Urban School*, 148.

94. "Favor a Paid Commission," *BG*, March 20, 1905, 3.

95. "Trade Schools," *BG*, April 15, 1905, 3.

96. "Printers Resent Mayor's Action," *BG*, November 26, 1906, 12.

97. "Opposes Mayor's School Measure," *BG*, February 6, 1905, 4; Arthur G. Powell, *The Uncertain Profession: Harvard and the Search for Educational Authority* (Cambridge: Cambridge University Press, 1980), 71–72.

98. "No Short Cut Wanted," *BG*, March 13, 1905, 8.

99. "Defends Idea," *BG*, March 9, 1905, 7; "Favor a Paid Commission," *BG*, March 20, 1905, 3; "Initial Step for Industrial School," *BH*, December 6, 1906, 9; Lazerson, *Origins of the Urban School*, 149–158, 163, 171; Powell, *The Uncertain Profession*, 49.

100. "Initial Step for Industrial School," *BH*, December 6, 1906, 9.

101. "New Industrial School in Lawrence," *BG*, June 7, 1908, SM4.

102. "Protests to Council," *BG*, June 18, 1906, 3.

103. Lazerson, *Origins of the Urban School*, 155–176.

104. *ARS 1909* (Boston: Printing Department, 1909), 42–44; *ARS 1910* (Boston: Printing Department, 1910), 54–56, 78–79, 92–103; "Training for Work Urged, Industrial Education Discussed," *BG*, April 25, 1910, 2.

105. *ARS 1910*, 54–56, 78–85.

106. "Germany Leads," *BG*, July 30, 1906, 12; *ARS 1910*, 37–43; *ARS 1913* (Boston: Printing Department, 1913), 8; *ARS 1915* (Boston: Printing Department, 1915), 13.

107. *ARS 1919* (Boston: Printing Department, 1919), 27.

108. "To Advise on School Policy," *BG*, January 25, 1911, 11.

109. "Mrs. Page Assails Trade Teaching," *BH*, May 16, 1910, 3; "Taxing Unmarried Women," *Ohio Law Reporter* 11, no. 23 (September 8, 1913): 228.

110. "To Advise on School Policy"; "CLU to Advise School Board," *BG*, February 6, 1911, 14; "Larger School Board Favored," *BG*, February 5, 1911, 3; "CLU Protest on Long Lease," *BG*, June 19, 1911, 14.

111. *ARSC 1911* (Boston: Printing Department, 1911), 36–39; *ARSC 1912* (Boston: Printing Department, 1912), 36; *ARS 1914* (Boston: Printing Department, 1914), 56, 159–160; *ARS 1915*, 13; *ARS 1917* (Boston: Printing Department, 1917), 10.

112. "School Plans Are Indorsed," *BG*, November 3, 1913, 9.

113. *ARS 1914*, 55–56, 207–208; *ARS 1915*, 53.

114. *ARS 1917*, 10; *ARS 1914*, 207; "Open and Non-Union Foundries," *The Review*, January 1908, 49–52.

115. "The Registered Attendance," *Transactions of the American Foundrymen's Association, Proceedings of the 22nd Annual Meeting, 1917*, 640.

116. Richard M. Abrams, *Conservatism in a Progressive Era: Massachusetts Politics, 1900–1912* (Cambridge, MA: Harvard University Press, 1964), 92–93, 238–239, 249–277; Stone, *Massachusetts Industries*, 1386–1390; "New England," *The Iron Age*, June 12, 1913, 1464; "Among the Manufacturers," *Steam* 12, no. 4 (October 1913): 116; "1919," p. 6, Case 5, Folder: Immigrants—Distribution, BCC.

117. "News from the Labor World," *BG*, January 5, 1913, 41.

118. "Abrahams Denies Request of CLU," *BG*, June 3, 1918, 5; "Labor Going into School Campaign," *BG*, April 21, 1913, 5; "After Voice in School Board," *BG*, March 6, 1916, 5; "Abrahams Named," *BG*, May 1, 1916, 9.

119. Hansen, "Caps and Gowns," 621–626.

120. "Industrial Education," *The Open Shop Review* 16, no. 6 (June 1919): 220–222.

121. George Seyler, "Training and Its Results," *The Open Shop Review* 18, no. 6 (June 1921): 213.

122. "The Institute and the Railroad Strike," *Technology Review* 23 (November 1921): 585; "Summons to Duty," *Harvard Crimson*, October 24, 1921; Norwood, "Student as Strikebreaker," 341–343.

123. "Trends: General Foundry and Machine Shop Products," 25, Box 12a, Folder: New England Industries, Surveys, Foundry and Machinery, 1924, BCC.

124. Carroll D. Wright, *The Census of Massachusetts 1880* (Boston: Wright & Potter, 1883), 580; *Annual Report on the Statistics of Manufactures 1920* (Boston: Wright & Potter, 1920), 35; Soltow, "Origins of Small Business Metal Fabricators"; Stone, *Massachusetts Industries*, 1313–1321, 1446, 1593–1594; Herndon, *Men of Progress*, 189.

125. "The Metal Working Industries of New England," 11, Box 12a, Folder: New England Industries, Surveys, Foundry and Machinery, 1924, BCC.

126. Ham, "Employment Relations," 183.

127. Roboff, *Boston's Labor Movement*, 18–19, 34–35; "Boston Building Trades Agreement, 1922," *Massachusetts Industrial Review* 9 (October 1922): 12; Council of State Governments, *Occupational Licensing Legislation in the States* (Chicago: 1313 East Sixtieth Street, 1952), 23; *Handbook of Labor Statistics 1929* (Washington, DC: GPO, 1929), 5–12; Julie Wurth, "In Illinois, Apprenticeships Are on the Rise," *News-Gazette* (Champaign, IL), January 6, 2020.

128. *Handbook of Labor Statistics 1929* (Washington, DC: GPO, 1929), 10–12.

129. Walter Gellhorn, *Individual Freedom and Governmental Restraints* (Baton Rouge: Louisiana State University Press, 1956), 199.

130. Dan Jacoby, "Plumbing the Origins of American Vocationalism," *Labor History* 37, no. 2 (March 1, 1996): 271n125; Herbert Roof Northrup, *Organized Labor and the Negro* (New York: Harper and Brothers, 1944), 24; IPUMS 1880–1940.

131. "Annual Directory of Labor Organizations in Massachusetts with Statistics of Membership 1932–1937," in *BSL 1938, LB,* no. 176 (1938): 90.

132. Horace Greeley Wadlin, "The Sweating System in Massachusetts," *Journal of Social Science; New York* 30 (October 1, 1892): 86; Eileen Boris, *Home to Work: Motherhood and the Politics of Industrial Homework in the United States* (Cambridge: Cambridge University Press, 1994), 52; Rosara Lucy Passero, "Ethnicity in the Men's Ready-Made Clothing Industry, 1880–1950: The Italian Experience in Philadelphia" (PhD diss., University of Pennsylvania, 1978), 163.

133. IPUMS 1880–1940.

134. Gamber, *The Female Economy,* 87, 193.

135. IPUMS 1880–1940.

136. *LB 1902,* no. 24, 115; *BSL 1894* (Boston: Wright & Potter, 1894), 294.

137. *BSL 1911* (Boston: Wright & Potter, 1913), 294, 311–316; Sarah Scovill Whittelsey, *Massachusetts Labor Legislation: An Historical and Critical Study* (Philadelphia: American Academy of Political and Social Science, 1900), 23–24; Wadlin, "The Sweating System in Massachusetts," 100; Carolyn D. McCreesh, *Women in the Campaign to Organize Garment Workers, 1880–1917* (New York: Garland, 1985), 40–51; Sarah Deutsch, *Women and the City: Gender, Space, and Power in Boston, 1870–1940* (New York: Oxford University Press, 2000), 161–219;

Robert Archey Woods, *The City Wilderness: A Settlement Study* (Boston: Houghton Mifflin, 1898), 87.

138. Vivien Hart, *Bound by Our Constitution: Women, Workers, and the Minimum Wage* (Princeton, NJ: Princeton University Press, 1994), 69; *BSL 1900* (Boston: Wright & Potter, 1900), 218.

139. *BSL 1894*, 283.

140. "Trade and Technical Education," in *Seventeenth Annual Report of the U.S. Commissioner of Labor, 1902* (Washington, DC: GPO, 1902), 111–119, 129; *The Work of NBSIS from 1881 to 1887* (Boston: Rand Avery Co., 1887), 7; "Female Help Wanted," *BG*, June 9, 1898, 10; "Female Help Wanted," *BG*, March 7, 1900, 11.

141. Deutsch, *Women and the City*, 184–187.

142. *The First Annual Report of the Boston Trade School for Girls* (Boston, 1905), 14; *The Second Annual Report of the Boston Trade School for Girls* (Boston, 1906), 22–25; *The Third Annual Report of the Boston Trade School for Girls* (Boston, 1907), 20–25; *The Fifth Annual Report of the Boston Trade School for Girls* (Boston, 1909), 28–35; John Daniels, *In Freedom's Birthplace: A Study of the Boston Negroes* (Boston: Houghton Mifflin, 1914), 379–380.

143. *ARSC 1870* (Boston: Alfred Mudge & Sons, 1871), 360–363.

144. *ARS 1913*, 99–101.

145. Lorinda Perry, *The Millinery Trade in Boston and Philadelphia: A Study of Women in Industry* (Binghamton, NY: Vail-Ballou Co., 1916), 106.

146. *ARS 1898* (Boston: Municipal Printing Office, 1898), 87–88; *ARS 1907* (Boston: Municipal Printing Office, 1907), 31.

147. *High School of Practical Arts Catalogue* (Boston, 1913), 2, Boston, Mass., High School Pamphlets, ca. 1913–1930, Widener Library, Harvard University, Cambridge, MA.

148. "HSPA Alumni Association Meeting Minutes, 1912–1940," 3, High School of Practical Arts Alumnae Association Records, Collection 0420.068, City of Boston Archives, Boston.

149. *ARS 1914*, 58.

150. *ARS 1914, 57*; *ARSC 1911*, 44–45; "Union Wages and Hours of Labor," *BSL 1914*, 22; May Allinson, *Dressmaking as a Trade for Women in Massachusetts* (Washington, DC: GPO, 1916), 135; Louise Marion Bosworth, *The Living Wage of Women Workers* (New York: Longmans, Green, and Co., 1911), 9.

151. "Clothing Makers Break with Union," *New York Times*, December 7, 1920, 17; "Boston Clothing Status," *Textile World Journal* 59, no. 5 (January 29, 1921): 26; *Fourteenth Census of the United States 1920*, vol. 4, *Population, Occupations* (Washington, DC: GPO, 1923), 138.

152. McCreesh, *Women in the Campaign to Organize Garment Workers*, xiii, 217; Tom Juravich, *Commonwealth of Toil: Chapters in the History of Massachu-*

setts Workers and Their Unions (Amherst: University of Massachusetts Press, 1996), 99; Green and Donahue, *Boston's Workers,* 102–103.

153. Annelise Orleck, *Common Sense and a Little Fire: Women and Working-Class Politics in the United States, 1900–1965* (Chapel Hill: University of North Carolina Press, 1995), 171–179; *Workers Education in the United States: Report of Proceedings, Second National Conference* (New York: Workers Education Bureau of America, 1922), 54–64. See also Tobias Higbie, *Labor's Mind: A History of Working-Class Intellectual Life* (Urbana: University of Illinois Press, 2018), 61–84.

154. Richard Freeland, *Academia's Golden Age: Universities in Massachusetts, 1945–1970* (Oxford: Oxford University Press, 1992), 77; John W. Servos, "The Industrial Relations of Science: Chemical Engineering at MIT, 1900–1939," *Isis* 71, no. 4 (1980): 536–537.

155. MCMA, *Proceedings of the One-Hundred and Twenty-Fourth Annual Meeting, January 15, 1919* (Boston: C. M. Barrows Co., 1919), 30.

156. The earliest state charters typically granted general degree-granting power, meaning that the institution could offer whatever type of degree it wanted. While the most common degrees were those derived from their European antecedents (BA, BS, MD), this legal leeway allowed for wide variation in degree types by the turn of the twentieth century. Subsequent school charters tended to be more specific about degree types as older universities sought to protect coveted degree types, including the BA. By the 1930s and 1940s, as new institutions sought to emulate the gold standard of elite schools, the range of degree types declined. See Alan L. Contreras, *The Legal Basis for Degree-Granting Authority in the United States* (Boulder, CO: State Higher Education Executive Officers, 2009), 5–12; Stephen Hopkins Spurr, *Academic Degree Structures: Innovative Approaches* (New York: McGraw-Hill, 1970), 14–15; Walter Crosby Eells, *Academic Degrees: Earned and Honorary Degrees Conferred by Institutions of Higher Education in the United States,* Bulletin 1960, No. 28 (Washington, DC: US Office of Education, 1960), 8–13; *Northeastern College Preliminary Announcement, 1916–17* (Boston: Trustees of Northeastern College, 1917), 3–6; *Catalog of the Cooperative School of Engineering 1920–21* (Boston: Northeastern College), 13; Everett A. Churchill, *History of Northeastern University, 1896–1927* (Boston: Boston YMCA, 1927), 14, 39–41, Frank Palmer Speare Papers, Archives and Special Collections, Northeastern University, Boston.

157. "Franklin Union Facing Crisis," *BG,* June 3, 1928, A4; "Franklin Union Reports Economies," *BG,* May 16, 1933, 2; *An Act Relative to the Membership of and Further Defining the Corporate Powers of the Franklin Foundation,* 1953 MA Acts Chap. 77.

158. "President's Address—Williston," *Journal of Proceedings and Addresses of the Fifty-Second Annual Meeting, National Education Association,* July 4–11,

1914, 579; "An Advocate of the Junior Technical School," *Power* 51, nos. 11–12 (March 20, 1920): 428.

159. "Wentworth to Give Associate Degree in Engineering," *BG*, July 22, 1956, 19.

160. "Education Report," 3–4, Box 180, Folder: Annual Report on Education Work 1927, DMC.

161. "R. F. McDonald," Box 333, Folder: Dept. 16; "Conversation—Mr. Wentworth & J. W. Riegel, September 20, 1929," and "Work Report," Box 333, Folder: Division T & G, DMC.

162. IPUMS 1940. The year 1940 was the first year total educational attainment was reported to the census. I use reported educational attainment of individuals over 60 to estimate rates at the turn of the century. These figures, especially for older cohorts, are likely overestimates, as many inflated the amount of education they received. Claudia Goldin, "America's Graduation from High School: The Evolution and Spread of Secondary Schooling in the Twentieth Century," *Journal of Economic History* 58 (1998): 365–367.

163. Hansen, "Caps and Gowns," 663–664.

164. Irving Lewis Horowitz, "The Metal Machining Trades in Philadelphia: An Occupational Survey" (PhD diss., University of Pennsylvania, 1939), 42–66.

165. Kliebard, *Schooled to Work,* 129–142; Hansen, "Caps and Gowns," 490–499, 543–545, 564–568; David L. Angus and Jeffrey Mirel, *The Failed Promise of the American High School, 1890–1995* (New York: Teachers College Press, 1999), 47, 73; Walter Licht, *Getting Work: Philadelphia, 1840–1950* (Philadelphia: University of Pennsylvania Press, 2000), 91–95; John Dale Russell, *Vocational Education,* Advisory Committee on Education (Washington, DC: GPO, 1938), 248–289; "Watson and Hurley Clash at School Board Meeting," *BG*, December 23, 1930, 25.

166. *ARS 1915*, 37; Susan Ginn, "Vocational Guidance in the Boston Public Schools," *Vocational Guidance Magazine* 3, no. 1 (October 1924): 3–14; Jacoby, *Employing Bureaucracy,* 77.

167. *ARS 1910*, 66.

168. *ARS 1922* (Boston: Printing Department, 1922), 58.

169. *The School, the Boy, and Industrial Employment* (Chicago: National Metal Trades Association, 1937), 4.

170. *ARS 1938* (Boston: Printing Department, 1938), 50–75.

171. See Chapter 4, Figures 4.8 and 4.9 for a detailed breakdown by course type.

172. "Annual Directory of Labor Organizations with Statistics of Membership 1926–1935," in *BSL 1936, LB,* no. 174 (1936): 85–86.

173. Roboff, *Boston's Labor Movement,* 46.

174. To calculate the percentages presented in Figure 3.2, I divided reported Boston union membership by the total Boston workforce listed in the US census

reports. Historians have presented different estimates for Boston union membership in the 1880s; this figure is estimated based on local reporting in 1881. See also Roboff, *Boston's Labor Movement*, 12; Green and Donahue, *Boston's Workers*, 36. After 1908, total union membership was reported annually by the Massachusetts Bureau of Statistics of Labor. "Labor Organizations," in *BSL* (Boston: Wright & Potter, 1908), 195–196; "Directory of Labor Organizations in Massachusetts," in *BSL, LB*, no. 196 (1953): 126.

175. Kathleen Thelen, *How Institutions Evolve: The Political Economy of Skills in Germany, Britain, the United States, and Japan* (Cambridge: Cambridge University Press, 2004); Hansen, "Caps and Gowns."

4. Becoming Pink Collar

1. *Inaugural Address of John F. Fitzgerald, 1906* (Boston: Municipal Printing Office), 33–37.

2. *Inaugural Address of John F. Fitzgerald, 1906*, 37.

3. Bertha Morton Stevens, *Private Commercial Schools: Manhattan and the Bronx* (New York: Public Education Association, 1918), 128–129.

4. Nancy Beadie, "Toward a History of Education Markets in the United States: An Introduction," *Social Science History* 32, no. 1 (2008): 47–73.

5. Claudia Goldin, "America's Graduation from High School: The Evolution and Spread of Secondary Schooling in the Twentieth Century," *Journal of Economic History* 58 (1998): 345–374; Tracy L. Steffes, *School, Society, and State: A New Education to Govern Modern America, 1890–1940* (Chicago: University of Chicago Press, 2012), 7.

6. Calculated by dividing total attendance reported by the school committee by the 14–17-year-old population. This chapter uses IPUMS USA (digitized individual-level data samples of the US decennial census) 100 percent samples for the censuses between 1880 and 1940, hereafter referred to as IPUMS plus the sample year (e.g., IPUMS 1880–1940, IPUMS 1900, etc.). Steven Ruggles, Sarah Flood, Ronald Goeken, Josiah Grover, Erin Meyer, Jose Pacas, and Matthew Sobek, IPUMS USA: Version 10.0 [dataset] (Minneapolis: IPUMS, 2020), https://doi.org/10.18128/D010.V10.0; *AS 1940* (Boston: Printing Department, 1940), 8; U.S. Bureau of the Census, "Table A-35: Age, by Race and Sex, for the City of Boston: 1940 and 1930," in *Sixteenth Census of the United States 1940, Population*, vol. 2, *Characteristics of the Population*, part 3 (Washington, DC: GPO, 1943) 670.

7. John L. Rury, *Education and Women's Work: Female Schooling and the Division of Labor in Urban America, 1870–1930* (Albany: State University of New York Press, 1991), 98–106.

8. Many political and economic histories of the United States largely ignore the role of secondary education. The role of the high school as a pathway into white-collar employment is a central focus of several studies including Ileen A. DeVault, *Sons and Daughters of Labor: Class and Clerical Work in Turn-of-the-Century Pittsburgh* (Ithaca, NY: Cornell University Press, 1990); Reed Ueda, *Avenues to Adulthood: The Origins of the High School and Social Mobility in an American Suburb* (Cambridge: Cambridge University Press, 1987), 153–186; David F. Labaree, *The Making of an American High School: The Credentials Market and the Central High School of Philadelphia, 1838–1939* (New Haven, CT: Yale University Press, 1988), 134–172.

9. These gender-equality metrics include higher labor-force participation rates among women, lower occupational segregation, and higher representation of women in elite managerial positions. Margarita Estévez-Abe, "Gendering the Varieties of Capitalism: Gender Bias in Skills and Social Policies," in *Political Economy of Japan's Low Fertility,* ed. Frances Rosenbluth (Stanford, CA: Stanford University Press, 2006), 63–86; Margarita Estévez-Abe, "Gendered Consequences of Vocational Training," in *The Political Economy of Collective Skill Formation,* ed. Marius R. Busemeyer and Christine Trampusch (Oxford: Oxford University Press, 2012), 259–283. However, other scholars have noted the need to distinguish between upper- and lower-class women, the latter of whom fare worse in liberal market economies. L. McCall and Ann Orloff, "Introduction to Special Issue of Social Politics: 'Gender, Class, and Capitalism,'" *Social Politics: International Studies in Gender, State & Society* 12, no. 2 (June 2005): 159–169.

10. IPUMS 1880–1940.

11. C. Wright Mills, *White Collar: The American Middle Classes* (New York: Oxford University Press, 1951). Not only does Mills use the male pronoun for the majority of his discussion of white-collar workers, but gendered anxieties shape his diagnosis throughout. The "new Little Man" has to perform the affective labor characteristic of women's' work: "He must smile and be affable" and express traits of "courtesy, helpfulness, and kindness." Selling his "personality" in this way turns him into a "standardized loser" (xvi–xvii). Many historical studies of this era's broad economic transformation focus primarily on the role of male managers rather than women white-collar workers, including Alfred D. Chandler Jr., *The Visible Hand: The Managerial Revolution in American Business* (Cambridge, MA: Harvard University Press, 1977); Richard Franklin Bensel, *The Political Economy of American Industrialization, 1877–1900* (Cambridge: Cambridge University Press, 2000). There are many excellent studies of women office and sales workers in particular, including Sharon Hartman Strom, *Beyond the Typewriter: Gender, Class, and the Origins of Modern American Office Work, 1900–1930* (Urbana: University of Illinois Press, 1992); Lisa M. Fine, *The Souls of*

the Skyscraper: Female Clerical Workers in Chicago, 1870–1930 (Philadelphia: Temple University Press, 1990); Susan Porter Benson, *Counter Cultures: Saleswomen, Managers, and Customers in American Department Stores, 1890–1940* (Urbana: University of Illinois Press, 1986).

12. "Twenty-fifth Reunion of the Class of 1915," 9, Carton 3, Folder 54, Girls' High School Association Records, Schlesinger Library, Radcliffe Institute, Harvard University, Cambridge, MA (hereafter GHSA).

13. Janet Levine, *Ellis Island Oral History Project, Interview of Esther Zarkin Rosoff*, Series EI, No. 106 (Alexandria, VA: Alexander Street Press, 2003).

14. Diane Ravitch, *Left Back: A Century of Battles over School Reform* (New York: Simon & Schuster, 2000), 88–129; David B. Tyack, *The One Best System: A History of American Urban Education* (Cambridge, MA: Harvard University Press, 1974), 191.

15. Claudia Dale Goldin, *Understanding the Gender Gap: An Economic History of American Women* (New York: Oxford University Press, 1990), 64, 107–112, 177.

16. Jürgen Kocka, *White Collar Workers in America, 1890–1940: A Social-Political History in International Perspective* (Beverly Hills, CA: Sage Publications, 1980), 144–153; Jerome P. Bjelopera, *City of Clerks: Office and Sales Workers in Philadelphia, 1870–1920* (Urbana: University of Illinois Press, 2005), 122–129.

17. Kocka, *White Collar Workers in America*, 144–148; Carol Srole, *Transcribing Class and Gender: Masculinity and Femininity in Nineteenth-Century Courts and Offices* (Ann Arbor: University of Michigan Press, 2010), 196–218; David Hogan, "'To Better Our Condition': Educational Credentialing and 'The Silent Compulsion of Economic Relations' in the United States, 1830 to the Present," *History of Education Quarterly* 36, no. 3 (1996): 256.

18. Walter Irving Firey, *Land Use in Central Boston* (Cambridge, MA: Harvard University Press, 1947), 233–244; Charles H. Trout, *Boston, the Great Depression, and the New Deal* (New York: Oxford University Press, 1977), xi.

19. U.S. Bureau of the Census, "Table 8: Total Gainful Workers 10 Years Old and Over, by Occupation, for the United States," *Comparative Occupations Statistics for the United States 1870–1940*, in *Sixteenth Census of the United States 1940, Population* (Washington, DC: GPO, 1943), 110–112.

20. In Boston these changes mostly reflected changes in the occupational structure rather than rising women's workforce participation, which increased slightly from 21 percent in 1880 to 26 percent by 1940. Men's workforce participation in Boston actually declined from 64 percent in 1880 to 60 percent in 1940. IPUMS 1880–1940.

21. U.S. Census Office, "Table 94: Total Persons Ten Years of Age and Over Engaged in Each Specified Occupation . . . ," in *Twelfth Census of the United States 1900*, vol. 2, *Population*, part 2 (Washington, DC: U.S. Census Office, 1902), 554.

22. "Secretarial Work No. 793," August 5, 1925, Folder 403, and "Duties of the Private Secretary," 1926, 24–33, Folder 503, Bureau of Vocational Information Records, 1908–1932, Schlesinger Library, Radcliffe Institute, Harvard University, Cambridge, MA (hereafter BVI); U.S. Census Office, "Table 116: Total Males and Females 10 Years of Age and Over Engaged in Selected Occupations . . . ," in *Eleventh Census of the United States 1890*, vol. 1, *Report on Population of the United States*, part 2 (Washington, DC: Government Printing Office, 1897), 568.

23. U.S. Bureau of the Census, "Table 8," Comparative Occupational Statistics, 110–112.

24. Lucile Eaves, *Training for Store Service* (Boston: Gorham Press, 1920), 24, 27, 57–61.

25. IPUMS 1880–1940; William A. Braverman, "The Emergence of a Unified Community, 1880–1917," in *The Jews of Boston*, ed. Jonathan D. Sarna, Ellen Smith, and Scott-Martin Kosofsky, (New Haven, CT: Yale University Press, 2005), 65–71.

26. Jewel Lightfoot and John Brady, *Report of Attorney General on American Telephone & Telegraph Co.* (Austin, TX: Austin Printing Co., 1911), 5.

27. Stephen Harlan Norwood, *Labor's Flaming Youth: Telephone Operators and Worker Militancy 1878–1923* (Urbana: University of Illinois Press, 1990), 26–38.

28. IPUMS 1900.

29. "The First Woman Typewriter," *The School Journal*, February 4, 1905, 138.

30. Margery W. Davies, *Woman's Place Is at the Typewriter: Office Work and Office Workers, 1870–1930* (Philadelphia: Temple University Press, 1982), appendix, 178–179.

31. Strom, *Beyond the Typewriter*, 273–275, 287–301; DeVault, *Sons and Daughters*, 58–60, 102, 142.

32. Jocelyn Wills, "Respectable Mediocrity: The Everyday Life of an Ordinary American Striver, 1876–1890," *Journal of Social History* 37, no. 2 (2003): 323–349; DeVault, *Sons and Daughters*, 158–159.

33. May Allinson, *The Public Schools and Women in Office Service* (Boston: WEIU, 1914), 105–122.

34. In 1880, married women with a spouse present in the household made up 5 percent of the women's workforce in Boston; by 1940, this percentage had

risen to 15 percent. The dramatic rise in married women's employment happened in the second half of the twentieth century; see Claudia Goldin, "The Quiet Revolution That Transformed Women's Employment, Education, and Family," *American Economic Review* 96, no. 2 (2006): 5. In contrast to Goldin's findings, in Boston in 1940, compared to the women's workforce as a whole, working married women had significantly lower levels of education, were underrepresented among professional or white-collar workers, and were overrepresented as factory operatives and service workers. IPUMS 1880–1940.

35. "Secretarial Work No. 782," October 22, 1925, Folder 403, BVI; Olivier Zunz, *Making America Corporate, 1870–1920* (Chicago: University of Chicago Press, 1990), 117–121.

36. Carol Srole, "A Position That God Has Not Particularly Assigned to Men': The Feminization of Clerical Work, Boston 1860–1915" (PhD diss., University of California, Los Angeles, 1984), 61, 584.

37. DeVault, *Sons and Daughters,* 167.

38. Levine, *Ellis Island Oral History Project.*

39. "Social Statistics of Workingwomen," *LB,* no. 18 (May 1901): 46.

40. IPUMS 1900.

41. Albert Benedict Wolfe, *The Lodging House Problem in Boston* (Boston: Houghton, Mifflin and Company, 1906).

42. IPUMS 1900–1940; Sarah Deutsch, *Women and the City: Gender, Space, and Power in Boston, 1870–1940* (New York: Oxford University Press, 2000), 91–103; Kathy Peiss, *Cheap Amusements: Working Women and Leisure in Turn-of-the-Century New York* (Philadelphia: Temple University Press, 1986).

43. James Hiram Bedford, *Vocational Interests of High School Students* (Berkeley: University of California, 1930), 19; Edward Earle Franklin, *The Permanence of the Vocational Interests of Junior High School Pupils* (Baltimore: Johns Hopkins Press, 1924), 21.

44. *ARS 1928* (Boston: Printing Department, 1928), 93.

45. "Secretarial Work No. 810," July 20, 1925, Folder 403, BVI.

46. Benson, *Counter Cultures,* 211.

47. Ruth Rosen, *Lost Sisterhood: Prostitution in America, 1900–1918* (Baltimore: Johns Hopkins University Press, 1982), 15; Val Marie Johnson, "'Look for the Moral and Sex Sides of the Problem': Investigating Jewishness, Desire, and Discipline at Macy's Department Store, New York City, 1913," *Journal of the History of Sexuality* 18, no. 3 (2009): 457–485; Walter Elmore Fernald, *Report of the Commission for the Investigation of the White Slave Traffic, So Called* (Boston: Wright & Potter, 1914), 22, 66; Thomas Herbert Russell, *The Girl's Fight for a Living: How to Protect Working Women from Dangers due to Low Wages* (Chi-

cago: M. A. Donohue, 1913), 61–62, 74–75; Srole, "'Position That God Has Not Particularly Assigned to Men,'" 569. See also Mary E. Odem, *Delinquent Daughters: Protecting and Policing Adolescent Female Sexuality in the United States, 1885–1920* (Chapel Hill: University of North Carolina Press, 1995).

48. Ethel Erickson, *The Employment of Women in Offices* (Washington, DC: GPO, 1934), 14.

49. US Commission on Industrial Relations, *Industrial Relations: Final Report and Testimony,* vol. 3 (Washington, DC: GPO, 1916), 2343.

50. Alice Kessler-Harris, "Where Are the Organized Women Workers?," *Feminist Studies* 3, no. 1/2 (1975): 94.

51. Kocka, *White Collar Workers in America,* 55–59.

52. Fine, *The Souls of the Skyscraper,* 15.

53. Marten Estey, "The Grocery Clerks: Center of Retail Unionism," *Industrial Relations* 7, no. 3 (May 1968): 254; Kocka, *White Collar Workers in America,* 67–68.

54. Kocka, *White Collar Workers in America,* 85–86, 144–153.

55. Srole, *Transcribing Class and Gender,* 196.

56. James Don Edwards, *History of Public Accounting in the United States* (East Lansing: Michigan State University, 1960), 69.

57. New England Shorthand Reporters' Association, *Proceedings of the New England Shorthand Reporters' Association 1889–1892* (Boston: Geo. H. Ellis, 1892), 9–19.

58. "October Meeting of the Boston Shorthand Club," *The Student's Journal* 21, no. 11 (November 1892): 2–3; "Annual Banquet of the Boston Shorthand Club," *The Student's Journal* 21, no. 12 (December 1892): 3; Srole, *Transcribing Class and Gender,* 202.

59. Srole, *Transcribing Class and Gender,* 204, 218.

60. YMCA Reports 1869–87, Box 1; YMCA Prospecti, 1884–1902, Box 20, YMCA of Greater Boston Records, Archives and Special Collections, Northeastern University, Boston.

61. Robert Archey Woods and Albert Joseph Kennedy, *Handbook of Settlements* (Boston: Charities Publication Committee, 1911), 105–135.

62. David J. Loftus, *Boston College High School, 1863–1983* (Boston: Addison C. Getchell, 1984), 21; *AS 1917* (Boston: Printing Department, 1917), 67.

63. *RCE 1890–'91,* vol. 2 (Washington, DC: GPO, 1894), 1462–1463; *Semi-AS 1890* (Boston: Rockwell & Churchill, 1890), 101.

64. "New Haven Collegiate and Commercial Institute," Small Broadside, Connecticut Historical Society Library, Hartford, CT; "Historical Sketch of the New Hampton Institute, 1876," and "New Hampton Literary Institution and

Commercial College Circular 1892," New Hampshire Historical Society, Concord, NH; "Kent's Hill Commercial College and Shorthand Institute Circular, 1885–86," Maine Historical Society, Portland, ME; Hon. E. R. French, *History of the Maine Wesleyan Female Seminary* (Portland, ME: Smith & Sale, 1919).

65. George Nixon Comer, *Book-Keeping Rationalized: Adapted to All Kinds of Business* (Boston: Comer's Commercial College, 1873).

66. *Annual Catalogue of Comer's Commercial College 1860* (Boston: Damrell & Moore, 1860), 12.

67. *Annual Register of Comer's Commercial College 1874* (Boston: Rand, Avery & Co, 1874), 10.

68. *Annual Catalogue of Comer's Commercial College 1860*, 4; *Annual Prospectus of Comer's Commercial College 1896* (Boston: 666 Washington St, 1896), 10–34.

69. *Annual Prospectus of Comer's Commercial College 1896*, 7, 49; *RCE 1890–'91*, vol. 2, 1462.

70. *RCE 1890–1891*, vol. 2, 1462–1463; *RCE 1901*, vol. 2 (Washington, DC: Government Printing Office, 1902), 2282–2283; *RCE 1913*, vol. 2 (Washington DC: Government Printing Office, 1914), 587–588; *BSE 1918–20, Statistics* (Washington, DC: GPO, 1923), 337–338; *Boston Almanac and Business Directory 1880* (Boston: Sampson, Davenport & Co., 1880), 438–444; *Boston Almanac and Business Directory 1893* (Boston: Sampson, Murdock & Co., 1893), 602–607; *The Boston Directory Supplement & Business Directory 1903* (Boston: Sampson, Murdock & Co., 1903), 687–691; *Boston Register and Business Directory 1921* (Boston: Sampson, Murdock & Co., 1921), 738–739, 762–767.

71. "Schools. Colleges. Etc," *BG*, February 7, 1915, 31.

72. *The Semma, 1944* (Boston: The Fisher School, 1944); "Schools, Colleges, Etc.," *BH*, September 22, 1903, 12; *RCE 1906*, vol. 2 (Washington, DC: GPO, 1908), 1111.

73. Ralph M. Hower, *The History of an Advertising Agency: N. W. Ayer & Son at Work, 1869–1939* (Cambridge, MA: Harvard University Press, 1939), 209–213.

74. *Twenty-Second Annual Prospectus of the Bryant & Stratton Commercial School 1882* (Boston: Rockwell & Churchill, 1882), 23–24.

75. "Burdett College Journal, Vol. XXXIII No. 1," Case 20: Education, Folder: Private Commercial School for Profit Survey 1914, Boston Chamber of Commerce Records, 1872–1949, Special Collections, Baker Library, Harvard Business School, Boston (hereafter BCC).

76. *Thirty-ninth Annual Prospectus of the Bryant & Stratton Commercial School 1900–1901* (Boston: Rockwell & Churchill Press, 1900), 36–37.

77. Burdett College Employment Service, *Man Power Highly Developed and Ready for Action: Capable Candidates for Business* (Boston: 18 Boylston Street,

1923), in Burdett College Misc. Pamphlets, Widener Library, Harvard University, Cambridge, MA.

78. Allinson, *The Public Schools and Women*, 40.

79. *Catalogue and Prospectus of Miss Pierce's Shorthand School* (Boston: Miss Pierce's Shorthand School, circa 1900), 3, 8.

80. *Annual Prospectus of the Bryant & Stratton Commercial School* (Boston: Rockwell & Churchill, 1901), 60.

81. *Annual Prospectus of the Burdett College of Business and Shorthand 1893* (Boston: Burdett College, 1893).

82. *How to Make More Money $* (Providence, RI: Bryant-Stratton College, 1926); *Your Next Step* (Boston: Bryant & Stratton School, 1930).

83. *Catalogue and Prospectus of Miss Pierce's Shorthand School* (Boston: Miss Pierce's Shorthand School, circa 1900), 25; Moses King, *How to See Boston* (Boston: Macullar, Parker & Co., 1895), 34.

84. *Annual Prospectus of the Burdett College of Business and Shorthand 1893*, 34–36.

85. "Secretarial Work No. 828," June 2, 1925, Folder 404, BVI.

86. Stevens, *Private Commercial Schools*, 72–74.

87. Charles Eliot, "Commercial Education," *Educational Review* 18, no. 5 (December 1899): 417.

88. "Our Trade at Stake," *BH*, October 31, 1899, 12.

89. *An Act to Protect the Name and Credit of Certain Educational Institutions*, 1893 MA Acts Chap. 0355, https://archives.lib.state.ma.us/handle/2452/86257.

90. "Private Commercial Schools for Profit," Case 20: Education, Folder: Private Commercial School for Profit Survey 1914, BCC.

91. A. J. Angulo, *Diploma Mills: How for-Profit Colleges Stiffed Students, Taxpayers, and the American Dream* (Baltimore: Johns Hopkins University Press, 2016), 47–52; Bertha Morton Stevens, *Boys and Girls in Commercial Work* (Philadelphia: Survey Committee of the Cleveland Foundation, 1916); City Club of Chicago, *A Report on Vocational Training in Chicago and in Other Cities* (Chicago: City Club of Chicago, 1912).

92. "United States District Court," in *Department Reports of the Commonwealth of Massachusetts*, vol. 4 (Bureau of Department Reports, 1917), 689–690.

93. *ARS 1900* (Boston: Municipal Printing Office, 1900), 64–66; Helen Rich Norton, *Department-Store Education* (Washington, DC: GPO, 1917), 59–61; "Commercial Education," *BH*, April 11, 1887, 4; "Commercial Education—A New Departure," *BH*, April 29, 1901, 6.

94. *ARS 1880* (Boston: Rockwell & Churchill, 1881), 21.

95. Henry William Blair, *Report of the Committee of the Senate upon the Relations between Labor and Capital,* vol. 4 (Washington, DC: GPO, 1885), 457; *ARS 1898* (Boston: Municipal Printing Office, 1898), 88, 93; *ARSC 1902* (Boston: Municipal Printing Office, 1902), 29–30; *ARS 1907* (Boston: Municipal Printing Office, 1907), 81–90.

96. "The Evening High School," *BH,* April 15, 1886, 5.

97. *ARSC 1911* (Boston: Printing Department, 1911), 41–43.

98. Allinson, *The Public Schools and Women,* 42–49.

99. In Figures 4.6 and 4.7, the jump in academic courses around 1924 likely reflects a change in how enrollments were tallied. Whereas students taking commercial courses in Boston's Central Evening High School had been classified as commercial students, in 1924 all students in Central were classified as academic, even though some were in commercial courses. Two-thirds of Central students were men, and this school enrolled the highest number of men of any evening high school, making the jump particularly pronounced for the men's chart. *AS 1924–1926* (Boston: Printing Department, 1924–1926), 51–53; *ARS 1924* (Boston: Printing Department, 1924), 74–75; *ARS 1929* (Boston: Printing Department, 1929), 284.

100. *ARS 1920* (Boston: Printing Department, 1920), 43. For evening high school curriculum, see *ARS 1898,* 88, 93; *ARS 1904* (Boston: Municipal Printing Office, 1904), 123–124; *ARS 1929* (Boston: Printing Department, 1929), 283–284.

101. Before 1898, school appropriations were made by the city council; after 1898, they were made directly by the school committee. *ARS 1915* (Boston: Printing Department, 1915), 9; Appendix, *ARSC 1897* (Boston: Rockwell & Churchill, 1898), 3–4; *Annual Report of the Business Agent 1910* (Boston: Printing Dept., 1910), 5–8; *Annual Report of the Business Manager on Cost of Public School Education 1929* (Boston: Printing Office, 1929), 3–4; National Bureau of Economic Research, Index of the General Price Level for United States [M04051US-M324NNBR], retrieved from FRED, Federal Reserve Bank of St. Louis, https://fred.stlouisfed.org/series/M04051USM324NNBR, June 15, 2020.

102. *Auditor of Accounts' Annual Report of the Receipts and Expenditures of the City of Boston 1879–80* (Boston: Rockwell & Churchill, 1880), 20–21; *Report of the City Auditor 1930* (Boston: Printing Department, 1931), 317, 319.

103. *ARS 1921* (Boston: Printing Department, 1921), 16; *ARS 1923* (Boston: Printing Department, 1923), 89.

104. Frank Victor Thompson, *Commercial Education in Public Secondary Schools* (Yonkers-on-Hudson, NY: World Book Co., 1915), 13–14.

105. *ARSC 1898* (Boston: Municipal Printing Office, 1898), 18–19; *ARS 1928,* 45.

106. *ARS 1900,* 64–66; *ARSC 1906* (Boston: Municipal Printing Office, 1906), 32–33.

107. In Figures 4.8 and 4.9, "Commercial" indicates that these students were pursuing a commercial course of study, including subjects such as bookkeeping, typewriting, and shorthand. Some students were in a school devoted to commercial instruction (the High School of Commerce for men, or the Clerical School for women), or they took these subjects within a commercial department of their high school. "College-prep" refers to students enrolled in Latin schools (Boston Latin for men or Girls' Latin for women) or a college preparatory sequence in their high school. "Industrial" indicates those who attended a specialized trade, mechanical arts, or practical arts (including domestic arts) school or who enrolled in an industrial or cooperative course of study in their high school. "General" refers to students enrolled in the standard academic high school curriculum.

108. Allinson, *The Public Schools and Women*, 13, 31–33, 155.

109. *ARS 1928*, 88–93.

110. *ARS 1939* (Boston: Printing Department, 1939), 76.

111. *ARS 1913* (Boston: Printing Department, 1913), 151.

112. "Secretarial Work No. 823," August 3, 1925, Folder 404, BVI.

113. Gail Bederman, *Manliness and Civilization: A Cultural History of Gender and Race in the United States, 1880–1917* (Chicago: University of Chicago Press, 1995), 170–215; Kristin L. Hoganson, *Fighting for American Manhood: How Gender Politics Provoked the Spanish-American and Philippine-American Wars* (New Haven, CT: Yale University Press, 1998); Matthew Frye Jacobson, *Barbarian Virtues: The United States Encounters Foreign Peoples at Home and Abroad, 1876–1917* (New York: Hill and Wang, 2000).

114. "Talk on Salesmanship," *BH*, February 13, 1907, 16.

115. "Germany Leads," *BG*, July 30, 1906, 12.

116. "Boston's New High School of Commerce," *BG*, September 10, 1906, 6.

117. James E. Downey, "'Education For Business:' The Boston High School of Commerce," *Journal of Political Economy* 21, no. 3 (1913): 221.

118. Louisa Iarocci, *The Urban Department Store in America, 1850–1930* (New York: Routledge, 2017), 170–172.

119. Thompson, *Commercial Education*, 11.

120. *ARSC 1906*, 49–51; "Thompson to Be Head of School of Commerce," *BG*, April 3, 1906, 3.

121. *ARS 1910* (Boston: Printing Department, 1910), 105–106; *AS 1910* (Boston: Printing Department, 1910), 33.

122. *Inaugural Address of John F. Fitzgerald, 1906*, 36–39; "Agree Boston Needs School of Commerce," *BG*, February 3, 1906, 1; James J. Connolly, *The Triumph of Ethnic Progressivism: Urban Political Culture in Boston, 1900–1925* (Cambridge, MA: Harvard University Press, 2009), 84.

123. "Business Men Asked to Help," *BG*, November 28, 1906, 7; "Broadside at Fitzgerald: Storrow Accuses Him of Underground Methods," *BG*, December 5, 1909, 1; "Fitzgerald in Answer: Disavows Responsibility for Storrow Stories," *BG*, December 6, 1909, 1.

124. *AS 1915* (Boston: Printing Department, 1915), 8.

125. Norton, *Department-Store Education*, 7–9.

126. Norton, *Department-Store Education*, 60–63; *ARS 1913*, 105–114; *ARS 1914* (Boston: Printing Department, 1914), 61–66, 170–171.

127. *ARSC 1910* (Boston: Printing Department, 1910), 46–47; "Boston Clerical School for Girls: Only School of Its Kind," *BG*, January 10, 1915, SM11; *ARS 1915*, 8.

128. "Ask Building for Clerical School," *BG*, May 13, 1925, 22.

129. Catholic schools played a more prominent role in commercial instruction in cities such as Philadelphia, described in Walter Licht, *Getting Work: Philadelphia, 1840–1950* (Philadelphia: University of Pennsylvania Press, 2000), 78.

130. Paula M. Kane, *Separatism and Subculture: Boston Catholicism, 1900–1920* (Chapel Hill: University of North Carolina Press, 1994), 3–4, 145–200; Donna Merwick, *Boston Priests, 1848–1910: A Study of Social and Intellectual Change* (Cambridge, MA: Harvard University Press, 1973), 143–196; James W. Sanders, *Irish vs. Yankees: A Social History of the Boston Schools* (Oxford: Oxford University Press, 2018), 115–116, 125–153; *AS 1930* (Boston: Printing Department, 1930), 6–7; *Biennial Survey of Education, 1924–1926* (Washington, DC: GPO, 1928), 1151; *Biennial Survey of Education, 1928–1930*, vol. 2 (Washington, DC: GPO, 1932), 809.

131. *The Boston Academy of Notre Dame* (Boston, 1923), 6–10, and *The Boston Academy of Notre Dame* (Boston, 1927), 6–18, Gutman Library Special Collections, Harvard University, Cambridge, MA.

132. "Secretarial Work No. 818," 1925, Folder 403, BVI; Charles W. Parton, *From Sanderson's to Alley's: A Biography of the West Tisbury General Store* (Barnardsville, NC: Charles William Parton, 1992), 31.

133. *Information for School Principals and Instructors* (Boston: Bryant & Stratton Commercial School, 1933), 6.

134. Scott Adams Fisher, "The Development and Recession of the Private Junior College Including Fisher Junior College: A Case Study" (PhD diss., Harvard Graduate School of Education, Harvard University, 1983), 1–75, 146.

135. "First Commencement," *BG*, June 14, 1906, 4; Norton, *Department-Store Education*, 49–63.

136. Collegiate business programs will be discussed further in Chapter 6.

137. Many commercial courses were shorter than a full school year, and therefore these different school types are not comparable in terms of length of course or quality of course. However, assuming that students were not enrolled

simultaneously in different schools, enrollment data provides a good estimate of student preferences for and the popularity of each type. The years shown in Figure 4.10 reflect available data.

138. Edwin Garfield Knepper, *History of Business Education in United States* (Bowling Green, OH: Edwards Brothers, 1941), 192.

139. IPUMS 1940.

140. Allinson, *The Public Schools and Women*, 36–39, 127, 147; Thompson, *Commercial Education*, 116; Eaves, *Training for Store Service*, 44; D. H. Fletcher, "Report of Committee on Commercial Education," July 1914, Case 20, BCC.

141. "Secretarial Work No. 788," July 24, 1925, Folder 403, BVI.

142. "Address of Mrs. Nanette R. Calver," March 23, 1940, 1, Carton 3, Folder 52, GHSA.

143. Allinson, *The Public Schools and Women*, 65; Norton, *Department-Store Education*, 33–35.

144. Norwood, *Labor's Flaming Youth*, 35–41.

145. C. R. Dooley, "Round Table Discussion June 5th, 1917," in *The National Association of Corporation Schools Fifth Annual Convention: Addresses, Reports, Bibliographies and Discussions* (New York: Andrew H. Kellogg Company, 1917), 192.

146. "Secretarial Work No. 848," July 20, 1925, Folder 404, BVI.

147. Allinson, *The Public Schools and Women*, 64–65, 156; Eaves, *Training for Store Service*, 39–41, 46–49, 82–83. See also Angel Kwolek-Folland, *Engendering Business: Men and Women in the Corporate Office, 1870–1930* (Baltimore: Johns Hopkins University Press, 1998), 41–69.

148. Norwood, *Labor's Flaming Youth*, 42–43.

149. "Secretarial Work," Employee Questionnaires, 1925, Folder 404, BVI.

150. Allinson, *The Public Schools and Women*, 96.

151. IPUMS 1940.

152. *ARS 1928*, 69–78.

153. Goldin, *Understanding the Gender Gap*, 109–112.

154. Norwood, *Labor's Flaming Youth*, 42–43.

155. Letter from Alice O'Meara to James J. Phelan, June 3, 1921, Box 9, Folder 82, "General Reports—Policies of the Bureau, 1913–1928," Women's Educational and Industrial Union Records, 1894–1955, Schlesinger Library, Radcliffe Institute, Harvard University, Cambridge, MA.

156. Norwood, *Labor's Flaming Youth*, 42–43; Benson, *Counter Cultures*, 209.

157. U.S. Bureau of the Census, "Table 1," in *Fourteenth Census of the United States 1920*, vol. 4, *Population, Occupations* (Washington, DC: GPO, 1923), 943–944.

158. Allinson, *The Public Schools and Women*, 113–114; Benson, *Counter Cultures*, 191–193.

159. Kocka, *White Collar Workers in America*, 171–172.

160. George E. Berkley, *The Filenes* (Boston: Branden Books, 1998), 74; Allon Gal, *Brandeis of Boston* (Cambridge, MA: Harvard University Press, 1980), 60–62.

161. Mary La Dame, *The Filene Store: A Study of Employees' Relation to Management in a Retail Store* (New York: Russell Sage Foundation, 1930), 119–123, 139–145, 189–196, 200–227, 332–333.

162. US Commission on Industrial Relations, *Industrial Relations*, 3:2309, 2237–2238, 2276–2279, 4:3385.

163. Allinson, *The Public Schools and Women*, 102–109.

164. US Commission on Industrial Relations, *Industrial Relations*, 3:2285.

165. Berkley, *The Filenes*, 120.

166. Kocka, *White Collar Workers in America*, 155–157.

167. Edward Cowdrick, *Manpower in Industry* (New York: H. Holt & Co., 1924), 153.

168. Eaves, *Training for Store Service*, 57–58.

169. Kocka, *White Collar Workers in America*, 158–160, 330n13.

170. Norwood, *Labor's Flaming Youth*, 91–103.

171. Norwood, *Labor's Flaming Youth*, 169–198, 283, 285; U.S. Bureau of the Census, "Table 15," in *Fourteenth Census of the United States 1920*, vol. 4, *Population, Occupations* (Washington, DC: GPO, 1923), 85; "Statistics of Labor Organizations in MA, 1918–1920," in *BSL 1921* (Boston: Wright & Potter, 1921), 27; "Telephone Strike Won by Workers," *New York Times*, April 21, 1919, 1.

172. Norwood, *Labor's Flaming Youth*, 180–197, 283–293, 301–303.

173. Benson, *Counter Cultures*, 248–258.

174. US Commission on Industrial Relations, *Industrial Relations*, 4:3382.

175. Cowdrick, *Manpower in Industry*, 154.

176. Benson, *Counter Cultures*, 228.

177. Sloan Wilson, *The Man in the Gray Flannel Suit* (New York: Simon and Schuster, 1955).

5. Professional Ladders

1. Gleason Leonard Archer, *The Educational Octopus: A Fearless Portrayal of Men and Events in the Old Bay State, 1906–1915* (Boston: Gleason L. Archer, 1915), 8.

2. David F. Labaree, *The Trouble with Ed Schools* (New Haven, CT: Yale University Press, 2004); Jurgen Herbst, *And Sadly Teach: Teacher Education and*

Professionalization in American Culture (Madison: University of Wisconsin Press, 1989); Amitai Etzioni, *The Semi-Professions and Their Organization: Teachers, Nurses, Social Workers* (New York: Free Press, 1969).

3. Magali Sarfatti Larson, *The Rise of Professionalism: Monopolies of Competence and Sheltered Markets,* new ed. (New Brunswick, NJ: Transaction Publishers, 2013), xxiv; Randall Collins, *The Credential Society: An Historical Sociology of Education and Stratification* (1979; repr., New York: Columbia University Press, 2019), 177–184; Burton J. Bledstein, *The Culture of Professionalism: The Middle Class and the Development of Higher Education in America* (New York: W. W. Norton, 1976).

4. Sociologists of gender and professionalization have pointed to the reproduction of inequalities not only through exclusion but also through inclusionary practices. Celia Davies, "The Sociology of Professions and the Profession of Gender," *Sociology* 30, no. 4 (1996): 661–678; Latonya J. Trotter, "Making a Career: Reproducing Gender within a Predominately Female Profession," *Gender & Society* 31, no. 4 (August 2017): 503–525.

5. William K. Selden, *Accreditation: A Struggle over Standards in Higher Education* (New York: Harper, 1960), 29–44, 55–81; R. D. Anderson, *European Universities from the Enlightenment to 1914* (Oxford: Oxford University Press, 2004), 88–102; Hal Hansen, "Caps and Gowns: Historical Reflections on the Institutions That Shaped Learning for and at Work, 1800–1945" (PhD diss., University of Wisconsin-Madison, 1997), 464–469.

6. This chapter uses IPUMS USA (digitized individual-level data samples of the US decennial census) 100 percent samples for the censuses between 1880 and 1940, hereafter referred to as IPUMS plus the sample year (e.g., IPUMS 1880–1940, IPUMS 1900, etc.). Steven Ruggles, Sarah Flood, Ronald Goeken, Josiah Grover, Erin Meyer, Jose Pacas, and Matthew Sobek, IPUMS USA: Version 10.0 [dataset] (Minneapolis: IPUMS, 2020), https://doi.org/10.18128/D010.V10.0.

7. T. Goebel, "The Uneven Rewards of Professional Labor: Wealth and Income in the Chicago Professions, 1870–1920," *Journal of Social History* 29, no. 4 (June 1, 1996): 749–777.

8. IPUMS 1940.

9. *ARSC 1870* (Boston: Alfred Mudge & Son, 1871), 177; *ARSC 1902* (Boston: Municipal Printing Office 1902), 6.

10. *ARS 1899* (Boston: Municipal Printing Office, 1899), 49.

11. Polly Kaufman, "Julia Harrington Duff: An Irish Woman Confronts the Boston Power Structure, 1900–1905," *Historical Journal of Massachusetts* 18, no. 2 (1990): 117–118.

12. *ARS 1888* (Boston: Rockwell & Churchill, 1889), 240.

13. *ARS 1881* (Boston: Rockwell & Churchill, 1883), 13; *ARS 1889* (Boston: Rockwell & Churchill, 1890), 27–30, 42–44; *ARS 1899,* 49; *ARS 1903* (Boston: Municipal Printing Office, 1903), 96.

14. *ARS 1889,* 29; IPUMS 1900.

15. Jerome Karabel, *The Chosen: The Hidden History of Admission and Exclusion at Harvard, Yale, and Princeton* (Boston: Houghton Mifflin, 2006), 48; "Lowell Will Head Harvard," *BG,* January 14, 1909, 2; *ARS 1899,* 47.

16. *Proceedings of the School Committee,* June 28, 1904, 291; "Mrs Duff's Rap," *BG,* November 12, 1902, 4; Kaufman, "Julia Harrington Duff," 118, 131.

17. *ARSC 1878* (Boston: Rockwell & Churchill, 1878), 28; *ARSC 1879* (Boston: Rockwell & Churchill, 1879), 28; *ARSC 1893* (Boston: Rockwell & Churchill, 1893), 15; *ARS 1896* (Boston: Rockwell & Churchill, 1897), 54.

18. *ARSC 1898* (Boston: Municipal Printing Office, 1898), 19–22; "Women Candidates for the School Board," *The Woman's Journal,* December 1, 1900, 381.

19. *ARS 1903* (Boston: Municipal Printing Office, 1903), 90–93; *ARSC 1907* (Boston: Municipal Printing Office, 1907), 13.

20. Because Boston was a college town that attracted many students from outside the city, it is not surprising that its college-going rate rose much faster than the national rate. In 1930 nationally, 7 percent of 18–24-year-olds were in college. Thomas D. Snyder, *120 Years of American Education: A Statistical Portrait* (Washington, DC: National Center for Education Statistics, 1993), 65; IPUMS 1930; U.S. Bureau of the Census, "Table 12: Population by Age, Color, Nativity, and Sex, for Urban Places of 10,000 or more: 1930," in *Fifteenth Census of the United States 1930, Population,* vol. 3, *Reports by States,* part 1, *Alabama–Missouri* (Washington, DC: GPO, 1932), 1083; *BSE 1928–1930,* vol. 2 (Washington, DC: GPO, 1932), 442–444.

21. *Proceedings of the School Committee of the City of Boston 1902* (Boston: Rockwell & Churchill, 1902), 124.

22. Appendix, *ARSC 1880* (Boston: Rockwell & Churchill, 1881), 86.

23. *ARSC 1902,* 39–40.

24. Arthur G. Powell, *The Uncertain Profession: Harvard and the Search for Educational Authority* (Cambridge: Cambridge University Press, 1980), 30–31.

25. Powell, *The Uncertain Profession,* 31–33.

26. Hugh Hawkins, *Between Harvard and America: The Educational Leadership of Charles W. Eliot* (New York: Oxford University Press, 1972), 152–156.

27. Powell, *The Uncertain Profession,* 32; Patricia A. Moore, *The First Hundred Years: 1885–1985* (Winchester, MA: New England Association of Schools and Colleges, 1986), 16; Selden, *Accreditation,* 30–34.

28. Marc A. VanOverbeke, *The Standardization of American Schooling: Linking Secondary and Higher Education, 1870–1910* (New York: Palgrave Macmillan, 2008), 134–135.

29. Powell, *The Uncertain Profession*, 24–25; VanOverbeke, *The Standardization of American Schooling*, 117–126.

30. Selden, *Accreditation*, 33.

31. Selden, *Accreditation*, 35; VanOverbeke, *The Standardization of American Schooling*, 165–166.

32. Powell, *The Uncertain Profession*, 22, 36–38, 57; VanOverbeke, *The Standardization of American Schooling*, 140–141.

33. Kaufman, "Julia Harrington Duff," 116.

34. Powell, *The Uncertain Profession*, 71–75; Mina Carson, *Settlement Folk: Social Thought and the American Settlement Movement, 1885–1930* (Chicago: University of Chicago Press, 1990), 65; Kaufman, "Julia Harrington Duff," 116; William Alan Braverman, "The Ascent of Boston's Jews, 1630–1918" (PhD diss., Harvard University, 1990), 229–230; Barbara Miller Solomon, *Ancestors and Immigrants: A Changing New England Tradition* (Cambridge, MA: Harvard University Press, 1956), 100–140; David B. Tyack, *The One Best System: A History of American Urban Education* (Cambridge, MA: Harvard University Press, 1974), 126–176.

35. "Mrs. Duff's Ire," *BG*, March 26, 1902, 1; *Proceedings of the School Committee of the City of Boston 1902* (Boston: Rockwell & Churchill, 1902), 115–126.

36. *Proceedings of the School Committee 1902*, 116–119.

37. *Proceedings of the School Committee 1902*, 120–126.

38. *ARS 1903*, 98; *Report of the Committee on Salaries* (Boston: Municipal Printing Office, 1902), 4–5.

39. *ARSC 1902*, 41–42; *ARS 1909* (Boston: Printing Department, 1909), 89–99; Lucile Eaves, *Old-Age Support of Women Teachers* (Boston: Spartan Press, 1921), 41.

40. "First Public Reception," *BG*, April 30, 1898, 9; "Teachers' Union," *BG*, January 30, 1903, 7; Powell, *The Uncertain Profession*, 71.

41. "Opposes Mayor's School Measure," *BG*, February 6, 1905, 4.

42. Powell, *The Uncertain Profession*, 72, 101.

43. A moniker given to Storrow by City Counselor Mr. McCullough, a representative of the heavily Irish neighborhood of South Boston. *Report of Proceedings of the City Council of Boston, 1906–1907* (Boston: Municipal Printing Office, 1907), 312.

44. *ARS 1906* (Boston: Municipal Printing Office, 1906), 9–10, 14–23; *ARS 1907*, 25–27.

45. "Is Cheered by 2000 Persons," *BG*, December 9, 1907, 6.

46. Powell, *The Uncertain Profession*, 72.

47. *ARS 1908* (Boston: E. W. Doyle, Printer, 1908), 90–100.

48. Powell, *The Uncertain Profession*, 132; *ARS 1919* (Boston: Printing Department, 1919), 74–78.

49. "Trade Schools," *BG*, April 15, 1905, 3; Richard Freeland, *Academia's Golden Age: Universities in Massachusetts, 1945–1970* (Oxford: Oxford University Press, 1992), 36–37.

50. Paula M. Kane, *Separatism and Subculture: Boston Catholicism, 1900–1920* (Chapel Hill: University of North Carolina Press, 1994), 3–4; Allon Gal, *Brandeis of Boston* (Cambridge, MA: Harvard University Press, 1980), 115; Donna Merwick, *Boston Priests, 1848–1910: A Study of Social and Intellectual Change* (Cambridge, MA: Harvard University Press, 1973), 143–196.

51. "Proposes Free State College," *BG*, September 8, 1913, 4.

52. "Clash on Plan of Popular Education," *BH*, May 16, 1909, 7; *Report of the Board of Education Relative to the Establishment of a State University* (Boston: Wright & Potter, 1915).

53. "The Boston Trade Union College," *Harvard Alumni Bulletin* 21, no. 26 (April 3, 1919): 520; *Workers Education in the United States: Report of Proceedings, Second National Conference* (New York: Workers Education Bureau of America, 1922), 49.

54. Kathleen Murphy, "Boston Teachers Organize, 1919–65" (Ed.D. diss., Harvard Graduate School of Education, Harvard University, 1981), 37.

55. Stephen Norwood, *Labor's Flaming Youth: Telephone Operators and Worker Militancy, 1878–1923* (Urbana: University of Illinois, 1990), 228–230.

56. "Boston's New College, Open Next Week, the Only One of Its Kind," *BG*, March 30, 1919, 52; "Trade Union College Opens Next Week," *BG*, September 29, 1919, 11; *Workers Education in the United States: Report of Proceedings, First National Conference* (New York: Workers Education Bureau of America, 1921), 3, 15–17, 90–91, 142; *Workers Education in the United States, Second National Conference*, 3.

57. After its closure, the BTUC was revived as a modest lecture series under the newly established Greater Boston Council for Workers Education in 1934. "Trade Union College May Be Revived," *BG*, September 10, 1934, 2; "Conference Plans to Educate Workers," *BG*, May 27, 1934, A7; "CLU Educational Courses Announced," *BG*, January 21, 1935.

58. *Workers Education in the United States, First National Conference*, 90.

59. The Intercollegiate Socialist Society became the League of Industrial Democracy in 1921, the parent organization of the 1960s Students for a Democratic Society. Max Horn, *The Intercollegiate Socialist Society, 1905–1921: Origins of the Modern American Student Movement* (Boulder, CO: Westview Press, 1979), xi; Drew Pendergrass, "The Boys in Crimson," *Harvard Crimson*, November 10, 2016; Upton Sinclair, *The Goose-Step: A Study of American Education* (Pasadena, CA: Author, 1923), 82–91.

60. Murphy, "Boston Teachers Organize, 1919–65," 36–76.

61. *ARS 1919*, 28.

62. "Will Consider State University Proposal," *BG*, October 19, 1922, 15.

63. Freeland, *Academia's Golden Age*, 37–38; "Historical Note," Boston State College Collection 1852–2007, University Archives and Special Collections, Joseph P. Healey Library, University of Massachusetts Boston.

64. *ARS 1922* (Boston: Printing Department, 1922), 17–19; "Historical Note," Boston State College Collection 1852–2007.

65. *Boston University Year Book, 1915–1916* (Boston, 1915), 125–126, 367; *Boston University Year Book, 1919–1920* (Boston, 1919), 405–412; AS 1918 (Boston: Printing Department, 1918), 7; *RCE 1880* (Washington, DC: GPO, 1882), 656; *RCE 1900–01*, vol. 2 (Washington, DC: GPO, 1902), 1660–1661; *BSE 1928–1930*, vol. 2, 443; Kathleen Kilgore, *Transformations: A History of Boston University* (Boston: Boston University, 1991), 132–133.

66. Donovan, *History of Boston College*, 166, 304, 364.

67. Powell, *The Uncertain Profession*, 48–50, 57–58, 72, 80, 110, 128; Henry Greenleaf Pearson, *Son of New England: James Jackson Storrow, 1864–1926* (Boston: T. Todd Co., 1932), 50n1.

68. Powell, *The Uncertain Profession*, 101, 133–136, 154–155; *BSE 1928–1930*, vol. 2, 443.

69. Powell, *The Uncertain Profession*, 57, 64–66, 108–109, 138–139; "Appointments Secured 1929–30," in Graduate School of Education Placement Office Records 1919–1932, Box 1, Folder: Annual Report, University Archives, Harvard University, Cambridge, MA.

70. Mark L. Savickas, "Meyer Bloomfield: Organizer of the Vocational Guidance Movement (1907–1917)," *Career Development Quarterly* 57, no. 3 (March 2009): 262–269.

71. Powell, *The Uncertain Profession*, 118–123.

72. Powell, *The Uncertain Profession*, 98–106; Records of the Psycho-Educational Clinic, 1927–1947, University Archives, Harvard University, Cambridge, MA.

73. Joseph F. Kett, *Merit: The History of a Founding Ideal from the American Revolution to the Twenty-First Century* (Ithaca, NY: Cornell University Press, 2013), 140–146; F. W. Taussig, *Principles of Economics*, vol. 2 (New York: Macmillan, 1915), 235–236.

74. Frank Ballou, "The Function of a Department of Educational Investigation and Measurement in a School System," *School and Society* 1, no. 6 (February 6, 1915): 181; *ARS 1915* (Boston: Printing Department, 1915), 28–29, 84–118; "Is Cheered by 2000 Persons," *BG*, December 9, 1907, 6; Frank Ballou, *The Appointment of Teachers in Cities* (Cambridge, MA: Harvard University Press, 1915), viii.

75. *ARS 1915,* 89–100; *ARS 1921* (Boston: Printing Department, 1915), 29; Frank Ballou, *Scales for the Measurement of English Compositions* (Cambridge, MA: Harvard University Press, 1914), 3.

76. Dorothy M. O'Brien, "Oration," in *The Alpha: The First Year Book of the Boston Normal School* (Boston: Boston Normal School, 1917), 75–76.

77. "Historical Note," Boston State College Collection 1852–2007; "To Consider 3 Plans," *BG,* March 9, 1938, 3; Labaree, *The Trouble with Ed Schools,* 29–34.

78. John William Leonard, *Who's Who in America* (Chicago: A. N. Marquis & Co., 1899), xii; Gerard W. Gawalt, "The Impact of Industrialization on the Legal Profession in Massachusetts, 1870–1900," in *The New High Priests: Lawyers in Post–Civil War America,* ed. Gerard W. Gawalt (Westport, CT: Greenwood Press, 1984), 100.

79. Dennis P. Ryan, "Beyond the Ballot Box: A Social History of the Boston Irish, 1845–1917" (PhD diss., University of Massachusetts Amherst, 1978), 97–102; Robert Bocking Stevens, *Law School: Legal Education in America from the 1850s to the 1980s* (Chapel Hill: University of North Carolina Press, 1987), 74–75; Jerold S. Auerbach, *Unequal Justice: Lawyers and Social Change in Modern America* (New York: Oxford University Press, 1976), 40–62; Timothy J. Gilfoyle, "'America's Greatest Criminal Barracks': The Tombs and the Experience of Criminal Justice in New York City, 1838–1897," *Journal of Urban History* 29, no. 5 (July 2003): 531–536; Robert A. Silverman, *Law and Urban Growth: Civil Litigation in the Boston Trial Courts, 1880–1900* (Princeton, NJ: Princeton University Press, 2014), 3–46, 69–71, 133–135.

80. Douglas Lamar Jones, *Discovering the Public Interest: A History of the Boston Bar Association* (Canoga Park, CA: Boston Bar Association and CCA Publications, 1993), 53–58.

81. Stevens, *Law School,* 51–54; William R. Johnson, *Schooled Lawyers: A Study in the Clash of Professional Cultures* (New York: New York University Press, 1978), 103–107; Kett, *Merit,* 177–179.

82. Daniel R. Coquillette, *On the Battlefield of Merit: Harvard Law School, the First Century* (Cambridge, MA: Harvard University Press, 2015), 438, 473–475. The doctor of law (JD) degree replaced the bachelor of laws (LLB) degree in 1969 for Harvard's same three-year law program. David Hollander, "Law Faculty Approves Awarding J.D. Degree in Place of the LL.B," *Harvard Crimson,* March 12, 1969.

83. Stevens, *Law School,* 74–75.

84. Stevens, *Law School,* 52–56, 63.

85. Johnson, *Schooled Lawyers,* 62–63, 83–84.

86. Wayne Hobson, "Symbol of the New Profession: Emergence of the Large Law Firm, 1870–1915," in Gawalt, *The New High Priests,* 16.

87. Johnson, *Schooled Lawyers*, 103, 116.

88. Hobson, "Symbol of the New Profession," 19–20.

89. Benjamin D. Raub, "Placement Work in Law Schools," *Duke Bar Association Journal* 5 (1940): 18.

90. "Vocational Preferences in the Class of 1923, 1924, 1925, 1926," Box 94, Folder: Vocational Studies, Harvard, 1924–1929, Records of the Office of Career Services, 1913–1985, Harvard University Archives, Harvard University, Cambridge, MA (hereafter OCS).

91. Marcia Graham Synnott, *The Half-Opened Door: Discrimination and Admissions at Harvard, Yale, and Princeton, 1900–1970* (Westport, CT: Greenwood Press, 1979), xvii; Coquillette, *On the Battlefield*, 476–508, 608; Karabel, *The Chosen*, 90–110.

92. IPUMS 1900; Jones, *Discovering the Public Interest*, 43, 64, 76–78.

93. Stevens, *Law School*, 59–60, 192–196.

94. Coquillette, *On the Battlefield*, 499–504; David J. Loftus, *Boston College High School, 1863–1983* (Boston: Addison C. Getchell, 1984), 23–25.

95. Coquillette, *On the Battlefield*, 500–507; Loftus, *Boston College High School*, 25; "The School of Law," *Boston College Bulletin* 3, no. 3 (1931): 179–182.

96. Archer, *The Educational Octopus*, 103; Stevens, *Law School*, 79–80; J. Clay Smith Jr., *Emancipation: The Making of the Black Lawyer, 1844–1944* (Philadelphia: University of Pennsylvania Press, 1999), 76; L. J. Pettijohn, *Twenty-Second Biennial Report of the Secretary of State of the State of Kansas, 1919–1920* (Topeka: Kansas State Printing Plant, 1920), 75; "Legal Directory," *The Crisis* 46, no. 12 (December 1939), 379; J. J. Boris, ed., *Who's Who in Colored America* (New York: Who's Who in Colored America Corp., 1927), 5; Year: *1910*; Census Place: *Boston Ward 10, Suffolk, Massachusetts*; Roll: *T624_617*; Page: *11A*; Enumeration District: *1405*; FHL microfilm: *1374630*; Year: *1910*; Census Place: *Boston Ward 10, Suffolk, Massachusetts*; Roll: *T624_617*; Page: *11A*; Enumeration District: *1405*; FHL microfilm: *1374630*.

97. Archer, *The Educational Octopus*, 114–115; *Annual Report of the Boston YMCA, 1904*, 62–63, Young Men's Christian Association of Greater Boston Records, 1833–2014, M13 Box 2, Folder: Annual Report 1904, Northeastern University Archives, Boston.

98. Thomas Koenig and Michael Rustad, "The Challenge to Hierarchy in Legal Education: Suffolk and the Night Law School Movement," *Research in Law, Deviance & Social Control* 7 (1985): 197; "Biographical Note," Gleason Archer Personal Papers (MS 108) 1880–1996, Moakley Archive and Institute, Suffolk University, Boston.

99. Archer, *The Educational Octopus*, 12–16, 43–50, 59–63, 116.

100. Koenig and Rustad, "The Challenge to Hierarchy," 203–205.

101. Archer, *The Educational Octopus,* 151–159.

102. Archer, *The Educational Octopus,* 103–107, 173–188, 278.

103. Ryan, "Beyond the Ballot Box," 100–105; Archer, *The Educational Octopus,* 160–163, 194.

104. Archer, *The Educational Octopus,* 206–211, 246–251.

105. *An Act Relative to the Granting of Degrees by Colleges and Other Institutions of Learning,* April 12, 1912, MA Acts Chap. 481.

106. Archer, *The Educational Octopus,* 253–273.

107. The act exempted institutions that already had these designations in their names. *An Act Relative to the Granting of Degrees by Colleges and Other Institutions of Learning,* July 9, 1919, MA Acts Chap. 293.

108. IPUMS 1940.

109. Virginia G. Drachman, *Sisters in Law: Women Lawyers in Modern American History* (Cambridge, MA: Harvard University Press, 1998), 27–36; Jones, *Discovering the Public Interest,* 58–59.

110. Felice Batlan, *Women and Justice for the Poor: A History of Legal Aid, 1863–1945* (New York: Cambridge University Press, 2015), 37–46.

111. Jones, *Discovering the Public Interest,* 73–75.

112. Auerbach, *Unequal Justice,* 41–52; Reginald Heber Smith, *Justice and the Poor* (New York: Carnegie Foundation for the Advancement of Teaching, 1919), 114, 138.

113. Batlan, *Women and Justice,* 135–153.

114. Jones, *Discovering the Public Interest,* 85; Drachman, *Sisters in Law,* 248.

115. Ronald Chester, *Unequal Access: Women Lawyers in a Changing America* (South Hadley, MA: Bergin & Garvey, 1985), 9, 21–22; Jones, *Discovering the Public Interest,* 77. "Cora E. Bigelow: Teacher Half-Century Becomes Lawyer," *BG,* October 22, 1943, 32.

116. Stevens, *Law School,* 194.

117. Chester, *Unequal Access,* 10–11. Portia admitted its first male students through a master's program in 1926. In 1969 Portia won accreditation as a law school from the ABA and became the New England School of Law. Portia Law School Archives 1908–1968, New England Law Library, Boston.

118. Anne Witz, "Patriarchy and Professions: The Gendered Politics of Occupational Closure," *Sociology* 24, no. 4 (1990): 682; Auerbach, *Unequal Justice,* 295.

119. Ellen Condliffe Lagemann, *Private Power for the Public Good: A History of the Carnegie Foundation for the Advancement of Teaching* (Middletown, CT: Wesleyan University Press, 1983), 75–77.

120. Stevens, *Law School,* 38, 112–114; Todd Savitt and North Carolina, "Abraham Flexner and the Black Medical Schools," *Journal of the National Medical Association* 98, no. 9 (2006): 10.

121. Johnson, *Schooled Lawyers*, 157; Stevens, *Law School*, 114.

122. Johnson, *Schooled Lawyers*, 121; Stevens, *Law School*, 115; Gleason Leonard Archer, *Is a College Monopoly of the Legal Profession Desirable?* (Boston: Gleason L. Archer, 1927).

123. Stevens, *Law School*, 115, 174; Archer, *Is a College Monopoly Desirable?*

124. Jones, *Discovering the Public Interest*, 96–97; Koenig and Rustad, "Challenge to Hierarchy," 201; Stevens, *Law School*, 177–180.

125. David L. Robbins, *Suffolk University* (Charleston, SC: Arcadia Publishing, 2006), 7.

126. IPUMS 1930–1940.

127. Jones, *Discovering the Public Interest*, 115.

6. Placement in Corporate America

1. Excelsior Insurance Co., "Job Specifications and Requirements," 1933–1935, Box 36, Folder: Excelsior Insurance Company, Records of the Office of Career Services, 1913–1958, Harvard University Archives, Harvard University, Cambridge, MA (hereafter OCS).

2. James Dwinell to Robert C. Hosmer, March 11, 1935, Box 36, Folder: Excelsior Insurance Company, OCS.

3. Anthony J. Mayo, *Paths to Power: How Insiders and Outsiders Shaped American Business Leadership* (Boston: Harvard Business School Press, 2006), 122.

4. Christopher Newfield, *The Great Mistake: How We Wrecked Public Universities and How We Can Fix Them* (Baltimore: Johns Hopkins University Press, 2016); Derek Bok, *Universities in the Marketplace: The Commercialization of Higher Education* (Princeton, NJ: Princeton University Press, 2009); Elizabeth Popp Berman, *Creating the Market University: How Academic Science Became an Economic Engine* (Princeton, NJ: Princeton University Press, 2011); Ethan Schrum, *The Instrumental University: Education in Service of the National Agenda after World War II* (Ithaca, NY: Cornell University Press, 2019).

5. Roger L. Geiger, *To Advance Knowledge: The Growth of American Research Universities, 1900–1940* (New York: Oxford University Press, 1986).

6. David F. Noble, *America by Design: Science, Technology, and the Rise of Corporate Capitalism* (Oxford: Oxford University Press, 1979); Clyde W. Barrow, *Universities and the Capitalist State: Corporate Liberalism and the Reconstruction of American Higher Education, 1894–1928* (Madison: University of Wisconsin Press, 1990).

7. This chapter uses IPUMS USA (digitized individual-level data samples of the US decennial census) 100 percent samples for the censuses between 1880

and 1940, hereafter referred to as IPUMS plus the sample year (e.g., IPUMS 1880–1940, IPUMS 1900, etc.). Steven Ruggles, Sarah Flood, Ronald Goeken, Josiah Grover, Erin Meyer, Jose Pacas, and Matthew Sobek, IPUMS USA: Version 10.0 [dataset] (Minneapolis: IPUMS, 2020), https://doi.org/10.18128/D010.V10.0.

8. Jerome Karabel, *The Chosen: The Hidden History of Admission and Exclusion at Harvard, Yale, and Princeton* (Boston: Houghton Mifflin, 2006); Marcia Graham Synnott, *The Half-Opened Door: Discrimination and Admissions at Harvard, Yale, and Princeton, 1900–1970* (Westport, CT: Greenwood Press, 1979). See also Peter Dobkin Hall, "Rediscovering the Bourgeoisie: Higher Education and Governing-Class Formation in the United States, 1870–1914," in *The American Bourgeoisie: Distinction and Identity in the Nineteenth Century,* ed. Sven Beckert and Julia B. Rosenbaum (New York: Palgrave Macmillan, 2010), 167–192.

9. Rakesh Khurana, *From Higher Aims to Hired Hands: The Social Transformation of American Business Schools and the Unfulfilled Promise of Management as a Profession* (Princeton, NJ: Princeton University Press, 2007), 43–50.

10. A brief mention of these services is made in David O. Levine, *The American College and the Culture of Aspiration, 1915–1940* (Ithaca, NY: Cornell University Press, 1988), 62–64, 125; Pamela Walker Laird, *Pull: Networking and Success since Benjamin Franklin* (Cambridge, MA: Harvard University Press, 2009), 153–154.

11. As a marker of class position, about 7 percent of owners and managers in Boston, or half a percentage of the male workforce, employed a live-in domestic worker or employee in their homes in 1930. Nationally, employment of domestic workers fell by about 30 percent between 1900 and 1930, making this a metric of slightly higher status in 1930 than earlier decades. George J. Stigler, *Domestic Servants in the United States, 1900–1940* (New York: National Bureau of Economic Research, April 1946), 4; IPUMS 1930.

12. Richard S. Tedlow, "The American CEO in the Twentieth Century: Demography and Career Path," Working Paper 03-097 (Boston: Division of Research, Harvard Business School, 2003), 54–55.

13. Mayo, *Paths to Power,* 84, 95, 187–215; Susie Pak, *Gentlemen Bankers: The World of J. P. Morgan* (Cambridge, MA: Harvard University Press, 2013), 80–106.

14. E. Digby Baltzell, *Philadelphia Gentlemen: The Making of a National Upper Class* (Glencoe, IL: Free Press, 1958), 293.

15. Theodore P. Gerber and Sin Yi Cheung, "Horizontal Stratification in Postsecondary Education: Forms, Explanations, and Implications," *Annual Review of Sociology* 34, no. 1 (August 2008): 299–318.

16. Lauren A. Rivera, *Pedigree: How Elite Students Get Elite Jobs* (Princeton, NJ: Princeton University Press, 2015); Karen Ho, *Liquidated: An Ethnography of Wall Street* (Durham, NC: Duke University Press, 2009).

17. "The Harvard Graduate in the Business World," undated, p. 3, Henry S. Dennison Papers, Box 1, Folder: "The Harvard Graduate in the Business World," Baker Library, Harvard Business School, Harvard University, Boston.

18. Thorstein Veblen, *The Higher Learning in America: A Memorandum on the Conduct of Universities by Business Men* (New York: B. W. Huebsch, 1918), 191–218.

19. Janet Levine, *Ellis Island Oral History Project, Interview of Esther Zarkin Rosoff*, Series EI, No. 106 (Alexandria, VA: Alexander Street Press, 2003).

20. Elizabeth Hafkin Pleck, *Black Migration and Poverty: Boston 1865–1900* (New York: Academic Press, 1979), 151–157.

21. C. Wright Mills, *The Power Elite* (New York: Oxford University Press, 1956), 54. See also Sven Beckert, *The Monied Metropolis: New York City and the Consolidation of the American Bourgeoisie, 1850–1896* (Cambridge: Cambridge University Press, 2001).

22. Steven B. Levine, "The Rise of American Boarding Schools and the Development of a National Upper Class," *Social Problems* 28, no. 1 (October 1980): 74.

23. Levine, "The Rise of American Boarding Schools," 90; Karabel, *The Chosen*, 45.

24. Samuel Eliot Morison, *Three Centuries of Harvard, 1636–1936* (Cambridge, MA: Harvard University Press, 1936), 330.

25. Charles Eliot, "Commercial Education," *Educational Review* 18, no. 5 (December 1899): 417–421.

26. Hugh Hawkins, *Between Harvard and America: The Educational Leadership of Charles W. Eliot* (New York: Oxford University Press, 1972), 202–204, 219.

27. Jeffrey L. Cruikshank, *A Delicate Experiment: The Harvard Business School, 1908–1945* (Boston: Harvard Business School Press, 1987), 26.

28. Khurana, *From Higher Aims to Hired Hands*, 111.

29. "Committee on Choice of Vocations," "Vocational Preferences in the Class of 1923, 1924, 1925, 1926," and "1931 Questionnaire #3," Box 94, Folder: Vocational Studies, Harvard, 1924–1929, OCS; "Table IV," Box 96, Folder: Vocational Survey, Class of 1935–1938, 3 Years after Graduation, OCS.

30. Louisa L. McCrady, "Development of a University Appointment Office," May 18, 1922, 809–815, Box 30, Folder: Alumni Placement Service, Harvard, General Printed Matter, OCS; *Reports of the President and Treasurer of Harvard*

College 1900–01 (Cambridge, MA: Harvard University, 1902), 10–12; Morison, *Three Centuries of Harvard,* 295.

31. "Alumni Placement Service," *Alumni Bulletin,* September 26, 1929, 10, Box 30, Folder: Alumni Placement Service, Harvard, General Printed Matter, OCS.

32. The pool of alumni registered with the service included graduates with more than a bachelor's degree and graduates one or more years out of college. Even out of a pool of several classes, however, 100-200 annual placements represented a substantial proportion. *Report of the President and Treasurer of Harvard College 1903–04* (Cambridge, MA: Harvard University, 1904), 353; *Report of the President and Treasurer of Harvard College 1905–06* (Cambridge, MA: Harvard University, 1907), 353; *Report of the President and Treasurer of Harvard College 1910–11* (Cambridge, MA: Harvard University, 1912), 266; *Report of the President and Treasurer of Harvard College 1917–18* (Cambridge, MA: Harvard University, 1919), 283, 287.

33. Louisa L. McCrady, "Development of a University Appointment Office," 811; "Geographical Distribution of Harvard Classes, 1923–1932," and "Report to the Harvard Alumni Employment Committee," 1–3, Box 94, Folder: Vocational Studies, Harvard 1924–1929, OCS.

34. James Dwinell to Helen Porter, March 2, 1936, Box 46, Folder U, OCS.

35. "Suppose You Hired One Man a Year," January 22, 1931, Box 30, Folder: Alumni Placement Service, Harvard, General Printed Matter, OCS.

36. Helen MacMurtrie Voorhees, *History of the Eastern College Personnel Officers, 1926–1952* (Boston: T. Todd Co., 1952), 1–5. See Miriam Carpenter to Walter Daly, September 21, 1926, and October 22, 1926; and Daly to Carpenter, September 14, 1926, and October 25, 1926, Box 1, Folder: ECPO, Graduate School of Education Placement Office Records, Harvard University Archives, Harvard University, Cambridge, MA.

37. "Report to the Harvard Alumni Employment Committee," Box 94, Folder: Vocational Studies, OCS; "The Alumni Employment Office," *Harvard Alumni Bulletin,* June 21, 1928, Box 30, Folder: Alumni Placement Service, Harvard, General Printed Matter, OCS.

38. Voorhees, *History of the Eastern College Personnel Officers,* 9.

39. Stuart Clement to R. W. Warfield, November 17, 1937, and Ralph Wolf to Donald Moyer, January 25, 1940, Box 48, Folder: Yale University, OCS.

40. F. G. Atkinson to Donald Moyer, September 20, 1940, Box 43, Folder: Procter & Gamble Co., OCS.

41. David M. Watt to Donald Moyer, October 29, 1940, Box 43, Folder: Procter & Gamble Co., OCS.

42. Voorhees, *History of the Eastern College Personnel Officers,* 5; "Obituary," *Paper Trade Journal* 105, no. 2 (November 22, 1937): 107.

43. "Alumni Employment Office," 24, Box 30, Folder: Alumni Placement Services, Harvard General Printed Matter, OCS.

44. Levine, *The American College,* 63.

45. Everett A. Teal and Robert F. Herrick, eds., *The Fundamentals of College Placement* (Bethlehem, PA: College Placement Council, 1962), 219–234.

46. Walworth Company, "Job Specifications and Requirements," April 16, 1934, Box 48, Folder: Walworth Company; Lever Brothers Company, "Job Specifications and Requirements," November 18, 1929, January 16, 1930, and August 2, 1938, Box 39, Folder: Lever Brothers Company, OCS.

47. "Concentrators in Physics" and "Concentrators in Math," "Ec. 26b" 1937–1940, Box 30, Folder: Info re Business Recruiters and Student Concentrators, OCS.

48. Kendall Mills Co., "Job Specifications and Requirements," June 27, 1934, and April 28, 1939; and Warren Eustis to J. F. Dwinell, November 12, 1940, Box 38, Folder: Kendall Mills, OCS.

49. John W. Servos, "The Industrial Relations of Science: Chemical Engineering at MIT, 1900–1939," *Isis* 71, no. 4 (1980): 531–538.

50. William H. Walker, "The Technology Plan," *Science* 51, no. 1319 (1920): 357–359.

51. *MIT Annual Report of the President and Treasurer 1903* (Boston: Geo. H. Ellis Co., 1904), 28; *Bulletin of the Massachusetts Institute of Technology: Reports of the President and Treasurer 1912,* vol. 47, no. 2 (January 1912): 29–30.

52. *RCE 1910,* vol. 2 (Washington, DC: Government Printing Office, 1911), 890–891; *BSE 1918–20, Statistics* (Washington, DC: GPO, 1923), 337–338.

53. *Bulletin of the Massachusetts Institute of Technology: Reports of the President and Treasurer 1911,* vol. 46, no. 2 (January 1911): 73; *Bulletin of the Massachusetts Institute of Technology: Reports of the President and Treasurer 1918,* vol. 53, no. 2 (January 1918): 70; *MIT Reports of the President and Treasurer 1920* (Cambridge: The Technology Press, 1920), 48.

54. Bruce Sinclair, "Mergers and Acquisitions," in *Becoming MIT: Moments of Decision,* ed. David Kaiser (Cambridge, MA: MIT Press, 2010), 42–51.

55. "Mechanic Arts High Criticised," *BG,* December 15, 1910, 4.

56. Sinclair, "Mergers and Acquisitions," 45–46.

57. Morton Keller, *Making Harvard Modern: The Rise of America's University* (Oxford: Oxford University Press, 2001), 13–14; Owen Johnson, "Social Usurpation of Our Colleges, Part II," *Collier's* 49 no. 10 (May 25, 1912): 12–13.

58. Sinclair, "Mergers and Acquisitions," 49.

59. James Bossard and J. Dewhurst, *University Education for Business: A Study of Existing Needs and Practices* (Philadelphia: University of Pennsylvania Press, 1931), 93.

60. Noble, *America by Design,* 316.

61. "Mechanic Arts High Criticised," 4; Daniel Nelson, *A Mental Revolution: Scientific Management since Taylor* (Columbus: Ohio State University Press, 1992), 86–87.

62. Karl L. Wildes, *A Century of Electrical Engineering and Computer Science at MIT, 1882–1982* (Cambridge, MA: MIT Press, 1985), 30, 48.

63. John B. Rae, "Engineering Education as Preparation for Management: A Study of M.I.T. Alumni," *Business History Review* 29, no. 1 (March 1, 1955): 67.

64. "Committee on Choice of Vocations: Table 1: Class of 1924," Box 94, Folder: Vocational Studies, Harvard, 1924–1929, OCS; "Classes of 1935–36–37–38," Box 96, Folder: Vocational Survey, Class of 1935–1938, 3 Years after Graduation, OCS.

65. Chandler Hovey to Donald Moyer, February 14, 1936; "Kidder Peabody & Co," March 16, 1936; Chandler Hovey to George Plimpton, April 13, 1937; and Chandler Hovey to George Plimpton, April 30, 1937, Box 39, Folder: Kidder, Peabody and Co., OCS.

66. "Committee on Choice of Vocations: Table 1: Class of 1924," Box 94, Folder: Vocational Studies, Harvard, 1924–1929, OCS; "Classes of 1935-36-37-38," Box 96, Folder: Vocational Survey, Class of 1935–1938, 3 Years after Graduation, OCS.

67. Procter & Gamble Distributing Co., "Job Specifications and Requirements," April 21, 1931, and Procter & Gamble Distributing Co., "Job Specifications and Requirements," January 18, 1934, Box 43, Folder: Procter & Gamble Co., OCS.

68. Dennison Manufacturing Company, "Job Specifications and Requirements," April 29, 1940, Box 35, Folder: Dennison Manufacturing Company, OCS.

69. James F. Dwinell to Robert Hosmer, September 5, 1939, Box 36, Folder: Excelsior Insurance Company, OCS.

70. Letter from David Watt to Donald Moyer, December 6, 1940, Box 43, Folder: Procter & Gamble Co., OCS.

71. Paula S. Fass, *The Damned and the Beautiful: American Youth in the 1920s* (New York: Oxford University Press, 1977), 152. See also Nicholas L. Syrett, *The Company He Keeps: A History of White College Fraternities* (Chapel Hill: University of North Carolina Press, 2009).

72. George Biddle, *An American Artist's Story* (Boston: Little, Brown & Co., 1939), 81.

73. J. F. Dwinell to Mr. Wallace, April 30, 1931, Box 31, Folder: American Steel & Wire Co., OCS.

74. Donald Moyer to Chandler Hovey, February 12, 1936, Box 39, Folder: Kidder, Peabody, and Co., OCS.

75. Synnott, *The Half-Opened Door*, 112; Edward S. Martin, "Undergraduate Life at Harvard," *Scribner's Magazine* 21, no. 5 (May 1897): 538–544.

76. Levine, "Boarding Schools," 74; Baltzell, *Philadelphia Gentlemen*, 292–326; Mills, *The Power Elite*, 62–68.

77. Levine, "Boarding Schools," 86; Johnson, "Social Usurpation Part II," 11.

78. Levine, "Boarding Schools," 87.

79. Owen Johnson, "The Social Usurpation of Our Colleges, Part I," *Collier's* 49, no. 9 (May 18, 1912): 11.

80. Owen Johnson, "The Social Usurpation of Our Colleges, Part V," *Collier's* 49, no. 14 (June 22, 1912): 22.

81. William Bruce Leslie, *Gentlemen and Scholars: College and Community in the "Age of the University," 1865–1917* (University Park: Pennsylvania State University Press, 1992), 190.

82. Morison, *Three Centuries of Harvard*, 409.

83. Biddle, *An American Artist's Story*, 82.

84. Mark F. Bernstein, *Football: The Ivy League Origins of an American Obsession* (Philadelphia: University of Pennsylvania Press, 2001), xii–xiii; Mitchell L. Stevens, *Creating a Class: College Admissions and the Education of Elites* (Cambridge, MA: Harvard University Press, 2009), 106–112.

85. Leslie, *Gentlemen and Scholars*, 194–199.

86. Fass, *The Damned and the Beautiful*, 143.

87. J. F. Dwinell to Robert Hosmer, September 5, 1939, Box 36, Folder: Excelsior Company, OCS; Donald Moyer to R. R. Wallace, May 27, 1931, Box 31, Folder: American Steel and Wire, OCS; J. F. Dwinell to S. T. McCall, March 14, 1939, Box 31, Folder: American Brake Shoe and Foundry Company, OCS; J. F. Dwinell to Harold L. Young, July 2, 1936, Box 36, Folder: The Employers Group, OCS.

88. "Job Specifications and Requirements," February 10, 1930, Box 43, Folder: Procter & Gamble Co., OCS.

89. "Job Specifications and Requirements," September 12, 1933, Box 39, Folder: Kendall Mills, Bauer and Black, OCS.

90. Memo from GFP January 25, 1939, and H. E. P. to Placement Office, February 20, 1941, Box 39, Folder: International Business Machine, OCS.

91. J. F. Dwinell to Mr. Eustis, March 21, 1941, Box 39, Folder: Kendall Mills, Bauer and Black, OCS.

92. J. F. Dwinell to R. H. White, May 23, 1933, and May 29, 1933, Box 39, Folder: Landers, Frary and Clark, OCS.

93. R. H. White to Donald Moyer, February 8, 1937, and April 13, 1936; and Donald Moyer to R. H. White, April 15, 1936, Box 39, Folder: Landers, Frary and Clark, OCS.

94. Donald Moyer to Donald Bridgman, May 16, 1941, Box 31, Folder: American Telephone and Telegraph Co., OCS.

95. In examining most of the Harvard placement office correspondence with business employers between 1929 and 1941, I did not come across the mention of any African American students.

96. William A. Braverman, "The Emergence of a Unified Community, 1880–1917," in *The Jews of Boston,* ed. Jonathan D. Sarna, Ellen Smith, and Scott-Martin Kosofsky (New Haven, CT: Yale University Press, 2005), 74.

97. Synnott, *The Half-Opened Door,* 58–110.

98. Karabel, *The Chosen,* 51–52, 97–98.

99. "J. F. Dwinell, '02," *Harvard Alumni Bulletin,* June 1930, 33, Box 30, Folder: Alumni Placement Service, Harvard, General Printed Matter, OCS.

100. "J. F. Dwinell, '02."

101. J. F. Dwinell to Robert Hosmer, September 26, 1936, Box 36, Folder: Excelsior Company, OCS.

102. A point well illustrated today by Anthony Abraham Jack, *The Privileged Poor: How Elite Colleges Are Failing Disadvantaged Students* (Cambridge, MA: Harvard University Press, 2019).

103. "College Men in the Bell System with Degrees from Harvard University, 1896–1939," Box 31, Folder: American Telephone and Telegraph Company, OCS.

104. "Dennison Mfg. Co.," February 20, 1934, Box 35, Folder: Dennison Manufacturing Company, OCS; "Harvard Placement Service, September 26, 1926, Box 30, Folder: Alumni Placement Service, Harvard, General Printed Matter, OCS.

105. Frank Bobst to Miss Mork, May 2, 1930, Box 39, Folder: John Hancock Mutual Life Insurance, OCS.

106. H. A. Deering to Harvard Alumni Placement Service, January 24, 1936, Box 39, Folder: Lever Brothers, OCS.

107. "Job Specifications and Requirements," November 7, 1930, and February 28, 1933, Box 43, Folder: Procter & Gamble Co., OCS.

108. R. L. to Mr. Moyer, October 31, 1936, Box 39, Folder: Landers, Frary & Clark, OCS.

109. Richard Plumley to Donald H. Moyer, July 18, 1938, Box 48, Folder: Yale and Towne Mfg. Co., OCS.

110. Donald Moyer to Charles E. Barry, April 18, 1940, Box 36, Folder: Wm. Filene's Sons Co., OCS.

111. Box 90, Folder: Commercial Banking; Box 92, Folder: Advertising; and Box 93, Folder: Manufacturing; Folder: Sales, OCS.

112. "Job Specifications and Requirements," January 10, 1933, Box 39, Folder: Lichtner Associates, The Wm. O., OCS.

113. Harold T. Young to J. F. Dwinell, August 7, 1936, Box 36, Folder: Employers' Group, OCS.

114. Waldo Adler to George Plimpton, July 18, 1935, and Waldo Adler to George Plimpton, Box 31, Folder: Adler, Waldo, and Company, OCS; "Job Specifications and Requirements," September 6, 1932, Box 43, Folder: Procter & Gamble Co., OCS.

115. F. G. Atkinson to J. F. Dwinell, May 4, 1936, Box 43, Folder: Procter & Gamble Co., OCS.

116. "No. 133," November 23, 1940, Box 92, Folder: Actuarial Work, OCS.

117. "No. 218," October 19, 1938, Box 92, Folder: Advertising, OCS; "No. 247," 1938, and "No. 203," October 27, 1939, Box 92, Folder: Advertising, OCS; "No. 117," January 9, 1939, Box 92, Folder: Accounting, OCS.

118. "No. 172," 1939, Box 92, Folder: Accounting, OCS; "No. 239," 1939, Box 92, Folder: Advertising, OCS.

119. "No. 36," circa 1930, and "No. 134," circa 1930, Box 90, Folder: Investments, OCS; "No. 287," circa 1930, Box 90, Folder: Insurance, OCS.

120. "No. 251," 1939, Box 92, Folder: Advertising, OCS.

121. "No. 239," 1938, Box 92: Actuarial Work, OCS.

122. "No. 239," 1939, Box 92, Folder: Advertising, OCS; "No. 246," 1938, Box 92, Folder: Actuarial Work, OCS.

123. "No. 247."

124. "No. 177," circa 1930, Box 90, Folder: Insurance, OCS.

125. "No. 142," 1937, Box 92, Folder: Advertising, OCS; "No. 133," 1937, Box 92, Folder: Actuarial, OCS.

126. "No. 279," 1936, Box 93, Folder: Sales, OCS.

127. "What the Employment Department Should Be in Industry," April 2–3, 1917, Henry S. Dennison Papers, Box 1, Folder: "What the Employment Department Should be in Industry," Baker Library, Harvard Business School, Boston, MA; Khurana, *From Higher Aims to Hired Hands*, 46, 111–121.

128. Louis D. Brandeis, *Business: A Profession* (Boston: Small, Maynard & Co., 1914); Morison, *Three Centuries of Harvard*, 471–472.

129. Cruikshank, *A Delicate Experiment*, 30–35, 41–54.

130. Khurana, *From Higher Aims to Hired Hands*, 97–98.

131. "Placement Statistics as of October 1 Following Graduation," Box 3, Vol. 10, HBS Placement Office Records, Baker Library, Harvard Business School, Boston; *BSE 1928–1930*, vol. 2 (Washington, DC: GPO, 1932), 442–444.

132. Melvin Copeland, *And Mark an Era: The Story of the Harvard Business School* (Boston: Little, Brown, 1958), 291–293.

133. "Placement Statistics 1926–1929," Box 1, Vol. 1, HBS Placement Office Records, Baker Library, Harvard Business School, Boston.

134. Copeland, *And Mark an Era*, 36, 86, 90.

135. "Trips by School Staff for Placement Office 1932–1946," Vertical File AA, HBS Placement Office Records, Baker Library, Harvard Business School, Boston; Mayo, *Paths to Power*, 131.

136. "A Statement of Fact Relative to House Bill 1463," Box 1, Folder: House Bill #1463 1911, School Commerce and Finance Records, 1910–1927, Northeastern University Archives and Special Collections, Northeastern University, Boston; *School of Commerce and Finance Catalogue 1914–15* (Boston: YMCA, 1915), 11; *School of Commerce and Finance Catalogue 1920–1921* (Boston: YMCA, 1921), 6.

137. *The Year Book 1914–15* (Boston: Boston University, 1914), 319–322; Eleanor Rust Collier, *The Boston University College of Business Administration, 1913–1958* (1959), Boston University Archives, Boston University, Boston.

138. David L. Robbins, *Suffolk University* (Charleston, SC: Arcadia Publishing, 2006), 7–8.

139. *Boston College School of Business Administration 1938–1939* (Boston: Boston College, 1939), 8–9; *Boston College Bulletin 1912–1913* (Boston: Boston College, 1913), 8.

140. "In Joint Sessions," *BH*, December 29, 1900, 9.

141. Marc A. VanOverbeke, *The Standardization of American Schooling: Linking Secondary and Higher Education, 1870–1910* (New York: Palgrave Macmillan, 2008), 166–167; Patricia A. Moore, *The First Hundred Years: 1885–1985* (Winchester, MA: New England Association of Schools and Colleges, 1986), 36.

142. Eleanor Rust Collier, *The Boston University College of Business Administration, 1913–1958* (1959), Boston University Archives, Boston; Hilda McLeod Jacob and Maine State Library, "Rev. Everett William Lord Correspondence," Maine Writers Correspondence, Paper 320 (2015); "Twenty-Four Girls Will Be Secretaries," *BG*, February 11, 1917, 8; "First Class in Secretaryship," *BG*, June 17, 1923, 2; *BSE 1924–1926* (Washington, DC: GPO, 1928), 890–891.

143. *BC School of Business Administration 1938–1939* (Boston: Boston College Intown, 1939), 9.

144. Abbe Carter Goodloe, "Undergraduate Life at Wellesley," *Scribner's Magazine* 23, no. 5 (May 1898): 520–537; Barbara Miller Solomon, *In the Company of Educated Women: A History of Women and Higher Education in America* (New

Haven, CT: Yale University Press, 1985), 71–77; Helen Lefkowitz Horowitz, *Campus Life: Undergraduate Cultures from the End of the Eighteenth Century to the Present* (New York: Knopf, 1987), 193–219; Margaret Freeman, "Instruction in Living Beautifully: Social Education and Heterosocializing in White College Sororities," in *Rethinking Campus Life: New Perspectives on the History of College Students in the United States,* ed. Christine A. Ogren and Marc A. VanOverbeke (New York: Springer, 2018), 115–140.

145. "Emmanuel College Class Entertained," *BG,* June 6, 1923, 5; "Emmanuel College Presents Degrees," *BG,* June 8, 1923, 12; "School of St. Agnes," *BG,* February 25, 1927, 14; "Emmanuel Girls Wallop Regis College, 39–9," *BG,* March 12, 1929, 25; "Regis College at Weston Opens Its First Commencement," *BG,* June 8, 1931, 5; James W. Sanders, *Irish vs. Yankees: A Social History of the Boston Schools* (Oxford: Oxford University Press, 2018), 139–140.

146. Goodloe, "Undergraduate Life at Wellesley," 520–537; Alice Katharine Fallows, "Undergraduate Life at Smith College," *Scribner's Magazine* 24, no. 1 (July 1898): 53–54; Kathleen Kilgore, *Transformations: A History of Boston University* (Boston: Boston University, 1991), 87.

147. Robert D. Mare, "Educational Assortative Mating in Two Generations," California Center for Population Research, January 13, 2013; Hans-Peter Blossfeld and A. Timm, *Who Marries Whom? Educational Systems as Marriage Markets in Modern Societies* (Dordrecht: Kluwer, 2012).

148. IPUMS 1940.

149. Solomon, *In the Company of Educated Women,* 120–130.

150. "The Worker and the Chance to Work," *BG,* May 8, 1910, 46; "Department of Vocational Advice and Appointment," 9, and "Appointment Bureau," 1–5, Box 13, Folder: Histories of Appointment Bureau, 1920, n.d., WEIU Additional Records, 1877–2004, Schlesinger Library, Harvard University, Cambridge, MA (hereafter WEIU Additional).

151. Contemporary studies show that the rates of women in managerial positions in the United States and other liberal market economies are actually higher than comparative rates in many European countries. While more comparative historical research is needed, it is likely that in the early twentieth century, although limited, managerial opportunities for women in the United States were more prevalent than in Europe. Margarita Estévez-Abe, "Gender Bias in Skills and Social Policies: The Varieties of Capitalism Perspective on Sex Segregation," *Social Politics: International Studies in Gender, State & Society* 12, no. 2 (2005): 202.

152. "College Placements," Box 9, Folder: A.B. College Placements, October 1911–December 1914; "College Placements," Box 9, Folder: A.B. College Placements, January 1919–December 1921; and "College Placements," Box 9, Folder: A.B. College Placements, January 1922–February 1925, WEIU Additional.

153. "The Woman Secretary," 1926, 262–268, Folder 507, Bureau of Vocational Information Records, 1908–1932, Schlesinger Library, Radcliffe Institute, Harvard University, Cambridge, MA (hereafter BVI); "No. 783 Secretarial Work," "No. 794 Secretarial Work," and "No. 797 Secretarial Work," Secretarial Work Employee Questionnaire, 1925, Folder 403, BVI.

154. Anne Witz, "Patriarchy and Professions: The Gendered Politics of Occupational Closure," *Sociology* 24, no. 4 (1990): 682.

Conclusion

1. Spencer Miller Jr., *Labor and Education* (Washington DC: American Federation of Labor, 1939), 20.

2. Nancy Hoffman and Robert Schwartz, *Gold Standard: The Swiss Vocational Education and Training System* (Washington, DC: National Center on Education and the Economy, 2015); Nancy Hoffman, *Schooling in the Workplace: How Six of the World's Best Vocational Education Systems Prepare Young People for Jobs and Life* (Cambridge, MA: Harvard Education Press, 2011); Elizabeth Redden, "Importing Apprenticeships," *Inside Higher Ed*, August 8, 2017; Nicholas Wyman, "Why We Desperately Need to Bring Back Vocational Training in Schools," *Forbes*, September 1, 2015; Harold Sirkin, "What Germany Can Teach the U.S. about Vocational Education," *Bloomberg*, April 29, 2013.

3. Marius R. Busemeyer, *Skills and Inequality: Partisan Politics and the Political Economy of Education Reforms in Western Welfare States* (Cambridge: Cambridge University Press, 2015), 7.

4. Fernanda Zamudio-Suaréz, "Why Politicians Love to Talk about Training Welders," *Chronicle of Higher Education*, April 14, 2017.

5. Victor E. Ferrall, *Liberal Arts at the Brink* (Cambridge, MA: Harvard University Press, 2011).

6. Margarita Estévez-Abe, Torben Iversen, and David Soskice, "Social Protection and the Formation of Skills: A Reinterpretation of the Welfare State," in *Varieties of Capitalism: Institutional Foundations of Comparative Advantage*, ed. Peter A. Hall and David Soskice (Oxford: Oxford University Press, 2001), 162; Torben Iversen and David Soskice, "An Asset Theory of Social Policy Preferences," *American Political Science Review* 95, no. 4 (December 1, 2001): 875–893.

7. Critiques of the general / specific dichotomy include Wolfgang Streeck, "Skills and Politics: General and Specific," Discussion Paper 11 / 1 (Cologne, Germany: MPIfG, 2011); Aleksandr Christenko, Žilvinas Martinaitis, and Simonas Gaušas, "Specific and General Skills: Concepts, Dimensions, and Measurements," *Competition & Change* 24, no. 1 (January 2020): 44–69.

8. Tressie McMillan Cottom, *Lower Ed: The Troubling Rise of For-Profit Colleges in the New Economy* (New York: New Press, 2017).

9. Michael Hout, "Social and Economic Returns to College Education in the United States," *Annual Review of Sociology* 38, no. 1 (August 11, 2012): 379–400; David H. Autor and David Dorn, "The Growth of Low-Skill Service Jobs and the Polarization of the US Labor Market," *American Economic Review* 103, no. 5 (August 2013): 1553–1597.

10. Lauren A. Rivera, *Pedigree: How Elite Students Get Elite Jobs* (Princeton, NJ: Princeton University Press, 2015); Daniel Markovits, *The Meritocracy Trap: How America's Foundational Myth Feeds Inequality, Dismantles the Middle Class, and Devours the Elite* (New York: Penguin Press, 2019), 11.

11. Elise Gould, "State of Working America Wages 2019: A Story of Slow, Uneven, and Unequal Wage Growth over the Last 40 Years," Economic Policy Institute, February 20, 2020, https://files.epi.org/pdf/183498.pdf.

12. Barry T. Hirsch, "Sluggish Institutions in a Dynamic World: Can Unions and Industrial Competition Coexist?," *Journal of Economic Perspectives* 22, no. 1 (February 2008): 155–156.

13. U.S. Department of Labor, Bureau of Labor Statistics, "Union Members—2019," news release, January 22, 2020, https://www.bls.gov/news.release /pdf/union2.pdf; Michael Sainato, "'We Can't Afford Healthcare': US Hospital Workers Fight for Higher Wages," *The Guardian*, February 17, 2020; Reid J. Epstein, "Major Nurses' Union Backs Bernie Sanders and His Push for 'Medicare for All,'" *New York Times*, November 12, 2019; Stan Karp and Adam Sanchez, "The 2018 Wave of Teacher Strikes," *Rethinking Schools* 32, no. 4 (Summer 2018), https://rethinkingschools.org/articles/the-2018-wave-of-teacher-strikes/; Sarah Jaffe, "The Chicago Teachers Strike Was a Lesson in 21st-Century Organizing," *The Nation*, November 16, 2019; Lauren Hilgers, "The New Labor Movement Fighting for Domestic Workers' Rights," *New York Times*, February 21, 2019; Anna Orso, "Law Protecting Philadelphia Domestic Workers Takes Effect as They're Losing Jobs in Droves," *Philadelphia Inquirer*, May 30, 2020.

14. Jeb Bush and Terry McAuliffe, "Retraining, Instead of Layoffs, Will Speed Economic Recovery," *USA Today*, May 28, 2020; Jaclyn Diaz, "Democrat Wants Job-Training Funds to Top Great Recession Level," *Bloomberg Law*, May 1, 2020; Pablo Illanes et al., "Retraining and Reskilling Workers in the Age of Automation," McKinsey & Co., January 2018, https://www.mckinsey.com/featured -insights/future-of-work/retraining-and-reskilling-workers-in-the-age-of -automation#.

15. Harvey Kantor and Robert Lowe, "Educationalizing the Welfare State and Privatizing Education: The Evolution of Social Policy since the New Deal,"

in *Closing the Opportunity Gap: What America Must Do to Give Every Child an Even Chance,* ed. Prudence L. Carter and Kevin G. Welner (Oxford: Oxford University Press, 2013), 25–39.

16. Lauren Camera, "Striking for the Common Good," *U.S. News & World Report,* November 1, 2019.

Acknowledgments

This book began with a puzzle. Reading the writings of John Dewey, I was moved by his vision of education as a means of transforming society and democratizing the economy. Generations later, however, we are no closer to realizing it. Rather, the most striking parallels between his time and ours are the extremely high levels of socioeconomic inequality and a lack of power for most workers on the job. Why did education fall so far short of this transformative vision? To answer this question, I was pulled into historical research well beyond the confines of schools and into the broader political and economic transformation of pathways into work. Only within this larger frame can we understand why social reform through education has repeatedly failed to provide substantive equality and gain insight into what might move us toward economic democracy in the present.

The production of scholarly knowledge requires the support of an extensive educational system that is, as this book argues, an extremely unequal one. I benefited from the training I received at an institution that very effectively concentrates wealth and power into the hands of a few. During my time in graduate school, I found a home within the academic labor movement, which opened my eyes to the ways in which inequality is reproduced within the walls of the ivory tower, as well as the ways that collective action can push back. The research that would eventually become this book was deeply shaped by what I learned organizing with the Harvard Graduate Students Union–UAW as much as it was through academic seminars and workshops.

I had the good fortune of having incredible mentors, colleagues, and friends along the way. Jim Kloppenberg, who first introduced me to John Dewey, has modeled for me what dedication to teaching, a deep commitment to democratic practice, and rigorous historical scholarship looks like. From him I learned the importance of understanding rather than judging the past to illuminate the present, and I am grateful for his continued guidance and friendship. Claudia Goldin encouraged me to pursue quantitative historical data analysis, challenged me to define terms carefully, and asked me tough questions throughout the process. Julie Reuben offered incisive feedback and pushed me toward historical and analytical nuance. Kathleen Thelen's conceptual clarity immensely improved the framing of this project. Hal Hansen, Harvey Kantor, and Joseph Kett generously offered their time, expertise, and honest criticism, which helped sharpen my arguments. Many other historians provided vital feedback and mentorship for which I am grateful, including Margo Anderson, Nancy Beadie, Sven Beckert, Jackie Blount, Eileen Boris, Angus Burgin, Dorothy Sue Cobble, Miriam Cohen, Eli Cook, Nancy Cott, Sarah Deutsch, Jack Dougherty, Ansley Erickson, Bryant Etheridge, Wendy Gamber, Michael Glass, William Goldsmith, Kelly Goodman, Patricia Graham, Ethan Hutt, Anthony Jack, Andy Jewett, William Jones, Nick Juravich, Matthew Kelly, Emily Labarbera-Twarog, Lisa McGirr, Yael Merkin, Sonya Michel, Premilla Nadasen, Christopher Nichols, Christine Ogren, Daniel Perlstein, Charles Petersen, William Reese, Noah Rosenblum, John Rury, Andrew Seal, Jon Shelton, Tracy Steffes, Walter Stern, Derek Taira, Mitch Troutman, and Katherine Turk. I could not have completed this project without the historical insight and camaraderie of an incredible community of graduate students, especially Ella Antell, Aaron Bekemeyer, Andy Donnelly, Sam Klug, Eva Payne, and Andrew Pope. Anonymous reviewers for the *History of Education Quarterly* and Harvard University Press supplied indispensable comments, and countless other participants of conferences, workshops, and seminars at which I shared parts of this research offered invaluable advice. As a work of history that aims to speak to social scientists, policymakers, journalists, educators, and organizers, this book also benefited from the wisdom and encouragement of Lois Beckett, David Bills, Justin Bloesch, Ellora Derenoncourt, Nicholas Hayes, Alex Kindel, Peter Meyer, Thomas Ponniah, Utpal Sandesara, Robert Schwartz, and Mitchell Stevens.

This project would not have been possible without the financial support and the incredible community of scholars of the National Academy of Education / Spencer Foundation. Additional financial assistance was provided by the New England Regional Fellowship Consortium, UMass Boston, the Taubman Center at the Harvard Kennedy School of Government, the Boston Area Research Initiative, Harvard University, and Lake Forest College. I also wish to thank the archivists and librarians at the Harvard University Archives, Gutman Library, Baker Library, Schlesinger Library, UMass Boston, MIT, Northeastern University, Boston University, Massachusetts Historical Society, Boston Public Library, Boston Athenaeum, New England Genealogical Society, Boston City Archives, Massachusetts State Archives, Maine Historical Society, New Hampshire Historical Society, and the Connecticut Historical Society, whose labor and historical expertise made the research for this book possible.

My editor, Andrew Kinney, helped me distill my arguments to make the case that history matters. I want to thank him, Mihaela Pacurar, and the Harvard University Press staff for guiding me through the publishing process. Suzanne Smith provided several rounds of detailed edits that immensely improved the book. Thank you as well to John Donohue of Westchester Publishing Services for his meticulous copy editing, and to Justin Mueller for preparing the index. Sue Davenport, Reid Higginson, Angelica Nierras, and Shuyu Wang also assisted with final proofing; all remaining flaws are mine alone. Detailed information about my use of quantitative data sources, as well as a bibliography, can be accessed at tinagroeger.com/educationtrap. A portion of Chapter 6 was previously published as "A Good Mixer: University Placement in Corporate America, 1890–1940," *History of Education Quarterly* 58, no. 1 (February 2018): 33–64.

The wonderful community of scholars and friends at Lake Forest College have inspired me with their deep commitment to mentorship and pedagogy, and have exemplified the transformative power of education.

Thank you to my students, who have shared with me their own hopes and aspirations for the future, and reflected in person and over Zoom how history may shed light on the path forward. Special thanks to my fellow historians Noah Blan, Shiwei Chen, Carol Gayle, Anna Jones, Courtney Joseph, Dan LeMahieu, and Brian McCammack for your friendship and support.

I am grateful for the rich intellectual community of Chicagoland historians who have been invaluable interlocutors over the past few years, including Peter Cole, Michael Ebner, Timothy Gilfoyle, Brad Hunt, Daniel Immerwahr, Destin Jenkins, Nick Kryczka, Ruby Oram, Leisl Orenic, and Ellie Shermer. My colleagues in the academic labor movement have been models of how activism can inform scholarship, and why historical perspective is necessary for activism. Thank you to Adom Getachew, Toni Gilpin, Benjamin Johnson, Robert Johnston, Niha Singh, and Gabe Winant for your friendship and inspiration. I also want to thank my many comrades in the Chicago Democratic Socialists of America, my political home since moving to the city, for articulating a vision of a democratic future for all and putting in tireless hours to move us closer to it.

My parents, Margarita and Chris, and my sister, Lena, have been my constant cheerleaders, and the concerns of this project have been shaped by decades of discussion with them. Thank you for your endless patience and love. Lena also generously applied her talents to design the wonderful charts and map in this book. To my baby nephew, Sebastian: our generation is working on it, but I know we'll need your help. Thank you to Corinne Lorian, John Bashaw, and Zoe and John Lindstrom for being my second family. And finally, to my partner, Rudi: thank you for your encouragement, generosity, patience, moral clarity, and love. In some of the battles we have taken on together, it is easy to be overwhelmed with cynicism. I am lucky to be able to carry on the fight by your side.

Index